International Academy of Noosphere
the Baltic branch

V. Aladjev, M. Shishakov, V. Vaganov

Functional and procedural programming in Mathematica

Lulu Press – 2020

Functional and procedural programming in Mathematica. V. Aladjev, M. Shishakov, V. Vaganov.– USA: Lulu Press, 352 p., 2020.

Software presented in the book contains a number of useful and effective receptions of the procedural and functional programming in ***Mathematica*** that extend the system software and allow sometimes much more efficiently and easily to program the software for various purposes. Among them there are means that are of interest from the point of view of including of their or their analogs in ***Mathematica,*** at the same time they use approaches, rather useful in programming of various applications. In addition, it must be kept in mind that the classification of the presented tools by their appointment in a certain measure has a rather conditional character because these tools can be crossed substantially among themselves by the functionality.

The freeware package ***MathToolBox*** containing the above means is attached to the present book. The ***MathToolBox*** not only contains a number of useful procedures and functions, but can serve as a rather useful collection of programming examples using both standard and non–standard techniques of functional–procedural programming.

The book is oriented on a wide enough circle of the users from computer mathematics systems, researchers, teachers and students of universities for courses of computer science, physics, mathematics, and a lot of other natural disciplines. The book will be of interest also to the specialists of industry and technology which use the computer mathematics systems in own professional activity. At last, the book is a rather useful handbook with fruitful methods on the procedural and functional programming in the ***Mathematica*** system.

Printed by Lulu Press

May 31, 2020

Contents

This book completes our multi–year cycle of book publications on general theory of statistics, computer science, cellular automata *(homogeneous structures)*, ***Maple*** and ***Mathematica*** along with creation of software for the latest two computer mathematics systems ***Maple*** and ***Mathematica*** [42] and [16] accordingly.

 This book completes a multi-year cycle of our publications in five areas: General theory of statistics, Information science, Cellular automata, ***Maple*** and ***Mathematica*** along with creation of software for ***Maple*** and ***Mathematica.***

For contacts: aladjev@europe.com, aladjev@yandex.ru, aladjev@mail.ru

Introduction

*Systems of computer mathematics (**SCM**)* find wide enough application in a whole number of natural, economic and social sciences such as: *technologies, chemistry, informatics, mathematics, physics, education, economics, sociology, etc.* Systems ***Mathematica*** and ***Maple,*** and some others are more and more demanded for learning of mathematically oriented disciplines, in scientifical researches and technologies. ***SCM*** are main tools for scientists, teachers, researchers, and engineers. The investigations on the basis of ***SCM,*** as a rule, well combine algebraical methods with advanced computing methods. In this sense, ***SCM*** are a certain interdisciplinary area between informatics and mathematics in which researches will be concentrated on the development of algorithms for algebraic *(symbolical)* and numerical calculations, data processing, and development of programming languages along with software for realization of algorithms of this kind and problems of different purpose basing on them.

It is possible to note that among modern ***SCM*** the leading positions are undoubtedly taken by the ***Maple*** and ***Matematica*** systems, alternately being ahead of each other on this or that indicator. The given statement is based on our long-term use in different purposes of both systems – ***Maple*** and ***Mathematica*** and also work on preparation and edition of the book series and some papers in *Russian* and *English* in this direction [1-42]. At the same time, as a result of expanded use of the above systems were created the package ***MathToolBox*** for ***Mathematica*** and library ***UserLib6789*** for ***Maple*** [16,42]. All tools from the above library and package are supplied with *freeware* license and have open program code. Programming of many projects in ***Maple*** and ***Mathematica*** substantially promoted emergence of a lot of system tools from the above library and package. So, openness of ***MathToolBox*** package code allows both to modify the tools containing in it, and to program on their basis own tools, or to use their components in various appendices. Experience of use of library and package showed efficiency of such approach.

In particular, ***MathToolBox*** package contains more than ***1320*** tools of different purpose which eliminate restrictions of a number of standard tools of ***Mathematica*** system, and expand its software with new tools. In this context, this package can serve as a certain additional tool of procedural and functional programming, especially useful in the numerous appendices where certain nonstandard evaluations have to accompany programming. At that, tools represented in this package have a direct relationship to certain principal questions of procedural and functional programming in ***Mathematica*** system, not only for the decision of applied problems, but, above all, for creation of software extending frequently used facilities of the system, eliminating their defects or extending ***Mathematica*** with new facilities. The software presented in the package contains a lot of rather useful and effective receptions of programming in the ***Mathematica,*** and extends its software that allows to program the tasks of various purpose more simply and more effectively. A number of tools of the given package is used in the examples illustrating these or those provisions of the book.

In the book basic objects of programming in ***Mathematica*** – functions and procedures are considered that consist the base of functional–procedural programming. The given book considers some principal questions of *procedural–functional* programming in ***Mathematica,*** not only for decision of various applied tasks, but, as well, for creation of software expanding frequently used facilities of the system and/or eliminating their limitations, or expanding the system with new facilities. The important role of functions and procedures take place at creation of effective and legible user software.

The book is oriented on a wide enough circle of the users of the ***CMS,*** researchers, mathematicians, physicists, teachers and students of universities for courses of mathematics, computer science, physics, chemistry, etc. The book will be of interest to the specialists of industry and technology, economics, medicine and others too, that use the ***CMS*** in own professional activity.

Chapter 1: The user functions in Mathematica

Function is one of basic concepts of mathematics, being not less important object in programming systems, not excluding ***Mathematica*** system, with that difference that function - as a subject to programming - very significantly differs from strictly mathematical concept of function, considering specific features of programming in the ***Mathematica*** system.

Mathematica has a large number of functions of different purpose and operations over them. Each function is rather well documented and supplied with the most typical examples of its application. Unfortunately, unlike ***Maple,*** the program code of the ***Mathematica*** functions is closed that significantly narrows a possibility of deeper mastering the system and acquaintance with the receptions used by it and a technique of programming.

Truth, with rare exception, ***Mathematica*** allows to make assignments that override the standard built-in functions and meaning of ***Mathematica*** objects. However, program codes of the built-in functions of the system remain closed for the user. Names of built-in functions submit to some general properties, namely: names consist of complete *English* words, or standard mathematical abbreviations. In addition, the first letter of each name is capitalized. Functions whose names end with ***Q*** letter as a rule usually *"ask a question"*, and return either *True* or *False*.

Many important functions of the ***Mathematica*** system can be found in our books [1-15], that provide detailed discussions of the built-in functions, the features of their implementation along with our tools [16] which expand or supplement them. A full arsenal of functionality can be found in the system manual. Here we will cover the basic issues of organizing user functions in ***Mathematica*** along with some tools that provide a number of important operations over user-defined functions. Moreover, it is possible to get acquainted with many of them in package ***MathToolBox*** [16] and in certain our books [1-15]. We pass to definition of the main functional user objects.

1.1. ***The classical functions, defined intuitively.*** Functions of this type are determines by expressions as follows:

(a) **F[x_, y_, z_, ...] := ℜ[x, y, z, ...]**

(b) **F[x_ /; TestQ[x], y_, z_ /; TestQ[z], ...] := ℜ[x, y, z, ...]**

Definition allows two formats *(a)* and *(b)* from which the first format is similar to the format of a classical mathematical function *f(x, y, z, ...) = ℜ(x, y, z, ...)* from ***n*** variables with that difference that for formal arguments ***x,y,z,...*** the object template are used "_" which can designate any admissible expression of the system while ***ℜ(x,y,z,...)*** designate an arbitrary expression from variables ***x,y,z ...,*** including constants and function calls, for example:

```
In[1425]:= F[x_, y_, z_] := a*x*b*y + N[Sin[2019]]
In[1426]:= F[42, 77, 2019]
Out[1426]= 0.864461 + 3234*a*b
```

Whereas the second format unlike the first allows to hold testing of actual arguments obtained at function call ***F[x, y, z]*** for validity. It does a testing expression ***TestQ[x]*** attributed to formal argument e.g. ***x*** – if at least one testing expression on a relevant argument returns *False,* then function call is returned unevaluated, otherwise the function call returns the required value, if at evaluation of expression **ℜ** was no an erroneous or especial situation, for example:

```
In[8]:= F[x_ /; IntegerQ[x], y_, z_Symbol] := a*x*b*y + c*z
In[9]:= F[77, 90, G]
Out[9]= 6930*a*b + c*G
In[10]:= F[77, 90, 56]
Out[10]= F[77, 90, 56]
```

At the same time, for an actual argument its ***Head,*** e.g. *List, Integer, String, Symbol,* etc, as that illustrates the above example, can act as a test. At standard approach the concept of a function does not allow the use of *local* variables. As a rule ***Mathematica*** system assumes that all variables are global. This means that every time you use a name e.g. ***w,*** the ***Mathematica*** normally assumes that you are referring to the same object. However, at program writing, you may not want all variables to be global. In this case, you need the *w* in different points of a program to be treated as a *local* variable. At the same time, local variables in function definition can be set using *modules*. Within *module* you can give a list of variables which are to be treated as local. This goal can be achieved with help of *blocks* too. A simple example illustrates the told:

```
In[47]:= F[x_, y_] := x*y + Module[{a = 5, b = 6}, a*x + b*y]
In[48]:= F[42, 77]
Out[48]= 3906
In[49]:= {a, b} = {0, 0}
Out[49]= {0, 0}
In[50]:= F[42, 77]
Out[50]= 3906
In[51]:= S[x_, y_] := x*Block[{a = 5, b = 6}, a/b*y^2]
In[52]:= S[42, 47]
Out[52]= 77315
In[53]:= {a, b} = {0, 0}; S[42, 47]
Out[53]= 77315
```

In addition, pattern object "___" or "__" is used for formal arguments in a function definition can stand for any sequence of zero or more expressions or for any nonempty sequence of expressions accordingly, for example:

```
In[2257]:= G[x__] := Plus[x]
In[2258]:= G[500, 90, 46]
Out[2258]= 636
In[2259]:= G1[x___] := Plus[x]
In[2260]:= {G1[], G1[42, 47, 67]}
Out[2260]= {0, 156}
```

Lack of such definition of function is that the user cannot use local variables, for example, the coefficients of polynomials and other symbols other than calls of *standard* functions or local symbols determined by the artificial reception described above *(otherwise function will depend on their current values in the current session with* ***Mathematica*** *system)*. So, at such function definition expression ℜ should depend only on formal arguments. But in a number of cases it is quite enough. This function definition is used to give a more complete view of this object and in certain practical cases it is indeed used [9-12,16].

Meanwhile, using our procedure [16] with program code:

```
In[2274]:= Sequences[x__] := Module[{a = Flatten[{x}], b},
                        b = "Sequence[" <> ToString1[a] <> "]";
                        a = Flatten[StringPosition[b, {"{", "}"}]];
            ToExpression[StringReplace[b, {StringTake[b, {a[[1]],
              a[[1]]}] -> "", StringTake[b, {a[[-1]], a[[-1]]}] -> ""}]]]
```

that extends the standard built-in *Sequence* function and useful in many applications, it is possible to represent another way to define the user functions, modules, and blocks, more precisely their headers based on constructions of format:

<*Function name*>@Sequences[*formal args*] := ℜ

The following a rather simple example illustrates the told:

```
In[75]:= G@Sequences[a_Integer, b_Symbol, c_] := a+b+c
In[76]:= Definition[G]
Out[76]= G[a_Integer, b_Symbol, c_] := a + b + c
In[77]:= G[6.7, 5, 7]
Out[77]= G[6.7, 5, 7]
In[78]:= G[67, m, 7]
Out[78]= 74 + m
```

Naturally, in real programming, this definition of functions is not practical, serving only the purposes of possible methods of defining said objects. In the meantime, such extension of the built-in tool allows to compare the capabilities of both tools in determining the underlying objects of the system.

Along with the above types of functions, the ***Mathematica*** uses also the ***Compile*** function intended for compilation of the functions which calculate numeric expressions at quite certain assumptions. The ***Compile*** function has the **4** formats of coding, each of which is oriented on a certain compilation type:

Compile*[{*x1, x2,...*}, *G*]** – *compiles a function for calculation of an expression* **G** *in the assumption that all values of arguments* ***xj *{**j** =*

1, 2, ... } have numerical character;

Compile*[{{*x1, t1*}, {*x2, t2*}, {*x3, t3*}, ... }, *G*]** *– compiles a function for calculation of an expression* ***G *in the assumption that all values of* ***xj*** *arguments have type* ***tj*** *{j = 1, 2, 3,... } accordingly;*

Compile*[{{*x1, p1, w1*}, {*x2, p2, w2*},... }, *J*]** *– compiles a function for calculation of an expression* ***J *in the assumption that values of* ***xj*** *arguments are* ***wj*** *ranks of array of objects, each of that corresponds to a type* ***pj*** *{j = 1, 2, 3,... };*

Compile*[*s, W,* {{*p1, pw1*}, {{*p2, pw2*}, ... }]** *– compiles a function for calculation of a certain expression* ***W *in the assumption that its* ***s*** *subexpressions that correspond to the* ***pk*** *templates have the* ***pwj*** *types accordingly {k = 1, 2, 3, ... }.*

The ***Compile*** function processes procedural and functional objects, matrix operations, numeric functions, functions for lists processing, etc. Each ***Compile*** function generates a special object ***CompiledFunction.*** The function call ***Compile*[..., *Evaluate*[*w*]]** is used to specify the fact that ***w*** expression should be evaluated symbolically before compilation. For testing of functions of this type a rather simple ***CompileFuncQ*** function is used [8], whose call ***CompileFuncQ*[x]** returns *True* if a ***x*** represents the ***Compile*** function, and *False* otherwise. The fragment represents source code of the ***CompileFuncQ*** function with examples of its use.

```
In[7]:= V := Compile[{{x, _Real}, {y, _Real}}, x*y]; K := (#1*#2) &;
  A := Function[{x, y}, x/y]; H[x_] := Block[{}, x]; H[x_, y_] := x + y;
  SetAttributes["H", Protected]; P[x__] := Plus[Sequences[{x}]];
  GS[x_/; IntegerQ[x], y_/; IntegerQ[y]] := Sin[78] + Cos[42];
  Sv[x_/; IntegerQ[x], y_/; IntegerQ[y]] := x^2 + y^2;
  Sv = Compile[{{x, _Integer}, {y, _Real}}, (x + y)^6];
  S := Compile[{{x, _Integer}, {y, _Real}}, (x + y)^3];
  G = Compile[{{x, _Integer}, {y, _Real}}, (x/y)];
In[8]:= CompileFuncQ[x_] := If[SuffPref[ToString1[Definition3[x]],
                        "Definition3[CompiledFunction[{", 1], True, False]
In[9]:= Map[CompileFuncQ, {Sv, S, G, V, P, A, K, H, GS, Sv}]
Out[9]= {True, True, True, True, False, False, False, False, False, True}
```

The ***CompileFuncQ*** function expands testing possibilities of the functional objects in ***Mathematica,*** by representing a certain interest first of all for the system programming.

Thus, as a reasonably useful version of the built-in ***Compile*** function, one can represent the ***Compile1*** procedure whose call ***Compile1***[*f, x, y*] returns a function of the classical type whose body is defined by an algebraic *y* expression, whereas *f* defines a name of the generated function and *x* defines the list of types attributed to the parameters of an expression *y*. The factual *x* argument is specified in the format {{*a, Ta*}, *b*, {*c, Tc*},...}, where {*a, b, c,...*} defines parameters of the *y* expression, whereas {*Ta, Tc,...*} defines the testing *Q*-functions while single elements of *x* defines validity of any expression for corresponding parameter.

```
In[10]:= Compile1[f_/; SymbolQ[f], x_/; ListQ[x], y_] :=
Module[{a = ToString1[y], b, c, d, g, h, t}, b = FactualVarsStr1[a];
          b = Select[b, ! SameQ[#[[1]], "System`"] &][[1]][[2 ;; -1]];
                    SetAttributes[g, Listable]; g[t_] := ToString[t];
              t = Map[ToString, Map[If[ListQ[#], #[[1]], #] &, x]];
                              c = ToString[f] <> "["; d = Map[g, x];
                  Do[h = d[[j]]; If[ListQ[h] && MemberQ[b, h[[1]]],
           c = c <> h[[1]] <> "_/;" <> h[[2]] <> "[" <> h[[1]] <> "],",
       If[MemberQ[b, h], c = c <> h <> "_,", 77]], {j, Length[d]}];
                                          t = Complement[b, t];
             If[t != {}, Do[c = c <> t[[j]] <> "_,", {j, Length[t]}], 78];
         c = StringTake[c, {1, -2}] <> "] := " <> a; ToExpression[c];
                                                    Definition[f]]
In[11]:= Compile1[f, {x, {n, IntegerQ}, {M, RationalQ}, {h, RealQ}},
                                 (Sin[h] + a*x^b)/(c*M - Log[n])]
Out[11]= f[x_, n_/; IntegerQ[n], M_/; RationalQ[M], h_/; RealQ[h],
                          a_, b_, c_] := (a*x^b + Sin[h])/(c*M - Log[n])
In[12]:= N[f[t, 77, 7/8, 7.8, m, n, p], 3]
Out[12]= (0.998543 + m*t^n)/(-4.34 + 0.875*p)
```

Fragment above represents source code of the procedure.

1.2. ***The user pure functions.*** First of all, we will notice that so-called ***functional programming*** isn't any discovery of the ***Mathematica*** system, and goes back to a number of software that appeared long before the above system. In this regard, it is pertinently focused slightly more in details the attention on the concept of functional programming in historical aspect. While here we only will note certain moments characterizing specifics of the paradigm of functional programming. We will note only that the foundation of functional programming has been laid approximately at the same time, as *imperative programming* that is the most widespread now, i.e. in the thirties years of the last century. *A. Church (USA)* – the author of **λ**–calculus and one of founders of the concept of *Cellular Automata* in connection with his works in field of infinite automata and mathematical logic along with *H. Curry (England)* and *M. Schönfinkel (Germany)* that have developed the mathematical theory of combinators, with good reason can be considered as the founders of mathematical foundation of functional programming. In additiom, functional programming languages, especially the purely functional ones such as the *Hope* and *Rex,* have largely been used in academical circles rather than in commercial software. Whereas prominent *functional* programming languages such as *Lisp* have been used in the industrial and commercial applications. Today, *functional programming paradigm* is also supported in a number of domain-specific programming languages, for example, by the ***Mathem***-language of the ***Mathematica.*** From a rather large number of languages of functional programming it is possible to note the following languages that exerted a great influence on progress in this field, namely: *Lisp, Scheme, ISWIM,* family *ML, Miranda, Haskell,* etc. By and large, if the *imperative* languages are based on operations of assignment and cycle, the *functional* languages on recursions. The most important advantages of the functional languages are considered in our books in detail [8-14], namely:

– programs on functional languages as a rule are much shorter and simpler than their analogues on the imperative languages;

– almost all modern functional languages are strictly typified and ensure the safety of programs; at that, the strict typification allows to generate more effective code;

– in a functional language the functions can be transferred as an argument to other functions or are returned as result of their calls;

– in pure functional languages (which aren't allowing by–effects for the functions) there is no an operator of assigning, the objects of

such language can't be modified or deleted, it is only possible to create new objects by decomposition and synthesis of the existing objects. In the pure functional languages all functions are free from by–effects.

Meanwhile, *functional* languages can imitate certain useful *imperative* properties. Not every functional languages are pure forasmuch in a lot of cases the admissibility of *by–effects* allows to essentially simplify programming. However today the most developed functional languages are as a rule pure. With many interesting enough questions concerning a subject of functional programming, the reader can familiarize oneself, for example, in [15]. Whereas with an quite interesting critical remarks on functional languages and possible ways of their elimination it is possible to familiarize oneself in [8-15,22].

A number of concepts and paradigms are quite specific for *functional* programming and absent in *imperative* programming. Meanwhile, many programming languages, as a rule, are based on several paradigms of programming, in particular imperative programming languages can succesfully use also concepts of functional programming. In particular, as an important enough concept are so–called the ***pure functions,*** whose results of run depends only on their *actual* arguments. Such functions possess certain useful properties a part of which it is possible to use for *optimization* of program code and parallelization of calculations. In principle, there are no special difficulties for programming in the functional style in languages that aren't the functional. The ***Mathematica*** language supports the mixed paradigm of functional and procedural programming. We will consider the elements of *functional programming* in ***Mathematica*** in whose basis the concept of the *pure* function lays. The ***pure*** functions – one of the basic concepts of functional programming which is a component of programming system in ***Mathematica*** in general.

Typically, when a function is called, its name is specified, whereas pure functions allow to specify functions which can be applied to arguments without having to define their explicit names. If a certain function ***G*** is used repeatedly, then can define the function using definition, considered above, and refer to the function by its name **G.** On the other hand, if some function is intend to use only once, then will probably find it better to give the function in format of *pure function* without ever naming it. The reader that is familiar with formal logic or the *LISP* programming language, will recognize ***Mathematica*** *pure* functions as being like λ expressions or *not named functions*. Note, that *pure functions* are also close to the pure mathematical notion of operators. ***Mathematica*** uses the following formats for definition of pure functions, namely:

(a) ***Function***[*x, **body***]
(b) ***Function***[{*x1, x2, …, xn*}*, **body***]
(c) ***body*** **&**

Format *(**a**)* determines pure function in which ***x*** in function *body* is replaced by any given argument. An arbitrary admissible expression from variable ***x***, including also constants and calls of functions acts as a body. Format *(**b**)* determines a pure function in which variables ***x1, x2, …, xn*** in function body is replaced by the corresponding arguments. Whereas format *(**c**)* determines a function body containing formal arguments denoted as **#** or **#1, #2, #3,** etc. It is so-called ***short*** format. Note, the pure functions of formats *(**a**)*, *(**b**)* do not allow to use the *typification* mechanism for formal arguments similarly to the *classical* functions, namely constructs of type *"**h_…**"* are not allowed. This is a very serious difference between *pure* function and *classical* function whereas otherwise, already when evaluating the definition of any pure function with typed formal arguments, ***Mathematica*** identifies the erroneous situations.

The calls of pure functions of the above formats are defined according to simple examples below, namely:

```
In[2162]:= Function[x, x^2 + 42][25]
Out[2162]= 667
In[2163]:= Function[{x, y, z}, x^2 + y^2 + z^2][42, 75, 77]
Out[2163]= 13318
In[2164]:= #1^2 + #2^2 &[900, 50]
Out[2164]= 812500
In[2165]:= Function[x_Integer, x^2 + 42]
          Function::flpar: Parameter specification x_Integer in ….
```

When ***Function[body]*** or ***body &*** is applied to a set of *formal* arguments, **#** *(or* ***#1****)* is replaced by the first argument, **#2** by the second, and so on while ***#0*** is replaced by the function itself. If there are more arguments than ***#j*** in the function supplied, the remaining arguments are ignored. At that, **##** defines sequence of all given arguments, whereas ***##n*** stands for arguments from number ***n*** onward. ***Function*** has attribute *HoldAll* and function body is evaluated only after the formal arguments have been replaced by actual arguments. Function construct can be nested in any way. Each is treated as a scoping construct, with named inner variables being renamed if necessary. Furthermore, in the call ***Function[args, body, attrs]*** as optional argument ***attrs*** can be a single attribute or a list of attributes, e.g. *HoldAll, Protected* and so on, while the call ***Function[Null, body, attrs]*** represents a function in which the arguments in function body are given using slot **#,** etc. Such format of a pure function is very useful when a one–time call of the function is required.

Note that unlike the format *(c)*, the formats *(a)* and *(b)* of a pure function allow use as the body rather complex program constructions, including local variables, cycles, definitions of blocks, modules and functions. A fairly simple example quite visually illustrates what has been said:

```
In[7]:= {a, b} = {0, 0}
Out[7]= {0, 0}
In[8]:= Function[{x, y, z}, Save["tmp", {a, b}]; {a, b} = {42, 47};
                                              g[h_, g_] := h*g;
If[x <= 6, Do[Print[{a, b, y^z}], z], x+y+z]; {(a+b)*(x+y+z)+
        g[42, 47], Get["tmp"], DeleteFile["tmp"]}[[1]]][1, 2, 3]
        {42, 47, 8}
        {42, 47, 8}
        {42, 47, 8}
Out[8]= 2508
In[9]:= {a, b}
Out[9]= {0, 0}
In[10]:= g[42, 47]
Out[10]= 1974
```

So, in the given example the locality of variables ***a*** and ***b*** is provided with saving their initial *(up to a function call)* values at the time of function call by their saving in the temporary *"tmp"* file, their redefinitions in the course of execution of a function body with the subsequent uploading of initial values of ***a*** and ***b*** from the *"tmp"* file to the current session of ***Mathematica*** with removal of the *"tmp"* file from the file system of the computer. Such mechanism completely answers the principle of locality of variables in a function body. This example also illustrates the ability to define a new function in the body of a pure function with its use, both within the body of the source function and outside of the function.

At using of the pure functions, unlike traditional functions, there is no need to designate their names, allowing to code their definitions directly in points of their call that is caused by that the results of the calls of pure functions depend only on values of the actual arguments received by them. Selection from a list ***x*** of elements that satisfy certain conditions and elementwise application of a function to elements of the list ***x*** can be done by constructions of the view ***Select*[*x, test*[#] &]** and ***Map*[*F*[#] &, *x*]** respectively as illustrate the following examples, namely:

```
In[3336]:= Select[{a, 72, 77, 42, 67, 2019, s, 47, 500}, OddQ[#] &]
Out[3336]= {77, 67, 2019, 47}
In[3337]:= Map[(#^2 + #) &, {1, 2, 3, 4, 5, 6, 7, 8, 9, 10, 11, 12}]
Out[3337]= {2, 6, 12, 20, 30, 42, 56, 72, 90, 110, 132, 156}
```

At use of the short form of a pure function it is necessary to be careful at its coding because the *ampersand (&)* has quite low priority. For example, expression ***#1 + #2 – #3 + #2*#4 &*** without parentheses is correct whereas, in general, they are obligatory, in particular, at use of a pure function as the right part of a rule as illustrate very simple examples [10-12]. The universal format of a call of pure *f* function is defined as *f* @@ {*args*}, for instance:

```
In[4214]:= OddQ[#] || PrimeQ[#] || IntegerQ[#] & @@ {77}
Out[4214]= True
```

In combination with a number of functions, in particular, ***Map, Select*** and some others the use of pure functions is rather convenient, therefore the question of converting the traditional functions into the pure functions seems an quite topical; for its decision various approaches, including creation of the program converters can be used. Thus, we used pure functions a rather widely at programming of a lot of problems of various types of the applied, and the system character [1-16,22].

Unlike a number of convertors of classical functions to pure function, procedure below allows to keep the testing functions of the general kind for arguments of the converted functions

W[*x_/; Test*[*x*], *y_H, z_, h__H1, t___, ...*] := 𝔑[*x, y, z, h, t, ...*]

by converting of a classical ***W*** function to pure function of short format, i.e. the procedure call ***FuncToPureFunction*[*W*]** returns the pure function in the following kind

If[*Test*[*#1*] && *HQ*[#2] && True && *H1Q*[#4] && True && ..., 𝔑[*#1, #2, #3, #4, #5, ...*], *IncorrectArgs*[*Sequential numbers of incorrect factual arguments*]] &

where {*heads* ***H*** and ***H1***} can absent. In addition, for arguments of type {*h__H1, t___*} the resultant pure function considers only their first factual value. At the same time, only one of the {*Real, List, Complex, Integer, Rational, String, Symbol*} list is allowed as a head ***H*** for a ***y*** expression. In a case of inadmissibility of at least one argument and/or its testing *(for example, incorrect head* ***H*** *or* ***H1****)* the call of the pure function returns the formal call of the kind ***IncorrectArgs*[*n1, n2,..., np*]**, where {*n1, n2,..., np*} determine sequential numbers of incorrect arguments. With source code of the ***FuncToPureFunction*** procedure with typical examples of its application that a quite clearly illustrate the results returned by the procedure can be found below [8-12,16].

```
In[5]:= FuncToPureFunction[x_/; FunctionQ[x]] :=
  Module[{a, b = ProcBody[x], c = 1, d, g, h, p, s = Map[ToString,
      {Complex, Integer, List, Rational, Real, String, Symbol}]},
    a = ArgsBFM1[x]; g = Map[{Set[d, "#" <> ToString[c++]]; d,
                StringReplaceVars[#[[2]], #[[1]] -> d]} &, a];
                  h = Map[If[! StringFreeQ[#[[2]], #[[1]]], #[[2]],
  If[#[[2]] == "Arbitrary", "True", If[MemberQ[s, #[[2]]], #[[2]] <>
                          "Q[" <> #[[1]] <> "]", "False"]]] &, g];
```

```
p = Map["(" <> # <> ")" &, h]; p = Riffle[p, "&&"];
a = Map[#[[1]] &, a]; c = Map[#[[1]] &, g];
a = StringReplaceVars[b, GenRules[a, c]];
ToExpression["If[" <> p <> "," <> a <> "," <>
"IncorrectArgs@@Flatten[Position[" <>
ToString[h] <> ", False]]" <> "]&"]]

In[6]:= f[x_/; IntegerQ[x], y_/; y == 77, z_List, t_, p__, h___] :=
x*y*h + Length[z]*t
In[7]:= FuncToPureFunction[f]
Out[7]= If[IntegerQ[#1] && #2 == 77 && ListQ[#3] && True &&
True && True, #1*#2*#6 + Length[#3]*#4,
IncorrectArgs @@ Flatten[Position[{IntegerQ[#1], #2 == 77,
ListQ[#3], True, True, True}, False]]] &
```

It should be noted that pure functions allow for a kind of *parameterization* based on constructions of the following format:

<*Name[params]*> := <*Pure function, containing params*>

where ***Name*** – a name of pure function and ***params*** determines parameters entering the function body. Calls of pure functions parameterized in this way have the following format:

Name[params][actual args]

The following simple example illustrates the told:

```
In[2215]:= T[n_, m_] := Function[{x, y, z}, n*(x + m*y + z)]
In[2216]:= T[42, 47][1, 2, 3]
Out[2216]= 4116
In[2217]:= G[p_, n_] := p*(#1^2 + #2^2*#3^n) &
In[2218]:= G[5, 2][5, 6, 7]
Out[2218]= 8945
In[2219]:= With[{p=5, n=2}, p*(#1^2 + #2^2*#3^n) &][5,6,7]
Out[2219]= 8945
```

In a number of applications such parameterization is quite useful, allowing to customize the tool for application based on parameter values. Some useful tools for working with the user functions are presented below, whereas a wider range of such tools are available for classical functions which are suitable also for many user procedure processing. This should be borne in mind when discussing issues related to the procedures.

1.3. Some useful tools for work with the user functions. For work with functions ***Mathematica*** has a wide range of tools for working with functions, including user ones. Here we present a number of tools for working with user functions that do not go to the standard set. First of all, it is of particular interest to test a symbol or expression to be a function. Some of the tools in this direction are presented in our package ***MathToolBox*** [16,9-12]. The most common tool of this type is the function ***FunctionQ,*** whose definition in turn contains ***QFunction*** and ***QFunction1*** procedures and function ***PureFuncQ*** of the same type, whose call on a symbol or expression ***x*** returns *True,* if ***x*** is a function and *False* otherwise. Program code of the ***FunctionQ*** function can be presented as follows:

```
In[25]:= FunctionQ[x_] := If[StringQ[x], QFunction1[x] ||
  PureFuncQ[ToExpression[x]], PureFuncQ[x] || QFunction[x]]
In[26]:= y := #1^2 + #2^2 &; {FunctionQ[#1^2 + #2^2 &],
                                              FunctionQ[y]}
Out[26]= {True, True}
In[27]:= z = Function[{x, y, z}, If[x <= 6, Do[Print[y^z], z],
                                                  x + y + z]];
In[28]:= FunctionQ[Function[{x, y, z}, If[x <= 6,
                                   Do[Print[y^z], z], x + y + z]]]
Out[28]= True
In[29]:= FunctionQ[z]
Out[29]= True
In[30]:= PureFuncQ[Function[{x, y, z}, If[x <= 6,
                                   Do[Print[y^z], z], x + y + z]]]
Out[30]= True
In[31]:= PureFuncQ[#1^2 + #2^2 &]
Out[31]= True
In[32]:= G[x_] := Plus[Sequences[x]]
In[33]:= {FunctionQ[G], PureFuncQ[G]}
Out[33]= {True, False}
```

At the same time, the function call ***PureFuncQ[w]*** allows to identify object ***w*** to be a pure function, returning *True,* if ***w*** is a pure function, and *False* otherwise. This tool along with others provide strict differentiation of such basic element of functional and procedural programming, as a ***function*** [8-16].

The question of determining the formal arguments of user function is of quite certain interest. Built-in tools of the system do not directly solve this issue and we have created a number of tools for the purpose of determining the formal arguments of the function, module and block. For a function, this problem is solved e.g. by the ***ArgsF*** function with program code:

```
In[47]:= ArgsF[x_] := If[PureFuncQ[x], ArgsPureFunc[x],
If[FunctionQ[x], Args[x], ToString1[x] <> " - not function"]]
In[48]:= GS@Sequences[a_Integer, b_Symbol, c_] := a+b+c
In[49]:= ArgsF[GS]
Out[49]= {a_Integer, b_Symbol, c_}
In[50]:= H := #1^2 + #2^2*#3^4 &
In[51]:= ArgsF[H]
Out[51]= {"#1", "#2", "#3"}
In[52]:= T := Function[{x, y, z}, x + y + z]; ArgsF[T]
Out[52]= {"x", "y", "z"}
In[53]:= ArgsF[Agn]
Out[53]= "Agn - not function"
```

The call ***ArgsF[x]*** returns the list of formal arguments in the string format of function ***x***, including pure function, if ***x*** is not a function, the call returns the corresponding message. The ***ArgsF*** function uses the testing tools ***FunctionQ*** and ***PureFuncQ*** along with tools ***Args, ArgsPureFunc,*** and ***ToString1*** with which it is possible to get acquainted in [1-12], while the interested reader can get acquainted here with a number of tools *(that complement the built-in system tools)* for work with the user functions.

For converting of a pure function of formats ***(a)*** and ***(b)*** to format ***(c)*** the ***PureFuncToShort*** procedure with the following program code serves:

```
In[4220]:= PureFuncToShort[x_/; PureFuncQ[x]] :=
                                        Module[{a, b, c, d},
     If[ShortPureFuncQ[x], x, a = ArgsPureFunc[x]; d = a;
          b = Map[ToExpression, a]; Map[ClearAll, a];
                                  a = Map[ToExpression, a];
          c = Quiet[GenRules[a, Range2[#, Length[a]]]];
     {ToExpression[ToString1[ReplaceAll[x[[2]], c]] <> "&"],
```

```
ToExpression[ToString[d] <> "=" <> ToString1[b]]}[[1]]]]
In[4221]:= G := Function[{x, y, z}, p*(x + y + z)];
In[4222]:= PureFuncToShort[G]
Out[4222]= p*(#1 + #2 + #3) &
```

The procedure call ***PureFuncToShort***[*w*] returns the result of converting of a pure function *w* to its short format. In turn, the ***PureFuncToFunction*** procedure is intended for converting of a pure function to classical. The following example presents its program code with a simple example of its application:

```
In[7]:= PureFuncToFunction[x_/; PureFuncQ[x], y_/; !HowAct[y]]:=
                              Module[{a = ArgsPureFunc[x], b, c},
  If[ShortPureFuncQ[x], b = (StringReplace[#1, "#" -> "x"] &) /@ a;
               c = StringReplace[ToString1[x], GenRules[a, b]];
                   b = ToExpression /@ Sort[(#1 <> "_" &) /@ b];
            ToExpression[ToString1[y[Sequences[b]]] <> ":=" <>
                   StringTake[c, {1, -3}]], a = (#1 <> "_" &) /@ a;
ToExpression[ToString1[y[Sequences[ToExpression /@ a]]] <> ":="
                                        <> ToString1[x[[2]]]]]]]
In[8]:= t := p*(#1^2 + #2^2*#3^n) &
In[9]:= PureFuncToFunction[t, H]
In[10]:= Definition[H]
Out[10]= H[x1_, x2_, x3_] := p*(x1^2 + x2^2*x3^n)
```

The procedure call with two arguments *x* and *H* where *x* - a pure function and *H* - an undefined symbol, converts the pure *x* function to a classical function named *H*.

We have programmed a number of procedures that ensure the mutual conversion of classical, pure and pure functions of the short format. In particular, the ***CfToPure*** procedure allows the classical functions to be converted into pure functions of the short format [12-16]. Calling the ***CfToPure***[*f*] procedure returns the result of converting a classical function *f* to its equivalent in the form of a pure function of short format. The procedure uses a number of techniques useful in practical programming, which are recommended to the reader. The fragment below represents source code of the ***CfToPure*** procedure and examples of its use.

```
In[4]:= {x, y, z} = {42, 47, 67};
```

```
In[5]:= F[x_Integer, y_, z_/; IntegerQ[z]] := (x^2 + y^3) +
                                  (y^2 - x*y*z)/Sqrt[x^2 + y^2 + z^2]

In[6]:= CfToPure[f_/; FunctionQ[f]] := Module[{a, b, c, d},
                          a = Map[ToString[#] <> "@" &, Args[f]];
   a = Map[StringReplace[#, "_" ~~ ___ ~~ "@" -> ""] &, a];
                                        d = "###"; Save2[d, a];
             b = Map["#" <> ToString[#] &, Range[Length[a]]];
                             Map[Clear, a];  c = GenRules[a, b];
 c = Map[ToExpression[#[[1]]] -> ToExpression[#[[2]]] &, c];
                     a = StringReplace[Definition2[f][[1]],
Headings[f][[2]] <> " := " -> ""]; a = ToExpression[a <> " &"];
                 {ReplaceAll[c][a], Get[d], DeleteFile[d]}[[1]]]

In[7]:= CfToPure[F]
Out[7]= (x^2 + y^3) + (y^2 - x*y*z)/Sqrt[x^2 + y^2 + z^2] &
In[8]:= {x, y, z}
Out[8]= {42, 47, 67}
In[9]:= G[x_Integer, y_List, z_/; IntegerQ[z]] := N[Sin[x]/
Log[Length[y]] + (y^2 - x*y*z)^(x+z)/Sqrt[x^2+y^2+z^2]]
In[10]:= CfToPure[G]
Out[10]= N[Sin[#1]/Log[Length[#2]] + (#2^2 - #1*#2*#3)^
                         (#1 + #3)/Sqrt[#1^2 + #2^2 + #3^2]] &
```

As in a function body along with formal arguments global variables and calls of functions can enter, then the problem of determination them is of a certain interest to any function. In this regard the ***GlobalsInFunc*** function can be useful enough with the following program code:

```
In[2223]:= VarsInFunc[x_] := Complement[Select[VarsInExpr[
                    ToString2[Definition[x]]], ! SystemQ[#] &],
                                      {ToString[x]}, ArgsBFM[x]]
                              GlobalsInFunc[x_] := If[PureFuncQ[x],
     Complement[VarsInExpr[x], Flatten[{ArgsPureFunc[x],
              "Function"}]], If[FunctionQ[x], VarsInFunc[x],
                                     "Argument - not function"]]

In[2224]:= F[x_, y_, z_] := a*x*b*y + N[Sin[2019]]
In[2225]:= GlobalsInFunc[F]
```

```
Out[2225]= {"a", "b"}
In[2226]:= G := Function[{x, y, z}, p*(x + y + z)];
In[2227]:= GlobalsInFunc[G]
Out[2227]= {"p"}
In[2228]:= T := p*(#1^2 + #2^2*#3^n) &
In[2229]:= GlobalsInFunc[T]
Out[2229]= {"n", "p"}
```

The call ***GlobalsInFunc[x]*** returns the list of global symbols in string format entering a function ***x*** definition *(pure or classical)* and other than the built-in symbols of ***Mathematica,*** if ***x*** is not a function, than the call returns the corresponding message. The function uses the tools of our ***MathToolBox*** package [7,8,16], in particular the function whose call ***VarsInFunc[x]*** returns the list of global symbols in string format entering a *classical* function ***x*** definition and other than the built-in symbols of the system.

Generally, the user functions do not allow to use the local variables, however a simple artificial reception allows to do it. Sequential list structure of execution of operations when the list is evaluated element-wise from left to right is for this purpose used, i.e. function is represented in the following format:

***Name[args]* := {*Save*["#", {*locals*}], {*locals = values*}, *function body*, *Get*["#"], *DeleteFile*["#"]}[[3]]**

The presented format is rather transparent and well illustrates essence of the method of use in user function of local variables. The following simple example illustrates told:

```
In[9]:= GS[x_, y_, z_] := {Save["#", {a, b, c}], {a=2, b=7, c=6},
          a*x + b + y + c*z, Get["#"], DeleteFile["#"]}[[3]]
In[10]:= {a, b, c} = {1, 2, 3}
Out[10]= {1, 2, 3}
In[11]:= GS[42, 47, 67]
Out[11]= 540
In[12]:= {a, b, c}
Out[12]= {1, 2, 3}
```

In some cases, the given approach may prove to be quite useful in practical programming.

Meanwhile, a rather significant remark needs to be made regarding the objects multiplicity of definitions with the same name. As noted repeatedly, ***Mathematica*** system differentiates objects, above all, by their headers, if any. It is therefore quite real that we may deal with different definitions under the same name. This applies to all objects that have headers. In view of this circumstance, we have programmed a number of tools for various cases of application [1-16]. First of all, we need a tool of testing the presence of such multiplicity for a particular object *(function, module, block)*. This function is successfully performed by the ***MultipleQ*** procedure with program code:

```
In[47]:= MultipleQ[x_ /; SymbolQ[x], j___] := Module[{a},
           a = ToString[InputForm[Definition[x]]];
           a = StringReplace[a, "\n \n" → "\[CircleDot]"];
           a = StringSplit[a, "\[CircleDot]"];
  If[{j} != {} && !ValueQ[j], j=a]; If[Length[a] > 1, True, False]]
In[48]:= G[x_, y_] := p*(x^2 + y^2); G[x_Integer, y_] := x*y
             G[x_, y_, z_] := x^2 + y^2 + z^2; G[x_, y_List] := x*y
In[49]:= MultipleQ[G, gs]
Out[49]= True
In[50]:= gs
Out[50]= {"G[x_Integer, y_] := x*y", "G[x_, y_List] := x*y",
      "G[x_, y_] := p*(x^2+y^2)", "G[x_, y_, z_] := x^2+y^2+z^2"}
In[53]:= MultipleQ1[x_ /; SymbolQ[x], j___] :=
                                Module[{a = Definition2[x]},
           If[{j} != {} && ! HowAct[j], j = a[[1 ;; -2]], 77];
                   If[Length[a[[1 ;; -2]]] == 1, False, True]]
In[54]:= MultipleQ2[x_Symbol] := If[Length[ToExpression[
           Unique1[Definition2[x], j]]][[1 ;; -2]]] > 1, True, False]
```

The call ***MultipleQ[x]*** returns *True* if symbol *x* has multiple definitions, and *False* otherwise. Through optional *j* argument the list of *x* definitions in string format is returned. ***MultipleQ1*** and ***MultipleQ2*** tools – functional analogues of the ***MultipleQ***.

At last, quite natural interest represents the existence of the user procedures and functions activated in the current session. Solution of the question can be received by tool of a procedure whose call ***ActBFMuserQ[]*** returns *True* if such objects exist in the current session, and *False* otherwise; the call ***ActBFMuserQ**[x]* thru optional ***x*** argument – *an undefinite variable* – returns the **2**-element nested list whose the first element contains name of the user object in the string format while the second defines list of its types in string format respectively. The fragment represents source code of the ***ActBFMuserQ*** with an example of its use.

```
In[7]:= ActBFMuserQ[x___ /; If[{x} == {}, True, If[Length[{x}] == 1
&& ! HowAct[x], True, False]]] := Module[{b = {}, c = 1, d, h,
a = Select[Names["`*"], ! UnevaluatedQ[Definition2, #] &]},
For[c, c <= Length[a], c++, h = Quiet[ProcFuncTypeQ[a[[c]]]];
          If[h[[1]], AppendTo[b, {a[[c]], h[[-1]]}], Null]];
  If[b == {}, False, If[{x} != {}, x = ReduceLists[b]]; True]]
In[8]:= V := Compile[{{x, _Real}, {y, _Real}}, (x^3 + y)^2];
  Art := Function[{x, y}, x*Sin[y]]; K := (#1^2 + #2^4) &;
  GS[x_ /; IntegerQ[x], y_ /; IntegerQ[y]] := Sin[90] + Cos[42];
  G = Compile[{{x, _Integer}, {y, _Real}}, x*y];
  H[x_] := Block[{}, x]; H[x_, y_] := x + y;
  SetAttributes["H", Protected]; P[x_] := Module[{}, x];
  P[y_] := Module[{}, y]; P[x__] := Plus[Sequences[{x}]];
  T42[x_, y_, z_] := x*y*z; R[x_] := Module[{a = 590}, x*a];
  GSV := (#1^2 + #2^4 + #3^6) &
In[9]:= ActBFMuserQ[]
Out[9]= True
In[10]:= {ActBFMuserQ[t77], t77}
Out[10]= {True, {{"Art", {"PureFunction"}},
  {"G", {"CompiledFunction"}}, {"GS", {"Function"}},
  {"H", {"Block", "Function"}}, {"P1", {"Function"}},
  {"R", {"Module"}}, {"K", "ShortPureFunction"},
  {"V", {"CompiledFunction"}},
  {"P", {"Module", "Module", "Function"}, {"T42", {"Function"}},
  {"GSV", "ShortPureFunction"}}}}
```

The ***ActBFMuserQ*** procedure is of interest as an useful tool first of all in the system programming.

Along with the presented tools a number of other useful tools for working with user functions and instructive examples of their application can be found in [1-16]. Here again it should be noted that the examples of tools presented in this book use the tools of the mentioned ***MathToolBox*** package [16] that has freeware license. Given that this package and its tools will be frequently mentioned below, we will briefly describe it.

The package contains more than ***1320*** tools which eliminate restrictions of a number of the standard ***Mathematica*** tools and expand its software with new tools. In this context, the package can serve as a certain additional tool of modular programming, especially useful in numerous applications where certain non-standard evaluations have to accompany programming. At the same time, tools presented in the package have the most direct relation to certain principal questions of procedure-functional programming in ***Mathematica,*** not only for decision of applied tasks, but, above all, for programming of software extending frequently used facilities of the system and/or eliminating their defects or extending the system with new facilities. Software presented in this package contains a number of useful enough and effective receptions of programming in ***Mathematica,*** and extends its software which allows in the system to programme the tasks of various purpose more simply and effectively. The additional tools composing the above package embrace a rather wide cyrcle of sections of the ***Mathematica*** system [15,16].

The given package contains definitions of some *functionally* equivalent tools programmed in various ways useful for use in practical programming. Along with this, they illustrate a lot of both efficient and undocumented features of ***Math***-language of the system. In our opinion, the detailed analysis of source code of the package software can be a rather effective remedy on the path of the deeper mastering of programming in ***Mathematica.*** Experience of holding of the master classes of various levels on the systems ***Mathematica*** and ***Maple*** in all evidence confirms expediency of joint use of both standard tools of the systems of computer mathematics, and the user tools created in the course of programming of various appendices. A lot of tools contained in the package and mentioned below were described in [1-15] in detail enough. We now turn to the procedural objects of the ***Mathematica*** system.

Chapter 2: The user procedures in Mathematica

Procedure is one of basic concepts of programming system of ***Mathematica,*** being not less important object in systems of programming as a whole. A *procedure* is an object implementing the well-known concept of *"black box"* when with known input *(actual arguments)* and output *(returned result)* while the internal structure of the object, generally speaking, is closed. ***Procedure*** forms the basis of the so-called *"procedural programming"* where in the future by the procedure we will understand such objects as ***module*** and ***block.*** Procedural programming is one of basic paradigms of ***Mathematica*** which in an essential degree differs from similar paradigm of the well-known *traditional* procedural programming languages. This circumstance is the cornerstone of certain system problems relating to *procedural* programming in ***Mathematica.*** Above all, similar problems arise in the field of distinctions in implementation of the above paradigms in the ***Mathematica*** and in the environment of traditional procedural languages. Along with that, unlike a number of traditional and built-in languages the built-in ***Math***–language has no a number of useful enough tools for operating with procedural objects. In our books [1-15] and ***MathToolBox*** package [16] are presented some such tools.

A number of the problems connected with similar tools is considered in the present chapter with preliminary discussion of the concept of *`procedure`* in ***Mathematica*** system as bases of its procedural paradigm. In addition, tools of analysis of this section concern only the user procedures and functions because definitions of all built–in system functions *(unlike, say, from the **Maple** system)* from the user are hidden, i.e. are inaccessible for processing by the standard tools of ***Mathematica*** system. Note that the discussion of *procedural* objects will take place relative to the latest version of ***Mathematica 12.1,*** which can dissonance with ***Mathematica*** of earlier versions. However this should not cause any serious misunderstandings. ***Math-****language* possesses a rather high level of immutability in relation to its versions.

2.1. Definition of procedures in Mathematica software

Procedures in ***Mathematica*** system are formally represented by program objects of the following 2 simple formats, namely:

M[x_/; Test$_x$, y_/; Test$_y$, ...] {:= | =} Module[{locals}, Module Body]

B[x_/; Test$_x$, y_/; Test$_y$, ...] {:= | =} Block[{locals}, Block Body]

i.e., procedures of both types represent the functions from two arguments – the procedure body *(Body)* and local variables *(locals)*. *Local* variables – the list of names, perhaps, with initial values which are attributed to them. These variables have the local character concerning the procedure, i.e. their values aren't crossed with values of the symbols of the same name outside of the procedure. All other variables in the procedure have global character, sharing field of variables of the ***Mathematica*** current session. In addition, in the procedure definition it is possible to distinguish six following component, namely:

- ***procedure name*** *(**M** and **B** in the both procedures definitions);*
- ***procedure heading*** *(**{M | B}[x_/; Test$_x$, y_/; Test$_y$, ...]** in the both procedures definitions);*
- ***procedural brackets*** **(Module[...]** *and* **Block[...])**;
- ***local variables*** *(list of local variables **{locals}**; can be empty list);*
- ***procedure (Module, Block) body;*** *can be empty;*
- ***testing Test$_x$ function*** *(the function call **Test[x]** returns True or False depend on permissibility of an actual **x** argument; can absent).*

When programmed, we typically try to program tasks as modular programs as possible to make them more readable and independent, and more convenient to maintain. One of ways of a solution of the given problem is use of the scope mechanism for variables, defining for them separate scopes. ***Mathematica*** provides 2 basic mechanisms for limiting the scope of variables in form of *modules* and *blocks,* hereinafter referred to as general term – ***procedures.*** *Procedures* along with *functions* play a *decisive* role in solving the issue of *optimal organization* of program code. Note, real programming uses modules much more frequently, but *blocks* are often more convenient in *interactive programming.*

Most traditional programming languages use a so-called *"lexical scoping"* mechanism for variables, which is analogous to the mechanism of modules in ***Mathematica.*** Whereas symbolic programming languages e.g. *LISP* allow also *"dynamic scoping"*, analogous to the mechanism used by blocks in ***Mathematica.*** When *lexical scoping* is used, variables are treated as local ones to a particular part of a program code. At a *dynamic scoping,* the values of the allocated variables are local only to a certain part of the program execution. A ***Module*** carries out processing of the body when it is carried out as a component of the general program code, any variable from locals in the module body is considered as local one. Then natural execution of the general program code continues. A ***Block,*** ignoring all expressions of a body, uses for it the current values of variables from locals. In the course of execution of body the *block* uses values of *locals* for variables, then *recovers* their original values after completion of the body. Most vividly these differences an example illustrates:

```
In[2254]:= {b, c} = {m, n};
In[2255]:= B[x_] := Block[{a = 7, b, c}, x*(a + b + c)];  B[7]
Out[2255]= 7*(7 + m + n)
In[2256]:= {b, c}
Out[2256]= {m, n}
In[2257]:= LocVars[x_String] := ToExpression[x <> "$" <>
                                 ToString[$ModuleNumber - 4]]
In[2258]:= M[x_] := Module[{a = 7, b, c}, x*(a + b + c)]; M[7]
Out[2258]= 7*(7 + b$21248 + c$21248)
In[2259]:= Map[LocVars, {"a", "b", "c"}]
Out[2259]= {a$21248, b$21248, c$21248}
```

Thus, ***Module*** is a scoping construct that implements *lexical* scoping, while ***Block*** is a scoping construct implements *dynamic* scoping of *local* variables. ***Module*** creates new symbols to name each of its local variables every time it is called. Call of ***LocVars*** function immediately after calling a module *(not containing calls of other modules)* with local variables *{a, b, c,...}* returns the list of variables ***Map[LocVars,*** *{"a", "b", "c",...}*] that were generated at the time the module was called.

In the context of testing blocks for procedural nature in the above sense, the ***LocVars1*** procedure may be of interest whose call ***LocVars1[x]*** returns *True* if ***x*** is a module or a block ***x*** has no local variables without initial values, or the list of local variables is empty, otherwise *False* is returned. While calling ***LocVars1[x,y]*** with the ***2nd*** optional argument ***y*** – *an indefined symbol* – through ***y*** additionally returns the **2**-element list whose the first element defines the list of all local variables of ***x***, while the ***2nd*** element defines the list of local variables without initial values. Below, fragment represents source code of the procedure with its use.

```
In[4]:= LocVars1[x_ /; BlockModQ[x], y___] := Module[{a, b, d = {}},
                                              a = Locals5[x, b];
   Do[AppendTo[d, If[Length[b[[k]]] < 2, a[[k]], Nothing]],
    {k, Length[a]}]; If[{y} != {} && SymbolQ[y], y = {a, d}, 7];
             If[ModuleQ[x], True, If[a == d, True, False]]]
In[5]:= B[x_] := Block[{a = 7, b, c = 8, d}, x*a*b*c*d];
                        B1[x_] := Block[{a, b, c, d}, x*a*b*c*d]
In[6]:= {LocVars1[B, t1], t1}
Out[6]= {False, {{"a = 7", "b", "c = 8", "d"}, {"b", "d"}}}
In[7]:= {LocVars1[B1, t2], t2}
Out[7]= {True, {{"a", "b", "c", "d"}, {"a", "b", "c", "d"}}}
In[8]:= G[x_] := Block[{}, x^2]; {LocVars1[G, t72], t72}
Out[8]= {True, {{}, {}}}
```

Considering importance of modular approach to software organization when a program code consists of set of the linked independent objects and reaction of objects is defined only by their *inputs*, in this quality to us the most preferable the *modules* are presented. In *general* software code of the *modular* structure, the output of the module is the input for another module. For this reason the lion share of tools of our package ***MathToolBox*** [16] is programmed in the form of modules.

Once again, pertinently to pay attention to one moment. A number of tools represented in the package are focused on the solution of identical problems, but they use various algorithms programmed with usage of various approaches. They not only illustrate variety of useful enough receptions but also revealing their shortcomings and advantages useful both in practical and system programming. In our opinion, such approach opens a rather wide field for *awakening* of creative activity of the reader in respect of improvement of his skills in the programming in ***Mathematica*** system. Now let's consider module components in more detail.

Let's note that in certain cases duplication of definitions of blocks, modules and functions under new names on condition of saving their former definitions invariable is required. So, for assignment of a name that is *unique* in the current session to the new means, the procedure whose call ***DupDef[x]*** returns a name *(unique in the current session)* whose definition will be equivalent to definition of the ***x*** symbol can be used. In addition, the given procedure successfully works with the means having multiple definitions too. The following fragment represents source code of the procedure with an example of its application.

```
In[3331]:= DupDef[x_/; BlockFuncModQ[x]] :=
         Module[{a = Flatten[{Definition1[x]}],
         b = Unique[ToString[x]]},
ToExpression[Map[StringReplace[#, ToString[x] <> "[" ->
         ToString[b] <> "[", 1] &, a]]; b]
In[3332]:= Gs[x_, y_] := x + y
In[3333]:= Gs[x_] := Module[{a = 77}, a*x^2]
In[3334]:= DupDef[Gs]
Out[3334]= Gs78
In[3335]:= Definition[Gs78]
Out[3335]= Gs78[x_, y_] := x + y
          Gs78[x_] := Module[{a = 77}, a*x^2]
```

In particular, the ***DupDef*** procedure is useful enough when debugging of the user software.

The call ***Definition[x]*** of the standard function in a number of cases returns the definition of some ***x*** object with the context corresponding to it what at a rather large definitions becomes badly foreseeable and less acceptable for subsequent program processing as evidently illustrates a number of examples [6-15]. Moreover, the name of an object or its string format also can act as an actual argument. For elimination of this shortcoming we defined a number of tools allowing to obtain definitions of the procedures or functions in a certain optimized format. As such means it is possible to note the following: ***DefOptimum, DefFunc, Definition1, Definition2, Definition3÷Definition5, DefFunc1, DefOpt, DefFunc2*** and ***DefFunc3.*** These means along with some others are represented in [4-9] and included in the ***MathToolBox*** package [16]. The following fragment represents the source code of the most used tool of them with an example of its application.

```
In[49]:= Definition2[x_ /; SameQ[SymbolQ[x], HowAct[x]]] :=
                              Module[{a, b = Attributes[x], c},
              If[SystemQ[x], Return[{"System", Attributes[x]}],
                       Off[Part::partw]]; ClearAttributes[x, b];
                  Quiet[a = ToString[InputForm[Definition[x]]];
             Mapp[SetAttributes, {Rule, StringJoin}, Listable];
    c = StringReplace[a, Flatten[{Rule[StringJoin[Contexts1[],
         ToString[x] <> "`"], ""]}]]; c = StringSplit[c, "\n \n"];
          Mapp[ClearAttributes, {Rule, StringJoin}, Listable];
                       SetAttributes[x, b]; a = AppendTo[c, b];
     If[SameQ[a[[1]], "Null"] && a[[2]] == {}, On[Part::partw];
    {"Undefined", Attributes[x]}, If[SameQ[a[[1]], "Null"] &&
   a[[2]] != {} && ! SystemQ[x], On[Part::partw]; {"Undefined",
    Attributes[x]}, If[SameQ[a[[1]], "Null"] && a[[2]] != {} &&
        a[[2]] != {}, On[Part::partw]; {"System", Attributes[x]},
                                        On[Part::partw]; a]]]]]
In[50]:= a[x_] := x + 6; a[x_, y_] := Module[{}, x/y]; a[t_Integer] := 7
In[51]:= SetAttributes[a, {Protected, Listable}]; Definition2[a]
Out[51]= {"a[t_Integer] := 7", "a[x_] := x + 6",
              "a[x_, y_] := Module[{}, x/y]", {Listable, Protected}}
```

The ***Definition2*** call on system functions returns the nested list, whose first element – *"System"*, while the second element – the list of attributes ascribed to a factual argument. On the user function or procedure ***x*** the call ***Definition2[x]*** also returns the nested list, whose first element – the optimized definitions of ***x*** *(in the sense of absence of contexts in them, at a series definitions in a case of multiplicity of **x** definition)*, whereas the second element – the list of attributes ascribed to ***x;*** in their absence the empty list acts as the second element of the returned list. In a case of *False* value on a test ascribed to a formal *x* argument, the procedure call ***Definition2*[*x*]** will be returned unevaluated. Analogously to the above procedures, the procedure ***Definition2*** processes the main both the erroneous, and especial situations.

Using the ***Definition2*** procedure and the list representation, we give an example of a simple enough ***Info*** procedure whose call ***Info*[*x*]** in a convenient form returns the complete definition of a symbol *x*, including its usage. While the call ***Info*[*x, y*]** with the second optional *y* argument – *an indefinite symbol* – through it additionally returns the usage for *x* symbol in string format. The following fragment represents the source code of the ***Info*** procedure with examples of its typical application.

```
In[3221]:= Info[x_/; SymbolQ[x], y___] :=
                    If[! HowAct[x], $Failed, {If[StringQ[x::usage],
        Print[If[{y} != {} && ! HowAct[y], y = x::usage, x::usage]],
              Print["Usage on " <> ToString[x] <> " is absent"]],
      ToExpression[Definition2[x][[1 ;; -2]]]; Definition[x]}[[-1]]]
In[3222]:= Info[StrStr]
The call StrStr[x] returns an expression x in string format if x is
different from string; otherwise, the double string obtained from an
expression x is returned.
Out[3222]= StrStr[x_] := If[StringQ[x], "\"" <> x <> "\"",
                                                   ToString[x]]
In[3223]:= x[x_] := x; x[x_, y_] := x*y; x[x_, y_, z_] := x*y*z
In[3224]:= Info[x]
          Usage on x is absent
Out[3224]= x[x_] := x
           x[x_, y_] := x*y
           x[x_, y_, z_] := x*y*z
In[3225]:= Info[StrStr, g47]
The call StrStr[x] returns an expression x in string format if x is
different from string; otherwise, the double string obtained from an
expression x is returned.
Out[3225]= StrStr[x_] := If[StringQ[x], "\"" <> x <> "\"", ToString[x]]
In[3226]:= g47
Out[3226]= "The call StrStr[x] returns an expression x in string
format if x is different from string; otherwise, the double string
obtained from an expression x is returned."
```

```
In[3227]:= Info[agn]
Out[3227]= $Failed
```

If the first ***x*** argument - an indefined symbol, the procedure call ***Info***[***x***] returns $*Failed*.

Another moment should be mentioned. In some cases, the above procedural objects can be represented in functional form based on the list structures of the format:

F[*x_, ..., z_*] := {*Save*[*w, a, b, c, ...*]; ***Clear***[*a, b, c, ...*]; ***Procedure body, Get***[*w*]; ***DeleteFile***[*w*]}[[-2]]

The ***Save*** function saves all values of *local* and *global* procedure variables in a certain ***w*** file, then clears all these variables, and then executes the ***procedure body***. Finally, ***Get*** function loads the ***w*** file into the current session, restoring {***a, b, c,...***} variables, and then deletes the ***w*** file. The result of the function call of the type described is the *second* list element, beginning with its end in a case if the procedure returns the result of the call through the last sentence of its body, which is a fairly frequent case. We can use {;|,} as the list element separators, depending on need. Thus, on the basis of the above design it is possible to program *functional* equivalents of quite complex procedures. An example is the functional equivalent of the ***SubsDel*** procedure described in section **3.4**.

```
In[77]:= SubsDel[S_/; StringQ[S], x_/; StringQ[x], y_/; ListQ[y] &&
                 AllTrue[Map[StringQ, y], TrueQ] &&
        Plus[Sequences[Map[StringLength, y]]] == Length[y],
   p_/; MemberQ[{-1, 1}, p]] := {Save["#$#", {"b", "c", "d", "h", "k"}];
       Clear[b, c, d, h, k]; {b, c = x, d, h = StringLength[S], k};
     If[StringFreeQ[S, x], Return[S], b = StringPosition[S, x][[1]]];
   For[k = If[p == 1, b[[2]] + 1, b[[1]] - 1], If[p == 1, k <= h, k >= 1],
             If[p == 1, k++, k--], d = StringTake[S, {k, k}];
        If[MemberQ[y, d] || If[p == 1, k == 1, k == h], Break[],
             If[p == 1, c = c <> d, c = d <> c]; Continue[]]];
   StringReplace[S, c -> ""], Get["#$#"]; DeleteFile["#$#"]}[[-2]]
In[78]:= SubsDel["12345avz6789", "avz", {"8", "5"}, 1]
Out[78]= "1234589"
```

A comparative analysis of both implementations confirms aforesaid.

It is well known [8-12,16], that the user package uploaded into the current session can contains tools *x* whose definitions obtained by means of the call ***Definition*[*x*]** aren't completely optimized, i.e. contain constructions of the kind ***j* <> "*x*`"** where ***j* –** a context from the system list **$***Packages*. We have created a number of tools [16] that solve various problems of processing unoptimized definitions of both individual means and means in the user packages located in files of {"***m***", "***mx***"} formats. So, the call ***DefFunc1*[*x*]** provides return of the optimized definition of an object *x* whose definition is located in the user package or ***nb*–**document and that has been loaded into the current session. At that, a name *x* should define an object without any attributes and options or with attributes and/or options. Fragment below represents source code of the ***DefFunc1*** procedure along with an example of its application.

```
In[7]:= Definition[ListListQ]
Out[7]= ListListQ[Global`ListListQ`L_] :=
     If[ListQ[Global`ListListQ`L] && Global`ListListQ`L != {} &&
                                Length[Global`ListListQ`L] >= 1 &&
                      Length[Select[Global`ListListQ`L, ListQ[#1] &&
              Length[#1] == Length[Global`ListListQ`L[[1]]] &]] ==
                                Length[Global`ListListQ`L], True, False]
In[8]:= DefFunc1[x_/; SymbolQ[x] || StringQ[x]] :=
            Module[{a = GenRules[Map14[StringJoin, {"Global`",
     Context[x]}, ToString[x] <> "`"], ""], b = Definition2[x][[1]]},
   ToExpression[Map[StringReplace[#, a] &, b]]; Definition[x]]
In[9]:= DefFunc1[ListListQ]
Out[9]= ListListQ[L_] := If[ListQ[L] && L != {} &&
                Length[L] >= 1 && Length[Select[L, ListQ[#1] &&
        Length[#1] == Length[L[[1]]] &]] == Length[L], True, False]
```

So, the procedure call ***DefFunc1*[*x*]** in an optimized format returns the definition of an object *x* contained in a package or a notebook loaded into the current session. The object name is set in string format or symbol format depending on the object type *(procedure, function, global variable, procedure variable, etc.)*. Thus, in the **2*nd*** case the definition is essentially more readably, above all, for rather large source codes of procedures, functions, along with other objects. The ***TypesTools*** procedure is rather useful.

Calling ***TypesTools[x]*** procedure returns the three-element list whose elements are sub-lists containing names in the string format of tools with context ***x*** in the terms of the objects such as ***Functions, Procedures,*** and ***Others,*** accordingly. During the procedure run, lists of the form *{n, "Name"}* are intermediately output, where ***n*** is the number of the tool being tested from the tools list with context ***x,*** and ***Name*** is the name of the tool being tested. The following fragment represents the source code of the ***TypesTools*** procedure, followed by its application.

```
In[3325]:= TypesTools[x_/; ContextQ[x]] := Module[{a = {},
               b = {}, c = {}, d = CNames[x], t, j}, Monitor[j = 1;
   While[j <= Length[d], Pause[0.1]; t = d[[j]]; If[QFunction[t],
  AppendTo[a, t], If[ProcQ[t], AppendTo[b, t], AppendTo[c, t]]];
                                         j++], {j, t}]; {a, b, c}]
In[3326]:= TypesTools["AladjevProcedures`"]
           {1, "AcNb"}
           ==============
           {1317, "$Version2"}
Out[3326]:= {{"AcNb", "ActBFM", ..., "XOR1"},
           {"ActCsProcFunc", ..., "$SysContextsInM1"},
           {"AddDelPosString", "Args", ..., "$Version2"}}
```

Calling ***ContextMonitor[x]*** procedure during its execution outputs the lists of the form ***{n, N, Tp, PI}*** where ***n*** is the number of the tool being tested from the tools list with context ***x, N*** – is the name of the tool being tested, ***Tp*** – its type *{Function, Block, Module, Other}* and ***PI*** – a progress indicator; returning nothing. The source code of the procedure is represented below.

```
ContextMonitor[x_/; ContextQ[x]] := Module[{c, d = CNames[x], t, j},
  Monitor[c = 0; Map[{t = #, c++, j = TypeBFM[#], Pause[0.5]} &, d],
  {c, t, If[! MemberQ[{"Block", "Function", "Module"}, j], "Other", j],
              ProgressIndicator[c, {1, Length[d]}]}];]
```

TypesTools **&** ***ContextMonitor*** procedures use the ***Monitor*** function whose call ***Monitor[x,y]*** generates a temporary monitor place in which the continually updated current ***y*** value will be displayed during the course of evaluation of ***x.*** Such approach may be a rather useful in many rather important applications.

2.2. *Headings of procedures in Mathematica software*

Procedures in ***Mathematica*** system are formally presented by ***Modules*** and ***Blocks*** whose program structure begins with a ***Heading,*** i.e. *heading* – the header part of a procedure definition, preceded to the sign {:= | =} of the delayed, as a rule, or instant assignment. The components of the heading are the procedure name and its formal arguments with patterns "_", possibly also with testing functions assigned to them.

It is necessary to highlight that in ***Mathematica*** system as correct procedural objects {*Block, Module*} only those objects are considered which contain the patterns of the formal arguments located in a certain order, namely:

1. *The coherent group of formal arguments with patterns "_" has to be located at the very beginning of the tuple of formal arguments in headings of the above procedural objects;*

2. *Formal arguments with patterns "__" or "___" can to finish the tuple of formal arguments; at that, couples of adjacent arguments with patterns consisting from {"__", "___"} are inadmissible because of possible violation of correctness (in context of scheduled computing algorithm) of calls of the above procedural objects as a simple enough fragment illustrates:*

```
In[1221]:= A[x_, y__, z__] := x*y^2*z^3
In[1222]:= {A[x, y, z], A[x, y, h, z], A[x, y, h, x, a, b]}
Out[1222]= {x*y^2*z^3, h^z^3*x*y^2, h^x^a^b^3*x*y^2}
In[1223]:= G[x_, y__, z___] := x + y + z
In[1224]:= {G[x, y, z], G[x, y, m, n, z], G[x, y, z, h]}
Out[1224]= {x + y + z, m + n + x + y + z, h + x + y + z}
```

Other rather simple examples illustrate told. Thus, the real correctness of tuple of *formal* arguments can be coordinated to their arrangement in the tuple in context of patterns {"_", "__", "___"}. At the same time, for all patterns for formal arguments the testing ***Test***$_x$ function of a rather complex kind can be used as the following evident fragment illustrates:

```
In[1567]:= Sg[x_/; StringQ[x], y__/; If[Length[{y}] == 1,
```

```
IntegerQ[y], MemberQ3[{Integer, List, String},
                              Map[Head, {y}]]]] := {x, y}
In[1568]:= Sg["agn", 72, 77, "sv", {a, b}]
Out[1568]= {"agn", 72, 77, "sv", {a, b}}
In[1569]:= Sg1[x_/; StringQ[x], y___/; If[{y} == {}, True,
  If[Length[{y}] == 1, IntegerQ[y], MemberQ3[{List, String,
                       Integer}, Map[Head, {y}]]]]] := {x, y}
In[1570]:= Sg1["agn", 72, 77, "sv", {a, b}, a + b]
Out[1570]= Sg1["agn", 72, 77, "sv", {a, b}, a + b]
```

Furthermore, a procedure and function headings in testing functions are allowed to use procedure and function definitions *(using the list structure)* that are activated in the current session at the time the objects containing them are called, for example:

```
In[1620]:= M1[x_/; {SetDelayed[h[a_], Module[{}, 42*a]],
  h[x] < 2020}[[2]], y_] := Module[{a=5, b=7}, a*x^2 + b*y^2]
In[1621]:= M1[42, 47]
Out[1621]= 24283
In[1622]:= Definition[h]
Out[1622]= h[a_] := Module[{}, 42*a]
```

Right there once again it should be noted one an essential moment. Definition of the testing $\boldsymbol{Test_x}$ function can be directly included to the procedure or function heading, becoming active in the current session by the first procedure or function call:

```
In[2]:= P[x_, y_/; {IntOddQ[t_] := IntegerQ[t] && OddQ[t],
                          IntOddQ[y]}[[-1]]] := x*y
In[3]:= P[72, 77]
Out[3]= 5544
In[4]:= Definition[IntOddQ]
Out[4]= IntOddQ[t_] := IntegerQ[t] && OddQ[t]
In[5]:= t = 77; Save["#", t]
In[6]:= P[x_/; Module[{}, If[x^2 < Read["#"], Close["#"];
                   True, Close["#"]; False]], y_] := x*y
In[7]:= P[8, 7]
Out[7]= 56
```

Generally speaking, ***Mathematica's*** syntax and semantics, when defining procedures *(modules and blocks)*, allow the use of procedure definitions in both the definition of test functions for formal arguments and the definitions of local variables, as the following fairly simple fragment illustrates quite clearly, while for classical functions similar assumptions are only possible for test functions, of cource.

```
In[9]:= Avz[x_ /; If[SetDelayed[g[t_], Module[{a = 42}, t^2 + a]];
                                    g[x] < 777, True, False]] :=
        Module[{a = SetDelayed[v[t_], Module[{b = 47, c = 67},
                                    b*t^3 + c]]}, a = 77; a*v[x]]
In[10]:= Avz[7]
Out[10]= 1246476
In[11]:= Avz[100]
Out[11]= Avz[100]
In[12]:= Definition[g]
Out[12]= g[t_] := Module[{a = 42}, t^2 + a]
In[13]:= Definition[v]
Out[13]= v[t_] := Module[{b = 47, c = 67}, b*t^3 + c]
In[14]:= Context[g]
Out[14]= "AladjevProcedures`"
In[15]:= Context[v]
Out[15]= "Global`"
In[16]:= $Context
Out[16]= "Global`"
In[17]:= Contexts[]
Out[17]= {"AladjevProcedures`", "AladjevProcedures`BitGet1`",
          "AladjevProcedures`CharacterQ`", ...}
In[18]:= Length[%]
Out[18]= 1533
```

Procedures the definitions of which are contained in the test functions or in the local variables domain are activated in the current session when the procedure contains them is called. In addition, the symbol *v* defined in the local area has the current context, while the symbol ***g*** defined in the test function obtains the context being the first in the list ***Contexts*[]** of all contexts of the current session. The feasibility of using the above approach to defining procedures is discussed in some detail in [8,11,15].

In a number of tasks, substantially including debugging of the user software, there is a necessity of dynamic change of the testing functions for formal arguments of blocks, functions and modules in the moment of their call. The ***ChangeLc*** procedure allowing dynamically to monitor influence of testing functions of formal arguments of tools for correctness of their calls is for this purpose programmed. The following fragment submits the source code of the procedure with examples of its application.

```
In[4478]:= ChangeLc[x_/; StringQ[x] | | ListQ[x],
                              P_/; BlockFuncModQ[P], y___] :=
         Module[{a = ArgsBFM2[P], b = Definition1[P],
             p, c, d, g, n, m = Flatten[{x}], t = ToString[P]},
 p = Map[StringTake[#, Flatten[StringPosition[#, "_"]][[1]]] &, m];
         b = StringReplace[b, "Global`" <> t <> "`" -> ""];
    c = StringReplace[b, t <> "[" -> ToString[n] <> "[", 1];
              a = Select[a, SuffPref[#, p, 1] &];
              If[a == {}, P @@ {y},
              c = StringReplace[c, Rule1[Riffle[a, m]], 1];
              ToExpression[c]; t = n @@ {y};
       {If[SuffPref[ToString1[t], ToString[n] <> "[", 1],
 "Updating testing functions for formal arguments of " <>
       ToString[P] <> " is unsuitable", t], Remove[n]}[[1]]]]

In[4479]:= G[x_, y_, z_Integer] := x^2 + y^2 + z^2
In[4480]:= ChangeLc["y_/;IntegerQ[y]", G, 42, 47, 67]
Out[4480]= 8462
In[4481]:= ChangeLc["y_/;RationalQ[y]", G, 42, 47, 67]
Out[4481]= "Updating testing functions for formal
              arguments of G is unsuitable"
In[4482]:= ChangeLc["y_/;RationalQ[y]", G, 42, 47/72, 67]
Out[4482]= 32417761/5184
```

The procedure call ***ChangeLc[x, P, y]*** returns the result of a call ***P[y]*** on condition of replacement of the testing functions of arguments of a *block, module* or *function* ***P*** by the new functions determined by a string equivalent ***x*** or by their list. The string equivalent is coded in shape ***"x_/; TestQ[x]"***, ***x*** – an argument.

The task of checking formal arguments of blocks, modules, functions for their validity to admissible values plays a rather important role and this problem is solved by means of the test functions assigned to the corresponding formal arguments of the above objects. The first part of the next fragment represents an example of how to organize a system to test the *actual* values obtained when the ***Art*** procedure is called. At that, if the formal arguments receive invalid actual values, then procedure call is returned unevaluated with the corresponding message printing for the first of such formal arguments. Note that built-in means ***Mathematica*** also do quite so. Meantime, the task of checking all invalid values for formal arguments when calling the above objects is more relevant. Below is a possible approach to that.

```
In[2185]:= Art[x_ /; If[IntegerQ[x], True,
        Print["Argument x is not integer, but received: x = " <>
                                        ToString1[x]]; False],
                                        y_ /; If[ListQ[y], True,
        Print["Argument y is not a list, but received: y = " <>
                                        ToString1[y]]; False],
                                        z_ /; If[StringQ[z], True,
        Print["Argument z is not a string, but received: z = " <>
                                        ToString1[z]]; False]] :=
        Module[{a = 77}, N[x*(Length[y] + StringLength[z])/a]]
In[2186]:= Art[47, {a, b, c}, "RansIan"]
Out[2186]= 6.1039
In[2187]:= Art[47.42, 67, "abc"]
        Argument x is not integer, but received: x = 47.42
Out[2187]= Art[47.42, 67, "abc"]
In[2188]:= Art[47.42, 67, "abc"]
        Argument x is not integer, but received: x = 47.42
Out[2188]= Art[47.42, 67, "abc"]
In[2189]:= Art[500, 67, "abc"]
        Argument y is not a list, but received: y = 67
Out[2189]= Art[500, 67, "abc"]
In[2190]:= Art[500, {a, b, c}, 77]
        Argument z is not a string, but received: z = 77
Out[2190]= Art[500, {a, b, c}, 77]
```

The above approach is based on the following construction:

```
G[x_/; If[Test_x, $x$ = True, Print[...]; $x$ = False; True],
   y_/; If[Test_y, $y$ = True, Print[...]; $y$ = False; True], ......
   h_/; AllTrue[{$x$, $y$, ...}, # == True &]] := Module[{}, ...]
```

The ***Kr*** procedure is an example of using of the above approach.

```
In[2192]:= Kr[x_/; If[IntegerQ[x], $x$ = True,
           Print["Argument x is not integer, but received: x = " <>
                                   ToString1[x]]; $x$ = False; True],
                                     y_/; If[ListQ[y], $y$ = True,
           Print["Argument y is not a list, but received: y = " <>
                                   ToString1[y]]; $y$ = False; True],
                                     z_/; If[StringQ[z], $z$ = True,
           Print["Argument z is not a string, but received: z = " <>
                                   ToString1[z]]; $z$ = False; True],
                       h_/; AllTrue[{$x$, $y$, $z$}, # == True &]] :=
           Module[{a = 77}, N[x*(Length[y] + StringLength[z])/a]]
In[2193]:= Kr[47, {a, b, c}, "RansIan", 78]
Out[2193]= 6.1039
In[2194]:= Kr[42.47, 67, "abc", 78]
           Argument x is not integer, but received: x = 42.47
           Argument y is not a list, but received: y = 67
Out[2194]= Kr[42.47, 67, "abc", agn]
In[2195]:= Kr[42.47, 67, 90, 78]
           Argument x is not integer, but received: x = 42.47
           Argument y is not a list, but received: y = 67
           Argument z is not a string, but received: z = 90
Out[2195]= Kr[42.47, 67, 90, agn]
```

The final part of the above fragment represents the ***Kr*** procedure equipped with a system for testing the values of the *actual* arguments passed to the formal arguments when the procedure is called. At that, only three {*x, y, z*} arguments are used as the formal arguments used by the procedure body, whereas the **4**[th] additional argument ***h***, when the procedure is called obtains an arbitrary expression, and in the ***Kr*** body is not used. Argument ***h*** at the procedure header level tests the validity of the actual values obtained by formal arguments when the procedure is called. The argument allows to obtain information on all inadmissible values for formal arguments at the procedure call. The fragment is fairly transparent and does not require any clarifyings.

Based on the form of the *heading* shown above, it is possible to represent its rather useful extension, that allows to form the *function body* at the level of such heading. In general, the format of such header takes the following form:

```
G[x_/; If[Test[x], Save["#", a, b, c, ... ]; a = {x, True}; True,
Save["#", a, b, c, ... ]; Print["Argument x is not integer, but received:
                    x = " <> ToString1[x]]; a = {x, False}; True],
   y_/; If[Test[y], b = {y, True}; True,
Print["Argument y is not integer, but received:
                    y = " <> ToString1[y]]; b = {y, False}; True],
   z_/; If[Test[z], c = {z, True}; True,
Print["Argument z is not integer, but received:
                    z = " <> ToString1[z]]; c = {z, False}; True], ... ...
 ... ... ... ... ... ... ... ... ... ... ... ... ... ... ... ... ... ... ... ... ... ... ... ... ... ... ... ... ...
   h_/; If[AllTrue[{a[[2]],b[[2]], c[[2]]}, # == True &],
        Result = Function_Body[a[[1]], b[[1]], c[[1]]]; Get["#"];
DeleteFile["#"]; True, Get["#"]; DeleteFile["#"]; False]] := Result
```

where ***Test***[*g*] – a testing expression, testing an expression ***g*** on admissibility to be ***g*** as a valid value for the ***g*** argument and ***Result*** is the result of *Function_body* evaluation on formal arguments {*x,y,z,...*}. Let give a concrete filling of the above structural form as an example:

```
In[3338]:= ArtKr[x_/; If[IntegerQ[x], Save["#", a, b, c];
                        a = {x, True}; True, Save["#", a, b, c];
Print["Argument x is not Integer, but received:
                        x = " <> ToString1[x]]; a = {x, False}; True],
          y_/; If[RealQ[y], b = {y, True}; True,
Print["Argument y is not Real, but received:
                        y = " <> ToString1[y]]; b = {y, False}; True],
          z_/; If[RationalQ[z], c = {z, True}; True,
Print["Argument z is not Rational, but received:
                        z = " <> ToString1[z]]; c = {z, False}; True],
          h_/; If[AllTrue[{a[[2]], b[[2]], c[[2]]}, # == True &],
$Result$ = N[a[[1]]*b[[1]]*c[[1]]]; Get["#"]; DeleteFile["#"]; True,
          Get["#"]; DeleteFile["#"]; False]] := $Result$
In[3339]:= $Result$ = ArtKr[72, 77.8, 50/9, vsv]
Out[3339]= 31120.
```

```
In[3340]:= $Result$ =ArtKr[72, 77.8, 78, vsv]
          Argument z is not Rational, but received: z = 78
Out[3340]= ArtKr[72, 77.8, 78, vsv]
In[3341]:= ArtKr[72, 778, 78, vsv]
          Argument y is not Real, but received: y = 778
          Argument z is not Rational, but received: z = 78
Out[3341]= ArtKr[72, 778, 78, vsv]
In[3342]:= ArtKr[7.2, 77.8, 78, vsv]
          Argument x is not Integer, but received: x = 7.2
          Argument z is not Rational, but received: z = 78
Out[3342]= ArtKr[7.2, 77.8, 78, vsv]
In[3343]:= ArtKr[7.2, 900, 50, vsv]
          Argument x is not Integer, but received: x = 7.2
          Argument y is not Real, but received: y = 900
          Argument z is not Rational, but received: z = 50
Out[3343]= ArtKr[7.2, 900, 50, vsv]
```

The function call ***ArtKr[x, y, z, h]*** returns the result of evaluation of a *Function_Body* on actual arguments {*x, y, z*}. In addition, the call ***ArtKr[x, y, z, h]*** as a value for formal ***h*** argument obtains an arbitrary expression. Through the global variable ***$Result$***, the call ***ArtKr[x, y, z, h]*** additionally returns the same value. At that, the above structural form is based on the processing principle of actual arguments passed to an object *(block, function, module)*, namely – the values of actual arguments are processed by the corresponding testing functions from left to right until the first calculation *False* that is obtained by a testing function, after that the call of the object is returned as unevaluated, otherwise the result of the object calculation is returned.

Therefore, the test functions for the leading formal arguments of the form are formed in such way that they return *True* when fixing the real value of the test functions and the values passed to them. Whereas the test function for the auxiliary argument ***h*** determines both the evaluation of the object body and validity of the factual values for the principal arguments {*x, y, z*}, solving the task of returning the result of the calculation of the body of the object or returns the result of the call unevaluated. Fragment above is fairly transparent and does not require any clarifyings.

According to the scheme described above, ***Mathematica*** allows a number of useful modifications. In particular, the following form of organizing headers {*block, function, module*} having the following format may well be of interest:

S[x_/; {X_1; ...; X_p; {$Test_x$ | True}}[[1]],
y_/; {Y_1; ... ; Y_n; $Test_y$}[[1]],
..
z___/; {Z_1; ...; Z_t; $Test_z$}[[1]] := *Object*

In addition as {*X1,…,Xp; Y1,…,Yn;…; Z1,…,Zt*} act admissible offers of the ***Mathematica*** language, including calls of blocks, functions and modules whereas as {***Testx,Testy,…,Testz***} act the testing functions ascribed to the corresponding formal {*x,y,…,z*} arguments. In a case if there is no the test function for a formal argument *(i.e. argument allows any type of actual value)* instead of it is used *True.* Moreover, the test function for pattern "*x*___" or "*x*__" should refer to all formal arguments relating thereto. In a case of such patterns used in an object header should be used or *True,* or a special test function, for example, that is presented below. In a number of cases similar approach can be interesting enough. The procedure call ***TrueListQ***[*x, y*] returns *True* if a list *x* has elements whose types match to the corresponding elements of a list *y,* otherwise *False* is returned. If lengths of both lists are different, then the first ***Min***[*x, y*] their elements are analyzed. At that, the call with the third argument *z – an undefinite symbol –* additionally returns the list of elements positions of list *x* whose types different from the corresponding types from the *y* list. The source code of the procedure are represented below.

```
In[942]:= TrueListQ[x_/; ListQ[x], y_/; ListQ[y], z___] :=
                Module[{a = Length[x], b = Length[y], c = {}, t = {}},
              Do[If[SameQ[Head[x[[j]]], y[[j]]], AppendTo[c, True],
                 AppendTo[t, j]; AppendTo[c, False]], {j, Min[a, b]}];
            If[{z} != {} && SymbolQ[z], z = t; If[t == {}, True, False],
                                               If[t == {}, True, False]]]
In[943]:= TrueListQ[{77, 6, "abc"}, {Integer, Symbol, String}]
Out[943]= False
```

```
In[944]:= TrueListQ[{77, 7.8, "a"}, {Integer, Real, String}]
Out[944]= True
In[945]:= {TrueListQ[{a, 78, "2020"}, {Integer, Real, String}, g], g}
Out[945]= {False, {1, 2}}
```

The following simple *GW* procedure uses the ***TrueListQ*** in heading for definition of its optional formal *y* argument along with illustrative examples of the procedure calls.

```
In[63]:= GW[x_, y___ /; TrueListQ[{y}, {Integer, Real, Rational},
                                        agn]] := Module[{a = 78}, x*(y + a)]
In[64]:= GW[77]
Out[64]= 6006
In[65]:= GW[77, 78, 7.8, 7/8]
Out[65]= 12680.
In[66]:= {GW[77, 78, 42, 47], agn}
Out[66]= {GW[77, 78, 42, 47], {2, 3}}
```

As an instructive information, an example of a procedure whose heading is based on the principles mentioned above is presented. The procedure call ***Mn[x, y, z]*** returns the list of all arguments passed to the procedure without reference to them.

```
In[3349]:= Mn[x_ /; {WriteLine["#", x]; IntegerQ[x]}[[1]],
                              y_ /; {WriteLine["#", y]; ListQ[y]}[[1]],
                              z___ /; {WriteLine["#", z]; True}[[1]]] :=
  Module[{Arg}, Close["#"]; Arg = ReadString["#"]; DeleteFile["#"];
                              Arg = StringReplace[Arg, "\n" -> ","];
                                  Arg = StringTake[Arg, {1, -2}];
                     Arg = ToExpression[StringToList[Arg]]; Arg]
In[3350]:= Mn[77, {42, 47, 67}]
Out[3350]= {77, {42, 47, 67}}
In[3351]:= Mn[77, {42, 47, 67}, a + b]
Out[3351]= {77, {42, 47, 67}, a + b}
In[3352]:= Mn[m, {42, 47, 67}, a + b]
Out[3352]= Mn[m, {42, 47, 67}, a + b]
In[3353]:= Mn[m, {42, 47, 67}, a + b, 77, 78]
Out[3353]= Mn[m, {42, 47, 67}, a + b, 77, 78]
```

Another point should be emphasized. As already mentioned, when calling an object (block, function or module), the factual arguments passed to it in its heading are processed in the list order, i.e., from left to right in the list of formal arguments. In this regard, and in view of the foregoing, there is a rather real possibility of setting in definition of some formal argument of a test function, that can be used as test functions for subsequent formal arguments of the object *heading*. The following fragment represents a rather simple ***Av*** function whose heading contains definitions of two Boolean functions, used by a testing function for the last formal ***z*** argument of the ***Av*** function. At the same time, when you call function ***Av***, both Boolean functions ***B*** and ***V*** become active in the current session, as it is well shown in the examples below.

```
In[3442]:= Av[x_ /; {SetDelayed[B[t_], If[t <= 90, True, False]];
                                                          NumberQ[x]}[[1]],
             y_ /; {SetDelayed[V[t_], ! RealQ[t]]; RealQ[y]}[[1]],
             z_ /; B[z] && V[z] | | RationalQ[z]] := N[Sqrt[x*y/z]]
In[3443]:= {Av[77, 7.8`, 42/47], Av[77, 90, 500]}
Out[3443]= {25.9249, Av[77, 90, 500]}
In[3444]:= Definition[B]
Out[3444]= B[t_] := If[t <= 90, True, False]
In[3445]:= Definition[V]
Out[3445]= V[t_] := ! RealQ[t]
In[3446]:= {B[42], V[47]}
Out[3446]= {True, True}
In[3447]:= Ag[x_ /; {SetDelayed[W[t_], Module[{a = 77}, a*t^2]];
                                          IntegerQ[x]}[[1]]] := W[x] + x^2
In[3448]:= {Ag[42], W[42]}
Out[3448]= {137592, 135828}
In[3449]:= Definition[W]
Out[3449]= W[t_] := Module[{a = 77}, a*t^2]
```

Thus, in particular, the last example of the previous fragment also shows that the object ***W*** *(block, function, module)* defined in the header of another ***Ag*** object allows a correct call in the body of the ***Ag*** object yet when it is first called. When ***Ag*** is called, ***W*** becomes active in the current session. The above fragments are quite transparent and do not require any clarifyings. Technique presented in them are of some practical interest in programming of the objects headings and objects as a whole.

On the assumption of the general definition of a procedure, in particular, of modular type

$$M[x\_/; Test_x, y\_/; Test_y, ...] := \textbf{Module}[\{Locals\}, \textit{Procedure body}]$$

and of the fact that concrete definition of procedure is identified not by its ***name,*** but its ***heading*** we will consider a set of useful enough tools [16] that provide the various manipulations with the headings of procedures and functions and play a important part in the procedural and functional programming and, above all, of programming of problems of the system character.

Having defined such object useful in many appendices as the *heading* of a procedure or function in the form "*Name*[*List of formal arguments with the testing tools ascribed to them*]", naturally arises the question of creating of means for testing of the objects regarding their relation to the ***`Heading`*** type. We have created a number of tools [15,16] in the form of procedures ***HeadingQ ÷ HeadingQ3.*** At the same time, between pairs of the procedures {***HeadingQ, HeadingQ1***} and {***HeadingQ2, HeadingQ3***} principal distinctions exist. Meantime, considering standard along with some other unlikely encoding formats of the procedures and functions headings, the above four tools can be considered as rather useful testing tools in programming. In addition, from experience of their use and their time characteristics it became clear that it is quite enough to be limited oneself only by tools ***HeadingQ*** and ***HeadingQ1*** which cover a rather wide range of erroneous coding of headings. Meantime, taking into account the mechanism of expressions parse for their correctness, that ***Mathematica*** uses, creation of comprehensive means of testing of the headings is a rather difficult. Naturally, it is possible to use the non-standard receptions for receiving the testing tools for the headings having a rather wide set of the deviations from the standard ones, but such outlay often do not pay off by the received benefits.

In particular, the possibilities of the ***HeadingQ ÷ HeadingQ3*** procedures are overlaped by opportunities of the means whose call ***TestHeadingQ*** returns *True,* if a ***x*** represents the heading in string format of a block, module, function, and *False* otherwise. Whereas the procedure call ***TestHeadingQ*[x, y]** with the second optional ***y*** argument – *an indefinite variable* – thru it additionally returns information specifying the reasons of the incorrectness of a heading ***x***. At that, on ***x*** objects of the same name *(multiple objects)* the procedure call returns **$***Failed;* the extension of the procedure to case of the multiple objects does not cause much difficulty. The source code of the ***TestHeadingQ*** procedure and the comparative analysis of its use concerning the ***HeadingQ*** ÷ ***HeadingQ3*** tools say about its preference at programming in ***Mathematica*** [8,9,15]. So, of the detailed analysis follows, that the ***TestHeadingQ*** procedure on the opportunities surpasses the above testing tools of the same purpose.

In the light of real correctness of formal arguments that has been defined above and is caused by mutual arrangements of formal arguments in the context of patterns {"_", "__", "___"} we can significantly generalize the above group of procedures ***HeadingQ ÷ HeadingQ3,*** intended for testing of correctness of headings of the user blocks, functions & modules, additionally using the ***CorrTupleArgs*** procedure. For this purpose the tool ***HeadingsUQ*** can be used.

Calling the ***HeadingsUQ*[x]** procedure returns *True* if all components composing an object ***x*** in the context of the call ***Definition*[x]** have correct headings, and *False* otherwise. While the call ***HeadingsUQ*[x, y]** in addition through the **2*nd*** optional argument – *an indefined **y** symbol* – returns the list the elements of which are *True* if the heading of the appropriate component of ***x*** object is correct, or the list whose first element determines incorrect heading of a component of the ***x*** object, whereas the second element determines of the component number with this *heading* concerning the call ***Definition*[x].** The source code of the ***TestHeadingQ*** procedure with examples of its use can be found in [15,16]. The ***HeadingsUQ*** procedure rather exhaustively tests the correctness of the *headings* of blocks, functions and modules.

It is appropriate to make one quite substantial remark here. As you know, ***Mathematica*** does not allow to use the testing functions in block, function, and module headers that will use factual argument values that relate to other formal arguments as the following simple fragment rather visually illustrates.

```
In[7]:= V[x_/; IntegerQ[x], y_/; EvenQ[x] && IntegerQ[y]] := x/y
In[8]:= V[42, 77]
Out[8]= V[42, 77]
```

In the example shown, the testing function assigned to the second formal argument *y* cannot include the value passed to the first formal argument *x*, otherwise by causing the return of *V* function call unevaluated. We will offer here one interesting reception, allowing to solve similar and some other problems. Consider it with a rather simple example.

```
In[2296]:= V[x_/; {Save3["j", x], IntegerQ[x]}[[-1]],
y_/; {If[Get["j"]*y > 100, True, False], DeleteFile["j"]}[[1]]] := x*y
In[2297]:= V[42, 77]
Out[2297]= 3234
In[2298]:= V[7, 8]
Out[2298]= V[7, 8]
```

In order to pass an actual value (passed to the *x* argument when the *V* function is called) to a testing function of another *y* argumene, by the function ***Save3*** the value is stored in a certain temporary *j* file. Then call ***Get[j]*** allows to read the stored value from the file *j* in the required point of the testing function of *any* formal argument of the header, after necessity deleting file ***j***. To solve such problems, a ***Save3*** function is of interest – a version of the built-in ***Save*** function whose ***Save3[f, x]*** call saves in the *f* of the *txt*-format an expression *x* without returning anything.

```
In[2310]:= Save3[f_, x_] := {Write[f, x], Close[f]}[[1]]
In[2311]:= Save3["###", b*S + c*V + G*x]
In[2312]:= Get["##"]
Out[2312]= b*S + c*V + G*x
```

After calling ***Save3[f, x]***, the file with expression *x* remains closed and is loaded into the current session by function ***Get[f]***, returning the *x* value. Note that the ***Write*** function used by the ***Save3*** has a number of features discussed in detail in [8]. In the first place, this refers to preserving the sequence of expressions.

The following procedure serves as an useful enough tool at manipulating with functions and procedures, its call ***HeadPF[x]*** returns heading in string format of a block, module or function with a ***x*** name activated in the current session, i.e. the function in its traditional understanding with heading. Whereas on other values of the ***x*** argument the call is returned unevaluated. At the same time, the problem of definition of headings is actual also in a case of the objects of the above type of the same name which have more than one heading. In this case the procedure call ***HeadPF[w]*** returns the list of headings in string format of the subobjects composing a ***w*** object as a whole. The following fragment represents the source code of the ***HeadPF*** procedure along with a typical example of its application.

```
In[2225]:= M[x_/; x == "avzagn"] := Module[{a}, a*x];
          M[x_, y_, z_] := x*y*z;  M[x_String] := x;
          M[x_/; IntegerQ[x], y_String] := Module[{a, b, c}, x];
          M[x_, y_] := Module[{a, b, c}, "abc"; x + y]

In[2226]:= HeadPF[x_/; BlockFuncModQ[x]] := Module[{b,
        c = ToString[x], a = Select[Flatten[{PureDefinition[x]}],
        ! SuffPref[#, "Default[", 1] &]}, b = Map[StringTake[#,
       {1, Flatten[StringPosition[#, {" := ", " = "}]][[1]] - 1}] &, a];
                                   If[Length[b] == 1, b[[1]], b]]

In[2227]:= HeadPF[M]
Out[2227]= {"M[x_ /; x == \"avzagn\"]", "M[x_, y_, z_]",
      "M[x_ /; IntegerQ[x], y_String]", "M[x_String]", "M[x_, y_]"}
```

Here, it is necessary to make one essential enough remark concerning the means dealing with the ***headings*** of procedures and functions. The matter is that as it was shown earlier, the testing tools ascribed to the formal arguments, as a rule, consist of the earlier defined testing functions or the *reserved* keywords defining the type, for example, *Integer*. While as a side effect the built-in *Math*-language allows to use the constructions that can contain definitions of the testing tools, directly in the headings of procedures and functions. Certain interesting examples of that have been represented above. Meanwhile, despite of such opportunity, the programmed means are oriented, as a rule, on use for testing of admissibility of the factual arguments or the predefined means, or including the testing algorithms in the body of the procedures and functions. For this reason, ***HeadPF*** procedure presented above in such cases can return incorrect results. Whereas the ***HeadPFU*** procedure covers such peculiar cases. The procedure call ***HeadPFU[x]*** correctly returns the heading in string format of a block, module or function with a name ***x*** activated in the current session regardless of a way of definition of testing of factual arguments. The fragment below presents the source code of the ***HeadPFU*** procedure along with typical examples of its application.

```
In[2230]:= P[x_, y_ /; {IntOddQ[t_] := IntegerQ[t] && OddQ[t],
                                   IntOddQ[y]}[[-1]]] := x*y
In[2231]:= HeadPF[P]
Out[2231]= "P[x_, y_ /; {IntOddQ[t_]"
In[2232]:= HeadPFU[x_ /; BlockFuncModQ[x]] :=
       Module[{a = Flatten[{PureDefinition[x]}], b = {}, c, g},
        Do[c = Map[#[[1]] - 1 &, StringPosition[a[[j]], " := "]];
         Do[If[SyntaxQ[Set[g, StringTake[a[[j]], {1, c[[k]]}]]],
  AppendTo[b, g]; Break[], Null], {k, Length[c]}], {j, Length[a]}];
                              If[Length[b] == 1, b[[1]], b]]
In[2233]:= HeadPFU[P]
Out[2233]= "P[x_, y_ /; {IntOddQ[t_] := IntegerQ[t] && OddQ[t],
                                   IntOddQ[y]}[[-1]]]"
In[2234]:= V[x_ /; {Save3["#", x], IntegerQ[x]}[[-1]],
y_ /; {If[Get["#"]*y > 77, True, False], DeleteFile["#"]}[[1]]] := x*y
In[2235]:= HeadPFU[V]
Out[2235]= "V[x_ /; {Save3[\"#\", x], IntegerQ[x]}[[-1]],
 y_ /; {If[Get[\"#\"]*y > 77, True, False], DeleteFile[\"#\"]}[[1]]]"
```

In this regard the testing of a ***x*** object regarding to be of the same name is enough actually; the ***QmultiplePF*** procedure [16] solves the problem whose call ***QmultiplePF[x]*** returns *True*, if ***x*** is an object of the same name *(Function, Block, Module)*, and *False* otherwise. Whereas the procedure call ***QmultiplePF[x, y]*** with the second optional ***y*** argument – *an indefinite variable* – through ***y*** returns the list of definitions of all subobjects with a name ***x***.

Right there pertinently to note some more tools linked with

the ***HeadPF*** procedure. So, the ***Headings*** procedure is a rather useful expansion of the ***HeadPF*** procedure in a case of blocks, functions and modules of the same name but with the different headings. Generally, the call ***Headings*[*x*]** returns the nested list whose elements are the sublists which determine respectively headings of subobjects composing an object ***x;*** the first elements of such sublists defines the types of subobjects, whereas others define the headings corresponding to them. In a number of the appendices that widely use procedural programming, a rather useful is the ***HeadingsPF*** procedure that is an expansion of the previous procedure. Generally, the call ***HeadingsPF*[]** returns the nested list, whose elements are sublists that respectively define the headings of functions, blocks and modules, whose definitions have been evaluated in the current session; the first element of each such sublist determines an object type in the context {"*Block*", "*Module*", "*Function*"} while the others define the headings corresponding to it. The procedure call returns a simple list if any of sublists does not contain headings**;** at that, if in the current session the evaluations of definitions of objects of the specified three types weren't made, the call returns empty list. The call with any arguments is returned unevaluated. The following fragment represents source code of the ***HeadingsPF*** procedure along with an example of its typical application.

```
In[2310]:= HeadingsPF[x___/; SameQ[x, {}]] := Module[{a = {},
    d = {}, k = 1, b, c = {{"Block"}, {"Function"}, {"Module"}}, t},
      Map[If[Quiet[Check[BlockFuncModQ[#], False]],
        AppendTo[a, #], Null] &, Names["`*"]];
  b = Map[Headings[#] &, a]; While[k <= Length[b], t = b[[k]];
    If[NestListQ[t], d = Join[d, t], AppendTo[d, t]]; k++];
    Map[If[#[[1]] == "Block", c[[1]] = Join[c[[1]], #[[2 ;; -1]]],
     If[#[[1]] == "Function", c[[2]] = Join[c[[2]], #[[2 ;; -1]]],
        c[[3]] = Join[c[[3]], #[[2 ;; -1]]]]] &, d];
  c = Select[c, Length[#] > 1 &]; If[Length[c] == 1, c[[1]], c]]
In[2311]:= M[x_/; SameQ[x, "avz"], y_] := Module[{a, b, c}, y];
      L1[x_] := x; M[x_, y_, z_] := x + y + z; L[x_, y_] := x + y;
      M[x_/; x == "avz"] := Module[{a, b, c}, x];
      M[x_/; IntegerQ[x], y_String] := Module[{a, b, c}, x];
```

```
M[x_, y_] := Module[{a, b, c}, "agn"; x + y]; M[x_String] := x;
M[x_/; ListQ[x], y_] := Block[{a, b, c}, "agn"; Length[x] + y];
F[x_/; SameQ[x, "avz"], y_] := {x, y}; F[x_/; x == "avz"] := x
In[2312]:= HeadingsPF[]
Out[2312]= {{"Block", "M[x_ /; ListQ[x], y_]"},
{"Function", "F[x_ /; x === \"avz\", y_]", "F[x_ /; x == \"avz\"]",
"L[x_, y_]", "L1[x_]", "M[x_, y_, z_]", "M[x_String]"},
{"Module", "M[x_ /; x === \"avz\", y_]", "M[x_, y_]",
"M[x_ /; x == \"avz\"]", "M[x_ /; IntegerQ[x], y_String]"}}
```

In the light of possibility of existence in the current session of procedures and functions of the same name with different headings the problem of removal from the session of an object with the concrete heading is of a certain interest; this problem is solved by the procedure ***RemProcOnHead,*** whose the source code with an example of its application is represented below.

```
In[7]:= RemProcOnHead[x_/; HeadingQ[x] | | HeadingQ1[x] | |
     ListQ[x] && AllTrue[Map[HeadingQ[#] &, x], TrueQ]] :=
      Module[{b, c, d, p, a = HeadName[If[ListQ[x], x[[1]], x]]},
       If[! MemberQ[Names["`*"] | | ! HowAct[a], a], $Failed,
          b = Definition2[a]; c = b[[1 ;; -2]]; d = b[[-1]];
 ToExpression["ClearAttributes["<>a<> ","<>ToString[d]<>"]"];
                       y = Map[StandHead, Flatten[{x}]];
                       p = Select[c, ! SuffPref[#, x, 1] &];
                       ToExpression["Clear[" <> a <> "]"];
                       If[p == {}, "Done", ToExpression[p];
 ToExpression["SetAttributes["<>a <> "," <> ToString[d] <> "]"];
                                                    "Done"]]]
In[8]:= V[x_] := Module[{}, x^6]; V[x_Integer] := x^2
In[9]:= {RemProcOnHead["V[x_Integer]"],
                                        RemProcOnHead["V[x_]"]}
Out[9]= {"Done", "Done"}
In[10]:= Definition[V]
Out[10]= Null
```

The call ***RemProcOnHead***[*x*] returns "*Done*" with removing from the current session a procedure, function or their list with heading or with list of *x* headings that are given in string format; headings in call ***RemProcOnHead***[*x*] is coded according to the format ***ToString1***[*x*].

The task, closely adjacent to the headings, is to determine the arity of objects. For this purpose, we have created a number of means [8,9]. In particular, the ***ArityBFM1*** procedure defining *arity* of objects of the type {*module, classical function, block*} serves as quite useful addition to the procedure ***Arity*** and some others.

The procedure call ***ArityBFM1*[x]** returns the ***arity*** *(number of the formal arguments)* of a block, function or module ***x*** in the format of **4**–element list whose the ***1st***, the ***2nd***, the ***3rd*** elements define quantity of formal arguments with the patterns "_", "__" and "___" accordingly. While the ***4th*** element defines common quantity of formal arguments which can be different from the quantity of actual arguments. In addition, the ***x*** heading should has classical type, i.e. it should not include non–standard, but acceptable methods of headings definition. The unsuccessful procedure call returns **$***Failed.*

The following procedure serves for definition of arity of system functions. The procedure call ***AritySystemFunction*[x]** returns the **2**–element list whose ***1st*** element defines number of formal arguments, while the second element – quantity of admissible actual arguments. The call with the second optional ***y*** argument – *an indefinite variable* – thru it returns the generalized template of formal arguments.

```
In[3341]:= AritySystemFunction[x_, y___] := Module[{a, b, c, d, g, p},
   If[! SysFunctionQ[x], $Failed, a = SyntaxInformation[x];
   If[a == {}, $Failed, c = {0, 0, 0, 0}; b = Map[ToString, a[[1]][[2]]];
   b = Map[If[SuffPref[#, "{", 1], "_",
   If[SuffPref[#, {"Optional", "OptionsPattern"}, 1], "_.", #]] &, b];
   If[{y} != {} && ! HowAct[y],
   y = Map[ToExpression[ToString[Unique["x"]] <> #] &, b], 77];
   Map[If[# == "_", c[[1]]++, If[# == "_.", c[[2]]++,
   If[# == "__", c[[3]]++, c[[4]]++]]] &, b]; {p, c, d, g} = c;
   d = DeleteDuplicates[{p + d, If[d != 0 | | g != 0, Infinity, p + c]}];
   If[d != {0, Infinity}, d, Quiet[x[Null]]; If[Set[p, Messages[x]] == {}, d,
   p = Select[Map[ToString, Map[Part[#, 2] &, p]],
   ! StringFreeQ[#, " expected"] &]; p = Map[StringTake[#,
   {Flatten[StringPosition[#, ";"]][[1]] + 1, -2}] &, p];
   p = ToExpression[Flatten[StringCases[p, DigitCharacter ..]]];
   If[p == {}, {1}, If[Length[p] > 1, {Min[p], Max[p]}, p]]]]]]]

In[3342]:= {AritySystemFunction[If, g72], g72}
Out[3342]= {{2, 4}, {x16_, x17_, x18_., x19_.}}
```

2.3. *Optional arguments of procedures and functions*

When programming procedures and functions often there is an expediency to define some of their formal arguments as optional. In addition, in case of explicit lack of such arguments by a call of tools, they receive values *by default*. System built-in ***Mathematica*** functions use two basic methods for dealing with optional arguments that are suitable for the user tools too. The *first* method consists in that that a value of each argument ***x*** that is coded by pattern "_:" in the form ***x_:b*** should be replaced by ***b***, if the argument omitted. Almost all built-in system functions that use this method, omit arguments since the end of the list of formal arguments. So, simple function ***G[x_:5, y_:7] := {x, y}*** two optional arguments have, for which values by default – ***5*** and ***7*** respectively. As ***Mathematica*** system assumes that arguments are omitted since end of the list of formal arguments then we have not a possibility by positionally *(in general selectively)* do an argument as optional.

```
In[3376]:= G[x_: 5, y_: 6] := {x, y}
In[3377]:= {G[], G[42, 77], G[42]}
Out[3377]= {{5, 6}, {42, 77}, {42, 6}}
```

So, from a simple example follows that for function **G** from two optional arguments the call **G[42]** refers value by default to the second argument, but not to the first. Therefore this method has a rather limited field of application.

The second method of organization of optional arguments consists in use of explicit names for the optional arguments by allowing to give them values using transformation rules. This method is particularly convenient for means like ***Plot*** function which have a rather large number of optional arguments, only a few of which usually need to be set in a particular example. The typical method is that values for so-called named optional arguments can be specified by including the appropriate rules at the end of the arguments at a function call. At determining of the named optional arguments for a procedure or function ***g***, it is conventional to store the default values for these arguments as a list of transformation rules assigned to ***Options***[*g*]. So, as a typical example of definition for a tool with zero or more *named* optional arguments can be:

g[x_, y_, OptionsPattern[]] := Module[{}, x*y]

Then for this means a list of transformation rules assigned to ***Options***[*g*] is determined

Options[g] = {val1 -> a, val2 -> b}

Whereas expression ***OptionValue***[*w*] for a named optional argument *w* has to be included to the body of the tool, in order that this mechanism worked. Below is presented the definition of a function *g* that allows up to 2 named optional arguments:

```
In[2114]:= g[x_, y_, OptionsPattern[]] :=
        (OptionValue[val1]*x + OptionValue[val2]*y)/
        (OptionValue[val1]*OptionValue[val2])
In[2115]:= Options[g] = {val1 -> 42, val2 -> 47}
Out[2115]= {val1 -> 42, val2 -> 47}
In[2116]:= g[90, 500]
Out[2116]= 13640/987
In[2117]:= g[90, 500, val1 -> 77]
Out[2117]= 30430/3619
In[2118]:= g[90, 500, val1 -> 10, val2 -> 100]
Out[2118]= 509/10
```

From the represented example the second method of work with named optional arguments is rather transparent. You can to familiarize with optional arguments in more detail in [22].

Other way of definition of optional arguments of functions and procedures consists in use of the template "_.", representing an optional argument with a default value specified by built-in ***Default*** function – ***Default***[*w*] = ***Value***. Let's note, the necessary values for call ***Default***[*w*] for a tool *w* must always precede an optional argument of the *w* tool. Values defined for ***Default***[*w*] are saved in ***DefaultValues***[*w*]. Fragment below illustrates told:

```
In[1346]:= Default[w] = 5;
In[1347]:= w[x_., y_., z_.] := {x, y, z};  {w[], w[42, 47], w[42]}
Out[1347]= {{5, 5, 5}, {42, 47, 5}, {42, 5, 5}}
```

More detailed information on this way can be found in [15] and by a call ***?Default*** in the current session of ***Mathematica.*** At the same time all considered approaches to the organization of work with optional arguments do not give the chance to define values by default for an arbitrary tuple of formal arguments.

The reception described below on a simple example can be for this purpose used. Definition of a procedure **G** for which we going to make all three formal arguments ***x, y*** and ***z*** optional, is made out as follows: ***Res*** defines the list of formal arguments in string format, ***Def*** determines the list of values by default for all formal arguments, the procedure body is made out in the form ***"{Body}"***, moreover, of the **G** definition is complemented with an obligatory argument ***Opt*** which represents the binary list of signs whose elements correspond to ***Res*** list elements. The zero element of the ***Opt*** list determines non-obligation of the ***Res*** list element corresponding to it, and vice versa. After the specified definition of the procedure body *(**d**)* the ***StringReplaceVars*** [16] procedure which provides substitution in the procedure body of the actual arguments *(sign* ***1****)* or their values by default *(sign* ***0****)* is applied to it. So, the procedure call **G[*x, y, z, Opt*]** returns the simplified value of the *source* procedure body on the arguments transferred to it. The simple example visually illustrates told.

```
In[7]:= G[x_., y_., z_., Opt_] := Module[{Res = {"x", "y", "z"},
                         Def = Map[ToString1[#] &, {42, 47, 67}],
                      args = Map[ToString1[#] &, {x, y, z}], b, c, d},
  d = "Simplify[{b = (x + y)/(x + z); c = b*x*y*z; (b + c)^2}]";
  d = StringReplaceVars[d, Map[If[Opt[[#]] == 0, Res[[#]] ->
    Def[[#]], Res[[#]] -> args[[#]]] &, Range[Length[Res]]]];
                                              ToExpression[d][[1]]]
In[8]:= G[a, s, t, {0, 1, 1}]
Out[8]= ((42 + s)^2*(1 + 42*s*t)^2)/(42 + t)^2
In[9]:= G[a, s, t, {1, 1, 1}]
Out[9]= ((a + s)^2*(1 + a*s*t)^2)/(a + t)^2
In[10]:= G[a, s, t, {0, 0, 0}]
Out[10]= 138557641644601/11881
```

In certain cases the above reception can be rather useful.

The problem for testing of correctness of the tuple of formal arguments in the user *modules, blocks* or *functions* can be solved by procedure whose call **CorrTupleArgs[x]** returns *True* if tuple of formal arguments of a procedure or a function ***x*** is correct in the sense stated above, and *False* otherwise [8,16].

On the other hand, the problem of preliminary definition of correctness of the factual arguments passing to a procedure or a function is of a rather interesting. If tool has no mechanisms of testing of actual arguments passing to it at a call, then the call on *incorrect* actual arguments as a rule is returned unevaluated. The procedure ***TestActArgs*** is one of variants of solution of the problem, whose call ***TestActArgs[x, y]*** returns *empty* list if tuple of actual arguments meets the tuple of testing functions of the corresponding formal arguments of ***x***, otherwise the procedure call trough ***y*** returns the integer list of numbers of the formal arguments to which *inadmissible* actual arguments are supposed to be passed [1-16].

Meantime, use of the above procedure assumes that testing for correctness of actual arguments for formal arguments with patterns {"__", "___"} is carried out only for the first elements of tuples of actual arguments passing to formal arguments with the appropriate patterns. Whereas further development of the procedure is left to the interested reader as a useful exercise. In addition, it should be noted the important circumstance. If in the traditional programming languages the identification of an arbitrary procedure or function is made according to its *name*, in case of ***Math***-language the identification is made according to its *heading*. This circumstance is caused by that the definition of a procedure or function in the ***Math***-language is made by the manner different from traditional [1]. Simultaneous existence of procedures of the same name with different headings in such situation is admissible as it illustrates a simple fragment:

```
In[2434]:= M[x_, y_] := Module[{}, x + y];
       M[x_] := Module[{}, x^2]; M[y_] := Module[{}, y^3];
       M[x___] := Module[{}, {x}]
In[2435]:= Definition[M]
```

```
Out[2435]= M[x_, y_] := Module[{}, x + y]
            M[y_] := Module[{}, y^3]
            M[x__] := Module[{}, {x}]
```

At the call of procedure or function of the same name from the list is chosen the one, whose formal arguments of heading correspond to actual arguments of the call, otherwise the call is returned unevaluated, excepting simplifications of arguments according to the standard system agreements. At compliance of formal arguments of *heading* with actual ones the component of *x* procedure or function is caused, whose definition is the first in the list returned at the call ***Definition*[*x*];** particularly, whose definition has been evaluated in the ***Mathematica*** by the first. Therefore, in order to avoid possible misunderstandings in case of procedure override with a name ***x***, which includes a change of its header also, the call ***Clear*[*x*]** must first undo the previous procedure definition.

The works [1-16] present a range of interesting software for dealing with the headings and formal arguments that make up them. In particular, the following tools can be mentioned:

ProcQ*[*x*]** – *returns True if* ***x *is a procedure and False otherwise;*

BlockModQ*[*x*]** – *returns True if* ***x *is a name defining a block or module; otherwise False is returned. At that, thru optional argument* ***y*** *– an indefinite variable the call* ***BlockModQ*[*x, y*]** *returns the type of the object* ***x*** *in the context* of *{"Block", "Module"} on condition that main result is True;*

ArgsP*[*x*]** – *returns the list whose elements – formal arguments of Block or Module* ***x *– are grouped with the preceding words* ***Block*** *and* ***Module****. Groups arise in the case of multiple object definition* ***x;***

```
In[72]:= ArgsP[x_/; BlockModQ[x]] := Module[{b, c = {}, j,
                                               a = Headings[x]},
          a = If[MemberQ3[a, {"Module", "Block"}], a, {a}];
                                                     b = Length[a];
          Do[Map[AppendTo[c, If[StringFreeQ[#, "["], #,
          StringReplace[StringTake[#, StringLength[#] - 1],
          ToString[x] <> "[" -> "{"] <> "}"]] &, a[[j]]], {j, 1, b}];
                                                 ToExpression[c]]
```

```
In[73]:= M[x_/; IntegerQ[x]] := Module[{}, x^2];
 M[x_, y_] := Module[{}, x*y^3]; M[x__] := Module[{}, {x}];
 M[x_, y__] := Block[{a = 42, b = 47}, {a*x, b*y}]
In[74]:= ArgsP[M]
Out[74]= {Block, {x_, y__}, Module, {x_ /; IntegerQ[x]},
                                              {x_, y_}, {x__}}
```

RenameP[x, y] *– returns the empty list, renaming a Function, Block or Module* ***x*** *to a name, defined by the second argument* ***y*** *with its activation in the current session; note, object* ***x*** *remains unchanged*

```
In[32]:= RenameP[x_/; BlockFuncModQ[x], y_Symbol] :=
            ReplaceAll[ToExpression[Map[StringReplace[#,
               ToString[x] <> "[" -> ToString[y] <> "[", 1] &,
                            DefToStrM[x]]], Null -> Nothing]
In[33]:= M[x_/; IntegerQ[x]] := Module[{}, x^2];
 M[x_, y_] := Module[{}, x*y^3]; M[x__] := Module[{}, {x}];
 M[x_, y__] := Block[{}, {x, y}]
In[34]:= RenameP[M, Agn]
Out[34]= {}
In[35]:= Definition[Agn]
Out[35]= Agn[x_ /; IntegerQ[x]] := Module[{}, x^2]
         Agn[x_, y_] := Module[{}, x*y^3]
         Agn[x_, y__] := Block[{}, {x, y}]
         Agn[x__] := Module[{}, {x}]
```

Note that we have programmed a lot of other useful tools for different processing of both the headings, as a whole, and their separate components, first of all, formal arguments [1-16]. Some of these are used in examples given in this book. Before further consideration, it should be noted once again that, the block and module headings handling tools are also functionally suitable for the classical functions determined by the headings according to a general mechanism used by the blocks, modules, and classical functions. Thus, what is said about the procedure headings fully applies to functions, making it easy to convert the second ones to the first.

One of the main tasks at working with formal arguments is

to define them for the user procedures *(modules and blocks)* and functions. In this direction, we have created a number of means of various purposes. At the same time, the definition of testing functions for formal arguments may itself contain definitions of procedures and functions, which implies consideration is given to this circumstance in the development of means of processing formal arguments. So, the ***ArgsProcFunc*** procedure considers this circumstance illustrating it on an example of its application to the ***M*** procedure presented below.

The procedure call ***ArgsProcFunc[x]*** generally returns the nested list whose single elements define formal arguments in the string format, and 2–element sub–lists by the first element define formal arguments, while by the second define the testing functions assigned to them *(conditions of their admissibility)* also in the string format of a procedure, block or function ***x***.

```
In[1938]:= ArgsProcFunc[x_ /; BlockModQ[x]] :=
           Module[{a = Definition1[x], b, c = "", d, j, f, g},
           d = StringLength[g = ToString[x]];  c = g;
               For[j = d + 1, j <= StringLength[a], j++,
If[! SyntaxQ[g = g <> StringTake[a, {j, j}]], Continue[], Break[]]];
               b = StringReplace[g, c <> "[" -> ",", 1];
               b = StringInsert[b, ",", -1];  c = "";
Do[c = c <> StringTake[b, {j, j}]; If[SyntaxQ[c], Break[],
               Continue[]], {j, 1, StringLength[b]}];
               d = StringDrop[c, -2] <> ",";  c = {};
Label[Agn];    f = StringPosition[d, ","];
               f = DeleteDuplicates[Flatten[f]];
               For[j = 2, j <= Length[f], j++,
   If[SyntaxQ[g = StringTake[d, {f[[1]] + 1, f[[j]] - 1}]],
   AppendTo[c, g]; d = StringReplace[d, "," <> g -> "", 1];
               Goto[Agn], Continue[]]];
c = Map[StringReplace[#, GenRules[{"___", "__", " /;", "_:",
         "_.", "_"}, "@$@"], 1] &, c];
c = Map[StringTrim[#] &, Map[StringSplit[#, "@$@"] &, c]];
Map[If[Length[#] == 1, #[[1]], If[SuffPref[#[[2]], g = "/; ", 1],
         {#[[1]], StringReplace[#[[2]], g -> "", 1]}, #]] &, c]]
```

```
In[1939]:= M[x_, y_ /; {g[t_] := Module[{}, t^2], If[g[y] > 50,
                          True, False]}[[2]], r_: 77, p_., z___] :=
                          Module[{}, x*y*r*p/g[z]]
In[1940]:= {M[77, 8, 42, 72, 7], M[77, 7, 42, 72, 7]}
Out[1940]= {38016, M[77, 7, 42, 72, 7]}
In[1941]:= Definition[g]
Out[1941]= g[t_] := Module[{}, t^2]
In[1942]:= ArgsProcFunc[M]
Out[1942]= {"x", {"y", "{g[t_] := Module[{}, t^2], If[g[y] > 50,
                          True, False]}[[2]]"}, {"r", "77"}, "p", "z"}
```

It follows from the fragment that for a tool defined in the testing function of a formal argument, the availability domain is the entire current session, including the procedure body that generated it. ***ArgsProcFunc1*** and ***ArgsProcFunc2*** procedures, unlike ***ArgsProcFunc***, are based on other principles, returning the lists of formal arguments with testing functions ascribed to them, while thtough the second optional argument is returned the same list with elements in the string format.

```
In[19]:= ArgsProcFunc1[x_/; BlockFuncModQ[x], y___] :=
             Module[{a = Definition1[x], b, c = "", d, j, f, g},
               d = StringLength[g = ToString[x]];  c = g;
               For[j = d + 1, j <= StringLength[a], j++,
If[! SyntaxQ[g = g <> StringTake[a, {j, j}]], Continue[], Break[]]];
b = ToExpression["{" <> StringTrim[g, {c <> "[", "]"}] <> "}"];
If[{y} == {}, b, If[SymbolQ[y], b; y = Map[ToString1, b]]]]
In[20]:= ArgsProcFunc1[M, t]
Out[20]= {"x_", "y_ /; {g[t_] := Module[{}, t^2], If[g[y] > 50,
                   True, False]}[[2]]", "r_:77", "p_.", "z___"}
In[77]:= ArgsProcFunc2[x_/; BlockFuncModQ[x], y___] :=
     Module[{a = ToExpression[HeadPFU[x]], b = {}, c, k},
       Do[c = Quiet[Check[Part[a, k], Error, Part::partw]];
   If[c === Error, Return[If[{y} == {}, b, If[SymbolQ[y], b;
y = Map[ToString1, b], b]]], AppendTo[b, c]], {k, Infinity}]]
In[78]:= ArgsProcFunc2[M]
Out[78]= {x_, y_ /; {g[t_] := Module[{}, t^2], If[g[y] > 50,
                       True, False]}[[2]], r_ : 77, p_., z___}
```

The question of processing of the formal arguments with good reason can be considered as the first problem relating to the calculations of the tuples of formal arguments of the user functions, modules and blocks that have been activated in the current session directly or on the basis of download of packages containing their definitions. In our works [1-15] certain tools for the solution of this problem have been programmed in the form of procedures ***Args, Args0÷Args2,*** then we presented similar tools in narrower assortment and with the improved some functional characteristics. Above all, as a rather useful tool, we present the ***Args3*** procedure whose call ***Args3[x]*** returns the list of formal arguments of the user module, block or function ***x***. At the same time, the argument ***x*** can present an multiple object of the same name. The following fragment represents the sourse code of the ***Args3*** procedure with the most typical examples of its use.

```
In[3122]:= M[x_ /; SameQ[x, "avz"], y_] := Module[{a, b, c}, y];
    M[x_ /; x == "avz"] := Module[{a, b, c}, x];
    M[x_ /; IntegerQ[x], y_String] := Module[{a, b, c}, x];
    M[x_, y_] := Module[{a, b, c}, "agn"; x + y]; M[x_String] := x;
    M[x_ /; ListQ[x], y_] := Block[{a, b, c}, "agn"; Length[x] + y];
     F[x_ /; SameQ[x, "avz"], y_] := {x, y}
In[3123]:= Args3[s_ /; BlockFuncModQ[s]] :=
                                    Module[{a = Headings[s], b, c = 7},
       If[SimpleListQ[a], a = {a}, Set[c, 77]]; a = Map[#[[2]] &, a];
             b = Map[StringReplace[#, ToString[s] -> "", 1] &, a];
               b = Map[StringToList[StringTake[#, {2, -2}]] &, b];
                                     If[c == 77, b, Flatten[b, 1]]]
In[3124]:= Args3[M]
Out[3124]= {{"x_ /; ListQ[x]", "y_"}, {"x_", "y_", "z_"},
                                      {"x_ /; x === \"avz\"", "y_"}}
In[3125]:= Args3[F]
Out[3125]= {"x_ /; x === \"avz\"", "y_"}
In[3126]:= Args3[L]
Out[3126]= {"x_", "y_"}
```

At that, in a case of the returned nested list its sublists define tuples of formal arguments in the order that is defined by order of components of ***x*** object according to the call ***Definition[x]***.

The following procedure is an useful modification of our argument processing means. The call ***ArgsBFM1[x]*** generally returns the list of the *ListList* type whose two-element sublists in string format determine the name of a formal argument *(1st element)* and its admissibility test *(2nd element)* of block, function or module ***x***. Lack of the test is coded as "*Arbitrary*"; in addition, under lack of test is understood not only its actual lack, but also the optional or default patterns ascribed to a formal argument. The procedure successfully processes the objects of the same name too, i.e. objects with several headings. The next fragment represents source code of the ***ArgsBFM1*** procedure with typical examples of its application.

```
In[3336]:= ArgsBFM1[x_/; BlockFuncModQ[x]] :=
                    Module[{b, c, d, g = {}, t, a = ToString2[Args[x]]},
                               a = If[QmultiplePF[x], a, {a}];
                              Do[{b, c, d} = {{}, {}, {}}; t = a[[j]];
                              Do[AppendTo[b, If[ListQ[t[[k]]],
  Map[StringSplit[#, {"/;", "__", "___", "_", ":", "_:", "_."}] &, t[[k]]],
StringSplit[t[[k]], {"/;", "__", "___", "_", ":", "_:", "_."}]]], {k, Length[t]}];
                           Do[AppendTo[c, If[NestListQ[b[[k]]],
                  Map[Map[If[#1 == " " || #1 == "", Nothing,
                                StringTrim[#1]] &, #] &, b[[k]]],
Map[If[# == " " || #1 == "", Nothing, StringTrim[#]] &, b[[k]]]]],
                                                  {k, 1, Length[b]}];
                           Do[AppendTo[d, If[NestListQ[c[[k]]],
   Map[If[Length[#1] == 1, {#1[[1]], "Arbitrary"}, #1] &, c[[k]]],
      If[Length[c[[k]]] == 1, {c[[k]][[1]], "Arbitrary"}, c[[k]]]]],
             {k, 1, Length[c]}]; d = If[Length[d] == 1, d[[1]], d];
   AppendTo[g, d], {j, Length[a]}]; If[Length[g] == 1, g[[1]], g]]

In[3337]:= G[x_, y_List, z_ : 77, h___] := Module[{g = 72}, Body];
           G[x_, y_List, z_ : 78, {x1_, x2_List, x3_ : 90}, h___] :=
           Module[{v = 42, g = 47, a = 87, k = 96, s = 67}, Body]
In[3338]:= ArgsBFM1[G]
Out[3338]= {{{"x", "Arbitrary"}, {"y", "List"}, {"z", "78"},
{{"x1", "Arbitrary"}, {"x2", "List"}, {"x3", "90"}}, {"h", "Arbitrary"}},
{{"x", "Arbitrary"}, {"y", "List"}, {"z", "77"}, {"h", "Arbitrary"}}}
```

The procedure has a number of useful applications [16].

Several useful tools have been created to work with arguments of blocks, functions and modules [16]. One example is the procedure whose call ***Args2***[***x***] returns the list of formal arguments with testing functions assigned to them in string format for a module, function, or block ***x***. While calling ***Args2***[***x***, ***y***] with the second optional argument ***y*** – *an undefined symbol* – via it returns the list consisting of 2–element sub–lists whose elements in string format represent arguments and testing functions ascribed to them.

```
In[111]:= Default[Sg, 6, 42]; Sg[x_, y_Integer, z_/; EvenQ[z], t__,
                    h_: 0, g_.] := x*y + z + t + h*g
In[112]:= Args2[x_/; BlockFuncModQ[x], y___] :=
          Module[{a = Definition2[x][[1]], b = "", c, d = {}, t},
  a = StringReplace5[a, {ToString[x] <> "[" -> "{", "] := " -> "}"}, 1];
Do[If[SyntaxQ[b = b <> StringTake[a, {j}]], Break[], 7], {j, Infinity}];
                    b = StringToList[StringTake[b, {2, -2}]];
  If[{y} != {} && SymbolQ[y], c = Map[StringSplit[#, "_"] &, b];
              y = Map[If[Length[#] == 1, AppendTo[d, #],
                   If[SuffPref[#[[2]], t = " /; ", 1],
         AppendTo[d, {#[[1]], StringReplace[#[[2]], t -> ""]}],
                   If[SuffPref[#[[2]], ":", 1],
   AppendTo[d, {#[[1]], "Optional"}], If[SuffPref[#[[2]], ".", 1],
   AppendTo[d, {#[[1]], "Default"}], AppendTo[d, #]]]]]] &, c];
          y = DeleteDuplicates[Flatten[y, 1]];
          y = Map[If[Length[#] == 1, #[[1]], #] &, y], 7]; b]
In[113]:= Args2[Sg, sv]
Out[113]= {"x_", "y_Integer", "z_/; EvenQ[z]", "t__", "h_:0", "g_."}
In[114]:= sv
Out[114]= {"x", {"y", "Integer"}, {"z", "EvenQ[z]"}, "t",
                    {"h", "Optional"}, {"g", "Default"}}
In[115]:= StringReplace5[x_String, y_/; ListRulesQ[y],
  z_Integer] := Module[{a = x}, Do[a = StringReplace[a, y[[j]], z],
                    {j, Length[y]}]; a]
In[116]:= StringReplace5["12345612345", {"2" -> "a", "4" -> "b",
                    "c" -> "d"}, 1]
Out[116]= "1a3b5612345"
```

The call ***StringReplace5***[***x***, ***y***, ***z***] unlike the ***StringReplace*** of the same call format returns result of replacements *only* the first *z* entries of left part of each rule from a list ***y*** onto its right part in a string ***x***.

It is worth noting that the permissibility of **W** constructions that include modules, blocks and functions including built-in ones, provided that ***BooleanQ*[*W*] = *True*,** makes it possible to conveniently include various kinds of diagnostic information in such constructs, as illustrated by the following simple example:

```
In[3337]:= T[x_/; If[x > 50, {Print["Invalid first argument:
                     it must be greater than 50"], False}, True],
  y_/; If[IntegerQ[y], True, Print["Invalid second argument:
                                  it must be an integer"]; False],
  z_/; If[PrimeQ[z], {g[t_] := t^2, True}[[2]], {Print["Invalid
     third argument: it must be a prime"], False}]] := g[x*y*z]
In[3338]:= T[100, 7, 7]
           Invalid first argument: it must be greater than 50
Out[3338]= T[100, 7, 7]
In[3339]:= T[50, 42/77, 7]
           Invalid second argument: it must be an integer
Out[3339]= T[50, 6/11, 7]
In[3340]:= T[50, 77, 4]
           Invalid third argument: it must be a prime
Out[3340]= T[50, 77, 4]
In[3341]:= T[50, 77, 7]
Out[3341]= 72630250
In[3342]:= Definition[g]
Out[3342]= g[t_] := t^2
```

Thus, the testing function for a formal ***x*** argument can be an arbitrary expression ***w*[*x*]**, for that the ratio ***BooleanQ*[*W*[*x*]] = *True*** will be true. Moreover, in addition to printing of *diagnostic* information, testing expressions ***w*[*x*]** may include definitions of *modules, blocks* and *functions* whose definitions are activated only if the actual argument ***x*** is valid, making their available in the body of an original procedure or function and in the current session as a whole. This possibility is illustrated in the above function ***T*** by the function ***g*** activated only at call ***T*[*x, y, z*]** with valid values for the formal arguments {***x, y, z***}. So, definitions of formal arguments of modules, blocks, functions allow a rather wide range of testing expressions to be used for them.

Here it is necessary to make an essential remark concerning the tools that deal with arguments of procedures and functions. The matter is that as it was shown earlier, testing tools ascribed to the formal arguments, as a rule, consist of the earlier defined testing functions or the reserved key words defining the type, for example, ***Integer***. Whereas as a side effect the builtin ***Math-language*** allows to use the constructions that contain definitions of the testing means, directly in headings of the procedures and functions. Interesting examples of that have been represented above. Meanwhile, despite of such possibility, the programmed means are oriented, as a rule, on use for testing of admissibility of the factual arguments or the predefined means, or including the testing algorithms in the body of procedures and functions. For this reason, the ***Args*** procedure along with similar to it in such cases can return incorrect results. Whereas the procedure ***ArgsU*** covers such peculiar cases. The procedure call ***ArgsU[x]*** regardless of way of definition of testing of factual arguments in the general case returns the nested list whose elements are **3**–element sublists of strings; the ***1st*** element of such sublists is the name of formal argument, the *second* element defines template ascribed to this formal argument, and the ***3rd*** element defines a testing function, construction including definition of the testing function, a key word, or an optional value, otherwise the third element is the empty string, i.e. "". The next fragment presents source code of the ***ArgsU*** procedure with examples of its use.

```
In[7]:= ArgsU[x_ /; BlockFuncModQ[x]] :=
                    Module[{a = HeadPFU[x], b, c, d = {}, g},
        a = StringTake[a, {StringLength[ToString[x]] + 2, -2}];
                                    c = StringPartition2[a, ","];
b[t_] := {StringTake[t, {1, Set[g, Flatten[StringPosition[t, "_"]][[1]]] - 1}],
StringTake[t, {g, -1}]}; c = Quiet[Map[StringTrim@b@# &, c]];
c = Quiet[Map[{#[[1]], StringReplace[#[[2]], " /; " -> "", 1]} &, c]];
                             Map[If[SuffPref[#[[2]], "___", 1],
AppendTo[d, {#[[1]], "___", StringTrim2[#[[2]], "_", 1]}],
                                     If[SuffPref[#[[2]], "__", 1],
AppendTo[d, {#[[1]], "__", StringTrim2[#[[2]], "_", 1]}],
                                          If[SuffPref[#[[2]], "_:", 1],
AppendTo[d, {#[[1]], "_:", StringReplace[#[[2]], "_:" -> "", 1]}],
```

```
                                        If[SuffPref[#[[2]], "_.", 1],
AppendTo[d, {#[[1]], "_.", StringReplace[#[[2]], "_." -> "", 1]}],
                                        If[SuffPref[#[[2]], "_", 1],
AppendTo[d, {#[[1]], "_", StringTrim2[#[[2]], "_", 1]}]]]]]] &, c];
                                        If[Length[d] == 1, d[[1]], d]]
In[8]:= Ak[x_, h_/; IntegerQ[h], y_/; {IntOddQ[t_/; IntegerQ[t]] :=
        Module[{}, IntegerQ[t] && OddQ[t]], IntOddQ[y]}[[-1]],
                                        p_ : 77, t_.] := x*y*h*p*t
In[9]:= Args[Ak]
        ToExpression::sntx: Invalid syntax in or before
        "{x_, h_ /; IntegerQ[h], y_ /; {IntOddQ[t_ /; IntegerQ[t]}".
Out[9]= $Failed
In[10]:= ArgsU[Ak]
Out[10]= {{"x", "_", ""}, {"h", "_", "IntegerQ[h]"},
{"y", "_", "{IntOddQ[t_/; IntegerQ[t]] := Module[{}, IntegerQ[t] &&
       OddQ[t]], IntOddQ[y]}[[-1]]"}, {"p", "_:", "77"}, {"t", "_.", ""}}
```

The *ArgsTypes* procedure [8] serves for testing of the formal arguments of block, function or module activated in the current session. So, the call ***ArgsTypes*[*x*]** returns the nested list, whose **2**-element sublists in the string format define names of formal arguments and their *admissible* types *(in the broader sense the tests for their admissibility with initial values by default)* respectively. In lack of a type an argument it is defined as ***"Arbitrary"*** which is characteristic for arguments of pure functions and arguments without the tests and/or initial values ascribed to them and also which have format patterns {*"__", "___"*}. The fragment below represents source code of the ***ArgsTypes*** procedure along with typical examples of its application.

Moreover, the ***ArgsTypes*** procedure successfully processes the above cases *"objects of the same name with various headings"*, returning the nested two-element lists of the formal arguments concerning the subobjects composing an object ***x***, in the order defined by the ***Definition*** function. And in this case **2**-element lists have the format, represented above while for objects with empty list of formal arguments the empty list is returned, i.e. **{}**. Unlike ***ArgsTypes*** of the same name this procedure processes objects, including pure functions and *Compile* functions.

2.4. Local variables in Mathematica procedures

The list of local variables of the procedure in its definition is located at once behind the open parenthesis "[". This list can be as empty, and to contain variables *(perhaps with their initial values)* which scope is limited to a framework of the procedure, i.e. values of variables from the mentioned list of locals in the current session up a procedure call match their values after exit from the procedure. All other variables of a procedure that are not entering the locals list rely as the *global* for the procedure in scope of the current session with the system.

At the same time *initial values* for local variables can be both simple and rather complex expressions. In particular, through local variables it is possible to define procedures and functions available in the current session *beyond* the procedure containing their definitions as illustrates a simple example:

```
In[85]:= P[x_, y_] := Module[{a = SetDelayed[b[c_],
              Module[{}, c^2]], d = 7, c = 8}, b[x] + d*x + c*y]
In[86]:= P[42, 47]
Out[86]= 2434
In[87]:= Definition[b]
Out[87]= b[c_] := Module[{}, c^2]
In[88]:= P1[x_, y_] := Module[{a = b[c_] := Module[{}, c^2],
                              d = 7, c = 8}, b[x] + d*x + c*y]
In[89]:= P1[42, 47]
Out[89]= 2434
In[90]:= P1[x_, y_, b_/; ! ValueQ[b]] := Module[{d = 7, c = 8,
              a = b[c_] := Module[{}, c^2]}, b[x] + d*x + c*y]
In[91]:= P1[42, 47, Name]
Out[91]= 2434
In[92]:= Definition[Name1]
Out[92]= Name[c_] := Module[{}, c^2]
In[93]:= P[x_, y_, b_/; ! ValueQ[b]] := Module[{d = 7,
                   a = SetDelayed[b[c_], Module[{}, c^2]],
                   c = If[b[x] < 100, 0, 7]}, b[x] + d*x + c*y]
In[93]:= P[200, 10, Name]
Out[93]= 41960
```

Variable ***b*** in this example is *global* while the *local* variable ***a*** can be used arbitrary in procedure body without influencing on the variable of the same name outside of the procedure. At last, a simple modification of the above example allows to define in addition in procedure ***P1*** a name for procedure ***b*** generated in its local variables. Note that a procedure or function generated in the list of local variables can successfully be called in initial values of other local variables of the procedure as appears from the above example.

We have created a number of tools to work with local user procedure variables [8,16]. Among them, ***LocalsMod*** procedure is of some interest.

```
In[2441]:= Avz[x_] := Module[{t, a = 77, b = k + t, d = Jn[x],
                 c = {m, {h, g}}}, a[t_] := t^2 + a*d; a[x] + d^2]
In[2442]:= LocalsMod[x_/; BlockModQ[x]] :=
              Module[{a = Definition1[x], b, c = {}, d, j, f, g},
b = Flatten[StringPosition[a, {"Module[", "Block["}, 1]][[-1]];
b = StringTake[a, {1, b}]; b = StringReplace[a, b -> ""];
                          Do[c = c <> StringTake[b, {j, j}];
If[SyntaxQ[c], Break[], Continue[]], {j, 1, StringLength[b]}];
d = "," <> StringDrop[StringDrop[c, 1], -1] <> ",";  c = {};
Label[Agn];           f = StringPosition[d, ","];
                      f = DeleteDuplicates[Flatten[f]];
                      For[j = 2, j <= Length[f], j++,
  If[SyntaxQ[g = StringTake[d, {f[[1]] + 1, f[[j]] - 1}]],
  AppendTo[c, g]; d = StringReplace[d, "," <> g -> "", 1];
                              Goto[Agn], Continue[]]];
c = Map[If[StringFreeQ[#, "="], {StringTrim[#], "Null"},
              {g = Flatten[StringPosition[#, "=", 1]][[1]],
              {StringTake[#, {1, g - 2}],
  StringTake[#, {g + 2, StringLength[#]}]}}[[2]]] &, c];
  SetAttributes[StringTrim, Listable];
                             Map[StringTrim[#] &, c]]
In[2443]:= LocalsMod[Avz]
Out[2443]= {{"t", "Null"}, {"a", "77"}, {"b", "k + t"},
                    {"d", "Sin[x]"}, {"c", "{m, {h, g}}"}}
```

The previous fragment represents the source code of the procedure with an example of its use. Thus, the procedure call ***LocalsMod***[*x*] returns a nested list whose two-element sub-lists as the *first* element defines a local variable of a procedure ***x*** in the string format, whereas the *second* element defines the initial condition assigned to it in the string format. If condition is not presented, then the second element is *"Null"*. If procedure ***x*** has no local variables, then the call ***LocalsMod***[*x*] returns the empty list, i.e. {}. The procedure has a number of useful applications.

Between the main objects *(function, block, module)* there is a mutual converting of one object to another if not to take global and local variables into account. Because of an opportunity and expediency of use of mechanism of *local* variables is reasonable convertings of both classical, and pure functions to procedures *(blocks, modules)*. The ***MathToolBox*** package [4-7,16] provides a number of tools for different conversion cases. As an example of certain practical interest, the ***FunctToProc*** procedure can be cited. The procedure call ***FuncToProc***[*x, N*] returns nothing, at the same time transforming a classical or pure function ***x*** to the procedure with name ***N*** with the same set of formal arguments along with a set of local variables created from global variables of the function ***x***. Simple examples illustrate the application of the ***FuncToProc*** procedure.

```
FuncToProc[x_, N_] := Module[{a, b=GlobalsInFunc[x], c},
        If[PureFuncQ[x], PureFuncToFunction[x, N];
      c = DefToStr[N], If[FunctionQ[x], c = DefToStr[x],
          Return["The first argument – not function"]]];
                c = StringInsert[c, "Module[" <>
            ToString[ToExpression[b]] <> ", ",
          StringPosition[c, ":=", 1][[1]][[2]] + 2];
   ToExpression[StringReplacePart[c, ToString[N],
        StringPosition[c, "[", 1][[1]][[1]] – 1] <> "]"]]
```

```
In[10]:= G := Function[{x, y, z}, p*(x + y + z)]
In[11]:= T := p*(#1^2 + #2^2*#3^n) &
In[12]:= F[x_, y_] := x*y + Module[{a = 5, b = 6}, a*x + b*y]
In[13]:= FuncToProc[G, H]
```

```
In[14]:= Definition[H]
Out[14]= H[x_, y_, z_] := Module[{p}, p*(x + y + z)]
In[15]:= FuncToProc[T, V]
In[16]:= Definition[V]
Out[16]= V[x1_, x2_, x3_] := Module[{n, p}, p*(x1^2 +
                                                    x2^2*x3^n)]
In[17]:= FuncToProc[F, W]
In[18]:= Definition[W]
Out[18]= W[x_, y_] := Module[{a, b}, x*y + Module[{a = 5,
                                                    b = 6}, a*x + b*y]]
```

```
DefToStr[x_/; SymbolQ[x] || StringQ[x]] := Module[{a, c,
   b = "*" <> ToString[x]}, c = Map[If[StringFreeQ[#, b], #,
 StringTake[#, {1, Flatten[StringPosition[#, b]][[1]] - 1}]] &,
StringSplit[ToString[InputForm[Definition[x]]], "\n \n"]];
                                   If[Length[c] == 1, c[[1]], c]]
```

```
In[19]:= DefToStr[F]
Out[19]= "F[x_, y_] := x*y + Module[{a = 5, b = 6}, a*x + b*y]"
```

Along with a number of tools from the package [3-5,16], the procedure uses a procedure whose call ***DefToStr***[***x***] returns the *Input*-expression of a symbol ***x*** definition in string format, that, generally speaking, the built-in ***ToString*** function is not able to do. Meanwhile, a rather significant remark needs to be made regarding the ***DefToStr*** tool. As noted repeatedly, ***Mathematica*** system differentiates objects not by their names, but by their headers, if any. It is therefore quite real that we may deal with different definitions under the same name. This applies to all objects that have headers. In view of this circumstance, we have developed a number of funds for various cases of application [1-16]. This can be fully attributed to the above ***DefToStr*** tool, whose call on a symbol having multiple definitions produce a correct result, i.e. the ***DefToStr*** procedure solves this problem. In the case of multiplicity of a symbol definition the procedure call ***DefToStr***[***x***] returns the list of *Input*-expressions of a symbol ***x*** definitions in string format, that the builtin ***ToString*** function generally speaking, is not able to do. In some cases, the method may be useful in practical programming. Note, that the actual *x* argument in ***DefToStr[x]*** call must be of type *Symbol* or *String (if for x there are headers)* or *String (if for x there are no headers)*, while on built-in system functions its call returns attributes ascribed to them. This procedure is rather demanded when processing multiple definitions of a function, block or module.

```
In[11]:= G[x_, y_] := p*(x^2 + y^2)
In[12]:= G[x_, y_, z_] := (x^2 + y^2 + z^2)
In[13]:= G[x_, y_, z_/; IntegerQ[z]] := Module[{}, x*y +
                                        42*x^2 + 47*y^2 + z^3]
In[14]:= F[x_, y_] := x*y + 42*x^2 + 47*y^2
In[15]:= DefToStr[G]
Out[15]= {"G[x_, y_] := p*(x^2 + y^2)",
          "G[x_, y_, z_ /; IntegerQ[z]] := Module[{}, x*y +
                                        42*x^2 + 47*y^2 + z^3]",
          "G[x_, y_, z_] := x^2 + y^2 + z^2"}
In[16]:= DefToStr[F]
Out[16]= "F[x_, y_] := x*y + 42*x^2 + 47*y^2"
```

Experience has shown that the use of the procedure is quite effective in many applications.

For work with local and global variables of procedures we created a number of enough useful tools that are absent among the built-in system tools [16]. Their detailed description can be found in [1-15]. In particular, the ***GlobalToLocalInit*** procedure provides expansion of the list of local variables of a procedure at the expense of its global variables. Moreover, for the local variables received from global variables the initial values rely those that at the time of the procedure call had global variables. In the absence of global variables the procedure call returns the corresponding message. The call ***GlobalToLocalInit[x]*** returns nothing, generating in the current session the procedure with name *$$x* with the updated list of local variables. The following program fragment illustrates told:

```
In[712]:= GS[x_, y_, z_/; IntegerQ[z]] := Module[{a= 72,
      b = 77}, t*(x^2 + n*y^2 + v*Sin[p]*T[z]*z^2)/g*W[a, b]]
```

```
In[713]:= {t, n, p, v} = {2, 7, 6, 9}; T[x_] := x^2; W[x_, y_] := x*y;
In[714]:= GlobalToLocalInit[x_ /; BlockModQ[x]] :=
            Module[{a = Args[x], b, c, d, f},  b = DefToStr[x];
                                           c = ArgsLocalsGlobals1[x];
                      Quiet[d = Select[Flatten[Select[c[[3]],
                 ! "System`" == #[[1]] &]], ! ContextQ[#] &]];
                      d = Select[d, ! BlockFuncModQ[#] &];
                    If[d == {}, Return["No global variables"],
                        Map[If[! Definition[#] === Null, #,
                       ToExpression[# <> "= " <> #]] &, d]];
       ToExpression["Save[\"#\"," <> ToString1[d] <> "]"];
          f = ReadString["#"]; DeleteFile["#"];
          f = Select[StringSplit[f, "\r\n"], # != " " &];
          c = StringReplace[b, HeadPF[x] -> "", 1];
          c = SubStrSymbolParity1[c, "{", "}"][[1]];
          f = StringReplace[StringReplace[ToString[c] <>
                         ToString[f], "}{" -> ", "], "{, " -> "{"];
        ToExpression["$$" <> StringReplace[b, c -> f, 1]]]]
In[715]:= GlobalToLocalInit[GS]
In[716]:= Definition[$$GS]
Out[716]= $$GS[x_, y_, z_ /; IntegerQ[z]] := Module[{a = 72,
                                b = 77, n = 7, p = 6, t = 2, v = 9},
          (t*(x^2 + n*y^2 + v*Sin[p]*T[z]*z^2)*W[a, b])/g]
In[4852]:= {m, n, p} = {42, 47, 67};
In[4853]:= A[x_, y_, z_] := Module[{a := 7, b := 5, c := 77},
                                         (a*x + b*y + c*z)*m*n*p]
In[4854]:= A[1, 2, 3]
Out[4854]= 32799984
In[4855]:= GlobalToLocalInit[A]
In[4856]:= Definition[$$A]
Out[4856]= $$A[x_, y_, z_] := Module[{a := 7, b := 5, c := 77,
              n = 47, p = 67, m = 42}, (a*x + b*y + c*z)*m*n*p]
In[4857]:= {m, n, p} = {77, 72, 52};
In[4858]:= $$A[1, 2, 3]
Out[4858]= 32799984
```

By the way, the last example with procedure ***A*** in addition illustrates a possibility of correct use of the delayed definitions instead of immediate for initial values of local variables.

A function or procedure defined in a procedure body with ***b*** name of local variable also is local whereas defined through a local variable becomes global tool in the current session of the system. The following example illustrates told:

```
In[2010]:= B[x_, y_] := Module[{a = 7, b, c := 77},
            If[x < y, b[t_] := t^2, b[t_] := t^3]; (a + c)*b[x*y]]
In[2011]:= B[7, 3]
Out[2011]= 777924
In[2012]:= Definition[b]
Out[2012]= Null
In[2013]:= J[x_, y_] := Module[{a = 7, b = {b[t_, c_] :=
            (t + c)^2, b}[[2]], c := 77}, (a + c)*b[x, y]]
In[2014]:= J[2, 3]
Out[2014]= 2100
In[2015]:= Definition[b]
Out[2015]= b[t_, c_] := (t + c)^2
```

The above mechanism works when determining headings and local variables of the functions, blocks and modules. At the same time, it must be kept in mind that presented mechanism with good reason can be carried to non-standard methods of programming which are admissible, correct and are a collateral consequence of the built-in ***Math***-language. Meantime, taking into account this circumstance to programming of processing tools of elements of procedures and functions *(headings, local variables, arguments, etc.)* certain additional demands are made. This mechanism can be considered facultative, i.e. optional to programming of procedures and functions. At the same time it must be kept in mind that definitions of the tools coded in the formal arguments and local variables become active in the all domain of the current session that isn't always acceptable. A reception correcting such situation presents the first example of previous fragment. The vast majority of tools presented in our package [16] don't use this mechanism. However certain our tools, represented in [1-15], use this mechanism, representing certain ways of its processing. Other example of processing of local variables – the procedure updating their initial values.

```
In[104]:= ReplaceLocalInit[x_ /; BlockModQ[x], y_List] :=
                    Module[{a = DefToStr[x], b, c, d, f = {}, k,
     h = If[NestListQ[y], y, {y}]}, c = ArgsLocalsGlobals1[x];
                              b = Map[If[Length[#] == 1, #,
   {StringReplace[#[[1]], " :" -> ""], #[[2]]}] &, Locals4[x]];
                                     k = Map[#[[1]] &, b];
                       If[b == {}, ToExpression["$" <> a],
                  d = Map[{#[[1]], ToString[#[[2]]]} &, h];
  f = Flatten[{b, d}, 1]; f = Gather[f, #1[[1]] === #2[[1]] &];
                  f = Map[If[Length[#] == 1, #[[1]], #] &, f];
            f = Map[If[NestListQ[#] && Length[#] == 2,
                        #[[2]][[1]] <> "=" <> #[[2]][[2]],
         If[Length[#] == 1 && MemberQ[k, #[[1]]], #[[1]],
               If[Length[#] == 2 && MemberQ[k, #[[1]]],
                  #[[1]] <> "=" <> #[[2]], Nothing]]] &, f];
         d = StringReplace[a, HeadPF[x] <> " := " -> "", 1];
                 d = SubStrSymbolParity1[d, "{", "}"][[1]];
ToExpression["$" <> StringReplace[a, d -> ToString[f], 1]]]]

In[105]:= B[x_] := Module[{a = 77, b, c := 72, d = 9}, Body]
In[106]:= ReplaceLocalInit[B, {{"a", 90}, {"b", 500},
                 {"c", 900}, {"p", 52}, {"g", 50}}]; Definition[$B]
Out[106]= $B[x_] := Module[{a=90, b=500, c=900, d=9}, Body]
In[107]:= H[x_, y_, z_] := Module[{}, y = x^2; z = x^3; x + 5]
In[108]:= ReplaceLocalInit[H, {{"a", 90}, {"b", 500},
                 {"c", 900}, {"p", 52}, {"g", 50}}]; Definition[$H]
Out[108]= $H[x_, y_, z_] := Module[{}, y = x^2; z = x^3; x + 5]
In[109]:= ReplaceLocalInit[B, {{"a", 90}, {"c", 900}, {"p", 52}}]
In[110]:= Definition[$B]
Out[110]= $B[x_] := Module[{a = 90, b, c = 900, d = 9}, Body]
```

The call ***ReplaceLocalInit***[***x***, {{"***a***", ***a1***}, ..., {"***p***", ***p1***}}] returns nothing, activating in the current session the procedure ***$x*** that relatively ***x*** has local variables *{a,...,p}* with the updated initial values *{a1,...,p1}*. The fragment illustrates the source code of the procedure with examples of its use. Other processing means of local variables of the user procedures can be found in [1-18,22]. They sometimes significantly complement the built-in software.

Also it is worth paying attention to one moment of rather local variables of procedures. The scope of local variables is the procedure in which they are determined and after a procedure call these variables are unavailable in the current ***Mathematica*** session. The local variables have ***Temporary*** attribute which is assigned to the variables which are created as local variables of a procedure; they are automatically removed when they are no longer needed. At that, local variables with attribute *Temporary* conventionally receive names of the format ***a$nnn,*** where ***a*** - a name of local variable that is defined at procedure creation and ***nnn*** - the number based on the current serial number defined by the system ***$ModuleNumber*** variable. Note, ***$ModuleNumber*** is incremented every time a procedure or built-in ***Unique*** function is called. A ***Mathematica*** session starts with ***$ModuleNumber*** set to ***1***, that can be redefined, but in order to avoid the possible conflict situations leading to decrease in efficiency, the user is not recommended to redefine ***$ModuleNumber*** variable. For the purpose of gaining access to local variables out of domain of the procedures containing them it is possible to use a reception that is based on redefinition of their ***Temporary*** attribute, namely on its cancelling. Let's illustrate told by a simple example:

```
In[37]:= Gs[x_, y_, z_] := Module[{a, b},
                 Print[{Map[Attributes[#] &, {a, b}], {a, b}}];
                       a[t_, n_, m_] := t*n*m; b := 78; b*x*y*z]
In[38]:= Gs[42, 47, 67]
              {{{Temporary}, {Temporary}}, {a$2666, b$2666}}
Out[38]= 10316124
In[39]:= Definition1[a$2666]
Out[39]= Null
In[40]:= b$2666
Out[40]= b$2666
In[41]:= Gs1[x_, y_, z_] := Module[{a, b, c}, Print[{a, b, c}];
                                          {a, b, c} = {x, y, z}; a*b*c]
```

```
In[42]:= Gs1[42, 47, 67]
         {a$2863, b$2863, c$2863}
Out[42]= 132258
In[43]:= {a$2863, b$2863, c$2863}
Out[43]= {a$2863, b$2863, c$2863}
In[44]:= Gs2[x_, y_, z_] := Module[{a, b, c}, Print[{a, b, c}];
           Map[ClearAttributes[#, Temporary] &, {a, b, c}];
                                   {a, b, c} = {x, y, z}; a*b*c]
In[45]:= Gs2[42, 47, 67]
         {a$2873, b$2873, c$2873}
Out[45]= 132258
In[46]:= {a$2873, b$2873, c$2873}
Out[46]= {42, 47, 67}
```

Procedure ***Gs*** uses *two* local variables *{a, b};* the first of them defines a name in function definition while the second defines simple integer variable. The procedure call returns an integer number with output of the nested list with attributes of local variables *{a, b}* and their values. It turns out that out of domain of the procedure local variables are indefinite ones.

Procedure call ***Gs1****[x, y, z]* returns an integer number along with output of the list of the local variables that are generated by the procedure from *{a, b, c}*. It turns out that out of domain of the procedure local variables *{a, b, c}* are indefinite ones.

The ***Gs2*** procedure differs from the ***Gs1*** procedure only in what in its body contains cancelling of ***Temporary*** attribute for all local variables *{a, b, c}*. Procedure call ***Gs2****[x, y, z]* returns an integer number along with output of the list of local variables that are generated by the procedure from *{a, b, c}*. It turns out that out of domain of the procedure local variables *{a, b, c}* are definite ones, obtaining quite concrete values. So, for ensuring access to local variables of a procedure out of its domain it is quite enough to cancel ***Temporary*** attribute for all *(or selected)* its local variables allowing to monitor intermediate calculations in the course of performing procedures. Such approach allows to provide monitoring of values of local variables of procedures that is especially important when debugging a rather large and complex software by transferring the local variables to the level of variables, unique for the current session. In certain cases this approach to debugging has quite certain advantages. For such purpose the simple ***LocalsInProc*** procedure which is based on the predetermined variable ***$ModuleNumber*** which determines the current serial number to be used for local variables that are created can appear quite useful. Any ***Mathematica*** session starts with ***$ModuleNumber*** set to ***1***, receiving the increment for each new local variable in the current session. The fragment below represents source code of the procedure with examples of use.

```
In[47]:= LocalsInProc[t_List] := Module[{a, b = Length[t]},
                  a = Map[ToString, ($ModuleNumber - 5)*
                                  Flatten[Tuples[{1}, b]]];
                  Map[t[[#]] <> "$" <> a[[#]] &, Range[b]]]
In[48]:= Agn2[x_] := Module[{a, b, c, d}, Print[{a, b, c, d}];
                        {a, b, c, d} = {42, 47, 67, 77}; x*a*b*c]
In[49]:= Agn2[77]
        {a$13366, b$13366, c$13366, d$13366}
Out[49]= 10183866
In[50]:= LocalsInProc[{"a", "b", "c", "d"}]
Out[50]= {a$13366, b$13366, c$13366, d$13366}
In[51]:= Avz[x_] := Module[{a, b, c}, Print[{a, b, c}];
                                  a[t_] := t^2; a[x]]; Avz[77]
        {a$49432, b$49432, c$49432}
Out[51]= 5929
In[52]:= LocalsInProc[{"a", "b", "c"}]
Out[52]= {"a$49432", "b$49432", "c$49432"}
```

The procedure call ***LocalsInProc*[*g*]** should follow directly a ***P*** procedure call, where ***g*** – the list of local variables of the ***P*** procedure, with return of the list of representations in form of ***x$nn*** *(**x** – a variable name and **nn** – an integer in string format)* that are generated for local variables of the ***P*** procedure. If ***g*** defines the empty list, i.e. procedure ***P*** has no local variables, then the call ***LocalsInProc*[{}]** returns the empty list, i.e. {}.

Additionally, a number of ***Locals*** ÷ ***Locals5*** tools have been programmed, using some useful programming techniques and returning local variables in various sections. A typical example is the procedure whose call ***Locals5[x]*** returns the list of local variables in string format with initial values assigned to them, for a module, or a block ***x***. While calling ***Locals5[x, y]*** with the second optional argument ***y*** – *an undefined symbol* – through it additionally returns the list consisting of two-element sub-lists whose elements in string format represent local variables and initial values ascribed to them. If there are no local variables, the empty list is returned. The fragment below represents the source code of the procedure with examples of its application.

```
In[422]:= Locals5[x_/; BlockModQ[x], y___] := Module[{a, b, c},
  a = StringJoin[Insert[Reverse[Headings[x]], " := ", 2]] <> "[";
      b = StringReplace[PureDefinition[x], a -> "", 1];
    Do[c = StringTake[b, k]; If[SyntaxQ[c], Return[c], 7],
                                {k, StringLength[b]}];
   If[c == "{}", c = {}, c = StrToList[StringTake[c, {2, -2}]]];
                              If[{y} == {}, c, If[SymbolQ[y],
             y = Map[StringSplit[#, " = "] &, c]; c, c]]]
In[423]:= M3[x_] := Block[{a = 90, b = 49, c, h}, h = 77; x*h];
  B1[x_] := Block[{a = 90, b = 50, c = {72, 77}, d = 42}, x*a*b*c*d];
                        B[x_] := Block[{}, x];  Locals5[M3]
Out[423]= {"a = 90", "b = 49", "c", "h"}
In[424]:= Locals5[B]
Out[424]= {}
In[425]:= Locals5[B1]
Out[425]= {"a = 90", "b = 50", "c = {72, 77}", "d = 42"}
In[426]:= Locals5[B1, agn]
Out[426]= {"a = 90", "b = 50", "c = {72, 77}", "d = 42"}
In[427]:= agn
Out[427]= {{"a", "90"}, {"b", "50"}, {"c", "{72, 77}"}, {"d", "42"}}
In[428]:= Locals5[B, vsv]; vsv
Out[428]= {}
In[429]:= Locals5[M3, art]; art
Out[429]= {{"a", "90"}, {"b", "49"}, {"c"}, {"h"}}
```

As an analogue of the above ***Locals5*** procedure we presents the ***Locals6*** procedure which uses certain useful programming techniques of the strings. The procedure has analogous formal arguments and its call returns results analogous to the call of the above ***Locals5*** procedure. The following fragment represents source code of the procedure with examples of its application.

```
In[3119]:= Locals6[x_ /; BlockModQ[x], y___] :=
    Module[{a = Definition2[x][[1]], b = Headings[x], c = "", d},
     a = StringReplace[a, b[[2]] <> " := " <> b[[1]] <> "[" -> ""];
 Do[If[SyntaxQ[c = c <> StringTake[a, {j}]], Break[], 7], {j, Infinity}];
     c = StringToList[StringTake[c, {2, -2}]];
     If[{y} != {} && SymbolQ[y],
     y = Map[{b =
     Quiet[Check[Flatten[StringPosition[#, "="]][[1]], {}]],
     If[b === {}, #, {StringTake[#, {1, b - 2}],
     StringTake[#, {b + 2, -1}]}]}[[2]] &, c], 7]; c]
In[3120]:= B[x_, y_] := Block[{a=5, b, c=7}, b = (a*x+b*c*y)/(x+y) +
     Sin[x + y]; If[b, 45, b, a*c]]
In[3121]:= SetAttributes[B, {Listable, Protected}]
In[3122]:= Locals6[B]
Out[122]= "{a = 5, b, c = 7}"
In[3123]:= Locals6[B, h7]
Out[3123]= {"a = 5", "b", "c = 7"}
In[3124]:= h7
Out[3124]= {{"a", "5"}, "b", {"c", "7"}}
In[3125]:= ModuleQ[StringReplaceVars]
Out[3125]= True
In[3126]:= Locals6[StringReplaceVars, g7]
Out[3126]= {"a = StringJoin[\"(\", S, \")\"]",
     "L = Characters[\"`!@#%^&*(){}:\\\"\\\\/|<>?~-=+[];:'.,
1234567890_\"]", "R = Characters[\"`!@#%^&*(){}:\\\"\\\\/|<>?~-
     =+[];:'., _\"]", "b", "c", "g = If[RuleQ[r], {r}, r]"}
In[3127]:= g7
Out[3127]= {{"a", "StringJoin[\"(\", S, \")\"]"},
     {"L", "Characters[\"`!@#%^&*(){}:\\\"\\\\/|<>?~-=+[];:'.,
     1234567890_\"]"},
     {"R", "Characters[\"`!@#%^&*(){}:\\\"\\\\/|<>?~-=+[];:'.,
     _\"]"}, "b", "c", {"g", "If[RuleQ[r], {r}, r]"}}
```

A number of other useful enough means for operating with local variables of modules and blocks can be found in [7,10-16].

At last, it makes sense to mention one method of *localization* of variables in procedures that in certain situations can be quite convenient. The structural organization of such procedures can be presented as follows, namely:

G[Args]* := Module[{}, *Save[f, {a, b, c, ...}]; Procedure body; {Res, Get[f], DeleteFile[f]}[[1]]]

A procedure can have a certain quantity of local variables or not have them in general whereas as other local variables any admissible variables are used, not excepting variables out of domain of the procedure, i.e. intersection of variables from the outside and in the procedure is allowed. For their *temporary* isolation *(on runtime of the procedure)* from external domain of the procedure their saving in a file *f* by ***Save*** function precedes the procedure body in which these variables are used like local variables. Whereas an exit from the procedure is made out by the three-element list where ***Res*** – a result of the procedure call, ***Get[f]*** – loading in the current session of file *f* with recovery of values of variables ***{a, b, c, ...}*** that were until the procedure call with the subsequent deleting of file *f.* The following fragment illustrates the above mechanism of localization of variables.

```
In[19]:= {a, b} = {42, 77}
Out[19]= {42, 77}
In[20]:= Gg[x_, y_] := Module[{}, Save["#$", {a, b, c}];
{a, b} = {47, 72}; {x*a/y*b, Get["#$"], DeleteFile["#$"]}[[1]]]
In[21]:= Gg[30, 21]
Out[21]= 33840/7
In[22]:= {a, b, c}
Out[22]= {42, 77, c}
```

At the same time, if the procedure has several possible exits then each exit should be issued in analogous way. In principle, the reception used for localization of variables described above within the framework of the procedure can be used not only in connection with its local variables.

In [15] we defined so-called *active* global variables as global variables to which in a *Block, Module* the assignments are done, whereas we understand the global variables different from the arguments as the *passive* global variables whose values are only used in objects of the specified type. In this regard tools which allow to evaluate the *passive* global variables for the user blocks and modules are being presented as a very interesting. One of similar means – the ***BlockFuncModVars*** procedure that solves even more general problem. The fragment represents the source code of the procedure ***BlockFuncModVars*** along with the most typical examples of its application.

```
In[24]:= BlockFuncModVars[x_ /; BlockFuncModQ[x]] :=
              Module[{d, t, c = Args[x, 90], a = If[QFunction[x], {},
              LocalsGlobals1[x]], s = {"System"}, u = {"Users"},
  b = Flatten[{PureDefinition[x]}][[1]], h = {}}, d = ExtrVarsOfStr[b, 2];
    If[a == {}, t = Map[If[Quiet[SystemQ[#]], AppendTo[s, #],
    If[BlockFuncModQ[#], AppendTo[u, #], AppendTo[h, #]]] &, d];
    {s, u = Select[u, # != ToString[x] &], c, MinusList[d, Join[s, u, c,
    {ToString[x]}]]}, Map[If[Quiet[SystemQ[#]], AppendTo[s, #],
    If[BlockFuncModQ[#], AppendTo[u, #], AppendTo[h, #]]] &, d];
    {Select[s, ! MemberQ[{"$Failed", "True", "False"}, #] &],
    Select[u, # != ToString[x] && ! MemberQ[a[[1]], #] &], c, a[[1]],
    a[[3]], Select[h, ! MemberQ[Join[a[[1]], a[[3]], c,
    {"System", "Users"}], #] &]}]]
In[25]:= A[m_, n_, p_ /; IntegerQ[p], h_ /; PrimeQ[h]] :=
              Module[{a = 77}, h*(m + n + p)/a +
              StringLength[ToString1[z]]/(Cos[c] + Sin[d])]
In[26]:= BlockFuncModVars[A]
Out[26]= {{"System", "Cos", "IntegerQ", "Module", "PrimeQ",
  "Sin", "StringLength"}, {"Users", "ToString1"}, {"m", "n", "p", "h"},
  {"a"}, {}, {"c", "d", "z"}}
```

The call ***BlockFuncModVars[x]*** returns the **6**–element list, whose the ***1st*** element – the list of *system* functions used by block or module *x*, whose ***1st*** element is ***"System"***, whereas other names are system functions in string format; the ***2nd*** element – the list of the user tools used by the block or module *x*, whose the ***1st*** element is ***"User"*** while the others define names of tools in the string format; the ***3rd*** element defines the list of formal arguments in the string format of the block or module *x;* the ***4th*** element – the list of local variables in the string format; the fifth element – the list of active global variables in string format; at last, the sixth element determines the list of passive global variables in the string format of the block or module *x.*

2.5. *Exit mechanisms of the user procedures (return results)*

The procedure body implements a particular calculation or processing algorithm using control sentences of ***Math***-language and its built-in functions along with other program tools. The result of successful execution of the procedure body is the exit from the procedure with purpose of return of its results to the current session of ***Mathematica*** system. In general, the return of results of procedure call can be organized by three manners: **(1)** through the last sentence of the procedure body, **(2)** through the system built-in ***Return*** function and **(3)** through its formal arguments, for example, procedures ***A, B*** and ***H*** accordingly:

```
In[7]:= A[x_] := Module[{a = 77, b = 72, c}, c = a + b; c*x]; A[1]
Out[7]= 149
In[8]:= B[x_, y_] := Module[{a = 77, b = 72, c}, c = a + b;
                         Return[77*x]; c*x; a*x + b*y]; B[1]
Out[8]= 77
In[9]:= H[x_, y_ /; ! ValueQ[y], z_ /; ! ValueQ[z]] :=
                 Module[{a = 77, b = 72, c}, c = a + b; y = c*x;
                       z = a*x^2; (a^2 + b^2)*x]; H[3, m, n]
Out[9]= 33339
In[10]:= {m, n}
Out[10]= {447, 693}
```

Depending on the algorithm logic realized by a procedure body, the procedure allows the use of several ***Return*** functions that return results of the procedure *(in general, the exit from the procedure)* at the required algorithm points. In principle, the use of ***Return***[] is allowed even in the list of local variables *(starting values)* as illustrates the following example:

```
In[27]:= B[x_, y_] := Module[{a = If[x < 10 && y > 10, x*y,
                 Return[{x, y}]], b = 5, c = 7}, a*b*c]: B[5, 15]
Out[27]= 2625
In[28]:= B[15, 15]
Out[28]= {525, 525}
```

Whereas the third case can be used for returning of some additional results of the procedure call *(values of local variables, intermediate evaluations, etc)*. In the present book and in [1-15] a number of examples of such approach has been illustrated. At that, formal arguments in heading of a procedure thru that it is planned to return results has to be of the form {g_, g__, g___} *(i.e. without a testing* ***Test***$_g$ *function)* and be indefinite symbols on which ***ValueQ[g]*** call returns *False*, or be coded in the form g_/; **!*ValueQ*[*g*]**. For practical reasons, it is recommended to use the latter option to return the result thru formal **g** argument so as not to introduce unpredictability into the results of the current session: so, in a case of simple definite **g** variable the erroneous situation arises in attempt of assignment of value for **g** in the procedure while for **g** variable as a heading name in the current session arises the multiplicity of definitions for it as illustrates a rather simple fragment:

```
In[3]:= y[t_] := t^2; z[t_] := Module[{}, t^3]
In[4]:= H[x_, y_, z_] := Module[{}, y = x^2; z = x^3; x + 5];
                                                      H[3, y, z]
Out[4]= 8
In[5]:= Definition[y]
Out[5]= y = 9
        y[t_] := t^2
In[6]:= Definition[z]
Out[6]= z = 27
        z[t_] := Module[{}, t^3]
In[7]:= Clear[y, z]; {y, z} = {72, 77};  H[3, y, z]
            Set::setraw: Cannot assign to raw object 72.
            Set::setraw: Cannot assign to raw object 77.
Out[7]= 8
```

Note that it is possible to use a mechanism represented by a fairly clear example to return intermediate results through the selected formal arguments with {__, ___} patterns:

```
In[2233]:= V[x_, y__] := Module[{a = 5, b = 7, c = {y}},
 If[Length[c] >= 2, ToExpression[ToString[c[[1]]] <> "=77"];
      ToExpression[ToString[c[[2]]] <> "=72"],
      ToExpression[ToString[c[[1]]] <> "=52"]]; (a + b)*x]
In[2234]:= Clear[b, c];  V[5, b, c]
```

```
Out[2234]= 60
In[2235]:= {b, c}
Out[2235]= {77, 72}
```

Further is being often mentioned about return of result of a function or a procedure as unevaluated that concerns both the standard built-in tools, and the user tools. In any case, the call of a procedure or a function on an inadmissible tuple of actual arguments is returned by unevaluated, except for the standard simplifications of the actual arguments. In this connection the ***UnevaluatedQ*** function providing testing of a procedure or a function regarding of the return of its call as unevaluated on a concrete tuple of actual arguments has been programmed. The function call ***UnevaluatedQ*[*F, x*]** returns *True* if the call ***F*[*x*]** will be returned unevaluated, and *False* otherwise; on an erroneous call ***F*[*x*]** *"ErrorInNumArgs"* is returned. The fragment presents source code of ***UnevaluatedQ*** function with examples of its use.

```
In[46]:= UnevaluatedQ[F_, x___] := If[! SymbolQ[F], True,
              ToString1[F[x]] === ToString[F] <> "[" <>
               StringTake[ToString1[{x}], {2, -2}] <> "]"]
In[47]:= Sin[1, 2]
Sin::argx: Sin called with 2 arguments; 1 argument is expected
Out[47]= Sin[1, 2]
In[48]:= UnevaluatedQ[Sin, 77, 72]
Out[48]= "ErrorInArgs"
In[49]:= G[x_Integer, y_String] := y <> ToString[x]
In[50]:= UnevaluatedQ[G, 77, 72]
Out[50]= True
```

The procedure presents an interest for program processing of the results of procedures and functions calls. The procedure was used by a number of means from our package [16].

As the results of exits from procedures, it is appropriate to consider also the various kinds of messages generated by the procedures as a result of erroneous and exceptional situations *(generated both by the system and programmed in the procedures)*. At the same time the issue of program processing of such *messages* is of a particular interest. In particular, the problem is solved by the procedure whose call ***MessagesOut*[x]** returns the message generated by a procedure or function **G** whose call given in the format ***x*="*G*[*z*]"**. Whereas the procedure call ***MessagesOut*[*x*,*y*]** with the ***2nd*** optional ***y*** argument – *an indefinite symbol* – thru it returns the messages in the format {*MessageName*, "*Message*"}. In the absence of any messages the empty list, i.e. {}, is returned. An unsuccessful procedure call returns $*Failed.*

All messages assigned to a symbol ***x*** *(Function,Module,Block)* along with its *usage (if any)* are returned by calling ***Messages*[x]**. Meantime, the returned result is not very convenient for further processing in program mode. Therefore, we have created some useful tools for this purpose [1-16]. In particular, the procedure call ***Usage*[x]** in the string format returns the usage ascribed to a symbol ***x*** *(built–in or user tool),* its source code and application examples are represented below, namely:

```
In[3107]:= Usage[x_Symbol] := Module[{a, b = Context[x],
                    c = ToString[x]}, ToExpression["?" <> c];
    a = ToExpression[StringJoin["Messages[", b, c, "]"]];
  If[a == {}, {}, b = StringSplit[ToString[a], "HoldPattern"];
           b = Select[b, ! StringFreeQ[#, c <> "::usage"] &];
           b = Flatten[StringSplit[b, " :> "]][[2]];
   If[SystemQ[x], StringDrop[b, -3], StringTrim[b, "}"]]]]
In[3108]:= Usage[ProcQ]
Out[3108]= "The call ProcQ[x] returns True if x is a
              procedure and False otherwise."
In[3109]:= Usage[While]
Out[3109]= "While[test, body] evaluates test, then body,
              repetitively, until test first fails to give True."
In[3110]:= Usage[Agn]
Out[3110]= {}
```

In this context, a simple procedure can be noted whose call ***ToFile*[*x*, *1*]** in the current session opens a file ***x*** to read, to that the system along with the screen writes all messages that occur. Whereas call ***ToFile*[*x*, *1*, *z*]** with the third optional argument ***z*** *(an arbitrary expression)* closes the ***x*** file, allowing in future to do analysis of the received messages.

```
In[42]:= ToFile[x_String, y_/; MemberQ[{1, 2}, y], z___] :=
Module[{a, b}, If[{z} == {}, b = OpenWrite[x]; Write["#", b];
 Close["#"]; If[y == 1, $Messages = Append[$Messages, b],
                    $Output = Append[$Output, b]];, $Output =
   ReplaceAll[$Output, Read["#"] -> Nothing]; Close["#"];
$Messages = ReplaceAll[$Messages, Read["#"] -> Nothing];
                   Close[x]; Quiet[DeleteFile[Close["#"]]; ]]]
In[43]:= MessageFile["C:\\temp\\Error.txt", 1]
=========================================
In[145]:= MessageFile["C:\\temp\\ Error.txt", 1, 7]
Out[145]= "C:\\temp\\Error.txt"
```

Moreover, the procedure calls with the second argument 2 are performed similarly, except that all messages output by the ***Print*** function are written to the *w* file until appear a procedure call with the third argument *z (an arbitrary expression)*.

Right there appropriate to note the ***Print1*** procedure which extends the capabilities of the built-in ***Print*** function, allowing additionally to output to the file the result of a call of the ***Print*** function. The call ***Print1[x, y, z]*** prints *z* as output additionally saving the *z* expression in the *x* file if *y* = *1* or closing the *x* file if *y*=2. A simple function ***IsOpenFile*** can be used in the procedure implementation, whose call ***IsOpenFile[x]*** returns *True* if a file *x* exists and is open for writing, and *False* otherwise.

```
In[2228]:= Print1[x_, y_/; MemberQ[{1, 2}, y], z___] :=
  Module[{a}, If[FileExistsQ[x], If[y == 1, Print[z], Close[x];
   $Output = ReplaceAll[$Output, Read["#"] -> Nothing];
   DeleteFile[Close["#"]]], a = OpenWrite[x]; Write["#", a];
     Close["#"]; $Output = Append[$Output, a]; Print[z]]]
In[2229]:= IsOpenFile[x_/; StringQ[x]] := ! StringFreeQ[
             StringReplace[ToString[InputForm[Streams[]]],
   "\\\\" -> "\\"], StringJoin["OutputStream[\"", x, "\","]]
In[2230]:= IsOpenFile["c:/print2.txt"]
Out[2230]= False
```

The following procedure generalizes the previous function for testing of openness of files on reading and writing. Namely, the procedure call ***IsInOutFile*[*x*]** returns *False* if a file ***x*** is closed or missing, whereas the list {*True*, *In*, *Out*}, {*True*, *In*}, {*True*, *Out*} otherwise, where *In* – the file for reading and *Out* – for writing.

```
In[3242]:= IsInOutFile[x_ /; StringQ[x]] := Module[{a =
 StringReplace[ToString[InputForm[Streams[]]],"\\\\"->"\\"]},
  If[! StringFreeQ[a, StringJoin["OutputStream[\"", x, "\","]] &&
     ! StringFreeQ[a, StringJoin["InputStream[\"", x, "\","]],
                                             {True, In, Out},
    If[! StringFreeQ[a, StringJoin["OutputStream[\"", x, "\","]],
                                                 {True, Out},
     If[! StringFreeQ[a, StringJoin["InputStream[\"", x, "\","]],
                                          {True, In}, False]]]]

In[3243]:= IsInOutFile["C:\\temp/Cinema_2019.doc"]
Out[3243]= {True, In}
```

However, note that *(as shown in* [1-15]) the coding of the file path is symbolic–dependent, for example, path "c:/tmp/kino" is not identical to "C:/Tmp\\Kino" i.e. the system will recognize them as different paths. This should be taken into account when programming file access tools. It is useful to use standardized datafiles path view as an easy approach [1-15].

Therefore, the output of messages, including ***Print*** function messages, can be ascribed fully to the return of results allowing further program processing along with their rendering on the display. Naturally, all procedure calls that complete by $*Failed* or $*Aborted* are processed programmatically. To recognize this return type it is possible to use the system function whose call ***FailureQ*[*x*]** returns *True* if ***x*** is equal to $*Failed* or $*Aborted.*

For more successful and flexible program processing of the main possible *erroneous* and *exception* situations that may occur in the procedure execution *(Block, Module),* it is recommended that the *messages* processing about them be programmed in the procedure, making it more reliable and steady against *mistakes.*

It should be noted that our tools for processing procedures and functions are oriented to the absence of attributes for them. Otherwise, the tools should be adapted to existence of attributes for the means being processed, which is easy to do.

2.6. *Tools for testing of procedures and functions*

Having defined procedures of two types *(Module and Block)* and functions, including pure functions, at the same time we have no standard tools for identification of objects of the given types. In this regard we created a series of means that allow to identify objects of the specified types. In the present section non-standard means for testing of procedural and functional objects are considered. In addition, it should be noted that the ***Mathematica*** – a rather closed system in contradistinction, for example, to its main competitor – the ***Maple*** system in which it is admissible to browse of source codes of its software which is located both in the main and in the auxiliary libraries. Whereas the ***Mathematica*** has no similar opportunity. In this connection the means presented below concerns only to the user functions and procedures loaded into the current session from a package *(**m**– or **mx**–file)*, or a document *(**nb**–file; also may contain a package)* and activated in it.

For testing of objects onto procedural type we proposed a number of means among which it is possible to mark out such as ***ProcQ, ProcQ1, ProcQ2.*** The procedure call **ProcQ[*x*]** provides testing of an object ***x*** be as a procedural object {"*Module*","*Block*"}, returning accordingly *True* or *False;* while the ***ProcQ1*** procedure is a useful enough modification of the ***ProcQ*** procedure, its call ***ProcQ1*[*x,t*]** returns *True,* if ***x*** – an object of the type *Block, Module* or *DynamicModule,* and *"Others"* or *False* otherwise; at that, the type of ***x*** object is returned through the factual ***t*** argument – an indefinite variable. The source codes of the above procedures, their description along with the most typical examples of their application are presented in our books and in our ***MathToolBox*** package [12-16]. A number of receptions used at their creation can be useful enough in the practical programming. The ***ProcQ*** procedure is an quite fast, processes attributes and options, but has certain restrictions, first of all, in a case of multiple objects of the same name. The fragment below represents source code the ***ProcQ*** procedure along with typical examples of its use.

```
In[7]:= ProcQ[x_] := Module[{a, atr = Quiet[Attributes[x]], b,
            c, d, h}, If[! SymbolQ[x], False, If[SystemQ[x], False,
                     If[UnevaluatedQ[Definition2, x], False,
              If[ListQ[atr] && atr != {}, ClearAllAttributes[x]];
          a = StringReplace[ToString[InputForm[Definition[x]]],
                     Context[x] <> ToString[x] <> "`" -> ""];
          Quiet[b = StringTake[a, {1, First[First[StringPosition[a,
                        {" := Block[{", " :=Block[{"}] - 1]]}];
                c = StringTake[a, {1, First[First[StringPosition[a,
                     {" := Module[{", " :=Module[{"}] - 1]]}];
                d = StringTake[a, {1, First[First[StringPosition[a,
         {" := DynamicModule[{", " :=DynamicModule[{"}] - 1]]}]];
         If[b === ToString[HeadPF[x]], SetAttributes[x, atr]; True,
         If[c === ToString[HeadPF[x]], SetAttributes[x, atr]; True,
         If[d === ToString[HeadPF[x]], SetAttributes[x, atr]; True,
                         SetAttributes[x, atr]; False]]]]]]]

In[8]:= Map[ProcQ, {Sin, a + b, ProcQ1, ProcQ, 77, ToString1}]
Out[8]= {False, False, True, True, False, True}
```

Generally, supposing existence of procedures of the above two types *(Module and Block)* in the ***Mathematica***, for ensuring of the reliability it is recommended to use the procedures of the *Module* type. From examples represented in [8,10-15] follows, if local variables of a modular object aren't crossed with domain of values of the variables of the same name which are external in relation to it, the absolutely other picture takes place in a case with the local variables of a block object, namely: *if initial values or values are ascribed to all local variables of such object in its body, they save effect in the object body; those variables of an object to which such values weren't ascribed accept values of the variables of the same name which are the external in relation to the block object.* So, at the listed conditions the modular and block objects relative to the local variables *(and in general as procedural objects)* can quite be considered as equivalent. Naturally, the told remains in force also for block objects with empty lists of the local variables. The specified reasons were used as a basis for the programming of the ***RealProcQ*** procedure presented by the following fragment.

```
In[2107]:= RealProcQ[x_ /; BlockModQ[x]] := Module[{a, b, c},
            If[ModuleQ[x], True,
  a = StringJoin[Insert[Reverse[Headings[x]], " := ", 2]] <> "[";
         b = StringReplace[PureDefinition[x], a -> "", 1];
      Do[c = StringTake[b, k]; If[SyntaxQ[c], Return[c], 7],
                  {k, StringLength[b]}];
        If[c == "{}", {}, c = StrToList[StringTake[c, {2, -2}]]];
                  c = Map[StringSplit[#, " = "] &, c];
  AllTrue[Map[If[Length[#] > 1, True, False] &, c], TrueQ]]]
In[2108]:= B[x_] := Block[{a = 90, b = 50, c = {72, 77}, d = 42},
                          x*(a*b*c*d)]; RealProcQ[B]
Out[2108]= True
In[2109]:= M[x_] := Block[{a = 90, b = 49, c, h}, h = 77; x*h];
In[2110]:= RealProcQ[M]
Out[2110]= False
```

Experience of use of the ***RealProcQ*** procedure confirmed its efficiency at testing objects of the type *Block* that are considered as real procedures. At that, we will understand an object of the type {*Module, Block*} as a *real* procedure that in the ***Mathematica*** software is functionally equivalent to a *Module*, i.e. is a certain procedure in its classical understanding. The call ***RealProcQ[x]*** returns *True* if a symbol ***x*** defines a *Module*, or a *Block* which is equivalent to a ***Module***, and *False* otherwise. In addition, it is supposed that a certain *block* is equivalent to a *module* if it has no the local variables or all its local variables have initial values or some local variables have initial values, while others obtain values by means of the operator "=" in the block body. From all our means solving the testing problem for procedural objects, the ***RealProcQ*** procedure with the greatest possible reliability identifies the set procedure in its classical understanding; thus, the real procedure can be of the type {*Module, Block*}.

In the context of providing of an object of the type {*Module, Block*} to be a *real* procedure recognized by the testing ***RealProcQ*** procedure, the ***ToRealProc*** procedure is of certain interest whose call ***ToRealProc[x, y]*** returns nothing, converting a module or a block ***x*** into the object of the same type and of the same name with the *empty* list of local variables that are placed in the object body at once behind the empty list of the local variables. At the same time all local variables of an object *x* are replaced with the symbols, unique in the current session, which are generated by means of the ***Unique*** function. In addition, along with a certain specified purpose the returned procedure provides a possibility of more effective debugging in interactive mode of procedure, allowing to do dynamic control of change of values of its local variables in the procedure run on concretefactual arguments. In addition to our means for testing of procedural objects, we can note a simple procedure, whose call ***UprocQ[x]*** returns *False* if an object *x* isn't a procedure or is an object of the same name [8].

Meanwhile, since the structural definitions of modules and blocks are identical, the ***ToRealProc1*** procedure that is based on this circumstance, has a simple implementation. The following fragment represents source code of the ***ToRealProc1*** procedure with examples of its application.

```
In[2229]:= B[x_] := Block[{a = 7, b, c = 8, d}, x*a*b*c*d];
In[2230]:= SetAttributes[B, {Protected, Listable, Orderless}]
In[2231]:= ToRealProc1[x_] := Module[{a = Attributes[x]},
                                    If[ModuleQ[x], x, If[BlockQ[x],
                              If[FreeQ[a, Protected], 7, Unprotect[x]];
                      ToExpression[StringReplace[Definition2[x][[1]],
  ":= Block[{" -> ":= Module[{", 1]]; SetAttributes[x, a]; x, $Failed]]]
In[2232]:= ToRealProc1[B]
Out[2232]= B
In[2233]:= Definition[B]
Out[2233]= Attributes[B] = {Flat, Listable, Orderless, Protected}
                          B[x_] := Module[{a = 7, b, c = 8, d}, x*a*b*c*d]
In[2234]:= ToRealProc1[vsv]
Out[2234]= $Failed
```

Calling the ***ToRealProc1[x]*** procedure returns the module name that is equivalent to a module *x* or a block *x*, retaining all attributes and structure of the original object *x*. The scope of the module created is the current session. As it was noted above, in general case between procedures of types "*Module*" and "*Block*" exist principal distinctions that do not allow a priori to consider a *block* structure as a procedure in its above meaning. Therefore the type of a procedure should be chosen rather circumspectly, giving preference to the procedures of the *"Module"* type [8,12].

As noted repeatedly, ***Mathematica*** does not distinguish the objects by names, but by headers, allowing objects of the same name with different headers and even types *(modules, functions, blocks)* to exist in the current session. First of all, it is useful to define the function whose call ***TypeBFM*[*x*]** returns the type of an object ***x*** *("Block","Function", "Module")*, or *$Failed* otherwise.

```
In[7]:= B[x_] := Block[{a=7, b}, x*a*b]; B[x_, y_] := Module[{a, b},
   x/y]; B[x_, y_, z_] := x^2 + y^2 + z^2; G[x_] := Module[{}, x*a]
In[8]:= TypeBFM[x_] := If[ModuleQ[x], "Module",
   If[FunctionQ[x], "Function", If[BlockQ[x], "Block", $Failed]]]
In[9]:= TypeBFM[G]
Out[9]= "Module"
In[10]:= TypeQ[x_, y___] := Module[{a, b, c = {}, d = {}, t},
 If[! SameQ[Head[x], Symbol], $Failed, a = Definition2[x][[1 ;; -2]];
                                   Map[{b = ToString[Unique[]],
                t = StringReplace[#, ToString[x] <> "[" -> b <> "[", 1],
   AppendTo[c, b], AppendTo[d, t]} &, a]; Map[ToExpression, d];
                                          Map[ToExpression, c];
                     If[{y} != {} && SymbolQ[y], b = Map[Headings, c];
                               y = Map[{#[[1]], StringReplace[#[[2]],
            "$" ~~ Shortest[__] ~~ "[" -> ToString[x] <> "["]} &, b];
   y = If[Length[y] == 1, Flatten[y], y], 7]; a = Map[TypeBFM, c];
                                    If[Length[a] == 1, a[[1]], a]]]
In[11]:= TypeQ[B]
Out[11]= {"Block", "Module", "Function"}
In[12]:= TypeQ[B, gs]
Out[12]= {"Block", "Module", "Function"}
In[13]:= gs
Out[13]= {{"Block", "B[x_]"}, {"Module", "B[x_, y_]"},
                                   {"Function", "B[x_, y_, z_]"}}
In[14]:= {TypeQ[G, gv], gv}
Out[14]= {"Module", {"Module", "G[x_]"}}
```

Whereas the ***TypeQ*** procedure is primarily intended to test procedural and functional objects having multiple definitions of the same name. Calling ***TypeQ[w]*** returns *$Failed* if ***w*** is not a symbol, whereas on ***w*** objects which have multiple definitions of the same name, the list is returned containing the subobject types that make up the ***w*** object in the form {*"Block", "Function", "Module"*}. While the calling ***TypeQ[w, j]*** with the ***2nd*** optional argument ***j*** – *an indefined symbol* – through ***j*** additionally returns the list in which for each subobject of object ***w*** corresponds the 2–element list whose first element defines its type, whereas the ***2nd*** element defines its header in the string format. The previous fragment represents the source code of the ***TypeQ*** procedure and typical examples of its application.

Meanwhile, procedures, being generally objects other than functions, allow relatively simply conversion of functions into procedures, whereas under certain assumptions it is possible to convert procedures into functions too. Particularly, on example of the modular objects consider a principal scheme for this type of conversion algorithm that is based on the list structure.

***Heading* := {*Save2[f*, {*locals, args*}], *Map*[*Clear*, {*locals, args*}], {*locals*}, *Procedure body*, {*Get*[*f*], *DeleteFile*[*f*]}}[[–2]]**

An algorithm of the ***ProcToFunc*** procedure, the original text of which together with examples of applications, is represented below, is based on the above scheme. The list view of a module is generated in the format containing the following components:

Heading – *the module or block heading;*

***Save2[f*, {*locals, args*}]** – *saving of values of the joint list of local variable names without initial values and arguments without testing functions in a file f;*

***Map*[*Clear*, {*locals, args*}]** – *clearing of the above arguments and local variables in the current session;*

{*locals*} – *the list of local variables with initial values, if any;*

Procedure body – *body of module or block;*

{*Get*[*f*], *DeleteFile*[*f*]} – *loading the f file to the current session, which contains the values of local variable names and arguments that were previously stored in it.*

With in mind the told, the procedure call ***ProcToFunc*[*j*]** does not return anything, converting a module or block ***j*** into a list format function of the same name with preserving of attributes of the module or block. The following fragment represents the source code of the procedure with examples of its application.

```
In[42]:= ProcToFunc[j_/; ProcQ[j]] := Module[{a, b, c, d, p},
   a = Map[ToString[#] <> "@" &, Args[j]];
   a = Map[StringReplace[#, "_" ~~ ___ ~~ "@" -> ""] &, a];
   If[ModuleQ[j], b = Map[#[[1]] &, Locals4[j]]; c = Join[a, b];
   d = Definition2[j][[1]]; d = StringReplace[d, "Module[" ->
   "{Save2[\"##\"," <> ToString1[c] <> "], Map[Clear, " <>
   ToString1[c] <> "],", 1]; d = StringReplacePart[d, "", {-1, -1}];
   d = d <> ", {Get[\"##\"], DeleteFile[\"##\"]}}[[-2]]";
   If[FreeQ[Attributes[j], Protected], ToExpression[d],
   Unprotect[j]; ToExpression[d]; SetAttributes[j, Protected]],
   b = Map[#[[1]] &, Locals4[j]]; c = Join[a, b];
   p = Map[If[Length[#] != 1, #[[1]], Nothing] &, Locals4[j]];
   p = Join[a, p]; d = Definition2[j][[1]];
   d = StringReplace[d, "Block[" ->
   "{Save2[\"##\"," <> ToString1[c] <> "], Map[Clear, " <>
   ToString1[p] <> "],", 1]; d = StringReplacePart[d, "", {-1, -1}];
   d = d <> ", {Get[\"##\"], DeleteFile[\"##\"]}}[[-2]]";
   If[FreeQ[Attributes[j], Protected], ToExpression[d],
   Unprotect[j]; ToExpression[d]; SetAttributes[j, Protected]]]]

In[43]:= {a, b, c, x, y} = {1, 2, 3, 4, 5};
In[44]:= M[x_/; IntegerQ[x], y_] := Module[{a = 5, b = 7, c},
   a = a*x + b*y; c = a*b/(x + y); If[x*y > 100, a, c]]
In[45]:= SetAttributes[M, {Protected, Listable, Flat}]
In[46]:= ProcToFunc[M]
In[47]:= Definition[M]
Out[47]= Attributes[M] = {Flat, Listable, Protected}
M[x_/; IntegerQ[x], y_] := {Save2["##", {"x", "y", "a", "b", "c"}],
   Clear /@ {"x", "y", "a", "b", "c"}, {a = 5, b = 7, c},
   a = a*x + b*y; c = (a*b)/(x + y);
   If[x*y > 100, a, c], {<< "##", DeleteFile["##"]}}[[-2]]
In[48]:= M[77, 72]
Out[48]= 889
```

```
In[49]:= {a, b, c, x, y}
Out[49]= {1, 2, 3, 4, 5}
In[50]:= B[x_, y_] := Block[{a = 5, b, c = 7}, a*x + b*c*y]
In[51]:= {a, b, c} = {72, 77, 67};
In[52]:= ProcToFunc[B]
In[53]:= Definition[B]
Out[53]= B[x_, y_] := {Save2["##", {"x", "y", "a", "b", "c"}],
                    Clear /@ {"x", "y", "a", "c"}, {a = 5, b, c = 7},
                 a*x + b*c*y, {<< "##", DeleteFile["##"]}}[[-2]]
In[54]:= B[42, 47]
Out[54]= 25543
In[55]:= {a, b, c}
Out[55]= {72, 77, 67}
```

Meantime, a module or block that is converted to a function must satisfy some of the conditions resulting from the inability to use certain built-in functions, such as ***Return***, in *Input* mode. Whereas ***Goto*** and ***Label*** are quite permissible, for example:

```
In[8]:= f[x_] := {n = x; Label[g]; n++; If[n < 100, Goto[g], n]}; f[5]
Out[8]= {100}
In[9]:= f[x_] := {n = x; Label[g]; n++; If[n < 100, Goto[g], Goto[j]];
                                                    Label[j]; n}; f[5]
Out[9]= {100}
```

As a rule, the primary limitation for such conversion is size of the procedure's source code, making the function obscure. In general, the representations of modules and blocks in list format is in many cases more efficient in time.

Note, that when programming the algorithm of converting of a block into function, it should be taken into account that due to the specifics of the local variables in the blocks *(as opposed to the modules)*, the function should save in a file the values of all local variables of the block, while the values of local variables with initial values of the block are cleared before the block *body* is executed when the resulting function is called. For the rest, the step of completing the resulting function is identical for the simulation of the block and module. In certain cases the above convertings can be rather useful.

2.7. The nested blocks and modules

In *Mathematica* along with simple procedures that aren't containing in its body of definitions of other procedures, the application of the so-called ***nested*** procedures, i.e. procedures whose definitions allow definitions of other procedures in their body. The nesting level of such procedures is defined by only a size of work field of the system. Therefore a rather interesting problem of determination of the list of subprocedures whose definitions are in the body of an arbitrary procedure of the type {*Block, Module*} arises. In this regard the ***SubProcs ÷ SubProcs3*** procedures have been programmed [16] that successfully solve the problem. Here consider the ***SubProcs3*** procedure whose call ***SubProcs3[x]*** returns the nested two-element list of the *ListList* type whose ***1st*** element defines the sublist of headings of blocks and modules composing a main procedure *x,* while the second element defines the sublist of the generated names of the blocks and modules composing the main procedure *x,* including itself procedure *x,* and that are activated in the current session of the ***Mathematica.*** The next fragment represents source code of the ***SubProcs3*** procedure with the most typical examples of its use.

```
In[20]:= G[x_] := Module[{Vg, H77}, Vg[y_] := Module[{}, y^3];
                    H77[z_] := Module[{}, z^4]; x + Vg[x] + H77[x]];
G[x_, z_] := Module[{Vt, H, P}, Vt[t_] := Module[{}, t^3 + t^2 + 7];
H[t_] := Module[{}, t^4]; P[h_] := Module[{a = 590}, a^2 + h^2];
x + Vt[x] + H[z]*P[x]]; SetAttributes[G, {Protected, Listable}]
In[21]:= SubProcs3[y_, z___] := Module[{u = {}, m = 1, Sv,
             v = Flatten[{PureDefinition[y]}]}, If[BlockFuncModQ[y],
      Sv[S_String] := Module[{a = ExtrVarsOfStr[S, 1], b, c = {}, d,
                                   t = 2, k = 1, cc = {}, n, p, j,
  h = {StringTake[S, {1, Flatten[StringPosition[S, " := "]][[1]] - 1}]}},
                          a = Select[a, ! SystemQ[Symbol[#]] &&
                                ! MemberQ[{ToString[G]}, #] &];
                  b = StringPosition[S, Map[" " <> # <> "[" &, a]];
     p = Select[a, ! StringFreeQ[S, " " <> # <> "["] &]; b = Flatten[
  Map[SubStrSymbolParity1[StringTake[S, {#[[1]], -1}], "[", "]"] &,
                     b]]; For[j = 1, j <= Length[p], j++, n = p[[j]];
```

```
For[k = 1, k <= Length[b] - 1, k++, d = b[[k]];
If[! StringFreeQ[d, "_"] && StringTake[b[[k + 1]], {1, 1}] == "[",
AppendTo[c, Map[n <> d <> " := " <> # <> b[[k + 1]] &,
{"Block", "Module"}]]]]]; c = DeleteDuplicates[Flatten[c]];
For[k = 1, k <= Length[c], k++, d = c[[k]];
If[! StringFreeQ[S, d], AppendTo[h, d], AppendTo[cc,
StringTake[d, {1, Flatten[StringPosition[d, " := "]][[1]] - 1}]]]];
{h, cc} = Map[DeleteDuplicates, {h, cc}];
p = Map[StringTake[#, {1, Flatten[StringPosition[#, "["]][[1]]}] &, h];
cc = Select[Select[cc, ! SuffPref[#, p, 1] &], ! StringFreeQ[S, #] &];
If[cc == {}, h, For[k = 1, k <= Length[cc], k++, p = cc[[k]];
p = StringCases[S, p <> " := " ~~ __ ~~ "; "];
AppendTo[h, StringTake[p,
{1, Flatten[StringPosition[p, ";"]][[1]] - 1}]]]]; Flatten[h]];
For[m, m <= Length[v], m++, AppendTo[u, Sv[v[[m]]]]];
u = Select[u, ! SameQ[#, Null] &]; u = If[Length[u] == 1, u[[1]], u];
If[{z} != {}, ToExpression[u]]; u, $Failed]]

In[22]:= SubProcs3[G]
Out[22]= {{"G[x_]", "Vg[y_] := Module[{}, y^3]",
"H77[z_] := Module[{}, z^4]"}, {"G[x_, z_]",
"Vt[t_] := Module[{}, t^3 + t^2 + 590]", "H[t_] := Module[{}, t^4]",
"P[h_] := Module[{a = 590}, a^2 + h^2]"}}
```

The ***SubProcs3*** procedure is a rather useful extension of the ***SubProcs ÷ SubProcs2*** procedures; its call ***SubProcs3[x]*** differs from a call ***SubProcs2[x]*** by the following 2 moments, namely: *(1)* the user block, function or module can act as an argument ***x***, and *(2)* the returned list as the first element contains heading of the ***x*** object while other elements of the list present definitions of functions, blocks and modules in string format entering into the ***x*** definition. In a case of the ***x*** object of the same name, the returned list will be the *nested* list whose sublists have the above mentioned format. In addition, the call ***SubProcs3[x, y]*** with the *second* optional ***y*** argument – *an arbitrary expression* – returns the above list and at the same time activates in the current session all objects of the above type, which enter into the ***x***. If function with heading acts as an object ***x***, only its heading is returned; the similar result takes place and in a case of the ***x*** object which doesn't contain subobjects of the above type whereas on the *x* object different from the user block, function or module, the call of the ***SubProcs3*** procedure returns *$Failed.*

In some cases there is a necessity of definition for a module or block of the subobjects of the type {***Block, Function, Module***}. The procedure call ***SubsProcQ[x, y]*** returns *True* if ***y*** is a global active subobject of an object ***x*** of the above-mentioned type, and *False* otherwise. However, as the ***Math*** objects of this type differ not by *names* as that is accepted in the majority of programming systems, but by headings then thru the third optional argument the procedure call returns the nested list whose sublists as first element contain headings with a name ***x***, whereas the second element contain the headings of subobjects corresponding to them with ***y*** name. On the ***1st*** two arguments {***x, y***} of the types, different from given in a procedure heading, the procedure call ***SubsProcQ[x, y]*** returns *False.* The fragment below represents source code of the ***SubsProcQ*** procedure along with an example of its typical application.

```
In[7]:= SubsProcQ[x_, y_, z___] := Module[{a, b, k=1, j=1, Res = {}},
  If[BlockModQ[x] && BlockFuncModQ[y],
  {a, b} = Map[Flatten, {{Definition4[ToString[x]]},
  Definition4[ToString[y]]}}];
  For[k, k <= Length[b], k++, For[j, j <= Length[a], j++,
  If[! StringFreeQ[a[[j]], b[[k]]], AppendTo[Res, {StringTake[a[[j]],
  {1, Flatten[StringPosition[a[[j]], " := "]][[1]] - 1}],
  StringTake[b[[k]], {1, Flatten[StringPosition[b[[k]]," := "]][[1]] - 1}]}],
  Continue[]]]]; If[Res != {}, If[{z} != {} && ! HowAct[z],
  z = If[Length[Res] == 1, Res[[1]], Res]; True], False], False]]
In[8]:= V[x_] := Block[{a, b, c}, a[m_] := m^2; b[n_] := n + Sin[n];
  c[p_] := Module[{}, p]; a[x]*b[x]*c[x]]; c[p_] := Module[{}, p];
  V[x_, y_] := Module[{a, b, c}, a[m_] := m^2; b[n_] := n + Sin[n];
  c[p_] := Module[{}, p]; a[x]*b[x]*c[x]]; c[p_] := Module[{}, p]; p[x_] := x
In[9]:= {SubsProcQ[V, c, g72], g72}
Out[9]= {True, {{"V[x_]", "c[p_]"}, {"V[x_, y_]", "c[p_]"}}}
```

Except the means considered in books [8-15], a number of means for operating with subprocedures is presented, here we will represent an useful ***SubsProcs*** procedure that analyzes the blocks and modules regarding presence in their definitions of subobjects of type {*Block, Module*}. The call ***SubsProcs[x]*** returns generally the nested list of definitions in the string format of all subobjects of type {*Block, Module*} whose definitions are in the body of an object ***x*** of type {*Block, Module*}. In addition, the first sublist determines subobjects of *Module* type, the second sublist defines subobjects of the *Block* type. In the presence of only one sublist the simple list is returned whereas in the presence of the ***1***–element simple list its element is returned. In a case of lack of subobjects of the above type, the call ***SubsProcs[x]*** returns the empty list, i.e. {} whereas on an object ***x***, different from *Block* or *Module*, the call ***SubsProcs[x]*** is returned unevaluated. Fragment represents source code of the ***SubsProcs*** procedure and a typical example of its application.

```
In[1125]:= P[x_, y_] := Module[{Art, Kr, Gs, Vg, a},
   Art[c_, d_] := Module[{b}, c + d]; Kr[n_] := Module[{}, n^2];
   Vg[h_] := Block[{p = 90}, h^3 + p]; Gs[z_] := Module[{}, x^3];
   a = Art[x, y] + Kr[x*y]*Gs[x + y] + Vg[x*y]]
In[1126]:= SubsProcs[x_/; BlockModQ[x]] := Module[{d, s = {}, g,
   k = 1, p, h = "", v = 1, R = {}, Res = {}, a = PureDefinition[x], j,
  m = 1, n = 0, b = {" := Module[{", " := Block[{"}, c = ProcBody[x]},
         For[v, v <= 2, v++, If[StringFreeQ[c, b[[v]]], Break[],
                d = StringPosition[c, b[[v]]]];
         For[k, k <= Length[d], k++, j = d[[k]][[2]];
              While[m != n, p = StringTake[c, {j, j}];
   If[p == "[", m++; h = h <> p, If[p == "]", n++; h = h <> p,
   h = h <> p]]; j++]; AppendTo[Res, h]; m = 1; n = 0; h = ""];
 Res = Map10[StringJoin, If[v == 1, " := Module[", " := Block["],
         Res]; g = Res; {Res, m, n, h} = {{}, 1, 0, "]"};
       For[k = 1, k <= Length[d], k++, j = d[[k]][[1]] - 2;
              While[m != n, p = StringTake[c, {j, j}];
                 If[p == "]", m++; h = p <> h,
         If[p == "[", n++; h = p <> h, h = p <> h]]; j --];
    AppendTo[Res, h]; s = Append[s, j]; m = 1; n = 0; h = "]"];
    Res = Map9[StringJoin, Res, g]; {g, h} = {Res, ""}; Res = {};
                     For[k = 1, k <= Length[s], k++,
       For[j = s[[k]], j >= 1, j --, p = StringTake[c, {j, j}];
   If[p == " ", Break[], h = p <> h]]; AppendTo[Res, h]; h = ""];
```

```
                    AppendTo[R, Map9[StringJoin, Res, g]];
                        {Res, m, n, k, h, s} = {{}, 1, 0, 1, "", {}}];
  R = If[Length[R] == 2, R, Flatten[R]]; If[Length[R] == 1, R[[1]], R]]
In[1127]:= SubsProcs[P]
Out[1127]= {{"Art[c_, d_] := Module[{b}, c + d]",
   "Kr[n_] := Module[{}, n^2]", "Gs[z_] := Module[{}, x^3]"},
                        {"Vg[h_] := Block[{p = 90}, h^3 + p]"}}
```

The ***SubsProcs*** procedure can be rather simply expanded, in particular, for definition of the *nesting* levels of *subprocedures,* and also onto *unnamed* subprocedures. Moreover, in connection with the problem of nesting of the blocks and modules essential enough distinction between definitions of the *nested* procedures in the ***Maple*** and ***Mathematica*** takes place. So, in the ***Maple*** the definitions of the subprocedures allow to use the lists of formal arguments identical with the main procedure containing them, while in the ***Mathematica*** similar combination is inadmissible, causing in the course of evaluation of determination of the main procedure erroneous situations [4-12]. Generally speaking, the given circumstance causes certain inconveniences, demanding a special attentiveness in the process of programming of the nested procedures. In a certain measure the similar situation arises and in a case of crossing of lists of formal arguments of the main procedure and the local variables of its subprocedures whereas that is quite admissible in the ***Maple*** [8,22-41]. In this context the ***SubsProcs*** procedure can be applied successfully to procedures containing subprocedures of the type {*Block, Module*} on condition of nonempty crossing of list of formal arguments of the main procedure along with the list of local variables of its subprocedures *(see also books on the* ***Maple*** *and* ***Mathematica*** *in our collections of works* [6,14,15]). There you can also familiarize yourself with examples of *nested* procedures, useful in practical programming of various problems.

In principle, on the basis of the above tools it is possible to programm a number of useful enough tools of operating with expressions using the nested objects of type *Block* and *Module.* Some from them can be found in [15,16].

Chapter 3: Programming tools of the user procedure body

So far, we have considered mainly questions of the external design of any procedure, practically without touching upon the questions of its internal content – the body of the procedure that in the definition of procedure *(module, block)* is located between the list *(may be empty)* of *local variables* and the *closing bracket* "]". The basic components of the tools used to program the body of user procedures are discussed below. To describe an arbitrary computational algorithm of structures that are based on purely sequential operations, completely insufficient means for control the computing process. The modern structural programming focuses on one of the most error–prone factors: program logic and includes **3** main components, i.e. top–down engineering, modular programming and structural coding. In addition, the first two components are discussed in sufficient detail in [3,15]. We will briefly focus here only on the third component.

The purpose of structural coding is to obtain the correct program ***(module)*** based on simple control structures. Control structures of sequence, branching, organization of cycles and function calls are selected as such basic structures *(procedures, programmes)*. Note here that all said structures allow only one input and one output. At the same time, the first of **3** specified control structures *(consecution, branching and cycle organization)* make the minimum basis, on the basis of which it is possible to create a correct program of any complexity with one input, one output, without cycles and unattainable commands. Detailed discussion of the bases of control programming structures can be found, in particular, in [15] and in other available literature on the basics of modern programming.

Consecution reflects the principle of consistent running of the proposals of either or another program until some proposal changing the sequence occurs. For example, a typical sequence control structure is a sequence of simple assignment sentences in a particular programming language. ***Branching*** characterizes choosing one of all possible paths for next calculations; typical offers providing this control structure are offers of ***"if A then B else C"*** format.

"Cycle" structure performs a repeat execution of the offers as long as the some logical condition is true; typical offers that provide this control structure, offers of ***Do, Do_while, Do_until*** are. Basic structures define, respectively, sequential *(**following**)*, conditional *(**branching**)* and iterative *(**loop**)* control transfer in programs [15]. It is shown, that any correct structured program theoretically of any complexity can be written only with using of control sequential structures, ***While***-cycles and ***if***-branching offers. Meantime, the extension of the set of specified tools in primarily by providing function calls along with mechanism of procedures can make programming very easy without breaking the structure programmes with increasing their modularity and robustness.

At the same time, combinations *(iterations, attachments)* of correct structured programs obtained on a basis of the specified control structure do not violate the principle of their degree of structure and correctness. Thus, the program of an arbitrary *complexity* and *size* can be obtained on a basis of an appropriate combination of extended basis *(function calls, cycle, consecution, procedure mechanism and branching)* of control structures. This approach allows to eliminate the use of *labels* and *unconditional* transitions in programs. The structure of such programs can be clearly traced from the beginning *(top)* to the end *(down)* in the absence of control transfers to the upper layers. So, exactly in light of this, it is languages of this type that represent a rather convenient linguistic support in the development of effective structured programs, combining the best traditions of modular-structural technology, that in this case is oriented towards the mathematical field of applications and is sufficient large number of programmatically unprofessional users from a range of the application fields, including not entirely mathematical focus.

In the following, the *"sentence"* or *"offer"* of ***Math***-language means the construction of the following simple form, namely: ***Math***-expression **";"** where any correct ***Mathematica*** language expression is allowed. Sentences are coded one after the other, each in a single string or multiple in one string; they in general are ended with separators ";", are processed strictly *sequentially* if the control structures of branching or loop do not define of a different order. The most widely used definition of a sentence of assignment is based on the operator "=" or ":=" accordingly of an immediate or delayed assignment which allow multiple assignments on a basis of list structure, namely:

$$\{a, b, c, d, \ldots\}\{= | :=\}\{m, n, p, k, \ldots\}$$

The basic difference between these formats consists in that the value ***g*** is evaluated at the time when expression ***g=a*** will be coded. On the other hand, a value ***g*** is not evaluated when the assignment ***g:=a*** is made, but is instead evaluated each time the value of ***g*** is requested. However, in some cases, computational constructs do not allow these formats to be used, in which case the following system built-in functions can be successfully used accordingly: ***Set[g,a]*** is equivalent of "***g=a***" and ***SetDelayed[g,a]*** is equivalent of "***g:=a***". So, in the list structure, the elements can be both comma-separated expressions and semicolon-separated sentences, for example:

```
In[2226]:= {g[t_] := t, s[t_] := t^2, v[t_] := t^3};
In[2227]:= Map[#[5] &, {g, s, v}]
Out[2227]= {5, 25, 125}
In[2228]:= Clear[g, s, v]
In[2229]:= {g[t_] := t; s[t_] := t^2; v[t_] := t^3};
In[2230]:= Map[#[5] &, {g, s, v}]
Out[2230]= {5, 25, 125}
```

Particularly at procedures writing the necessity to modify the value of a particular variable repeatedly often arises. The ***Mathematica*** provides special notations for modification of the variables values, and for some other often used situations. Let us give a summary of such notations:

k++	– increment the value of *k* by **1**
k––	– decrement the value of *k* by **1**
++*k*	– pre-increment value of *k* by **1**

--k – pre–decrement value of ***k*** by ***1***
k+=h – add ***h*** to the value of ***k***
k–=h – subtract ***h*** from ***k***
x=h* – multiply ***x*** by ***h***
x/=h – divide ***x*** by ***h***
PrependTo[g, e] – prepend ***e*** to a list ***g***
AppendTo[g, e] – append ***e*** to a list ***g***

Let us give examples for all these cases, namely:

```
In[2230]:= k = 77; k++; k
Out[2230]= 78
In[2231]:= k = 77; k--; k
Out[2231]= 76
In[2232]:= k = 77; ++k; k
Out[2232]= 78
In[2233]:= k = 77; --k; k
Out[2233]= 76
In[2234]:= k = 77; h = 7; k += h; k
Out[2234]= 84
In[2235]:= k = 77; h = 7; k -= h; k
Out[2235]= 70
In[2236]:= k = 77; h = 7; k *= h; k
Out[2236]= 539
In[2237]:= k = 77; h = 7; k /= h; k
Out[2237]= 11
In[2238]:= g = {a, b, c, d, e, h}; AppendTo[g, m]; g
Out[2238]= {a, b, c, d, e, h, m}
In[2239]:= g = {a, b, c, d, e, h}; PrependTo[g, m]; g
Out[2239]= {m, a, b, c, d, e, h}
```

Typically, a considerable or large part of a procedure body consists of sequential structures, i.e. blocks from sequences of assignment sentences of different types, possibly involving calls to built–in and user functions. In principle, the most of bodies of procedures can be implemented in the form of a sequential structure, excluding cycles. True, such organization can results in voluminous codes, so the following control structures are of particular interest, namely branching structures and cycles.

3.1. *Branching control structures in Mathematica*

Conditional branching structures. Complex computation algorithms and/or control *(first of all)* cannot has with a purely sequential scheme, however include various constructions that change the sequential order of the algorithm depending on the occurrence of certain conditions: ***conditional*** and ***unconditional*** transitions, loops and branching *(structure of such type is called control one)*. Thus, for the organization of control structures of branching type the ***Mathematica*** system has a number of tools provided by so-called ***If***-offer, having the following two coding formats, namely:

If[*CE, a, b*] – *returns **a**, if conditional expression **CE** gives True, and **b** if conditional expression **CE** gives False;*

If[*CE, a, b, c*] – *returns **a**, if conditional expression **CE** gives True, **b** if expression **CE** gives False and **c** if expression **CE** gives to neither True nor False.*

The meaning of the first format of ***If*** sentence is transparent, being represent in one form or another in many programming languages. Whereas the second format in the context of other ***Mathematica*** tools is not quite correct, namely. If a Boolean ***w*** expression does not make sense *True* or *False*, then ***If*[*w, a, b, c*]** *(by definition)* returns ***c,*** while call ***BooleanQ*[*w*]** returns *False* if an expression ***w*** does not equal neither *True* nor *False* and a call ***If*[*BooleanQ*[*w*],*a,b,c*]** will return ***b,*** defining a certain *dissonance,* which illustrates the following rather simple example:

```
In[3336]:= If[77, a, b, c]
Out[3336]= c
In[3337]:= If[BooleanQ[77], a, b, c]
Out[3337]= b
In[3338]:= BooleanQ[77]
Out[3338]= False
```

In our view, in order to resolve such situation, it is enough useful to define in ***Mathematica*** system a Boolean value other than *True* and *False,* similar to the *FAIL* value in ***Maple.*** In the ***Maple*** concept, the *FAIL* symbol is used by logic to define both an unknown and undefined value. At the same time, if it is used inside Boolean expressions with operators ***and, or*** and ***not,*** its behaviour is similar to the case of standard 3–digit logic. Many ***Maple*** procedures and functions, primarily of the testing type, return the *FAIL* symbol if they cannot clearly establish the truth or falsity of a Boolean expression. In addition, the ***If*** function allows an arbitrary level of nesting, whereas as ***a*** and ***b*** can be any sequences of valid ***Mathematica*** clauses. In the context of ***Mathematica*** syntax, both format of ***If*** function can participate in expressions forming.

The ***If*** clause is the most typical tool of providing branching algorithms. In this context, it should be noted that the ***if*** tool of the ***Maple*** language and ***If*** of the ***Mathematica*** language appear to be largely equivalent, however in the sense of readability it is somewhat easier to *perceive* rather complex *branching* algorithms implemented precisely by the ***if*** clauses of ***Maple.*** It is difficult to give preference to anyone in this regard.

Thus, the ***If*** function ris the most typical tool for ensuring of the branching algorithms. In this context it should be noted that ***If*** means of the ***Maple*** and ***Mathematica*** are considerably equivalent, however readability of difficult enough branching algorithms realized by means of ***if*** offers of the ***Maple*** is being perceived slightly more clearly. So, ***Maple*** allows conditional ***if*** offer of the following format, namely:

if l1 then v1 elif l2 then v2 elif l3 then v3 elif l4 then v4 ... else vk end

where *j–th lj* – a logical condition and *vj* – an expression whose sense is rather transparent and considered, for example, in [38]. This offer is convenient at programming of a lot of conditional structures. For definition of a similar structure in ***Mathematica,*** the ***IFk*** procedure whose source code with examples of its use represents the following fragment can be used, namely:

```
In[3212]:= IFk[x__] := Module[{a = {x}, b, c = "", d = "If[", e = "]",
                                        h = {}, k = 1}, b = Length[a];
                                              If[For[k, k <= b - 1, k++,
   AppendTo[h, b >= 2 && ListQ[a[[k]]] && Length[a[[k]]] == 2]];
      DeleteDuplicates[h] != {True}, Return[Defer[IFk[x]]], k = 1];
```

```
For[k, k <= b - 1, k++,
    c = c <> d <> ToString[a[[k]][[1]]] <> "," <>
        ToString[a[[k]][[2]]] <> ","];
c = c <> ToString[a[[b]]] <> StringMultiple[e, b - 1];
ToExpression[c]]
```

```
In[3213]:= IFk[{a, b}, {c, d}, {g, s}, {m, n}, {q, p}, h]
Out[3213]= If[a, b, If[c, d, If[g, s, If[m, n, If[q, p, h]]]]]
```

The call of ***IFk*** procedure uses any number of the factual arguments more than one; the arguments use the two-element lists of the form {*lj, vj*}, except the last. Whereas the last factual argument is a correct expression; in addition, a testing of a *lj* on *Boolean* type isn't done. The call of ***IFk*** procedure on a tuple of the correct factual arguments returns the result equivalent to execution of the corresponding ***Maple*** offer ***if.***

The ***IFk1*** procedure is an useful extension of the previous procedure which unlike ***IFk*** allows only *Boolean* expressions as factual arguments ***lj,*** otherwise returning the unevaluated call. In the rest, the ***IFk*** and ***IFk1*** are functionally identical. Thus, similarly to the ***Maple*** offer ***if,*** the procedures ***IFk*** and ***IFk1*** are quite useful at programming of the branching algorithms of the different types. With that said, the above procedures ***IFk, IFk1*** are provided with a quite developed mechanism of testing of the factual arguments transferred at the procedure call whose algorithm is easily seen from the source code *(see below).*

```
In[7]:= IFk1[x__] := Module[{a = {x}, b, c = "", d = "If[", e = "]",
    h = {}, k = 1}, b = Length[a];
  If[For[k, k <= b - 1, k++,
    AppendTo[h, b >= 2 && ListQ[a[[k]]] && Length[a[[k]]] == 2]];
    DeleteDuplicates[h] != {True},
    Return[Defer[IFk1[x]]], {h, k} = {{}, 1}];
  If[For[k, k <= b - 1, k++, AppendTo[h, a[[k]][[1]]]];
    Select[h, ! MemberQ[{True, False}, #] &] != {},
    Return[Defer[IFk1[x]]], k = 1];
  For[k = 1, k <= b - 1, k++,
    c = c <> d <> ToString[a[[k]][[1]]] <> "," <>
        ToString[a[[k]][[2]]] <> ","];
  c = c <> ToString[a[[b]]] <> StringMultiple[e, b - 1];
  ToExpression[c]]
```

```
In[8]:= IFk1[{False, b}, {False, d}, {False, s}, {True, G}, {False, p}, h]
Out[8]= G
```

Now, using the described approach fairly easy to program in ***Math***–language an arbitrary ***Maple*** construction describing the branching algorithms [27–41].

In a number of cases the simple ***Iff*** procedure with number of arguments in quantity ***1÷n*** which generalizes the standard ***If*** function is quite useful tool; it is very convenient at number of arguments, starting with **1**, what is rather convenient in those cases when calls of the ***Iff*** function are generated in a certain procedure automatically, simplifying processing of erroneous and especial situations arising at the call of such procedure at number of arguments from range **2..4**. The following fragment represents source code of the ***Iff*** procedure with an example. In addition, it must be kept in mind that all its factual arguments, since the second, are coded in string format in order to avoid their premature calculation at the call ***Iff*[*x*, ...]** when the factual arguments are being evaluated/simplified.

```
In[1114]:= Iff[x_, y__ /; StringQ[y]] := Module[{a = {x, y}, b},
                                                          b = Length[a];
  If[b == 1 | | b >= 5, Defer[Iff[x, y]],
   If[b == 2, If[x, ToExpression[y]],
    If[b == 3, If[x, ToExpression[y], ToExpression[a[[3]]]],
     If[b == 4, If[x, ToExpression[a[[2]]], ToExpression[a[[3]]],
                                           ToExpression[a[[4]]]], Null]]]]]
In[1115]:= a = {}; For[k = 1, k <= 77, k++, Iff[PrimeQ[k],
                                                   "AppendTo[a, k]"]]; a
Out[1115]= {2, 3, 5, 7, 11, 13, 17, 19, 23, 29, 31, 37, 41, 43, 47, 53,
                                                       59, 61, 67, 71, 73}
```

To a certain degree to the ***If*** constructions adjoins the ***Which*** function of the following format:

***Which*[*lc1, w1, lc2, w2, lc3, w3, ..., lck, wk*]**

which returns the result of evaluation of the first ***wj*** expression for which *Boolean* expression ***lcj*** *(j =* ***1..k****)* accepts *True* value. If some of the evaluated conditions ***lcj*** doesn't return {*True* | *False*} the function call is returned unevaluated while in a case of *False* for all ***lcj*** conditions *(j =* ***1..k****)* the function call returns *Null*, i.e.

nothing. At dynamical generation of a ***Which*** object the simple procedure ***WhichN*** can be a rather useful that allows any even number of arguments similar to the ***Which*** function, otherwise returning result unevaluated. In the rest, the ***WhichN*** is similar to the ***Which*** function; the following fragment represents source code of the ***WhichN*** procedure with a typical example of its use.

```
In[47]:= WhichN[x__] := Module[{a = {x}, c = "Which[", d,
      k = 1}, d = Length[a]; If[OddQ[d], Defer[WhichN[x]],
                     ToExpression[For[k, k <= d, k++, c = c <>
      ToString[a[[k]]] <> ","]; StringTake[c, {1, -2}] <> "]"]]]
In[48]:= f = 90; WhichN[False, b, f == 90, SV, g, h, r, t]
Out[48]= SV
```

The above procedures ***Iff, IFk, IFk1*** and ***Which*** represent a quite certain interest at programming a number of applications of various purpose, first of all, of the system character *(similar tools are considered in our collection* [15] *and package **MathToolBox**).*

<u>Unconditional transitions</u>. At that, control transfers of the unconditional type are defined in the language, usually, by the ***Goto*** constructions by which control is transferred to the ***Label*** point of the procedure specified by the corresponding ***Label.*** In ***Mathematica*** language, can to usage unconditional transitions based on the built-in ***Goto*** function encoded in the ***Goto[Label]*** format to organize the branching of algorithms along with the presented ***If*** clause. Meanwhile, in a number of cases, the use of this tool is very effective, in particular when it is necessary to load in ***Mathematica*** software the programs using *unconditional* transitions based on ***Goto*** offer. Particularly, *Fortran* programs, rather common in scientifical applications, are a fairly typical example. From our experience it should be noted that the use of ***Goto*** function greatly simplified immersion in ***Mathematica*** of *Fortran*-programs related to engineering and physical direction which rather widely use ***Goto***-constructions. Note that, unlike ***Mathematica,*** the ***goto*** function in ***Maple*** only makes sense in the procedure body, allowing from the ***goto(Label)*** call point to go to a sentence preceded by the specified ***Label.*** Meanwhile, in

Mathematica the **Goto** function is permissible also outside of procedures, although that makes little sense. There can be an arbitrary ***g*** expression as a ***Label,*** as the following rather simple fragment illustrates, namely:

```
In[1900]:= G = {}; p = 1; Label[agn]; AppendTo[G, p++];
                                          If[p <= 10, Goto[agn], G]
Out[1900]= {1, 2, 3, 4, 5, 6, 7, 8, 9, 10}
```

The above fragment illustrates a simple example of cyclic computations on a basis of ***Goto*** function without using built-in standard loop functions. However, such cyclic constructions (in the temporary relation) substantially concede to the cycles, for example, based on the built–in function ***Do,*** for example:

```
In[5]:= p = 0; Timing[Label[g]; If[p++ < 999999, Goto[g], p]]
Out[5]= {1.54441, 1000000}
In[6]:= p = 0; Timing[Do[p++, 1000000]; p]
Out[6]= {0.187201, 1000000}
```

Time differences are quite noticeable, starting with a cycle length greater than *4000* steps. However, cyclic constructions based on the unconditional ***Goto*** transition are in some cases quite effective at programming of the procedure bodies. Note another point is worth paying attention to, namely. It is known [20-41] that in ***Maple,*** an unconditional ***goto(Label)*** transition assumes a global variable as a ***Label,*** whereas the definition of ***Label*** as a local *(that not test as an error in the procedure definition calculation stage)* initiates an erroneous situation when calling the procedure. Whereas the ***Mathematica*** in an unconditional ***Goto[Label]*** transition as a ***Label*** allows both global variable and local along with an arbitrary expression, for example:

```
In[2254]:= Sv[k_Integer] := Module[{p = 0, g}, Label[g];
                                          If[p++ <= k, Goto[g], {g, p}]]
In[2255]:= Sv[10000]
Out[2255]= {g$16657, 10002}
In[2256]:= Sv1[k_Integer, x_] := Module[{p = 0}, Label[x];
                                          If[p++ <= k, Goto[x], {x, p}]]
In[2257]:= Sv1[10000, a*Sin[b] + c*Cos[d]]
Out[2257]= {c*Cos[d] + a*Sin[b], 10002}
```

Meanwhile, in order to avoid any misunderstandings, the ***Label*** is recommended to be defined as a local variable because the global ***Label*** calculated outside of a module will be always acceptable for the module, however calculated in the module body quite can distort calculations outside of the module. At that, multiplicity of occurrences of identical ***Goto*** functions into a procedure is a quite naturally and is defined by the realized algorithm while with the corresponding tags ***Label*** the similar situation, generally speaking, is inadmissible; in addition, it is not recognized at evaluation of a procedure definition and even at a stage of its performance, often substantially distorting the planned task algorithm. In this case only point of the module body that is marked by the first such ***Label*** receives the control. Moreover, it must be kept in mind that lack of a ***Label[j]*** for the corresponding call ***Goto[j]*** in a block or a module at a stage of evaluation of its definitions isn't recognized, however only at the time of performance with the real appeal to such ***Goto[j]***. Interesting examples illustrating the told can be found in [6-15].

In this connection the ***GotoLabel*** procedure can represent a quite certain interest whose call ***GotoLabel[j]*** allows to analyse a procedure ***j*** on the subject of formal correctness of use of ***Goto*** functions and the ***Label*** tags corresponding to them. So, the call ***GotoLabel[j]*** returns the nested **3**–element list whose the first element defines the list of all ***Goto*** functions used by a module ***j***, the second element defines the list of all tags *(excluding their multiplicity)*, the third element determines the list whose sublists determine ***Goto*** functions with the tags corresponding to them *(in addition, as the first elements of these sublists the calls of the* ***Goto*** *function appear, whereas multiplicities of functions and tags remain)*. The fragment below represents source code of the ***GotoLabel*** procedure along with typical examples of its application.

```
In[7]:= GotoLabel[x_/; BlockModQ[x]] := Module[{b, d, p, k = 1,
    c = {{}, {}, {}}, j, h, v = {}, t, a = Flatten[{PureDefinition[x]}][[1]]},
                                                b = ExtrVarsOfStr[a, 1];
  b = DeleteDuplicates[Select[b, MemberQ[{"Label", "Goto"}, #] &]];
          If[b == {}, c, d = StringPosition[a, Map[" " <> # <> "[" &,
```

```
{"Label", "Goto"}]]; t = StringLength[a];
For[k, k <= Length[d], k++, p = d[[k]]; h = ""; j = p[[2]];
While[j <= t, h = h <> StringTake[a, {j, j}];
If[StringCount[h, "["] == StringCount[h, "]"],
AppendTo[v, StringTake[a, {p[[1]] + 1, p[[2]] - 1}] <> h];
Break[]]; j++]]; h = DeleteDuplicates[v];
{Select[h, SuffPref[#, "Goto", 1] &],
Select[h, SuffPref[#, "Label", 1] &], Gather[Sort[v], #1 ==
StringReplace[#2, "Label[" -> "Goto[", 1] &]}]]
In[8]:= ArtKr[x_/; IntegerQ[x]] := Module[{prime, agn},
If[PrimeQ[x], Goto[9; prime], If[OddQ[x], Goto[agn],
Goto[Sin]]]; Label[9; prime]; Print[x^2]; Goto[Sin];
Print[NextPrime[x]]; Goto[Sin]; Label[9; prime]; Null]
In[9]:= GotoLabel[ArtKr]
Out[9]= {{"Goto[9; prime]", "Goto[agn]", "Goto[Sin]"},
{"Label[9; prime]"}, {{"Goto[9; prime]", "Label[9; prime]",
"Label[9; prime]"}, {"Goto[agn]"}, {"Goto[Sin]", "Goto[Sin]",
"Goto[Sin]"}}}
In[10]:= Map[GotoLabel, {GotoLabel, TestArgsTypes, CallsInMean}]
Out[10]= {{{}, {}, {}}, {{}, {}, {}}, {{}, {}, {}}}
In[11]:= Map[GotoLabel, {SearchDir, StrDelEnds, OP, BootDrive}]
Out[11]= {{{}, {}, {}}, {{}, {}, {}}, {{"Goto[ArtKr]"}, {"Label[ArtKr]"},
{{"Goto[ArtKr]", "Label[ArtKr]"}}}, {{"Goto[avz]"}, {"Label[avz]"},
{{"Goto[avz]", "Goto[avz]", "Goto[avz]", "Label[avz]"}}}}
```

We will note that existence of the nested list with the third sublist containing ***Goto***-functions without tags corresponding to them, in the result returned by means call ***GotoLabel[j]*** not necessarily speaks about existence of the function calls ***Goto[j]*** for which not exists any ***Label[j]*** tag. It can be, for example, in the case of generation of a value depending on some condition.

```
In[320]:= Av[x_Integer, y_Integer, p_/; MemberQ[{1, 2, 3}, p]] :=
Module[{}, Goto[p]; Label[1]; Return[x + y]; Label[2];
Return[N[x/y]]; Label[3]; Return[x*y]]
In[321]:= Map[Av[590, 90, #] &, {1, 2, 3, 4}]
Out[321]= {680, 6.55556, 53100, Av[590, 90, 4]}
In[322]:= GotoLabel[Av]
Out3[22]= {{"Goto[p]"}, {"Label[1]", "Label[2]", "Label[3]"},
{{"Goto[p]"}, {"Label[1]"}, {"Label[2]"}, {"Label[3]"}}}
```

For example, according to simple example of the previous fragment the call ***GotoLabel[Av]*** contains {"Goto[p]"} in the third sublist what, at first sight, it would be possible to consider as an impropriety of the corresponding call of ***Goto*** function. However, all the matter is that a value of actual ***p*** argument in the call ***Av[x,y,p]*** and defines a tag really existing in definition of the procedure, i.e. ***Label[p]***. Therefore, the ***GotoLabel*** module only at the *formal* level analyzes existence of the ***Goto*** functions, ***"incorrect"*** from its point of view with ***"excess"*** tags. Whereas refinement of the results received on a basis of a procedure call ***GotoLabel[W]*** lies on the user, above all, by means of analysis of accordance of source code of the ***W*** to the correctness of the required algorithm.

As a ***Label*** may be a correct sentence, for example:

```
In[9]:= a[x_, y_] := Module[{a, b, c}, If[x/y > 7, Goto[a], Goto[b]];
   Label[a[t_] := t^2; a]; c = a[x]; Goto[Fin]; Label[b[t_] := t^3; b];
                                              c = b[y]; Label[Fin]; c]
In[10]:= {a[7, 12], a[77, 7]}
Out[10]= {1728, 5929}
```

The structured paradigm of programming doesn't assume application in programs of the ***Goto*** constructions allowing to transfer control from bottom to top. At the same time, in some cases the use of ***Goto*** function is rather effective, for example, at needing of embedding into ***Mathematica*** of programs which use unconditional transitions on a basis of the ***goto*** offer. Thus, *Fortran* programs can be adduced as a typical example that are very widespread in scientific appendices. From our experience follows, that the use of ***Goto*** function allowed significantly to simplify embedding into ***Mathematica*** of a number of rather large *Fortran* programs relating to the engineering and physical applications that very widely use the goto constructions. Right there it should be noted that from our standpoint the function ***Goto*** of ***Mathematica*** is more preferable, than ***goto*** function of ***Maple*** in respect of efficiency in the light of application in the procedural programming of various appendices, including also appendices of the system character.

3.2. Cyclic control structures in Mathematica

One of the basic cyclic structures of ***Mathematica*** is based on the ***For*** function having the following coding format:

For[start of a loop variable, test, increment, loop body]

Starting from a given initial value of *loop variable*, the ***loop body*** that contains language sentences is cyclically computed, with the loop variable cyclically incremented by an ***increment*** until the *logical condition (**test**)* remains *True*. The control words ***Continue[]*** *(continuation)* and {***Break[]***, ***Return[]***} *(termination)* respectively are used to control the ***For***–cycle, as the following example well illustrates:

```
In[21]:= a := {7, 6, c, 8, d, f, g}; b := {a1, d, c1, 77, f1, m, n, t};
In[22]:= For[k = 1, k <= 1000, k++, p = a[[k]]; If[PrimeQ[p],
            Break[p], If[IntegerQ[p], Return[], Continue[]]]]
Out[22]= 7
In[23]:= For[k = 1, k <= 1000, k++, p = b[[k]]; If[PrimeQ[p],
           Break[p], If[IntegerQ[p], Return[p], Continue[]]]]
Out[23]= Return[77]
In[24]:= For[k = 1, k <= 1000, k++, p = b[[k]]; If[PrimeQ[p],
Break[], If[IntegerQ[p], Print[{k, p}]; Return[], Continue[]]]]
           {4, 77}
Out[24]= Return[]
In[25]:= A[x___] := Module[{}, For[k = 1, k <= Infinity,
        k++, p = b[[k]]; If[PrimeQ[p], Break[], If[IntegerQ[p],
                                        Return[p], Continue[]]]]]
In[26]:= A[]
Out[26]= 77
In[27]:= G[x_] := (If[x > 10, Return[x]]; x^2)
In[28]:= G[90]
Out[28]= 90
```

Meanwhile, note in mind that ***Return[]*** terminates the loop both outside and inside the procedure or function. In addition, in the first case, the loop ends by ***Return[]***, while in the second case the termination of the loop by ***Return*** allows by means of the call ***Return[E]*** additionally to return a certain ***E*** expression, for example, a result at the end of the loop. The ***For***-loop allows an arbitrary level of nesting, depending on the size of working area of the software environment. Moreover, in both cases by means of ***Break[gsv]*** can not only terminate the loop, but also return the required ***gsv*** expression.

In our books [1-3] the reciprocal functional equivalence of both systems is visually illustrated when the most important computing structures of ***Mathematica*** with this or that efficiency are simulated by ***Maple*** constructions and vice versa. Truly, in principle, it is a quite expected result because built-in languages of both systems are universal and in this regard with one or the other efficiency they can program an arbitrary algorithm. But in the time relation it is not so and at use of the loop structures of a rather large nesting level the ***Maple*** can have rather essential advantages before ***Mathematica.*** For confirmation we will give a simple example of a loop construction programmed both in the ***Maple,*** and the ***Mathematica*** system.

The results speak for themselves – if for the ***Maple 11*** the execution of the following ***for***–loop of the nesting *8* requires *7.8 s*, the ***Mathematica 12.1*** for execution of the same loop on base of ***For***–function requires already *51.372 s*, i.e. approximately *6.6* times more *(estimations have been obtained on **Dell OptiPlex 3020**, i5-4570 3.2 GHz with 64-bit Windows **7** Professional 6.1.7601 service pack 1 Build 7601)*. In addition, with growth of the nesting depth and range of a loop variable at implementation of the loops this difference rather significantly grows.

```
> t := time(): for k1 to 10 do for k2 to 10 do for k3 to 10 do for k4 to
10 do for k5 to 10 do for k6 to 10 do for k7 to 10 do for k8 to 10 do
900 end do end do end do end do end do end do end do end do:
time() – t;                                                    # (Maple 11)
   7.800
   In[8]= n = 10; t = TimeUsed[]; For[k1 = 1, k1 <= n, k1++,
                 For[k2 = 1, k2 <= n, k2++, For[k3 = 1, k3 <= n, k3++,
                 For[k4 = 1, k4 <= n, k4++, For[k5 = 1, k5 <= n, k5++,
                 For[k6 = 1, k6 <= n, k6++, For[k7 = 1, k7 <= n, k7++,
                  For[k8 = 1, k8 <= n, k8++, 500]]]]]]]]; TimeUsed[] - t
   Out[8]= 51.372
```

Our long experience [1-42] of using ***Maple*** and ***Matematica*** systems of different versions has clearly shown that, in general, programming of loops in the first system is more efficient in the temporal relation.

As another fairly widely used tool in ***Mathematica*** for the organization of cyclic calculations is the ***Do***-function, which has the following six coding formats, namely:

Do[*E*, *n*] – *evaluates an expression* ***E n*** *times;*

Do[*E*, {*j*, *p*}] – *evaluates* **E** *with variable* ***j*** *successively taking on the values* **1** *through* **k** *(in steps of* **1***);*

Do[*E*, {*j*, *k*, *p*}] – *starts with* ***j*** *=* ***k****;*

Do[*E*, {*j*, *k*, *p*, *dt*}] – *uses steps* ***dt****;*

Do[*E*, {*j*, {*k1*, *k2*,...}}] – *uses the successive values* ***k1, k2,...****;*

Do[*Exp*, {*j*, *j1*, *j2*}, {*k*, *k1*, *k2*},...] – *evaluates* ***Exp*** *looping over different values of* **k** *etc. for each* ***j****.*

In the above ***Do***-constructions, there can be both individual expressions and sequences of language sentences as ***E*** and ***Exp*** *(**body**)*. To exit the ***Do*** loop prematurely or continue it, the body of a loop uses functions ***Return, Break, Continue;*** in the case of the nested ***Do*** loop, control in such constructions is transferred to the external loop. Examples of ***Do***-loops of the above formats

```
In[11]:= t := 0; Do[t = t + 1, 1000000]; t
Out[11]= 1000000
In[12]:= t := 0; Do[t = t + k^2, {k, 1000}]; t
Out[12]= 333833500
In[13]:= t := 0; Do[t = t + k^2, {k, 1000, 10000}]; t
Out[13]= 333050501500
In[14]:= t := 0; Do[t = t + k^2, {k, 1000, 10000, 20}]; t
Out[14]= 16700530000
In[15]:= t := 0; Do[t = t + k^2 + j^2 + h^2, {k, 10, 100},
                                   {j, 10, 100}, {h, 10, 100}]; t
Out[15]= 8398548795
In[16]:= A[x_] := Module[{t = 0}, Do[If[t++ > x, Return[t],
                                   Continue[]], Infinity]]; A[900]
Out[16]= 902
```

```
In[17]:= A1[x_] := Module[{t = 0}, Do[If[t++ > x, Break[t],
                                    Continue[]], Infinity]]; A1[900]
Out[17]= 902
In[18]:= t = 0; Do[If[t++ > 100, Return[t], Continue[]], 1000]
Out[18]= 102
In[19]:= t = 0; Do[If[t++ > 100, Break[t], Continue[]], 1000]
Out[19]= 102
In[20]:= t := 0; k = 1; Do[t = t + k^2; If[k >= 30, Break[t],
                                     Continue[]], {k, 1000}]; {t, k}
Out[20]= {9455, 1}
```

Note that ***Break*** and ***Return*** make sense for exit of ***Do*** loop both within a procedure containing this loop, and outside it. At the same time, the loop variable is *local (see the last example of the previous fragment)*. Here is a list of several more ***Mathematica*** functions for cyclic computing:

While*[E, *body*]** – *evaluates* **E**, *then repetitively evaluates* ***body *until* **E** *to give True;*

```
In[3338]:= {t, v} = {0, {}}; While[t++; t <= 100,
                                   s = Total[AppendTo[v, t]]]; s
Out[3338]= 5050
```

Nest*[F, E, *n*]** – *returns the result of application of a function* **F** *to an* **E** *expression* ***n *times;*

```
In[3339]:= Nest[F, (a + b + c), 6]
Out[3339]= F[F[F[F[F[F[a + b + c]]]]]]
```

FixedPoint*[F, E]** – *starting with* **E, F** *is applied repeatedly until two nearby results will identical; in addition* ***FixedPoint*[F, E, *n*]** *stops after at most* ***n *steps.* ***FixedPoint*** *returns the last result it gets.*

```
In[3340]:= FixedPoint[Sqrt, 19.42, 15]
Out[3340]= 1.00009
```

The ***FixedPoint1*** procedure is a program equivalent of the ***FixedPoint*** based on ***Do*** loop:

```
In[5]:= FixedPoint1[f_, e_, n___] := Module[{a = e, b, p = 1},
          Do[b = f @@ {a}; If[SameQ[b, a], Return[], a = b; p++;
                Continue[]], If[{n} == {}, 10^10, n]]; {p - 1, b}]
In[6]:= FixedPoint1[Sqrt, 19.42, 15]
```

```
Out[6]= {15, 1.00009}
In[7]:= FixedPoint1[Sqrt, 19.42]
Out[7]= {52, 1.}
```

The procedure call ***FixedPoint1[f, e, n]*** returns the list of the form ***{p, FixedPoint[f, e, n]}***, where ***p*** is the number of steps of the procedure required to obtain the desired result, whereas ***n*** is optional argument similar to ***n*** of ***FixedPoint[f, e, n]***.

NestWhile[F, E, Test] – *starting with **E**, **F** is applied repeatedly until applying **Test** to the result gives False;*

```
In[1119]:= N[NestWhile[Sqrt, 90050, # > 7 &]]
Out[1119]= 4.16208
```

The ***NestWhile1*** procedure is a program equivalent of the ***NestWhile*** based on ***Do*** loop:

```
In[1132]:= NestWhile1[f_, e_, t_] := Module[{a = e, b, p = 1},
    Do[b = f @@ {a}; If[! t @@ {b}, Return[], a = b; p++;
        Continue[]], Infinity]; {p, b}]
In[1133]:= N[NestWhile1[Sqrt, 90050, # > 7 &]]
Out[1133]= {3., 4.16208}
```

The procedure call ***NestWhile1[f, e, t]*** returns the list of the form ***{p, NestWhile[f, e, t]}***, where ***p*** is the number of steps of the procedure required to obtain the desired result, whereas ***t*** is the ***t*** test analogous to ***t*** for ***NestWhile[f, e, t]***. At that, in addition to the presented format the ***NestWhile*** has additional five formats, with which the reader can familiarize in the ***Mathematica*** help.

TakeWhile[L, t] – *returns elements of a list **L** from the beginning of the list, continuing so long as **t** for the **L** elements gives True.*

```
In[1134]:= TakeWhile[{a, b, c, 7, e, r, 15, k, h, m, n, g, s, w},
        SymbolQ[#] || PrimeQ[#] &]
Out[1134]= {a, b, c, 7, e, r}
```

The ***TakeWhile1*** procedure is a program equivalent of the ***TakeWhile*** based on ***Do*** loop:

```
In[1135]:= TakeWhile1[L_List, t_] := Module[{p = {}},
    Do[If[t @@ {L[[j]]}, AppendTo[p, L[[j]]], Return[{j, p}]],
        {j, Length[L]}]]
```

```
In[1136]:= TakeWhile1[{a, b, c, 7, e, r, 15, k, h, m, n, k, h},
                       SymbolQ[#] || PrimeQ[#] &]
Out[1136]= {7, {a, b, c, 7, e, r}}
```

The procedure call ***TakeWhile1[L, T]*** returns the list of the form ***{p, TakeWhile[L, T]}***, where ***p*** is the number of steps of the procedure required to obtain the desired result, whereas ***T*** is the test analogous to ***T*** in ***TakeWhile[L, T]***.

Catch[exp] – *returns the argument of the first* ***Throw*** *call that is generated in the evaluation of an* ***exp*** *expression.*

```
In[4906]:= Catch[Do[If[j > 100 && PrimeQ[j], Throw[j]],
                    {j, Infinity}]]
Out[4906]= 101
```

At that, in addition to the presented format the ***Catch*** has additional two formats, with which the reader can familiarize in [15] or in the ***Mathematica*** help. The ***Break, Return, Goto*** and ***Continue*** functions are used to control whether the loop exits or continues, respectively. Other functions that make substantial use of cyclic computing can be found in the ***Mathematica*** help. In addition, most of them have rather simple program analogs using the basic functions ***Do, For*** of the loop along with function ***If*** of conditional transitions and functions of loop termination control ***Break, Return, Continue*** to organize cyclic calculations. Some instructive examples of similar program counterparts are presented above. The above largely applies to both simple and the nested loops whose attachments can alternating and shared different types of loops.

3.3. Special types of cyclic control structures in Mathematica

Along with the basic cyclic structures discussed above, the ***Mathematica*** has a number of useful special control structures of cyclic type, which allow to significantly simplify the solution of a number of important tasks. Such structures are realized on the basis of a number of built-in functions ***Map, MapAt, MapAll, MapIndexed, Select, Sum, Product,*** etc., allowing to describe the algorithms of mass tasks of processing and calculations in a very compact way. In addition, not only good visibility of programs is ensured, but also rather high efficiency of their execution. At the same time, first of all, the tools of the so-called ***Map*** group, among which the ***Map*** function is the most used, appear to be important. Consider this group a little more detailed.

The main ***Map*** function has two formats, namely:

Map[*F, exp*] *or* ***F/@exp*** *– returns the result of applying of* **F** *to each element of the first level of an expression* ***exp;***

Map[*F, exp, levels*] *– returns the result of applying of* **F** *to parts of an expression* ***exp*** *specified by* ***levels;*** as the values for the ***levels*** argument can be:

n	*– levels from* **1** *through* ***n***
Infinity	*– levels from* **1** *through Infinity*
{***n***}	*– level* ***n*** *only*
{***n1, n2***}	*– levels from* ***n1*** *through* ***n2***

Here are some examples of management by ***Map*** execution:

```
In[1]:= A[x_, y_] := Module[{t = {}}, Map[If[# <= x,
      AppendTo[t, F[#]], Goto[g]] &, Range[y]]; Label[g]; t]
In[2]:= A[7, 90]
Out[2]= {F[1], F[2], F[3], F[4], F[5], F[6], F[7]}
In[3]:= A1[x_, y_] := Module[{t = {}}, CheckAbort[Map[
      If[# <= x, AppendTo[t, F[#]], Abort[]] &, Range[y]], t]]
In[4]:= A1[7, 90]
Out[4]= {F[1], F[2], F[3], F[4], F[5], F[6], F[7]}
In[5]:= Map[g, Map[If[OddQ[#], #, Nothing] &, Range[18]]]
Out[5]= {g[1], g[3], g[5], g[7], g[9], g[11], g[13], g[15], g[17]}
In[6]:= t = {}; CheckAbort[Map[If[# <= 7, AppendTo[t, F[#]],
                                      Abort[]] &, Range[90]], t]
Out[6]= {F[1], F[2], F[3], F[4], F[5], F[6], F[7]}
In[7]:= Map[j, (a + b)/(c – d)*m*n, Infinity]
Out[7]= j[m]*j[n]*j[j[a] + j[b]]*j[j[j[c] + j[j[-1]*j[d]]]^j[-1]]
```

MapAll*[*f, exp*]** is equivalent to **Map[*f, exp,* {*0, Infinity*}].** At the same time, the call ***MapAll*[*f, exp, Heads -> True*]** returns the result of applying of ***f to heads in ***exp*** additionally. Whereas the ***MapIndexed*** function also has two formats, namely:

MapIndexed[*F, exp*] – *returns the result of applying of* ***F*** *to the elements of an expression* ***exp****, giving the part number of each element as the second argument to* ***F****;*

MapIndexed[*F, exp, levels*] – *returns the result of applying of* ***F*** *to all parts of* ***exp*** *on levels specified by* ***levels.***

As a program implementation of the ***MapIndexed*** function of the first format can be given:

```
In[20]:= MapIndexed[F, (a + b)/(c – d) + m*n]
Out[20]= F[(a + b)/(c – d), {1}] + F[m*n, {2}]
In[21]:= MapIndexed1[F_, e_] := Module[{p = 1}, Part[e, 0]
                              @@ Map[F[#, {p++}] &, Op[e]]]
In[22]:= MapIndexed1[F, (a + b)/(c – d) + m*n]
Out[22]= F[(a + b)/(c – d), {1}] + F[m*n, {2}]
```

The program implementation of the second format of the ***MapIndexed*** function we leave to the reader as a useful exercise.

The ***SubsetMap*** function has two formats, namely:

SubsetMap[*g, j, j1*] – *returns the result of replacing of elements of a* ***j*** *list by the corresponding elements (whose positions are defined by a list* ***j1****) of the list obtained by evaluating* **g[*j*]**.

SubsetMap[*g, j, L*] – *returns the result of replacing of elements* j_n *of an expression* ***j*** *at positions* **L** *on* **g[**j_n**]**.

Here are some examples of the ***SubsetMap*** use:

```
In[6]:= SubsetMap[Power[#, 3] &, {a, b, c, d, g, h, t}, {1,3,5,7}]
Out[6]= {a^3, b, c^3, d, g^3, h, t^3}
In[7]:= SubsetMap[Power[#, 7] &, {a, b, c, d, g, h, m, t}, 3;;7]
Out[7]= {a, b, c^7, d^7, g^7, h^7, m^7, t}
```

As a program implementation of the ***SubsetMap1*** function of the *first* format for case of lists as an argument ***j*** can be given:

```
In[9]:= SubsetMap1[F_, j_, L_] := Map[If[MemberQ[L,
                 Flatten[Position[j, #]][[1]]], g[#], #] &, j]
In[10]:= SubsetMap1[g, {a, b, c, d, g, h, m, t}, {3, 4, 5, 6, 7}]
Out[10]= {a, b, g[c], g[d], g[g], g[h], g[m], t}
```

The program realization of the more common cases of the ***SubsetMap*** function we leave to the reader as a useful exercise.

Frequently used functions such as ***Sum, Product, Delete*** and ***Select*** also may be carried to cyclic constructions. Function ***Sum*** has five formats of coding from which as an example give the following format:

Sum[*F[j]*, {*j*, {*j1, j2, j3,...*}}] – *returns the result of summarizing of an expression* ***F[j]*** *using successive values j1, j2, j3,... for* ***j***.

Here is function examples use and its program analogue:

```
In[3336]:= Sum[1/j^2, {j, {1, Infinity}}]
Out[3336]= 1
In[3337]:= Total[Map[1/#^2 &, {1, Infinity}]]
Out[3337]= 1
In[3338]:= Sum[(j + 1)/j^2, {j, {1, m}}]
Out[3338]= 2 + (1 + m)/m^2
In[3339]:= Total[Map[(# + 1)/#^2 &, {1, m}]]
Out[3339]= 2 + (1 + m)/m^2
```

Function ***Delete*** has three formats of coding do not causing any difficulties. Both functions allow multiple levels of nesting. Once again, the functions underlying cyclic constructions allow nesting. Function ***Select*** has two formats of coding, namely:

Select[*L, test*] – *returns the list of elements* ***Lj*** *of* ***L*** *list for which* ***test*** *gives True;*

Select[*L, test, n*] – *returns the list of the first* ***n*** *elements* ***Lj*** *of* ***L*** *list for which* ***test*** *gives True.*

Here is function examples use and its program analogue:

```
In[4272]:= Select[{a, b, 77, c, 7, d, 14, 5, n}, SymbolQ[#] &&
                                   ! SameQ[#, a] | | PrimeQ[#] &]
Out[4272]= {b, c, 7, d, 5}
In[4275]:= Select5[L_, test_, n___] := Module[{t},
                    t = Map[If[test @@ {#}, #, Nothing] &, L];
   If[{n} == {}, t, If[Length[t] >= n, t[[1 ;; n]], "Invalid third
                                                  argument value"]]]
In[4276]:= Select5[{a, b, 77, c, 7, d, 14, 5}, SymbolQ[#] &&
                                   ! SameQ[#, a] | | PrimeQ[#] &]
Out[4276]= {b, c, 7, d, 5}
In[4277]:= Select5[{a, b, 77, c, 7, d, 14, 5}, SymbolQ[#] &&
                                 ! SameQ[#, a] | | PrimeQ[#] &, 3]
```

```
Out[4277]= {b, c, 7}
In[4285]:= Select5[L_, test_, n___] := {Save["#77#", t],
    t = Map[If[test @@ {#}, #, Nothing] &, L], If[{n} == {}, t,
  If[Length[t] >= n, t[[1 ;; n]], "Invalid third argument value"]],
                          Get["#77#"], DeleteFile["#77#"]}[[-3]]
In[4286]:= t = 2020; Select5[{a, b, 77, c, 7, d, 14, 5},
         SymbolQ[#] && ! SameQ[#, a] | | PrimeQ[#] &, 3]
Out[4286]= {b, c, 7}
In[4287]:= t
Out[4287]= 2020
In[4288]:= Select5[{a, b, 77, c, 7, d, 14, 5}, SymbolQ[#] &&
                              ! SameQ[#, a] | | PrimeQ[#] &, 7]
Out[4288]= "Invalid third argument value"
In[8]:= Nest1[F_Symbol, x_, n_Integer] := {Save["#78#", a],
a = x, Do[a = F[a], n], a, Get["#78#"], DeleteFile["#78#"]}[[-3]]
In[9]:= a = 77; Nest1[G, m + n, 7]
Out[9]= G[G[G[G[G[G[G[m + n]]]]]]]
In[10]:= Nest2[F_List, x_] := {Save["#78#", a], a = x,
   Do[a = Reverse[F][[j]][a], {j, Length[F]}], a, Get["#78#"],
                                    DeleteFile["#78#"]}[[-3]]
In[11]:= {a, j} = {42, 77}; {Nest2[{F, G, H, S, V}, x], {42, 77}}
Out[11]= {F[G[H[S[V[x]]]]], {42, 77}}
```

The previous fragment also represents program realizations of the built-in ***Select (Select5)*** and ***Nest (Nest1)*** functions in the form of functions of the list format along with an extension of the ***Nest (Nest2)***. The function call ***Nest2[{a, b, c, d, ...}, x]*** where ***{a, b, c, d,...}*** – the list of symbols and ***x*** – an expression, returns ***a[b[c[d[... [x]...]]]]***. In these functions, the question of localizing variables by means of built-in ***Save, Get, DeleteFile*** functions may be of definite interest. It is shown [6] that for most built-in functions which provide the cyclic structures, it is possible to successfully program their analogues based on system ***Map, Do*** and ***If*** functions. Because of the importance of the ***Map*** function we have created a so-called ***Map***-group consisting of the ***Map1÷ Map24*** means which cover a wide range of applications [6,16].

3.4. *Mathematica tools for string expressions*

The ***Mathematica*** language provides a variety of functions for manipulating strings. Most of these functions are based on a viewing strings as a sequence of characters, and many of these functions are analogous to ones for manipulating lists. Without taking into account the fact that ***Mathematica*** has a rather large set of tools for work with string structures, the necessity of tools which are absent in it arises. Some of such tools are represented in the given section; among them are available both simple, and more difficult which appeared in the course of programming of tasks of various purpose as additional procedures and functions and simplifying or facilitating the programming. The section presents a number of tools providing usefulenough operations on strings which supplement and expand the standard system means. These means are widely used at programming of many tools in our package ***Mathematica,*** as well as in programming other applications. More fully these tools are presented in [16].

Examples throughout this book illustrate formalization of procedures in the ***Mathematica*** that reflects its basic elements and principles, allowing by taking into account the material to directly start creation, at the beginning, of simple procedures of different purpose that are based on processing of string objects. Here only procedures of so-called ***"system"*** character intended for processing of string structures are considered that, however, represent also the most direct applied interest for programming of various appendices. Moreover, the procedures and functions that have quite foreseeable volume of source code that allows to carry out their a rather simple analysis are represented here. Their analysis can serve as a rather useful exercise for the *reader* both who is beginning programming and already having rather serious experience in this direction. Later we will understand under ***"system"*** tools the actually built-in tools, and our tools oriented on *mass* application. In addition it should be noted that *string structures* are of special interest not only as *basic structures* with which the system and the user operate, but also as a basis, in particular, of dynamic generation of objects in ***Mathematica,*** including procedures and functions. The mechanism of *dynamic* generation is quite simple and enough in detail is considered in [8-15], whereas examples of its use can be found in source codes of tools of the present book. Below we will present a number of useful enough means for strings processing in ***Mathematica.***

The procedure call ***SuffPref***[*S, s, n*] provides testing of a *S* string regarding to begin *(n=1)*, to end *(n=2)* or both ends *(n=3)* be limited by a substring or substrings from a ***s*** list. In a case of establishment of such fact the ***SuffPref*** returns *True*, otherwise *False* is returned. Whereas the function call ***StrStr***[*x*] provides return an expression ***x*** different from a string, in string format, and a double string otherwise. In a number of cases the ***StrStr*** function is a rather useful at working with strings, in particular, with the standard ***StringReplace*** function. The following below represents source codes of the above tools along with examples of their application.

```
In[7]:= SuffPref[S_/; StringQ[S], s_/; StringQ[s] | | ListQ[s] &&
AllTrue[Map[StringQ, s], TrueQ], n_/; MemberQ[{1, 2, 3}, n]] :=
                    Module[{a, b, c, k = 1}, If[StringFreeQ[S, s], False,
              b = StringLength[S]; c = Flatten[StringPosition[S, s]];
                         If[n == 3 && c[[1]] == 1 && c[[-1]] == b, True,
                                                If[n == 1 && c[[1]] == 1, True,
                           If[n == 2 && c[[-1]] == b, True, False]]]]]
In[8]:= StrStr[x_] := If[StringQ[x], "\"" <> x <> "\"", ToString[x]]
In[9]:= Map[StrStr, {"RANS", a + b, IAN, {72, 77, 67}, F[x, y]}]
Out[9]= {"\"RANS\"", "a + b", "IAN", "{72, 77, 67}", "F[x, y]"}
In[10]:= SuffPref["IAN_RANS_RAC_REA_90_500", "90_500", 2]
Out[10]= True
```

If the ***StrStr*** function is intended, first of all, for creation of double strings, then the following simple procedure converts double strings and strings of higher nesting level to the classical strings. The procedure call ***ReduceString***[*x*] returns the result of converting of a string ***x*** to the usual classical string.

```
In[15]:= ReduceString[x_/; StringQ[x]] := Module[{a = x},
                Do[If[SuffPref[a, "\"", 3], a = StringTake[a, {2, -2}],
                                                Return[a]], {j, 1, Infinity}]]
```

```
In[16]:= ReduceString["\"\"\"\"\"{a + b, \"g\", s}\"\"\"\"\""]
Out[16]= "{a + b, \"g\", s}"
```

The ***SuffPrefList*** procedure [8,16] is a rather useful version of the above ***SuffPref*** procedure concerning the lists. At ***n=1***, the procedure call ***SuffPrefList***[*x, y, n*] returns the maximal subset common for the lists ***x*** and ***y*** with their beginning, whereas at ***n=2***, the procedure call ***SuffPrefList***[*x, y, n*] returns the maximal subset common for the lists ***x*** and ***y*** since their end, otherwise the call returns two-element sublist whose elements define the above limiting sublists of the lists ***x*** and ***y*** with the both ends; moreover, if the call ***SuffPrefList***[*x, y, n, z*] has fourth optional ***z*** argument – an arbitrary function from one argument, then each element of lists ***x*** and ***y*** is previously processed by a ***z*** function. The fragment below represents source code of the ***SuffPrefList*** procedure along with typical example of its application.

```
In[7]:= SuffPrefList[x_/; ListQ[x], y_/; ListQ[y],
                             t_/; MemberQ[{1, 2, 3}, t], z___] :=
  Module[{a = Sort[Map[Length, {x, y}]], b = x, c = y, d = {{}, {}}, j},
                  If[{z} != {} && FunctionQ[z] || SystemQ[z],
     {b, c} = {Map[z, b], Map[z, c]}, 6]; Goto[t]; Label[3]; Label[1];
Do[If[b[[j]] === c[[j]], AppendTo[d[[1]], b[[j]]], Break[]], {j, 1, a[[1]]}];
                             If[t == 1, Goto[Exit], 6]; Label[2];
          Do[If[b[[j]] === c[[j]], AppendTo[d[[2]], b[[j]]], Break[]],
          {j, -1, -a[[1]], -1}]; d[[2]] = Reverse[d[[2]]]; Label[Exit];
                    If[t == 1, d[[1]], If[t == 2, d[[2]], {d[[1]], d[[2]]}]]]]
In[8]:= SuffPrefList[{x, y, x, y, a, b, c, x, y, x, y}, {x, y, x, y}, 3]
Out[8]= {{x, y, x, y}, {x, y, x, y}}
```

StringTrim1÷ StringTrim3 procedures are useful extensions to the built-in ***StringTrim*** function. In particular, the procedure call ***StringTrim3***[***S, s, s1, s2, n, m***] returns the result of truncation of a ***S*** string by ***s*** symbols on the left *(**n=1**)*, on the right *(**n=2**)* or both ends *(**n=3**)* a for case of ***s1*** = "" and ***s2*** = "", at condition that truncating is done onto ***m*** depth. Whereas in a case of the ***s1*** and ***s2*** arguments different from empty string instead of truncatings the corresponding insertings of strings ***s1*** *(at the left)* and ***s2*** *(on the right)* are done. Thus, the arguments ***s1*** and ***s2*** – two string arguments for processing of the ends of the initial *S* string at the left and on the right accordingly are defined. In addition, in a case of *S* = "" or *s* = "" the procedure call returns the *S* string; at that, a single character or their string can act as the *s* argument. The fragment below represents source code of the ***StringTrim3*** procedure along with typical example of its application.

```
In[7]:= StringTrim3[S_String, s_String, s1_String, s2_String,
                              n_Integer, m_/; MemberQ[{1, 2, 3}, m]] :=
                                   Module[{a = S, b, c = "", p = 1, t = 1, h},
    If[S == "" || s == "", S, Do[b = StringPosition[a, s];
    If[b == {}, Break[], a = StringReplacePart[a, "",
    If[m == 1, {If[b[[1]][[1]] == 1, p++; b[[1]], Nothing]},
    If[m == 2, {If[b[[-1]][[2]] == StringLength[a], t++; b[[-1]],
         Nothing]}, {If[b[[1]][[1]] == 1, p++; b[[1]], Nothing],
   If[b[[-1]][[2]] == StringLength[a], t++; b[[-1]], Nothing]}]]]];
   If[a == c, Break[], 6]; c = a, {j, 1, n}]; h = {p, t} - {1, 1};
   If[m == 1, StringRepeat[s1, h[[1]]] <> c,
   If[m == 2, c <> StringRepeat[s2, h[[2]]],
     StringRepeat[s1, h[[1]]] <> c <> StringRepeat[s2, h[[2]]]]]]]]

In[8]:= StringTrim3["dd1dd1ddaabcddd1d1dd1dd1dd1dd1dd1",
                                         "dd1", "avz", "agn", 3, 3]
Out[8]= "avzavzddaabcddd1d1dd1dd1agnagnagn"
```

Thus, by varying of values of the actual arguments {*s, s1, s2, n, m*}, it is possible to processing of the ends of arbitrary strings in a rather wide range.

The call ***SequenceCases***[*x, y*] of the built-in function returns the list of all sublists in a *x* list that match a sequence pattern *y*. In addition, the default option ***Overlaps -> False*** is assumed, therefore the ***SequenceCases*** call returns only sublists which do not overlap. In addition to the function the following procedure is presented as a rather useful tool. The call ***SequenceCases1***[*x,y*] as a whole returns the nested list whose two-element sublists have the following format {*n, h*} where *h* – the sublist of a list *x* which is formed by means of maximally admissible continuous concatenation of a list *y*, and *n* – an initial position in the list *x* of this sublist. At that, the procedure call ***SequenceCases1***[*x,y,z*] with *3rd* optional *z* argument – *an undefinite symbol* – through *z* returns the nested list whose the *1st* element defines the sublists maximal in length in format *{m, n, p}*, where *m* – the length of a sublist and *n, p* – its first and end position accordingly, whereas the *2nd* element determines the sublists minimal in length of the above format with obvious modification. In a case of erroneous situations the procedure call returns *$Failed* or empty list. The following fragment represents the source code of the procedure with typical examples of its application.

```
In[7]:= SequenceCases1[x_/; ListQ[x], y_/; ListQ[y], z___] :=
                    Module[{a = SequencePosition[x, y], b = 6, c, t},
                            If[Length[y] > Length[x], $Failed,
     While[! SameQ[a, b], a = Gather[a, #1[[2]] == #2[[1]] – 1 &];
             a = Map[Extract[#, {{1}, {–1}}] &, Map[Flatten, a]];
          b = Gather[a, #1[[2]] == #2[[1]] – 1 &];
          b = Map[Extract[#, {{1}, {–1}}] &, Map[Flatten, b]]];
          b = Map[{#[[1]], Part[x, #[[1]] ;; #[[–1]]]} &, b];
          If[{z} == {}, b, c = Map[{#[[1]], Length[#[[2]]]} &, b];
                         c = Map8[Max, Min, Map[#[[2]] &, c]];
 z = {Map[If[Set[t, Length[#[[2]]]] == c[[1]], {c[[1]], #[[1]], #[[1]] +
     t – 1}, Nothing] &, b], Map[If[Set[t, Length[#[[2]]]] == c[[2]],
                  {c[[2]], #[[1]], #[[1]] + t – 1}, Nothing] &, b]};
             z = Map[If[Length[#] == 1, #[[1]], #] &, z]; b]]]
In[8]:= SequenceCases1[{a, x, y, x, y, x, y, x, y, x, y, x, y, x, y, a, m,
                        n, x, y, b, c, x, y, x, y, h, x, y}, {x, y}]
Out[8]= {{2, {x, y, x, y, x, y, x, y, x, y, x, y, x, y}}, {19, {x, y}},
                                   {23, {x, y, x, y}}, {28, {x, y}}}
In[9]:= SequenceCases1[{a, x, y, x, y, x, y, x, y, x, y, x, y, x, y, a, m,
                     n, x, y, b, c, x, y, x, y, h, x, y}, {x, y}, g]; g
Out[9]= {{14, 2, 15}, {{2, 19, 20}, {2, 28, 29}}}
```

Additionally to the built-in ***StringReplace*** function and the four our procedures ***StringReplace1÷StringReplace4***, extending the first, the following procedure represents undoubted interest. The procedure call ***StringReplaceVars[S, r]*** returns the result of replacement in a string *S* of all occurrences of the left sides of a rule or their list *r* onto the right sides corresponding to them. In a case of absence of the above left sides entering in the *S* string the procedure call returns initial *S* string. Distinctive feature of the procedure is the fact, that it considers the left sides of *r* rules as separately located expressions in the *S* string, i.e. framed by the special characters. The procedure is of interest at processing of strings. The following fragment represents source code of the *StringReplaceVars* procedure with typical examples of its use.

```
In[7]:= StringReplaceVars[S_/; StringQ[S], r_/; RuleQ[r] | |
                          ListRulesQ[r]] := Module[{a = "(" <> S <> ")",
  L = Characters["`!@#%^&*(){}:\"\\/|<>?~-=+[];:'., 1234567890_"],
     R = Characters["`!@#%^&*(){}:\"\\/|<>?~-=+[];:'., _"], b, c,
                                      g = If[RuleQ[r], {r}, r]},
                        Do[b = StringPosition[a, g[[j]][[1]]];
     c = Select[b, MemberQ[L, StringTake[a, {#[[1]] - 1}]] &&
                 MemberQ[R, StringTake[a, {#[[2]] + 1}]] &];
     a = StringReplacePart[a, g[[j]][[2]], c], {j, 1, Length[g]}];
                                       StringTake[a, {2, -2}]]

In[8]:= StringReplaceVars["Sqrt[t*p] + t^t", "t" -> "(a + b)"]
Out[8]= "Sqrt[(a + b)*p] + (a + b)^(a + b)"
In[9]:= StringReplaceVars["(125 123 678 123 90)", {"123" -> "abc",
                                  "678" -> "mn", "90" -> "avz"}]
Out[9]= "(125 abc mn abc avz)"
```

The following procedure – a version of the *StringReplaceVars* procedure that is useful in the certain cases. The procedure call *StringReplaceVars1[S, x, y, r]* returns the result of replacement in a string *S* of all occurrences of the left sides of a rule or their list *r* to the right sides corresponding to them. In a case of absence of the above left sides entering in the *S* string the procedure call returns the initial *S* string. Distinctive feature of this procedure with respect to the procedure *StringReplaceVars* is the fact that it considers the left sides of *r* rules which are separately located expressions in the *S* string, i.e. they are framed on the left by the characters from a string *x* and are framed on the right by means of characters from a string *y*. The procedure is of certain interest at strings processing, in particular, at processing of definitions in string format of blocks and modules. The following fragment represents an example of the *StringReplaceVars1* procedure use.

```
In[3317]:= StringReplaceVars1["{a = \"ayb\", b = Sin[x],
    c = {\"a\", 77}, d = {\"a\", \"b\"}}", "{( 1234567890", " })",
                                    {"a" -> "m", "b" -> "n"}]
Out[3317]= "{m = \"ayb\", n = Sin[x], c = {\"a\", 77},
                                    d = {\"a\", \"b\"}}"
```

Earlier it was already noted that certain functional facilities of the ***Mathematica*** need to be reworked both for purpose of expansion of domain of application, and elimination of certain shortcomings. It to the full extent concerns such an important enough function whose call ***ToString*[*x*]** returns the result of the converting of an arbitrary expression ***x*** to the string format. The standard function incorrectly converts expressions into string format, that contain string subexpressions if to code them in the standard way. By this reason we defined procedure ***ToString1*** whose call ***ToString1*[*x*]** returns the result of correct converting of an arbitrary expression ***x*** in the string format. The fragment below represents source codes of the ***ToString1*** procedure and ***ToString1*** function with examples of their use. In a number of appendices these means is popular enough.

```
In[1]:= ToString1[x_] := Module[{a = "###", b = "", c, k = 1},
                                        Write[a, x]; Close[a];
                    For[k, k < Infinity, k++, c = Read[a, String];
       If[SameQ[c, EndOfFile], Return[DeleteFile[Close[a]]; b],
                                b = b <> StrDelEnds[c, " ", 1]]]]
In[2]:= K[x_] := Module[{a = "r", b = " = "}, a <> b <> ToString[x]]
In[3]:= ToString[Definition[K]]
Out[3]= "K[x_] := Module[{a = r, b =  = }, a<>b<>ToString[x]]"
In[4]:= ToExpression[%]
        ToExpression::sntx: Invalid syntax in or before "K[x_] :=
        Module[{a = r, b =  = }, a<>b<>ToString[x]]".
Out[4]= $Failed
In[5]:= ToString1[Definition[K]]
Out[5]= "K[x_] := Module[{a = \"r\", b = \" = \"},
                                StringJoin[a, b, ToString[x]]]"
In[6]:= ToExpression[%]
In[7]:= ToString1[x_] := {Write["#$#", x], Close["#$#"],
                  ReadString["#$#"], DeleteFile["#$#"]}[[-2]]
```

```
In[8]:= ToString1[Definition[K]]
Out[8]= "K[x_] := Module[{a = \"r\", b = \" = \"},
                                   StringJoin[a, b, ToString[x]]]"
In[9]:= ToString2[x_] := Module[{a},
If[ListQ[x], SetAttributes[ToString1, Listable]; a = ToString1[x];
        ClearAttributes[ToString1, Listable]; a, ToString1[x]]]
In[10]:= ToString2[{{77, 7}, {4, {a, b, {x, y}, c}, 5}, {30, 23}}]
Out[10]= {{"77", "7"}, {"4", {"a", "b", {"x", "y"}, "c"}, "5"}, {"30", "23"}}
In[11]:= ToString5[x_] := Module[{a, b, c, d}, a[b_] := x;
  c = Definition1[a]; d = Flatten[StringPosition[c, " := ", 1]][[-1]];
                                          StringTake[c, {d + 1, -1}]]
In[12]:= ToString5[{{a, b, "c", "d + h"}, "m", "p + d"}]
Out[12]= "{{a, b, \"c\", \"d + h\"}, \"m\", \"p + d\"}"
In[13]:= ToString1[{{a, b, "c", "d + h"}, "m", "p + d"}]
Out[13]= "{{a, b, \"c\", \"d + h\"}, \"m\", \"p + d\"}"
In[26]:= {a, b} = {72, 77};
In[27]:= ToString6[x_] := {Save["#", "a"], ClearAll["a"],
                         a = Unique["$"], a[t_] := x, a = Definition1[a],
  StringTake[a, {Flatten[StringPosition[a, " := ", 1]][[-1]] + 1, -1}],
                                      {Get["#"], DeleteFile["#"]}}[[-2]]
In[28]:= ToString6[{{c, d, "c", "d + h"}, "m", "p + d", "m/n"}]
Out[28]= "{{c, d, \"c\", \"d + h\"}, \"m\", \"p + d\", \"m/n\"}"
In[29]:= ToString1[{{c, d, "c", "d + h"}, "m", "p + d", "m/n"}]
Out[29]= "{{c, d, \"c\", \"d + h\"}, \"m\", \"p + d\", \"m/n\"}"
In[30]:= {a, b}
Out[30]= {72, 77}
In[46]:= Unique3[x_, n_] :=
                          Module[{a = Characters[ToString[x]], b},
b = Map[StringJoin, {Select[a, LetterQ[#] &], Select[a, DigitQ[#] &]}];
     ToExpression[b[[1]] <> ToString[ToExpression[b[[2]]] - n]]]
In[47]:= Unique3[Unique["avz"], 7]
Out[47]= avz204
In[48]:= ToString7[x_] := {Unique3[Unique["g"], 0][t_] := x;
  Unique3[Unique["g"], 0] = Definition1[Unique3[Unique["g"], 0]];
                 StringTake[Definition1[Unique3[Unique["g"], 3]],
   {Flatten[StringPosition[Definition1[Unique3[Unique["g"], 4]],
                                     " := ", 1]][[-1]] + 1, -1}]}[[1]]
```

```
In[49]:= ToString7[{{c, d, "c", "d + h"}, "m", "p + d", "m/n"}]
Out[49]= "{{c, d, \"c\", \"d + h\"}, \"m\", \"p + d\", \"m/n\"}"
In[50]:= ToString1[{{c, d, "c", "d + h"}, "m", "p + d", "m/n"}]
Out[50]= "{{c, d, \"c\", \"d + h\"}, \"m\", \"p + d\", \"m/n\"}"
```

Immediate application of the ***ToString1*** procedure allows to simplify rather significantly the programming of a lot of tasks. In addition, examples of the previous fragment rather visually illustrate application of both means on the concrete example which emphases the advantages of our procedure. Whereas the ***ToString2*** procedure expands the previous procedure onto lists of any level of nesting. So, the call ***ToString2[x]*** on an argument ***x,*** different from list is equivalent to the call ***ToString1[x],*** while on a list ***x*** is equivalent to the procedure call ***ToString1[x]*** that is endowed with the *Listable* attribute. The call ***ToString3[j]*** serves for converting of an expression ***j*** into the string *InputForm* form. The function has a number of rather useful appendices. Whereas the call ***ToString4[x]*** is analogous to the call ***ToString1[x]*** if ***x*** is a symbol, otherwise string \"(\" **<>** ***ToString1[x]*** **<>** \")\" will be returned. At last, the ***ToString5*** procedure is a certain functional analogue of the ***ToString1*** procedure whose source code is based on a different algorithm that does not use the file access. While the ***ToString6*** function is a functional analogue of the ***ToString5*** procedure but with using of the file access. Meanwhile, using a procedure whose call ***Unique3[Unique[x], n]*** returns the name of a variable *unique* to the current session and which was earlier generated by a ***Unique[x]*** call chain ***n*** steps before the current time *(the **x** argument is either a letter or a string from them in string format)* it is possible to program the ***ToString7*** function in form of the list which is equivalent to the above ***ToString1*** procedure and does not use the file access. With source codes of the above **7** tools with examples of their application the interested reader can partially familiarize above and fully in [8,10-16]. Note, that the tools ***StrStr, ToString1 ÷ ToString7*** are rather useful enough at processing of expressions in the string format.

A number of the important problems dealing with strings processing do the ***SubsString*** procedure as a rather useful tool, whose call ***SubsString*[*s*, {*a*, *b*, *c*,... }]** returns the list of substrings of a string ***s*** which are limited by substrings **{*a*, *b*, *c*,... }**, whereas the procedure call ***SubsString*[*s*, {*a*, *b*, *c*, *d*, ... }, *p*]** with the third optional ***p*** argument – *a pure function in short format* – returns the list of substrings of the ***s*** string which are limited by substrings **{*a*, *b*, *c*, ... }**, meeting the condition defined by a pure ***p*** function.

Furthermore, the procedure call ***SubsString*[*s*, {*a*, *b*, *c*, ... }, *p*]** with the third optional ***p*** argument – *any expression different from pure function* – returns the list of substrings limited by substrings **{*a*, *b*, *c*, ... }**, with removed prefixes and suffixes **{*a*, *b*, *c*, *d*,... }[[1]]** and **{*a*, *b*, *c*, *d*,... }[[–1]]** accordingly. In absence in the string ***s*** of at least one of substrings **{*a*, *b*, *c*, *d*,... }** the procedure call returns the empty list. The following fragment represents source code of the procedure with typical examples of its application.

```
In[80]:= SubsString[s_ /; StringQ[s], y_ /; ListQ[y], pf___] :=
                                   Module[{a = "", b, c, k = 1},
          If[Set[c, Length[y]] < 2, s, b = Map[ToString1, y];
  While[k <= c – 1, a = a <> b[[k]] <> "~~ Shortest[__] ~~ "; k++];
        a = a <> b[[–1]]; b = StringCases[s, ToExpression[a]];
                If[{pf} != {} && PureFuncQ[pf], Select[b, pf],
     If[{pf} != {}, Map[StringTake[#, {StringLength[y[[1]]] + 1,
  –StringLength[y[[–1]]] – 1}] &, b], Select[b, StringQ[#] &]]]]]
In[81]:= SubsString["adfgbffgbavzgagngbArtggbKgrg",
                              {"b", "g"}, StringFreeQ[#, "f"] &]
Out[81]= {"bavzg", "bArtg", "bKg"}
In[82]:= SubsString["abcxx7xxx42345abcyy7yyy42345",
                                             {"ab", "42"}, 590]
Out[82]= {"cxx7xxx", "cyy7yyy"}
```

On the other hand, the ***SubsString1*** procedure is an useful enough ***SubsString*** procedure extension, being of interest at the programming of the problems connected with processing of the strings too. The procedure call ***SubsString1*[*s*, *y*, *f*, *t*]** returns the list of substrings of a string ***s*** that are limited by the substrings of a list ***y***; at that, if a testing pure function acts as ***f*** argument, the returned list will contain only the substrings satisfying this test. At that, at ***t* = *1*** the returned substrings are limited to ultra substrings of the *y* list, whereas at ***t* = *0*** substrings are returned without the limiting ultra substrings of the *y* list. At that, in the presence of the *5th* optional ***r*** argument – *any expression* – search of substrings in the ***s*** string is done from right to left, that as a whole simplifies algorithms of *search* of the required substrings. With source code of the ***SubsString1*** procedure and examples of its use the interested reader can familiarize in [8,9,14-16].

For operating with strings the ***SubsDel*** procedure is a quite certain interest whose call ***SubsDel*[*S*, *x*, *y*, *p*]** returns the result of removal from a string ***S*** of all sub-strings that are limited on the right *(at the left)* by a sub-string ***x*** and at the left *(on the right)* by the first met symbol in string format from the ***y*** list; in addition, search of ***y*** symbol is done to the left *(**p=-1**)* or to the right *(**p=1**)*. In addition, the deleted sub-strings will contain a sub-string ***x*** since one end and the first symbol met from ***y*** since other end. Moreover, if in the course of search the symbols from the ***y*** list weren't found until end of the ***S*** string, the rest of initial ***S*** string is removed. Fragment represents source code of the procedure ***SubsDel*** with typical example of its application [8,16].

```
In[2321]:= SubsDel[S_ /; StringQ[S], x_ /; StringQ[x],
   y_ /; ListQ[y] && AllTrue[Map[StringQ, y], TrueQ] &&
    Plus[Sequences[Map[StringLength, y]]] == Length[y],
           p_ /; MemberQ[{-1, 1}, p]] := Module[{b, c = x, d,
                                   h = StringLength[S], k},
 If[StringFreeQ[S, x], Return[S], b = StringPosition[S, x][[1]]];
 For[k = If[p == 1, b[[2]] + 1, b[[1]] - 1], If[p == 1, k <= h, k >= 1],
               If[p == 1, k++, k--], d = StringTake[S, {k, k}];
     If[MemberQ[y, d] | | If[p == 1, k == 1, k == h], Break[],
               If[p == 1, c = c <> d, c = d <> c]; Continue[]]];
                                   StringReplace[S, c -> ""]]
In[2322]:= SubsDel["12345avz6789", "avz", {"8", "5"}, 1]
Out[2322]= "1234589"
```

While the procedure call ***SubDelStr*[*x*, *t*]** provides removal from a string ***x*** of all sub-strings which are limited by numbers of the positions set by a list ***t*** of the *ListList* type from 2–element sublists. On incorrect tuples of actual arguments the procedure call is returned unevaluated. The following fragment represents source code of the procedure and an example of its application.

```
In[28]:= SubDelStr[x_ /; StringQ[x], t_ /; ListListQ[t]] :=
            Module[{k = 1, a = {}}, If[! t == Select[t, ListQ[#] &&
  Length[#] == 2 &] | | t[[-1]][[2]] > StringLength[x] | | t[[1]][[1]] < 1,
                                Return[Defer[SubDelStr[x, t]]],
  For[k, k <= Length[t], k++,AppendTo[a, StringTake[x, t[[k]]] -> ""]];
                                             StringReplace[x, a]]]

In[29]:= SubDelStr["123456789abcdfdh", {{3, 5}, {7, 8}, {10, 12}}]
Out[29]= "1269dfdh"
```

<u>Replacements and extractions in strings.</u> In a number of problems of strings processing, there is a need of replacement not simply of substrings but substrings limited by the certain substrings. The procedure solves one of such problems, its call ***StringReplaceS*[*S*, *s1*, *s2*]** returns the result of substitution into a ***S*** string instead of entries into it of substrings ***s1*** limited by ***"x"*** strings on the left and on the right from the specified lists ***L*** and ***R*** respectively, by ***s2*** substrings ***(StringLength*["x"]=1);** in a case of absence of such entries the procedure call returns the ***S*** string. The following fragment represents source code of the procedure ***StringReplaceS*** with an example of its application.

```
In[3822]:= StringReplaceS[S_ /; StringQ[S], s1_ /; StringQ[s1],
              s2_ /; StringQ[s2]] := Module[{a = StringLength[S],
  L = Characters["`!@#%^&*(){}:\"\\/|<>?~-=+[];:'., 1234567890"],
  R = Characters["`!@#%^&*(){}:\"\\/|<>?~=+[];:'., "], c = {}, k = 1,
                                    p, b = StringPosition[S, s1]},
                 If[b == {}, S, While[k <= Length[b], p = b[[k]];
            If[Quiet[(p[[1]] == 1 && p[[2]] == a) | | (p[[1]] == 1 &&
             MemberQ[R, StringTake[S, {p[[2]] + 1, p[[2]] + 1}]]) | |
            (MemberQ[L, StringTake[S, {p[[1]] - 1, p[[1]] - 1}]] &&
             MemberQ[R, StringTake[S, {p[[2]] + 1, p[[2]] + 1}]]) | |
(p[[2]] == a && MemberQ[L, StringTake[S, {p[[1]] - 1, p[[1]] - 1}]])],
              c = Append[c, p]]; k++]; StringReplacePart[S, s2, c]]]

In[3823]:= S = "abc& c + bd6abc[abc] - abc77*xyz^abc&78";
                          StringReplaceS[S, "abc", "xyz"]
```

```
Out[3823]= "xyz& c + bd6xyz[xyz] – abc77*xyz^xyz&78"
```

The above procedure, in particular, is a rather useful tool at processing of definitions of blocks and modules in respect of the operating with their formal arguments and local variables [14].

In a number of cases at strings processing it is necessary to extract from them the substrings limited by the symbol {"}, i.e. ***"strings in strings"***. This problem is solved by the procedure, whose call ***StrFromStr[x]*** returns the list of such substrings that are in a string ***x;*** otherwise, the call ***StrFromStr[x]*** returns the empty list, i.e. {}. The fragment below represents source code of the procedure along with a typical example of its application.

```
In[11]:= StrFromStr[x_String] := Module[{a = "\"", b, c = {}, k = 1},
          b = DeleteDuplicates[Flatten[StringPosition[x, a]]];
                      For[k, k <= Length[b] – 1, k++,
  AppendTo[c, ToExpression[StringTake[x, {b[[k]], b[[k + 1]]}]]];
                                              k = k + 1]; c]
In[12]:= StrFromStr["12345\"678abc\"xyz\"50090\"mnph"]
Out[12]= {"678abc", "50090"}
```

To the above procedure an useful ***UniformString*** function adjoins. The strings can contain the substrings bounded by "\"" in particular the *cdf/nb*-files in the string format. To make such strings by uniform, the simple function ***UniformString*** is used. The call ***UniformString[x]*** returns a string ***x*** in the *uniform* form, whereas the call ***UniformString[x, y]***, where ***y*** is an expression returns the list of substrings of the ***x*** string which are bounded by **"\""**. The following fragment represents source code of the ***UniformString*** function with examples of its application.

```
In[4]:= UniformString[x_/; StringQ[x], y___] :=
                      If[{y} == {}, StringReplace[x, "\"" -> ""],
                         Map[StringReplace[#, "\"" -> ""] &,
                  StringCases[x, Shortest["\"" ~~ __ ~~ "\""]]]]
In[5]:= UniformString["{\"ClearValues\", \"::\", \"usage\"}"]
Out[5]= "{ClearValues, ::, usage}"
In[6]:= UniformString["{\"ClearValues\", \"::\", \"usage\"}", 7]
Out[6]= {"ClearValues", "::", "usage"}
```

The above function is a rather useful tool at processing of

the string representation of *cdf/nb*–files which is based on their internal formats [14,22]. Unlike standard ***StringSplit*** function, the call ***StringSplit1[x, y]*** performs semantic splitting of a string ***x*** by symbol ***y*** onto elements of the returned list. The semantics is reduced to the point that in the returned list only substrings of the ***x*** string which contain the correct expressions are placed; in a case of lack of such substrings the procedure call returns the empty list. The ***StringSplit1*** procedure appears as a rather useful tool, in particular at programming of tools of processing of the headings of blocks, functions and modules. The comparative analysis of the ***StringSplit*** and ***StringSplit1*** tools speaks well for that. Fragment below represents source code of the ***StringSplit1*** procedure along with typical examples of its application.

```
In[7]:= StringSplit1[x_ /; StringQ[x], y_ /; StringQ[y] ||
                                          StringLength[y] == 1] :=
     Module[{a = StringSplit[x, y], b, c = {}, d, p, k = 1, j = 1},
    d = Length[a]; Label[G]; For[k = j, k <= d, k++, p = a[[k]];
  If[! SameQ[Quiet[ToExpression[p]], $Failed], AppendTo[c, p],
    b = a[[k]]; For[j = k, j <= d - 1, j++, b = b <> y <> a[[j + 1]];
  If[! SameQ[Quiet[ToExpression[b]], $Failed], AppendTo[c, b];
                              Goto[G], Null]]]]; Map[StringTrim, c]]

In[8]:= StringSplit1["x_String, y_Integer, z_/; FreeQ[{1, 2, 3, 4}, z]
||OddQ[z], h_, s_String, c_/; StringQ[c]||StringLength[c] == 1", ","]
Out[8]= {"x_String", "y_Integer", "z_/; FreeQ[{1, 2, 3, 4}, z] ||
OddQ[z]", "h_", "s_String", "c_ /; StringQ[c]||StringLength[c] == 1"}
```

<u>Substrings processing in strings.</u> At substrings processing in strings is often need of check of existence fact of substrings *overlaping* that entere to the strings. The call ***SubStrOverlapQ[x,y]*** returns *True,* if a string ***x*** contains overlapping substrings ***y*** or substrings from ***x*** matching the general string expression ***y***, and *False* otherwise. While the call ***SubStrOverlapQ[x, y, z]*** through optional ***z*** argument – *an indefinite symbol* – additionally returns the list of consecutive quantities of overlapings of the ***y*** sublist in the ***x*** string. The following fragment represents source code of the function with typical examples of its application.

```
In[7]:= SubStrOverlapQ[x_ /; StringQ[x], y_, z___] :=
```

```
MemberQ[{If[{z} != {} && NullQ[z], z = {}, 77],
    Map[If[Length[#] == 1, True,
  If[! NullQ[z], Quiet[AppendTo[z, Length[#]]], 78]; False] &,
    Split[StringPosition[x, y],
  MemberQ[Range[#1[[1]] + 1, #1[[2]]], #2[[1]]] &]]}[[2]], False]
In[8]:= {SubStrOverlapQ["dd1dd1ddaaaabcdd1d1dd1dd1dd1\
    dd1aaaaaadd1", "aa", g1], g1}
Out[8]= {True, {3, 5}}
In[9]:= {SubStrOverlapQ["AAABBBBBAABABBBBCCCBAA\
    AAAA", x_ ~~ x_, g2], g2}
Out[9]= {True, {2, 4, 3, 2, 5}}
```

The procedure ***SubStrSymbolParity*** represents undoubted interest at processing of definitions of functions or procedures given in the string format. The call ***SubStrSymbolParity***[*x,y,z,d*] with four arguments returns the list of substrings of a string ***x*** that are limited by one-character strings ***y, z*** *(**y ≠ z**);* in addition, *search* of such substrings in the string ***x*** is done from left to right *(**d = 0**)*, and from right to left *(**d = 1**)*. Whereas the procedure call ***SubStrSymbolParity***[*x,y,z,d,t*] with the 5th optional argument – *a positive number **t>0*** – provides search in a substring of ***x*** which is limited by a position ***t*** and the end of ***x*** string at ***d = 0***, and by the beginning of ***x*** string and ***t*** at ***d = 1***. In a case of receiving of inadmissible arguments the call is returned unevaluated, while at impossibility of extraction of demanded substrings the call returns $*Failed*. This procedure is an useful tool, in particular, at solution of tasks of extraction from definitions of procedures of the list of local variables, headings, etc. The following fragment represents source code of the ***SubStrSymbolParity*** procedure with typical examples of its application.

```
In[5]:= SubStrSymbolParity[x_ /; StringQ[x], y_ /; CharacterQ[y],
  z_ /; CharacterQ[z], d_ /; MemberQ[{0, 1}, d], t___ /; t == {} ||
    PosIntQ[{t}[[1]]]] :=
  Module[{a, b = {}, c = {y, z}, k = 1, j, f, m = 1, n = 0, p, h},
If[{t} == {}, f = x, f = StringTake[x,
If[d == 0, {t, StringLength[x]}, {1, t}]]];
If[Map10[StringFreeQ, f, c] != {False, False} || y == z, Return[],
    a = StringPosition[f, If[d == 0, c[[1]], c[[2]]]]];
```

```
For[k, k <= Length[a], k++,
j = If[d == 0, a[[k]][[1]] + 1, a[[k]][[2]] - 1];
h = If[d == 0, y, z]; While[m != n,
p = Quiet[Check[StringTake[f, {j, j}], Return[$Failed]]];
If[p == y, If[d == 0, m++, n++];
If[d == 0, h = h <> p, h = p <> h], If[p == z, If[d == 0, n++, m++];
If[d == 0, h = h <> p, h = p <> h],
If[d == 0, h = h <> p, h = p <> h]]];
If[d == 0, j++, j--]]; AppendTo[b, h]; m = 1; n = 0; h = ""]; b]
In[6]:= SubStrSymbolParity["123{abcdf}7{ran}8{ian}9", "{", "}", 0]
Out[6]= {"{abcdf}", "{ran}", "{ian}"}
In[7]:= SubStrSymbolParity["12{abf}6{ran}8{ian}9", "{", "}", 1, 25]
Out[7]= {"{abf}", "{rans}"}
```

Meantime, in many cases it is possible to use a simpler and reactive version of the above procedure, whose procedure call ***SubStrSymbolParity1****[x, y, z]* with three arguments returns the list of substrings of a string *x* that are limited by one-character strings *{y,z} (y≠z);* in addition, search of such substrings is done from left to right. In the absence of the required substrings the procedure call returns the empty list, i.e. {}. A simple procedure is an useful enough modification of the ***SubStrSymbolParity1*** procedure; its call ***StrSymbParity****[S,s,x,y]* returns the list whose elements are substrings of a string ***S*** which have format ***s1w*** on condition of parity of the minimum number of entries into a ***w*** substring of symbols ***x, y*** *(x≠y)*. In the lack of such substrings or identity of symbols *x, y,* the call returns the empty list [16]. The ***SubStrSymbolParity, SubStrSymbolParity1*** and ***StrSymbParity*** procedures are rather useful tools, for instance, at processing of definitions of modules and blocks given in string format. These procedures are used by a number of tools of our ***MathToolBox*** package [8-12,15,16].

The procedure below is a rather useful tool for ensuring of converting of strings of a certain structure into lists of strings. In particular, such problems arise at processing of arguments and local variables. The problem is solved a rather effectively by the ***StrToList*** procedure, providing converting of strings of the "*{xxxxxxxxx ... x}*" format into the list of strings received from a *"xxxxx ... x"* string parted by comma symbols. In absence in an initial string of both limiting symbols {"{", "}"} the string will be converted in list of symbols as a call ***Characters["xxx...x"]***. The next fragment presents source code of the ***StrToList*** procedure with examples of its application.

```
In[8]:= StrToList[x_/; StringQ[x]] := Module[{a, b = {}, c = {}, d,
    h, k = 1, j, y = If[StringTake[x, {1}] == "{" &&
    StringTake[x, {-1}] == "}", StringTake[x, {2, -2}], x]},
  a = DeleteDuplicates[Flatten[StringPosition[y, "="]] + 2];
  d = StringLength[y];
  If[a == {}, Map[StringTrim, StringSplit[y, ","]],
    While[k <= Length[a], c = ""; j = a[[k]];
      For[j, j <= d, j++, c = c <> StringTake[y, {j}];
        If[! SameQ[Quiet[ToExpression[c]], $Failed] &&
          (j == d | | StringTake[x, {j + 1}] == ","),
          AppendTo[b, c -> ToString[Unique[$g$]]]; Break[]]]; k++];
    h = Map[StringTrim, StringSplit[StringReplace[y, b], ","]];
    Map14[StringReplace, h, RevRules1[b]]]]
In[9]:= StrToList["Kr, a = 90, b = {x, y, z}, c = {n, m, {42, 47, 67}}"]
Out[9]= {"Kr", "a = 90", "b = {x, y, z}", "c = {n, m, {42, 47, 67}}"}
In[10]:= StrToList["{a = 500, b = 90, c = {m, n}}"]
Out[10]= {"a = 500", "b = 90", "c = {m, n}"}
```

The above procedure is intended for converting of strings of format "{*x...x*}" or "*x...x*" into the list of strings received from strings of the specified format which are parted by symbols "=" and/or comma. Fragment examples an quite visually illustrate the basic principle of performance of the procedure along with formats of the returned results. At last, the fragment uses quite simple and useful procedure, whose call ***RevRules*[*x*]** returns the rule or list of rules that are reverse to the rules defined by a *x* argument – a rule of form ***a* -> *b*** or their list [16]. The procedure can be also represented in the functional form, namely:

```
In[3327]:= RevRules1[x_/; RuleQ[x] | | ListQ[x] &&
  AllTrue[Map[RuleQ, x], TrueQ]] := Map[Rule[#[[2]], #[[1]]] &,
Flatten[{x}]][[If[Length[Flatten[{x}]] > 1, 1 ;; Length[Flatten[{x}]], 1]]]
In[3328]:= RevRules1[{a -> b, c -> d, n -> m}]
Out[3328]= {b -> a, d -> c, m -> n}
```

Note, that the ***RevRules1*** function is essentially used by the above ***StrToList*** procedure.

The following procedure is a rather useful means of strings processing in a case when it is required to identify in a string of occurrence of substrings of kind ***"abc...n"*** and ***"abc...np"***, ***p*** - a character. The procedure call ***SubsInString[x, y, z]*** returns ***0***, if substrings ***y*** and ***y<>z*** where ***y*** - a string and ***z*** - a character are absent in a string ***x; 1***, if ***x*** contains ***y*** and not contain ***y <> z; 2***, if ***x*** contains ***y <> z*** and not contain ***y***, and three otherwise, i.e. the ***x*** string contains both ***y*** and ***y <> z*** [8,9]. Whereas the procedure call ***CorrSubStrings[x, n, y]*** returns the list of substrings of string ***x*** that contain all formally correct expressions, at the same time, search is done beginning with ***n–th*** position of the ***x*** string from left to right if the third optional ***y*** argument is absent, and from right to left if the ***y*** argument – *any expression* – exists. Fragment represents source code of the ***CorrSubStrings*** procedure and an example of its typical application.

```
In[7]:= CorrSubStrings[x_ /; StringQ[x], n_ /; PosIntQ[n], y___] :=
                    Module[{a = {}, b = StringLength[x], c = ""},
      If[{y} != {}, Do[If[SyntaxQ[Set[c, StringTake[x, {j}] <> c]],
                              AppendTo[a, c], 7], {j, n, 1, -1}],
                 Do[If[SyntaxQ[Set[c, c <> StringTake[x, {j}]]],
                              AppendTo[a, c], 7], {j, n, b}]]; a]
In[8]:= CorrSubStrings["(a+b/x^2)/(c/x^3+d/y^2)+1/z^3", 29, 2]
Out[8]= {"3", "z^3", "1/z^3", "+1/z^3", "(c/x^3+d/y^2)+1/z^3",
                                     "(a+b/x^2)/(c/x^3+d/y^2)+1/z^3"}
```

In a number of cases there is a necessity of reducing to the set number of the quantity of entries into a string of its adjacent substrings. That problem is solved by the ***ReduceAdjacentStr*** procedure presented by the following fragment. The procedure call ***ReduceAdjacentStr[x, y, n]*** returns the string – the result of reducing to an quantity ***n ≥ 0*** of occurrences into a string ***x*** of its adjacent ***y*** substrings. If a string ***x*** not contain ***y*** substrings, then the call returns the initial ***x*** string; the call ***ReduceAdjacentStr[x, y, n, h]*** where ***h*** *– an arbitrary expression*, returns the above result on condition that at search of the ***y*** substrings in the ***x*** string the lowercase and uppercase letters are identified.

```
In[41]:= ReduceAdjacentStr[x_ /; StringQ[x], y_ /; StringQ[y],
                 n_ /; IntegerQ[n], z___] := Module[{a = {}, b = {},
   c = Append[StringPosition[x <> FromCharacterCode[0], y,
         IgnoreCase -> If[{z} != {}, True, False]], {0, 0}], h, k},
         If[c == {}, x, Do[If[c[[k]][[2]] + 1 == c[[k + 1]][[1]],
      b = Union[b, {c[[k]], c[[k + 1]]}], b = Union[b, {c[[k]]}]];
                 a = Union[a, {b}]; b = {}], {k, 1, Length[c] - 1}];
                         a = Select[a, Length[#] >= n &];
      a = Map[Quiet[Check[{#[[1]], #[[-1]]}, Nothing]] &,
         Map[Flatten, Map[#[[-Length[#] + n ;; -1]] &, a]]];
                         StringReplacePart[x, "", a]]]
In[42]:= ReduceAdjacentStr["abababcdcdxmnabmabab","ab",3]
Out[42]= "abababcdcdxmnabmabab"
```

In contrast to the ***LongestCommonSubsequence*** function the procedure call ***LongestCommonSubsequence1***[*x, y, J*] in a mode *IgnoreCase*->*J*∈{*True,False*} finds the *longest contiguous substrings* that are common to the strings ***x*** and ***y***. Whereas the procedure call ***LongestCommonSubsequence1***[*x,y,J,t*] additionally through an undefinite ***t*** variable returns the list of all *common contiguous* substrings. The procedure essentially uses the procedure whose call ***Intersection1***[*x,y,z,…,J*] returns the list of elements common to all lists of strings in the mode *IgnoreCase*->*J*∈{*True,False*}. The fragment below represents source codes of both procedures and typical examples of their application.

```
In[6]:= LongestCommonSubsequence1[x_ /; StringQ[x],
      y_ /; StringQ[y], Ig_ /; MemberQ[{False, True}, Ig], t___] :=
           Module[{a = Characters[x], b = Characters[y], c, d, f},
           f[z_, h_] := Map[If[StringFreeQ[h, #], Nothing, #] &,
                   Map[StringJoin[#] &, Subsets[z]][[2 ;; -1]]];
   c = Gather[d = Sort[If[Ig == True, Intersection1[f[a, x], f[b, y], Ig],
Intersection[f[a,x], f[b,y]]], StringLength[#1] <= StringLength[#2] &],
                 StringLength[#1] == StringLength[#2] &];
   If[{t} != {} && ! HowAct[t], t = d, Null]; c = If[c == {}, {}, c[[-1]]];
                   If[c == {}, {}, If[Length[c] == 1, c[[1]], c]]]
In[7]:= {LongestCommonSubsequence1["AaAaBaCBbBaCaccccC",
```

```
"CacCCbbbAaABaBa", False, gs], gs}
Out[7]= {{"AaA", "aBa", "Cac"}, {"a", "A", "b", "B", "c", "C", "aA",
  "Aa", "aB", "ac", "Ba", "Ca", "cC", "AaA", "aBa", "Cac"}}
In[8]:= {LongestCommonSubsequence1["Rans", "Ian", True, j], j}
Out[8]= {"an", {"a", "n", "an"}}
In[9]:= Intersection1[x__ /; AllTrue[Map[ListQ[#] &, {x}], TrueQ],
  Ig_ /; MemberQ[{False, True}, Ig]] :=
  Module[{b = Length[{x}], c = {}, d = {}},
  Do[AppendTo[c, Map[StringQ, {x}[[j]]]], {j, 1, b}];
  If[DeleteDuplicates[Flatten[c]] != {True}, $Failed,
  If[Ig == False, Intersection[x], Do[AppendTo[d,
  Map[{j, #, ToUpperCase[ToString[#]]} &, {x}[[j]]]], {j, 1, b}];
  c = Map[DeleteDuplicates,
  Gather[Flatten[Join[d], 1], #1[[3]] == #2[[3]] &]];
  c = Flatten[Select[c, Length[#] >= b &], 1];
  c = If[DeleteDuplicates[Map[#[[1]] &, c]] != Range[1, b], {},
  DeleteDuplicates[Map[#[[2]] &, c]]]]]]
In[10]:= Intersection1[{"AB", "XY", "cd", "Mn"}, {"ab", "cD", "MN",
  "pq", "mN"}, {"90", "mn", "Ag"}, {"500", "mn", "Av"}, True]
Out[10]= {"Mn", "MN", "mN", "mn"}
```

The ***LongestCommonSubsequence2*** procedure is a certain extension of the ***LongestCommonSubsequence1*** procedure for a case of a finite number of strings in which the search for longest common continuous substrings is done [8,11,14-16].

```
In[317]:= LongestCommonSubsequence2["ABxCDH", "ABxC",
  "ABxCDCABCdc", "xyzABXC", "xyzABxC", "mnpABxC", True]
Out[317]= {"ABxC", "ABXC"}
```

For work with strings the following procedure is a rather useful, whose call ***InsertN*[*S, L, n*]** returns the result of inserting into a string ***S*** after its positions from a list ***n*** of substrings from a list ***L;*** in a case ***n*** = {< ***1*** | ≥ ***StringLength*[*S*]**} a substring will be located before ***S*** string or in its end respectively. It is supposed that the actual arguments ***L*** and ***n*** may contain various number of elements, in such case the excess ***n*** elements are ignored. At that, processing of a string ***S*** is carried out concerning the list of positions for ***m*** insertions defined according to the relation ***m*** = ***DeleteDuplicates*[*Sort*[*n*]]**. The procedure call ***InsertN*[*S, L, n*]** with inadmissible arguments is returned as unevaluated. The procedure was used significantly in programming a number of ***MathToolBox*** package tools [16]. The next fragment represents source code of the procedure with examples of its application.

```
In[2220]:= InsertN[S_String, L_/; ListQ[L], n_/; ListQ[n] &&
                Length[n] == Length[Select[n, IntegerQ[#] &]]] :=
  Module[{a = Map[ToString, L], d = Characters[S], p, b, k = 1,
   c = FromCharacterCode[2], m = DeleteDuplicates[Sort[n]]},
        b = Map[c <> ToString[#] &, Range[1, Length[d]]];
          b = Riffle[d, b]; p = Min[Length[a], Length[m]];
         While[k <= p, If[m[[k]] < 1, PrependTo[b, a[[k]]],
             If[m[[k]] > Length[d], AppendTo[b, a[[k]]],
   b = ReplaceAll[b, c <> ToString[m[[k]]] -> a[[k]]]]]; k++];
                StringJoin[Select[b, ! SuffPref[#, c, 1] &]]]
In[2221]:= InsertN["123456789Rans_Ian", {Ag, Vs, Art, Kr},
                                              {6, 9, 3, 0, 3, 17}]
Out[2221]= "Ag123Vs456Art789KrRans_Ian"
In[2222]:= InsertN["123456789", {a, b, c, d, e, f, g, h, n, m},
                                              {4,2,3,0,17,9,18}]
Out[2222]= "a12b3c4d56789efg"
```

Contrary to the ***InsertN*** procedure the call of the procedure ***DelSubStr*[*S, L*]** provides removal from a string ***S*** of substrings, whose positions are set by a list ***L;*** the ***L*** list has nesting ***0*** or ***1,*** for example, {{3, 4}, {7}, {9}} or {1, 3, 5, 7, 9}, whereas the function call ***AddDelPosString*[*x, y, h, z*]** returns the result of truncation of a string ***x*** to the substring ***x*[[*1 ;; y*]]** if ***z*** – an arbitrary expression and ***x*[[*y ;; -1*]]** if {z} == {} with replacing of the deleted substring by a string ***h.*** In a case of an incorrect value ***y*** the call returns the initial ***x*** string or is returned unevaluated [16]. Both these tools are rather useful in a number of problems of strings processing of various structure and appointment.

The following procedure provides extraction from string of *continuous* substrings of length bigger than ***1.*** The procedure call ***ContinuousSubs*[*x*]** returns the nested list whose elements have format ***{s, {p11, p12},…,{pn1, pn2}}*** where ***s*** – a substring and ***{pj1, pj2}*** ***(j = 1..n)*** determine the first and last positions of copies of a continuous ***s*** substring that compose a string ***x.*** The procedure uses an auxiliary tool – the ***SplitIntegerList*** procedure whose call ***SplitIntegerList*[*x*]** returns the result of splitting of a strictly increasing ***x*** list of the *IntegerList* type into sublists consisting of strictly increasing tuples of integers. In addition, the procedure ***SplitIntegerList*** has other useful applications too [9,10-16].

```
In[6]:= ContinuousSubs[x_ /; StringQ[x]] := Module[{a},
    a = Select[DeleteDuplicates[Map[StringPosition[x, #] &,
                    Characters[x]]], Length[#] > 1 &];
        a = Map[DeleteDuplicates, Map[Flatten, a]];
                    a = Map[SplitIntegerList, a];
            a = Select[Flatten[a, 1], Length[#] > 1 &];
  a = Map[{StringTake[x, {#[[1]], #[[-1]]}], {#[[1]], #[[-1]]}} &, a];
      a = Gather[Sort[a, #[[1]] &], #1[[1]] === #2[[1]] &];
a = Map[If[Length[#] == 1, #[[1]], DeleteDuplicates[Flatten[#, 1]]] &, a];
                                        SortBy[a, First]]
In[7]:= ContinuousSubs["abbbssccchggxxx66xxggazzzaaabbbssz7"]
Out[7]= {{"66", {16, 17}}, {"aaa", {26, 28}}, {"bbb", {2, 4}, {29, 31}},
       {"ccc", {7,9}}, {"gg", {11,12}, {20,21}}, {"ss", {5, 6}, {32,33}},
       {"xx", {18, 19}}, {"xxx", {13, 15}}, {"zzz", {23, 25}}}
```

The procedure call ***SolidSubStrings*[*x*]** returns the nested list whose the first elements of **2**–element sublists define solid substrings of a string ***x*** which consist of identical characters in quantity **>** ***1***, while the second elements define their counts in the ***x*** string. In a case of lack of similar solid substrings the call returns the empty list, i.e. {}.

```
In[19]:= SolidSubStrings[x_ /; StringQ[x]] :=
Module[{a = DeleteDuplicates[Characters[x]], b, c={}, d=x, n=1},
              b = Map["[" <> # <> "-" <> # <> "]+" &, a];
 b = Map[Sort, Map[StringCases[x, RegularExpression[#]] &, b]];
   b = Reverse[Sort[DeleteDuplicates[Flatten[Map[Select[#,
                         StringLength[#] > 1 &] &, b]]]]];
                 Do[AppendTo[c, StringCount[d, b[[j]]]];
          d = StringReplace[d, b[[j]] -> ""], {j, 1, Length[b]}];
  Sort[Map[{#, c[[n++]]} &, b], OrderedQ[{#1[[1]], #2[[1]]}] &]]
In[20]:= SolidSubStrings["cccabaacdaammddddpphaaaaaccaaa"]
Out[20]= {{"aa", 2}, {"aaa", 1}, {"aaaaa", 1}, {"cc", 1}, {"ccc", 1},
          {"dddd", 1}, {"mm", 1}, {"pp", 1}}
```

In particular, the ***SubsStrLim*** procedure represents an quite certain interest for a number of appendices which significantly use procedure of extraction from the strings of substrings of an quite certain format. The next fragment represents source code of the ***SubsStrLim*** procedure and typical examples of its use.

```
In[1942]:= SubsStrLim[x_/; StringQ[x], y_/; StringQ[y] &&
StringLength[y] == 1, z_/; StringQ[z] && StringLength[z] == 1] :=
  Module[{a, b = x <> FromCharacterCode[6], c = y, d = {}, p, j,
   k = 1, n, h}, If[! StringFreeQ[b, y] &&
   ! StringFreeQ[b, z], a = StringPosition[b, y];
   n = Length[a]; For[k, k <= n, k++, p = a[[k]][[1]]; j = p;
   While[h = Quiet[StringTake[b, {j + 1}]]; h != z, c = c <> h; j++];
   c = c <> z; If[StringFreeQ[StringTake[c, {2, -2}], {y, z}],
   AppendTo[d, c]]; c = y]];
   Select[d, StringFreeQ[#, FromCharacterCode[6]] &]]

In[1944]:= SubsStrLim[DefOpt["SubsStrLim"], "{", "}"]
Out[1944]= {"{}", "{j + 1}", "{2, -2}", "{y, z}"}
In[1945]:= SubsStrLim[Definition2["DefOpt"][[1]], "{", "}"]
Out[1945]= {"{a = If[SymbolQ[x], If[SystemQ[x], b = \"Null\",
   ToString1[Definition[x]], \"Null\"]], b, c}"}
```

The call ***SubsStrLim[x, y, z]*** returns the list of substrings of a string ***x*** that are limited by symbols ***{y, z}*** provided that these symbols don't belong to these substrings, excepting their ends. In particular, the ***SubsStrLim*** procedure is a quite useful means at need of extracting from definitions of the functions, blocks or modules given in the string format of certain components that compose them which are limited by certain symbols, at times, significantly simplifying a number of procedures of processing of such definitions. Whereas the procedure call ***SubsStrLim1[x, y, z]*** which is an useful enough modification of the ***SubsStrLim*** procedure, returns list of substrings of ***x*** string that are limited by symbols ***{y, z}*** provided that these symbols or don't enter in substrings, excepting their ends, or along with their ends have identical number of entries of pairs ***{y, z}***, for example:

```
In[1947]:= SubsStrLim1["G[x_] := Block[{a = 7, b = 50, c = 900},
   (a^2 + b^3 + c^4)*x]", "{", "}"]
Out[1947]= {"{a = 7, b = 50, c = 900}"}
```

The next means are useful at work with string structures. The procedure call ***StringPat*[*x, y*]** returns the string expression formed by strings of a list ***x*** and objects {"_", "__", "___"}; the call returns ***x*** if ***x*** – a string. The procedure call ***StringCases1*[*x, y, z*]** returns the list of the substrings in a string ***x*** that match a string expression, created by the call ***StringPat*[*x, y*]**. While a function call ***StringFreeQ1*[*x, y, z*]** returns *True* if no substring in ***x*** string matches a string expression, created by the call ***StringPat*[*x, y*]**, and *False* otherwise. In the fragment below, source codes of the above tools with examples of their applications are presented.

```
In[87]:= StringPat[x_ /; StringQ[x] || ListStringQ[x],
          y_ /; MemberQ[{"_", "__", "___"}, y]]:= Module[{a = "", b},
               If[StringQ[x], x, b = Map[ToString1, x];
     ToExpression[StringJoin[Map[# <> "~~" <> y <> "~~" &,
                                        b[[1 ;; -2]]], b[[-1]]]]]]

In[88]:= StringPat[{"ab", "df", "k"}, "__"]
Out[88]= "ab" ~~ __ ~~ "df" ~~ __ ~~ "k"

In[89]:= StringFreeQ1[x_ /; StringQ[x], y_ /; StringQ[y] ||
           ListStringQ[y], z_ /; MemberQ[{"_", "__", "___"}, z]] :=
                                   If[StringQ[y], StringFreeQ[x, y],
                           If[StringCases1[x, y, z] == {}, True, False]]

In[90]:= StringFreeQ1["abcfghkaactabcfghkt", {"ab", "df", "k"}, "___"]
Out[90]= True

In[91]:= StringCases2[x_ /; StringQ[x], y_ /; ListQ[y] && y != {}] :=
                          Module[{a, b = "", c = Map[ToString, y]},
      Do[b = b <> ToString1[c[[k]]] <> "~~__~~", {k, 1, Length[c]}];
   a = ToExpression[StringTake[b, {1, -7}]]; StringCases[x, Shortest[a]]]

In[92]:= StringCases2["a1234b7890000c5a b ca1b2c3", {a, b, c}]
Out[92]= {"a1234b7890000c", "a b c", "a1b2c"}
```

Whereas the call ***StringCases2*[*x, y*]** returns a list of disjoint substrings in a string ***x*** that match the string expression of the format ***Shortest*[*j1*~~__~~*j2* ~~__~~... ~~__~~*jk*]**, where ***y*** = {*j1*, *j2*, ..., *jk*} and ***y*** is different from the empty list, i.e. {}. The above tools are essentially used by a number of means of the package ***MathToolBox***, enough frequently essentially improving the programming algorithms which deal with string expressions.

The following procedure along with independent interest appears as a rather useful tool, e.g., in a case of computer study of questions of the reproducibility of finite subconfigurations in **1**-dimensional *cellular automata (CA)* models. The procedure call ***StringEquiQ[x,y,n]*** returns *True* if strings ***x*** and ***y*** differ no more than in ***n*** positions, and *False* otherwise. At that, in the presence of the fifth optional ***z*** argument – *an undefinite symbol* – through it the message *"Strings lengths aren't equal"*, if lengths of strings ***x*** and ***y*** are different, or the nested list {{*n1*, {*x1*, *y1*}}, {*n2*, {*x2*, *y2*}}, ..., {*np*, {*xp*, *yp*}}} are returned whose **2**–element sublists define respectively numbers of positions *(nj)*, characters of a string ***x*** *(xj)* and characters of a string ***y*** *(yj)* which differ in ***nj*** positions *(j = 1..p)*. It must be kept in mind that the ***4th*** argument ***r*** defines the string comparison mode – lowercase and uppercase letters are considered as *different (r=True)*, or lowercase and uppercase letters are considered as equivalent *(r=False)*. The next fragment represents the source code of the ***StringEquiQ*** procedure with typical examples of its application.

```
In[7]:= StringEquiQ[x_ /; StringQ[x], y_ /; StringQ[y],
  n_ /; IntegerQ[n], r_: True, z___] := Module[{c = {}, d, m, p, x1, y1,
                                  a = StringLength[x], b = StringLength[y]},
                                   If[{z} != {} && ! HowAct[z], d = 77, Null];
                        If[r === True, x1 = x; y1 = y, x1 = ToLowerCase[x];
                                                         y1 = ToLowerCase[y]];
                                              If[x1 == y1, True, If[a != b,
       If[d == 77, z = "Strings are`t equal in lengths", Null]; False,
                                        {m, p} = Map[Characters, {x1, y1}];
          Do[If[m[[j]] != p[[j]], AppendTo[c, {j, {StringTake[x, {j}],
                                   StringTake[y, {j}]}}], Null], {j, 1, a}];
           If[d == 77, z = c, Null]; If[Length[c] > n, False, True]]]]]
In[8]:= StringEquiQ["Grsu_2018", "Grsu_2019", 2, False, v42]
Out[8]= True
In[9]:= v42
Out[9]= {{9, {"8", "9"}}}
In[10]:= StringEquiQ["Grsu_2019", "Grsu_4247", 2, False, g47]
Out[10]= False
In[11]:= g47
```

```
Out[11]= {{6, {"2", "4"}}, {7, {"0", "2"}}, {8, {"1", "4"}}, {9, {"9", "7"}}}
```

At this point, we conclude the problem related to processing of string expressions in the ***Mathematica*** whereas a rather large number of other useful enough tools of this purpose developed by us can be found in [4-16]. Our experience of use of the ***Maple*** and ***Mathematica*** for programming of tools for operating with string structures showed that standard tools of ***Maple*** by many essential indicators yield to the tools of the same type of ***Math***-language. For problems of this type the ***Math***-language appears simpler not only in connection with more developed tools, but also because the procedural and functional paradigm allows to use the mechanism of the pure functions. The item represents a number of tools expanding the built-in tools of system that are oriented on work with string structures. These and other means of this type are located in our package [16]. At that, their correct use assumes that this package is loaded into the current session, the need for which is due to the fact that many tools of package together with built-in means, make substantial use of the tools whose definitions are in the same package.

Expressions containing in strings. In a number of cases of expressions processing the problem of excretion of one or other type of expressions from strings is quite topical. In this relation a certain interest the ***ExprOfStr*** procedure represents, whose source code with examples of its use represents the following fragment. The procedure call ***ExprOfStr[w, n, m, L]*** returns the result of extraction from a string ***w*** limited by its ***n***-th position and the end, of the first correct expression provided that search is done on the left ***(m = -1)*** / on the right ***(m = 1)*** from the given position; at that, a symbol, next or previous behind the found expression must belong to a list ***L***. The call is returned in string format; in a case of the absence of a correct expression $*Failed* is returned while the procedure call on inadmissible arguments is returned unevaluated.

```
In[7]:= ExprOfStr[x_/; StringQ[x], n_/; IntegerQ[n] && n > 0,
   p_/; MemberQ[{-1, 1}, p], L_/; ListQ[L]] := Module[{a = "", b, k},
  If[n >= StringLength[x], Return[Defer[ExprOfStr[x,n,p,L]]], Null];
```

```
For[k = n, If[p == -1, k >= 1, k <= StringLength[x]],
If[p == -1, k--, k++], If[p == -1, a = StringTake[x, {k}] <> a,
a = a <> StringTake[x, {k}]]; If[! SyntaxQ[a], Null,
If[If[p == -1, k == 1, k == StringLength[x]] ||
MemberQ[L, Quiet[StringTake[x, If[p == -1, {k - 1}, {k + 1}]]]],
Return[a], Null]]]; $Failed]
In[8]:= ExprOfStr["12345;F[(a+b)/(c+d)]; A_2019", 7, 1, {"^", ";"}]
Out[8]= "F[(a+b)/(c+d)]"
```

The ***ExprOfStr1*** represents an useful enough modification of the previous procedure; its call ***ExprOfStr1[x, n, p]*** returns a substring of string ***x***, that is minimum on length and in that a boundary element is a symbol in ***n***–th position of a string ***x*** that contains a correct expression. At that, search of such substring is done from ***n***–th position to the right and until the end of the ***x*** string ***(p = 1)***, and from the left from ***n–th*** position of ***x*** string to the beginning of the string ***(p = –1)***. In a case of absence of such substring the call returns *$Failed,* while on inadmissible factual arguments the procedure call is returned unevaluated [10,16].

In a certain relation to the above procedures the ***ExtrExpr*** procedure adjoins, whose the call ***ExtrExpr[S, n, m]*** returns the omnifarious correct expressions in the string format which are contained in a substring of a string ***S*** limited by positions with numbers ***n*** and ***m***. In a case of absence of correct expressions the *empty* list is returned. The fragment below represents source code of the ***ExprOfStr*** procedure with an example of its use.

```
In[6]:= ExtrExpr[S_/; StringQ[S], n_/; IntegerQ[n],
m_/; IntegerQ[m]] := Module[{a = StringLength[S], b, c, h = {}, k, j},
If[! (1 <= m <= a && n <= m), {}, b = StringTake[S, {n, m}];
Do[Do[c = Quiet[StringTake[b, {j, m - n - k + 1}]];
If[ExpressionQ[c], AppendTo[h, c]; Break[], Null],
{k, 0, m - n + 1}], {j, 1, m - n}];
DeleteDuplicates[Select[Map[StringTrim2[#,
{"+", "-", " ", "_"}, 3] &, h], ! MemberQ[{"", " "}, #] &]]]]
In[7]:= ExtrExpr["z=(Sin[x*y]+Log[x])-F[x,y]; S[x_]:= x^2;", 4, 39]
Out[7]= {"Sin[x*y]+Log[x]", "in[x*y]+Log[x]", "n[x*y]+Log[x]",
"x*y", "y", "Log[x]", "og[x]", "g[x]", "x", "F[x,y]; S[x_]:= x^2",
```

```
"S[x_] := x^2", "x^2"}
```

Using procedures ***CorrSubStrings, RevRules, ExtrVarsOfStr, SubsInString, StringReplaceVars, ToStringRational*** [8,16], it is possible to offer one more tool of extraction from an expression of all formally correct subexpressions which are contained in it. The procedure call ***SubExprsOfExpr*[*x*]** returns the sorted list of every possible formally correct subexpressions of an expression ***x***. Meantime, if ***x*** expression contains no undefinite symbols, the procedure call returns the evaluated initial expression ***x***.

```
In[14]:= SubExprsOfExpr[x_] := Module[{b, c, c1, d = {}, h, f,
    p = 7000, a = StringReplace[ToStringRational[x], " " -> ""]},
    b = StringLength[a]; c = ExtrVarsOfStr[a, 1];
    If[c == {}, x, f = Select[c, ! StringFreeQ[a, # <> "["] &&
      StringFreeQ[a, # <> "[["] &];
    c1 = Map[# -> FromCharacterCode[p++] &, c];
    h = StringReplaceVars[a, c1];
    Do[AppendTo[d, CorrSubStrings[h, j]], {j, 1, b}];
    d = Map[StringTrim[#, ("+" | "-") ...] &, Flatten[d]];
    d = Map[StringReplaceVars[#, RevRules[c1]] &, d];
    Do[Set[d, Map[If[MemberQ[{0, 2}, SubsInString[#, f[[j]], "["]], #,
      Nothing] &, d]], {j, 1, Length[f]}];
    Sort[DeleteDuplicates[ToExpression[d]]]]]
In[15]:= SubExprsOfExpr[(a + bc)*Log[z]/(c + Sin[x])]
Out[15]= {a, bc, a + bc, c, x, z, Log[z], (a + bc)*Log[z], Sin[x],
    ((a + bc)*Log[z])/(c + Sin[x]), c + Sin[x]}
```

Three ***ExtrVarsOfStr ÷ ExtrVarsOfStr2*** procedures are of interest in extracting variables from strings. In particular, the procedure call ***ExtrVarsOfStr2*[*S, t*]** returns the sorted list of variables in the string format that managed to extract from a string ***S;*** at the absence of the similar variables the empty list, i.e. {} is returned. While the procedure call ***ExtrVarsOfStr2*[*S,t,x*]** with the third optional ***x*** argument – *the list of strings of length* **1** – returns the list of the variables of **S** on condition that at the above extracting, the elements from ***x*** list are not ignored. The following fragment represents source code of the ***ExtrVarsOfStr2*** procedure with typical examples of its application.

```
In[7]:= ExtrVarsOfStr2[S_/; StringQ[S], x___/; If[{x} == {}, True,
ListQ[x]]] := Module[{k, j, d = {}, p, a, q = Map[ToString, Range[0, 9]],
```

```
h = 1, c = "", L = Characters["`!@#%^&*(){}:\"\\/|<>?~-=+[];:'.,
1234567890_"], R = Characters["`!@#%^&*(){}:\"\\/|<>?~-=+[];:'., _"],
s = "," <> S <> ","}, a = StringLength[s];
  If[{x} == {}, 7, {L, R} = Map[Select[#, ! MemberQ[x, #] &] &, {L, R}]];
            Label[Gs]; For[k = h, k <= a, k++, p = StringTake[s, {k}];
                         If[! MemberQ[L, p], c = c <> p; j = k + 1;
                              While[j <= a, p = StringTake[s, {j}];
                   If[! MemberQ[R, p], c = c <> p, AppendTo[d, c];
                                   h = j; c = ""; Goto[Gs]]; j++]]];
              AppendTo[d, c]; d = Select[d, ! MemberQ[q, #] &];
  d = Select[Map[StringReplace[#, {"+" -> "", "-" -> "", "_" -> ","}] &,
          d], # != "" &]; d = Flatten[Select[d, ! StringFreeQ[s, #] &]];
  Sort[DeleteDuplicates[Flatten[Map[StringSplit[#, ", "] &, d]]]]]]
In[8]:= ExtrVarsOfStr2["(a*#1 + b*#2)/(c*#3 - i*#4) + j*#1*#4", {"#"}]
Out[8]= {"#1", "#2", "#3", "#4", "a", "b", "c", "i", "j"}
In[9]:= ExtrVarsOfStr2["(a*#1 + b*#2)/(c*#3 - d*#4) + m*#1*#4"]
Out[9]= {"a", "b", "c", "d", "m"}
```

The ***VarsInExpr*** procedure presents a rather useful version of the ***ExtrVarsOfStr ÷ ExtrVarsOfStr2*** procedures. Procedure call ***VarsInExpr[x]*** returns the sorted list of variables in string format, that managed to extract from an expression ***x;*** in a case of absence of such variables the empty list is returned. At that, it is supposed that the expression ***x*** can be encoded in the string format, i.e. in ***ToString[InputForm[x]].*** The fragment represents source code of the ***VarsInExpr*** procedure and examples of its use.

```
In[151]:= VarsInExpr[x_] :=
    Module[{a = StringReplace[ToStringRational[x], " " -> ""],
  b = Join[Range5[33 ;; 35, 37 ;; 47], Range[58, 64], Range[91, 96],
                                             Range[123, 126]]},
                   Sort[DeleteDuplicates[Select[StringSplit[a,
                          Map[FromCharacterCode[#] &, b]],
                                   SymbolQ[#] && # != "" &]]]]
In[152]:= VarsInExpr["(a + b)/(c + 590*d$) + Sin[c]*Cos[d + h]"]
Out[152]= {"a", "b", "c", "Cos", "d", "d$", "h", "Sin"}
In[153]:= VarsInExpr[(a + b/x^2)/Sin[x*y] + 1/z^3 + Log[y]]
Out[153]= {"a", "b", "Csc", "Log", "x", "y", "z"}
```

In general, the procedures ***ExtrVarsOfStr ÷ ExtrVarsOfStr2*** and ***VarsInExpr*** can be also rather useful for structural analysis of algebraical expressions. Whereas the ***SymbToExpr*** procedure applies symbols to specified sub-expressions located at certain levels of an expression ***x***. The procedure call ***SymbToExpr[x, d]*** returns the result of applying of symbols to ***n–th*** sub-elements located on ***m–th*** levels of an expression ***x***. The ***2nd*** argument ***d*** is a simple or nested list of format ***{{n,s1,n2,…,np},…,{r,sj,r1,…,rt}}***, where the ***1st*** element ***n*** of sublist ***{n,s1,n1,…,np}*** defines level of the expression ***x***, the ***2nd*** element ***s1*** defines an applied symbol, while its other elements ***{n1,…,np}*** define the positions numbers of subexpressions at this level. Procedure handles the erroneous situations conditioned by inadmissible levels, and positions of elements at them, printing appropriate messages. The fragment represents source code of the procedure and examples of its use.

```
In[6]:= SymbToExpr[x_, d_/; ListQ[d]] := Module[{agn, t = 0, res = x,
                                   h = If[NestListQ[d], d, {d}], k},
              Do[If[Level[x, {j}] != {}, t++, Break[]], {j, Infinity}];
                                     agn[y_, s_, n_, m_] := Module[{a},
  If[n > t, Print["Level number more than maximal " <> ToString[t]],
    If[Set[a, Cases[Level[y, {n}], Except[_Integer]]]; Length[a] < m,
    Print["Level " <> ToString[n] <> " no contain an element with
                                        number " <> ToString[m]],
          res = Replace[y, a[[m]] -> h[[j]][[2]] @@ {a[[m]]}, n]]]];
    Do[Do[agn[res, c, h[[j]][[1]], h[[j]][[k]]], {k, 3, Length[h[[j]]]}],
                                                 {j, Length[h]}]; res]
In[7]:= SymbToExpr[h + (x + y)/f[x, y^n]^g - m/n, {{4, s, 2, 3}, {2, h, 1, 2}}]
Out[7]= h - h[m]/n + (x + y)*h[f[x, s[y^n]]^-s[g]]
In[8]:= SymbToExpr[h + (x + y)/f[x, y^n]^g - m/n, {{4, S, 2, 3}, {2, V, 2, 8}}]
        "Level 2 no contain an element with number 8"
Out[8]= h + (x + y)*f[x, S[y^n]]^-S[g] - m*V[1/n]
In[9]:= SymbToExpr[h + (x + y)/f[x, y^n]^g – m/n, {{6, s, 3}, {5, T, 1, 2}}]
        "Level number more than maximal 5"
Out[9]= h - m/T[n] + f[x, T[y]^T[n]]^-g*(x + T[y])
```

In addition to the tools listed in this section, we have created a large number of other useful tools for strings processing, that can be found in [16]. The tools have proven their effectiveness in many applications.

3.5. *Mathematica tools for lists processing*

At programming of many problems the use not of separate expressions, but their sets made in the form ***lists*** is expedient. At such approach we can instead of calculations of the separate expressions to do the demanded operations as over lists in a whole – *unified objects* – and over their separate elements. Lists of various types represent important and one of the most often used structures in the ***Mathematica*** system.

The list is one of the underlying data structures supported by the ***Mathematica.*** The classic list structure has the following format, namely: ***List:=*** *{a, b, c, …, d}*, where as elements of ***List*** can be arbitrary expressions. When a list definition is calculated, its elements are calculated from left to right, remaining at their positions relative to the original list. Thus, in a list we have the possibility to pass the result of evaluation of an element to the following element of the list, accumulating an information in the last list element. In particular, list structures of the form {*a, b, c, …,* ***Test***}**[[–1]]** can act as test elements for formal arguments of blocks, functions, and modules, for example:

```
In[3333]:= A[x_/; {If[OddQ[x], Print["Odd number"],
                 Print["Even number"]], IntegerQ[x]}[[-1]]] := x^2
In[3334]:= A[77]
            Odd number
Out[3334]= 5929
```

In the meantime, mention should also be made of the list structure of form *{a; b; c; d; …; h}* along with the list structures with alternation of the delimiters {";", ","} of list elements which are of quite important too. The difference between this lists and the above list structure rather illustratively illustrates the next simple example:

```
In[2229]:= {a = b, b = c, c = d}
Out[2229]= {b, c, d}
In[2230]:= {a = b; b = c; c = d}
Out[2230]= {d}
In[2231]:= {a = b, b = c; c = d}
Out[2231]= {b, d}
```

```
In[2234]:= B[x_/; {h = x^3, If[OddQ[x], Print["Odd number"],
                 Print["Even number"]]; IntegerQ[x]}[[2]]] := x^2
In[2235]:= {B[78], h}
           Even number
Out[2235]= {6084, 474552}
```

The above considerations are quite transparent and do not require any clarifyings. Techniques represented in them are of some practical interest in programming of the objects headings and objects as a whole.

In the ***Mathematica*** many functions have *Listable* attribute saying that an operator, block, function, module ***F*** with *Listable* attribute are automatically applicable to each element of the list used respectively as their operand or argument. The call of the function ***ListableQ[x]*** returns *True* if a block, operator, function, module ***x*** has *Listable* attribute, and *False* otherwise [4,10-16]. At the formal level for a block, function and module ***F*** of arity ***1*** it is possible to note the following defining relation, namely:

Map[F, {a, b, c, d, ...}] ≡ {F[a], F[b], F[c], F[d], ...}

where in the left part the block, function and module ***F*** can be both with the *Listable* attribute, and without it whereas in the right part the existence of *Listable* attribute for block, function or module ***F*** is supposed. In addition, for blocks, functions and modules without the *Listable* attribute for receiving such effect the ***Map*** function is used. Meanwhile, for the nested lists, ***Map*** does not produce the desired result, as an example illustrates:

```
In[1529]:= Map[F, {a, b, {c, d, {m, n}}, t}]
Out[1529]= {F[a], F[b], F[{c, d, {m, n}}], F[t]}
```

Moreover, attributing the *Listable* attribute to the ***Map***, we not only do not solve the problem, but violate this function. On the other hand, a function extends the built-in function ***Scan*** onto lists. The call ***ScanList[x, y]*** evaluates ***x*** applied through each element of ***y*** *(see the source code and examples below):*

```
In[47]:= ScanList[x_, y_] := If[MemberQ[Attributes[x], Listable],
                 Map[x, y], SetAttributes[x, Listable]; {Map[x, y],
                                  ClearAttributes[x, Listable]}[[1]]]
In[48]:= ScanList[f, {a, b, {c, d, {m, n}}, t, {g, s}}]
```

```
Out[48]= {f[a], f[b], {f[c], f[d], {f[m], f[n]}}, f[t], {f[g], f[s]}}
In[49]:= x[t_] := N[Sin[t], 3]; ScanList[x, {42, 47, {67, 87, {6, 7}}, 3}]
Out[49]= {-0.917, 0.124, {-0.856, -0.822, {-0.279, 0.657}}, 0.141}
```

The problem is solved only by attributing of *Listable* attribute to ***F***, as the previous example illustrates. Using of *Listable* attribute allows to make processing of the nested lists, without breaking their internal structure. The procedure call ***ListProcessing[w, y]*** returns the list of the same internal structure as a list ***w*** whose elements are processed by means of an ***y*** function. A fragment below represents source code of the procedure with examples of its application.

```
In[2225]:= ListProcessing[x_/; ListQ[x], y_/; SystemQ[y] ||
                   ProcQ[y] || FunctionQ[y] || PureFuncQ[y]] :=
                   Module[{f = y, g}, g = Attributes[f]; Unprotect[f];
                        Attributes[f] = {}; SetAttributes[f, Listable];
                              If[PureFuncQ[f], f = Map[f[#] &, x],
    If[FreeQ[Attributes[y], Listable], SetAttributes[y, Listable];
                 f = y[x]; ClearAttributes[y, Listable], f = y[x]]]; f]
In[2226]:= x = {a, 7, d, c, {c, 5, s, {g, h, 8, p, d}, d}, 4, n};
                                            ListProcessing[x, #^3 &]
Out[2226]= {a^3, 343, d^3, c^3, {c^3, 125, s^3,
                    {g^3, h^3, 512, p^3, d^3}, d^3}, 64, n^3}
In[2227]:= ListProcessing[x, ToString]
Out[2227]= {"a", "7", "d", "c", {"c", "5", "s", {"g", "h", "8", "p", "d"},
                                                   "d"}, "4", "n"}
In[2228]:= gv[x_] := If[SymbolQ[x], gs, If[PrimeQ[x], s, x]];
                                            ListProcessing[x, gv]
Out[2228]= {gs, s, gs, {gs, s, gs, {gs, gs, 8, gs, gs}, gs}, 4, gs}
```

The procedure call ***ClusterSubLists[x]*** returns generally the nested list, whose **3**-element lists determine elements of a list ***x***, their positions and lengths of the sublists *(clusters)* that contain more than ***1*** identical element and that begin with this element. At the same time, the grouping of such sublists on base of their first element is made. In a case of lack of clusters in the ***x*** list the procedure call ***ClusterSubLists[x]*** returns the empty list, i.e. {}. The following fragment represents source code of the procedure ***ClusterSubLists*** with an example of its application.

```
In[3314]:= ClusterSubLists[x_/; ListQ[x]] :=
    Module[{a, b = {}, c, d, h = {}, g = {}, n = 1},
    a = Gather[Map[{#, n++} &, x], #1[[1]] == #2[[1]] &];
    a = Select[a, Length[#] > 1 &];
    Do[AppendTo[b, Map[#[[2]] &, a[[j]]]], {j, 1, Length[a]}];
    b = Map[Differences[#] &, b];
    Do[Do[If[b[[j]][[k]] == 1,
    g = Join[g, {a[[j]][[k]], a[[j]][[k + 1]]}], AppendTo[h, g]; g = {}],
    {k, 1, Length[b[[j]]]}]; AppendTo[h, g]; g = {}, {j, 1, Length[b]}];
    h = Map[If[# == {}, Nothing, DeleteDuplicates[#]] &,
    DeleteDuplicates[h]];
    ReduceLists[Map[ReduceLists, Gather[Map[Join[#[[1]],
    {Length[#]}] &, h], #1[[1]] === #2[[1]] &]]]]

In[3315]:= ClusterSubLists[{a, a, a, c, c, c, c, a, a, a, b, b, b, a, a, a,
    a, a, g, g, g, g, p, p, p, v, v, v, v, v, 77, 77, 77, 77, 77, 77, 77}]
Out[3315]= {{{a, 1, 3}, {a, 8, 3}, {a, 14, 5}}, {c, 4, 4}, {b, 11, 3}, {g, 19, 4},
    {p, 23, 3}, {v, 26, 5}, {77, 31, 7}}
```

In difference of standard ***Partition*** function the procedure ***PartitionCond***, supplementing its, allows to partition the list into sublists by its elements satisfying some testing function. The procedure call ***PartitionCond*[*x*, *y*]** returns the nested list consisting of sublists received by means of partition of a list ***x*** by its elements satisfying a testing ***y*** function. At the same time, these elements don't include in sublists. At absence in the ***x*** list of the separative elements an initial ***x*** list is returned. At that, at existing the third optional ***z*** argument – *an arbitrary expression* – the call ***PartitionCond*[*x*, *y*, *z*]** returns the above nested list on condition that the sequences of elements in its sublists will be limited by the ***z*** element. In addition, if the call contains four arguments and the fourth argument is ***1*** or **2** than the procedure call ***PartitionCond*[*x*, *y*, *z*, *h*= {*1* | 2}]** returns the above nested list on condition that the elements sequences in its sublists will be limited by the ***z*** element at the left *(**h** = **1**)* or at the right *(**h** = **2**)* accordingly, otherwise the procedure call is equivalent the call ***PartitionCond*[*x*, *y*]**. The fragment below represents the source code of the ***PartitionCond*** procedure with typical examples of its application [4-8,14-16].

```
In[2217]:= PartitionCond[x_ /; ListQ[x],
              y_ /; Quiet[ProcFuncBlQ[y, Unique["g"]]], z___] :=
                                          Module[{a, b, c, d},
   If[Select[x, y] == {}, x, If[{z} != {} && Length[{z}] > 1,
   If[{z}[[2]] == 1, c = {z}[[1]]; d = Nothing,
   If[{z}[[2]] == 2, c = Nothing; d = {z}[[1]], c = d = Nothing]],
   If[Length[{z}] == 1, c = d = {z}[[1]], c = d = Nothing]];
                                       a = {1, Length[x]}; b = {};
Do[AppendTo[a, If[(y) @@ {x[[j]]}, j, Nothing]], {j, 1, Length[x]}];
                                   a = Sort[DeleteDuplicates[a]];
Do[AppendTo[b, x[[a[[j]] ;; a[[j + 1]]]]], {j, 1, Length[a] - 1}];
b = ReplaceAll[Map[Map[If[(y) @@ {#}, Nothing, #] &, #1] &, b],
                                               {} -> Nothing]];
  Map[{a = #, Quiet[AppendTo[PrependTo[a, c], d]]}[[2]] &, b]]
In[2218]:= PartitionCond[{8, a, b, 3, 6, c, 7, d, h, 77, 72, d, s, 8, k,
                                     f, a, 9}, IntegerQ[#] &]
Out[2218]= {{a, b}, {c}, {d, h}, {d, s}, {k, f, a}}
In[2219]:= PartitionCond[{8, a, b, 3, 6, c, 7, d, h, 77, 72, d, s, 8, k,
                                  f, a, 9}, ! IntegerQ[#] &, gs]
Out[2219]= {{gs, 8, gs}, {gs, 3, 6, gs}, {gs, 7, gs}, {gs, 77, 72, gs},
                                   {gs, 8, gs}, {gs, 9, gs}}
```

The *Mathematica* at manipulation with the list structures has certain shortcomings among which impossibility of direct assignment to elements of a list of expressions is, for example:

```
In[36]:= {a, b, c, d, h, g, s, x, y, z}[[10]] = 590
... Set: {a,b,c,d,h,g,s,x,y,z} in the part assignment is not a symbol.
Out[36]= 590
```

In order to simplify the implementation of procedures that use similar direct assignments to the list elements, the following ***ListAssignP*** procedure is used, whose call ***ListAssignP[x, n, y]*** returns the updated value of a list ***x*** which is based on results of assignment of a value ***y*** or the list of values to ***n*** elements of the ***x*** list where ***n*** – one position or their list. Moreover, if the lists ***n*** and ***y*** have different lengths, their common minimum value is chosen. The ***ListAssignP*** procedure expands the functionality of the ***Mathematica,*** doing quite correct assignments to the list elements what the system fully doesn't provide. The ***ListAssign1*** procedure is a certain modification of the ***ListAssignP*** procedure its call is equivalent to the ***ListAssignP*** call. The source code of the ***ListAssignP*** procedure along with some examples of its use are represented below.

```
In[2138]:= ListAssignP[x_ /; ListQ[x], n_ /; PosIntQ[n] | |
                                              PosIntListQ[n], y_] :=
Module[{a = DeleteDuplicates[Flatten[{n}]], b = Flatten[{y}], c, k=1},
   If[a[[-1]] > Length[x], Return[Defer[ListAssignP[x, n, y]]],
                                    c = Min[Length[a], Length[b]]];
While[k <= c, Quiet[Check[ToExpression[ToString[x[[a[[k]]]]] <>
        " = " <> ToString1[If[ListQ[n], b[[k]], y]]], Null]]; k++];
                                      If[NestListQ1[x], x[[-1]], x]]
In[2139]:= ListAssignP[{x, y, z}, {1, 2, 3}, {42, 78, 2020}]
Out[2139]= {42, 78, 2020}
In[2140]:= Clear[x, y, z]; ListAssignP[{x, y, z}, 2, 590]
Out[2140]= {x, 590, z}
```

The following procedure carries out exchange of elements of a list that are determined by the pairs of positions. The call ***SwapInList[x,y]*** returns the exchange of elements of a list ***x*** that are determined by pairs of positions or their list ***y***. At the same time, if the ***x*** list is explicitly encoded at the procedure call, the updated list is returned, if the ***x*** is determined by a symbol *(that determines a list)* in the string format then along with returning of the updated list also value of the ***x*** symbol is updated in situ. The procedure processes the erroneous situation caused by the indication of non-existent positions in the ***x*** list with returning ***$Failed*** and the appropriate message. Note, it is recommended to consider a reception used for updating of the list in situ. The procedure is of a certain interest at the operating with lists. The fragment represents source code of the ***SwapInList*** procedure and examples of its use which rather visually illustrate the told.

```
In[716]:= SwapInList[x_ /; ListQ[x] | | StringQ[x] &&
ListQ[ToExpression[x]], y_ /; SimpleListQ[y] | | ListListQ[y] &&
   Length[y[[1]]] == 2] := Module[{a, b, c = ToExpression[x], d,
                                  h = If[SimpleListQ[y], {y}, y]},
d = Complement[DeleteDuplicates[Flatten[y]], Range[1, Length[c]]];
If[d != {}, Print["Positions " <> ToString[d] <> " are absent in list " <>
```

```
ToString[c]]; $Failed, Do[a = c[[h[[j]][[1]]]]; b = c[[h[[j]][[2]]]];
          c = ReplacePart[c, h[[j]][[1]] -> b];
          c = ReplacePart[c, h[[j]][[2]] -> a], {j, 1, Length[h]}];
     If[StringQ[x], ToExpression[x <> "=" <> ToString[c]], c]]]

In[717]:= SwapInList[{1, 2, 3, 4, 5, 6, 7, 8, 9}, {{1, 3}, {4, 6}, {8, 10}}]
          Positions {10} are absent in list {1, 2, 3, 4, 5, 6, 7, 8, 9}
Out[717]= $Failed
In[718]:= SwapInList[{1, 2, 3, 4, 5, 6, 7, 8, 9}, {{1, 3}, {4, 6}}]
Out[718]= {3, 2, 1, 6, 5, 4, 7, 8, 9}
```

In the ***Mathematica*** for grouping of expressions along with simple lists also more complex list structures in the form of the nested lists are used, whose elements are lists *(sublists)* too. In this regard the lists of the *ListList* type whose elements - *sublists* of identical length are of special interest. The ***Mathematica*** for simple lists has testing function whose call ***ListQ[j]*** returns *True,* if ***j*** - a list, and *False* otherwise. While for testing of the nested lists we defined the useful enough functions ***NestListQ, NestQL, NestListQ1, ListListQ*** [16]. These tools are quite often used as a part of the testing components of the headings of procedures and functions both from our ***MathToolBox*** package, and in the different blocks, functions and modules first of all that are used in different problems of the system character [4-15].

In addition to the above testing functions some functions of the same class that are useful enough in programming of tools to processing of the list structures of an arbitrary organization have been created [16]. Among them can be noted testing tools such as ***BinaryListQ, IntegerListQ, ListNumericQ, ListSymbolQ, PosIntListQ, ListExprHeadQ, PosIntListQ, PosIntQ.*** In particular, the call ***ListExprHeadQ[x,h]*** returns *True* if a list ***x*** contains only elements meeting the condition *Head*[*a*] = *h,* and *False* otherwise. At that, the testing means process all elements of the analyzed list, including all its sublists of any level of nesting. The above means are often used at programming of the problems oriented on the lists processing. These and other means of the given type are located in our ***MathToolBox*** package [16]. Their correct use assumes that the package is uploaded into the current session.

A number of problems dealing with the nested lists require to determine their maximum nesting level. In this direction, we have proposed a number of means. For example, the procedure call ***ListLevelMax*[x]** whose source code along with examples of its application are shown below, returns the maximum nesting level of a list ***x***. Whereas the procedure call ***ListLevelMax*[*x*, *y*]** with the **2*nd*** optional argument ***y*** – *an arbitrary symbol* – through ***y*** additionally returns the nested list whose **2**-elements sub-lists as the first argument define numbers of nesting levels of the ***x*** list, while as the **2*nd*** elements define the quantities of elements that are different from lists at corresponding levels.

```
In[1222]:= ListLevelMax[x_/; ListQ[x], y___] :=
                                    Module[{a = x, b = {}, t = 1},
        Do[AppendTo[b, {t, Length[Select[a, ! ListQ[#] &]]}];
           a = Select[a, ListQ[#] &]; If[a == {}, Break[], t++];
                                 a = Flatten[a, 1], {j, Infinity}];
                   If[{y} != {} && SymbolQ[y], y = b, 77]; t]
In[1223]:= ListLevelMax[{a, b, {c, {m, {c, {{b}}, d}, n}, d}, c, d}]
Out[1223]= 6
In[1224]:= ListLevelMax[{a, b, {c, {m, {c, {{b}}, d}, n}, d}, c, d}, gs]
Out[1224]= 6
In[1225]:= gs
Out[1225]= {{1, 4}, {2, 2}, {3, 2}, {4, 2}, {5, 0}, {6, 1}}
In[1226]:= ListLevelMax[{a, b, c, m, n, d, c, d}, gv]
Out[1226]= 1
In[1227]:= gv
Out[1227]= {{1, 8}}
```

The procedure call ***MaxLevel*[x]** returns the maximal level of nesting of a list ***x***; its source code is represented below:

```
In[1230]:= MaxLevel[x_/; ListQ[x]] := Module[{k},
          If[! NestListQ1[x], 1, For[k = 1, k <= Infinity, k++,
             If[Level[x, {k}] == {}, Break[], Continue[]]]; k]]
In[1231]:= MaxLevel[{a, b, {c, {m, {c, {{b}}, d}, n}, d}, c, d}]
Out[1231]= 7
In[1231]:= MaxLevel[{a, b, {c, {m, {c, {{}}, d}, n}, d}, c, d}]
Out[1231]= 6
In[1232]:= MaxLevelList[x_/; ListQ[x]] :=
```

```
                    Module[{b = 0, a = ReplaceAll[x, {} -> {77}]},
          Do[If[Level[a, {j}] == {}, Return[b], b++], {j, 1, Infinity}]]
In[1233]:= MaxLevelList[{a, b, {c, {m, {c, {{}}, d}, n}, d}, c, d}]
Out[1233]= 6
In[1234]:= MaxLevelList[{a, b, {c, {m, {c, {{b}}, d}, n}, d}, c, d}]
Out[1234]= 6
```

Meanwhile, it is appropriate to make a significant comment here about our means that use the built-in ***Level*** function, and without its using. The function call ***Level[expr, level]*** returns a list of all subexpressions of ***expr*** on levels specified by ***level***. At the same time the function call ***Level[expr, {level}]*** returns a list of all subexpressions of ***expr*** on a ***level***. Meanwhile, using the built-in ***Level*** function when the nested lists are used as an ***expr*** requires a certain care. For example, from the fragment below easily follows, you can obtain the incorrect results at using of the ***Level*** function when calculating the maximum nesting level of a list. In particular, on lists of form {… {} … } and {… *{a, b, c}* … }.

```
In[3342]:= Do [Print[Level[{{{{a, b, c}}}}, {j}]], {j, 1, 5}]
          {{{{a, b, c}}}}
          {{{a, b, c}}}
          {{a, b, c}}
          {a, b, c}
          {}
In[3343]:= MaxLevel[{{{{a, b, c}}}}]
Out[3343]= 4
In[3344]:= Do [Print[Level[{{{{}}}}, {j}]], {j, 1, 5}]
          {{{{}}}}
          {{{}}}
          {{}}
          {}
          {}
In[3345]:= MaxLevel[{{{{}}}}]
Out[3345]= 3
In[3346]:= ListLevelMax[{{{{a, b, c}}}}]
Out[3346]= 4
In[3347]:= ListLevelMax[{{{{}}}}]
Out[3347]= 4
```

```
In[3348]:= MaxLevel1[{{{{a, b, c}}}}]
Out[3348]= 4
In[3349]:= MaxLevel1[{{{{}}}}]
Out[3349]= 4
In[3350]:= Map[#[{{}}] &, {MaxLevel, ListLevelMax}]
Out[3350]= {1, 2}
```

It has been found that it is the use of an empty list {} as the last nesting level in the list that results in, among other things, an incorrect calculation of the maximum nesting level of a list. Therefore, in the development of the built-in ***Level*** function for lists, a simple ***Mlist*** function has been programmed, whose call ***Mlist*[*x*]** returns the replacement result in a list ***x*** of sub-lists of view {}, i.e. empty lists, to lists of view {*w*}, where *w* is a symbol unique to the current session. The following fragment presents the source code of the function with an example of its use along witx its use in the *MaxLevel2* procedure being a modification of the above *MaxLevel* procedure, eliminating said its drawback.

```
In[1240]:= Mlist[x_] := If[ListQ[x],
               ReplaceAll[x, {} -> ToString[{Unique["v77" ]}]], x]
In[1241]:= Mlist[{{}, {{{}}}, {}}]
Out[1241]= {"{v7711}", {{"{v7711}"}}, "{v7711}"}
In[1242]:= MaxLevel2[x_/; ListQ[x]] := Module[{a = Mlist[x], k},
              If[! NestListQ1[a], 1, For[k = 1, k <= Infinity, k++,
              If[Level[a, {k}] == {}, Break[], Continue[]]]]; k - 1]
In[1243]:= MaxLevel2[{a, b, {c, {m, {c, {{b}}, d}, n}, d}, c, d}]
Out[1243]= 6
In[1244]:= MaxLevel2[{a, b, {c, {m, {c, {{}}, d}, n}, d}, c, d}]
Out[1244]= 6
```

Meanwhile, it should be borne in mind that the use of the ***Mlist*** function has its limitations – its application may be quite appropriate in a case of tasks whose algorithm remains correct if the structural organization of a list is preserved, but without taking into account its content. This is a case when calculating the maximum nesting level of a list.

Note that in addition to the above means, several versions of similar means have been created: ***MaxLevel1, MaxLevelList, MaxNestLevel*** using other approaches [16].

Finally, based on the pure structure of the list, it is possible successfully solve a number of nested list processing problems, including calculating their maximum nesting level. At the same time, the ***pure structure*** of a list will be understood as a list, all elements of which are deleted, forming the corresponding list consisting only of characters {"{", "}"}. The following procedure solves the converting problem of a list to its pure structure. The sourse code of the ***PureListStr*** function is represented below.

```
In[2242]:= PureListStr[x_/; ListQ[x]] := Module[{f,
 a = Map[ToString[#] &, Flatten[x]]}, f[t_] := Quiet[Set[t, Nothing]];
 SetAttributes[f, Listable]; {Map[f[#] &, x], Map[ClearAll[#] &, a]}[[1]]]
In[2243]:= PureListStr[{a, b, c, d}]
Out[2243]= {}
In[2244]:= PureListStr[{{a, {a, b, c, {{{a, {}, b}}}}, b, {c, d}}}]
Out[2244]= {{{{{{{}}}}}, {}}}
In[2245]:= PureListStr[{{a, {a, {c, {h}}, b, c, {{{a, {n}, b}}}}, b, {c, d}}}]
Out[2245]= {{{{{}}, {{{{}}}}}, {}}}
```

The function call ***PureListStr***[*x*] returns the result of converting of a list *x* to its pure structure. So, the previous fragment additionally represents the examples of the above function application.

This function is a rather useful for lists processing problems. In particular, it makes it possible to calculate the *maximum* nesting level of a list based not on the built-in ***Level*** function, but on *pure structure,* as illustrated by example of the ***MaxLevel3*** procedure, whose source code along with examples of its use is represented below.

```
In[2249]:= MaxLevel3[x_/; ListQ[x]] :=
                              Module[{a = PureListStr[x], p = 1},
  Do[If[a == {}, Return[p], a = ReplaceAll[a, {} -> Nothing]; p++],
                                                  {j, Infinity}]]
In[2250]:= Map[MaxLevel3, {{}, {{{b}}}}]
Out[2250]= {1, 3}
In[2251]:= MaxLevel3[{a, b, {c, {m, {c, {{{{{}}}}}, d}, n}, d}, c, d}]
Out[2251]= 9
In[2252]:= MaxLevel3[{{a, {a, b, c, {{{a, {{b, c}}, b}}}}, b, {c, d}}}]
Out[2252]= 8
```

The procedure call ***MaxLevel3***[*x*] returns the maximal nesting level of a list *x;* examples presented above illustrate aforesaid.

Along with the task of determining the maximum nesting level of a list, the ***PureListStr*** procedure allows to calculate so-called ***isolated*** levels of the list, where as the isolated nesting levels are undestood the nesting levels in a list of isolated its sub-lists. The procedure call ***IsolLevelsList***[*x*] returns the list of the isolated nesting levels of a list *x,* while the call ***IsolLevelsList***[*x, y*] through optional argument *y – an arbitrary symbol –* additionally returns the maximal nesting level of the *x* list. Fragment below represents the source code of the ***IsolLevelsList*** procedure along with typical examples of its application.

```
In[2277]:= IsolLevelsList[x_/; ListQ[x]] :=
                    Module[{a = PureListStr[x], b, c, d = {}, h = "", k},
      b = StringTake[ToString[a], {2, -2}]; c = StringSplit[b, ","];
                                        c = Map[StringTrim[#] &, c];
                                                  Do[h = h <> c[[j]];
 If[SyntaxQ[h], AppendTo[d, MaxLevel3[ToExpression[h]]]; h = "",
                                                 Do[h = h <> c[[k]],
 If[SyntaxQ[h], AppendTo[d, MaxLevel3[ToExpression[h]]]; h = "",
                   Break[]]], {k, j, Length[c]}], {j, Length[c]}];
      If[{y} != {} && SymbolQ[y], y = Max[Map[# + 1 &, d]], 7];
                                                  Map[# + 1 &, d]]
In[2278]:= d = {{{}}, {}, {{{{}, {}}}}, {{{{{}, {}}}}}};
In[2279]:= IsolLevelsList[d]
Out[2279]= {3, 2, 5, 6}
In[2280]:= d1 = {{}, {{}}, {{{}, {}, {}}}, {{{{}, {}}}}};
In[2281]:= {IsolLevelsList[d1, gs], gs}
Out[2281]= {{2, 3, 4, 5}, 5}
In[2282]:= MaxLevel3[d1]
Out[2282]= 5
In[2283]:= {IsolLevelsList[{{{{{{{}}}}}}}, gs1], gs1}
Out[2283]= {{7}, 7}
In[2284]:= {IsolLevelsList[{{}, {c, {c, {{b, {m, {n}, d}, n, d}}, d}}}, j], j}
Out[2284]= {{2, 7}, 7}
```

In addition to the above-mentioned problems based on use of pure list structures, there are many other problems utilizing this methodology. A number of quite interesting tasks that use such an approach can be found, for example, in [6,8-15].

The procedure below gives an useful method of elements transposition of the list. The procedure call ***ListRestruct*[*x, y*]** returns the result of *mutual exchanges* of elements of a list *x* that are defined by the rule or their list *y* of the kind ***aj -> bj***, where ***aj*** – positions of elements of the list *x* and ***bj*** – their positions in the returned list, and vice versa. At that, the procedure excludes unacceptable rules from *y* list. The fragment represents source code of the ***ListRestruct*** procedure and examples of its use.

```
In[21]:= ListRestruct[x_List, y_/; RuleQ[y] || ListRulesQ[y]] :=
                                Module[{b = If[RuleQ[y], {y}, y], c, d},
  b = DeleteDuplicates[DeleteDuplicates[b, #1[[1]] === #2[[1]] &],
                                                  #1[[1]] === #2[[1]] &];
 c = Map[#[[1]] -> x[[#[[2]]]] &, b]; d = ReplacePart[x, c];
 c = Map[#[[1]] -> x[[#[[2]]]] &, RevRules[b]]; ReplacePart[d, c]]
In[22]:= ListRestruct[{1, 3, 77, 4, 5, 28, 3, 2, 6, 40, 4, 3, 20, 3},
                              {1 -> 6, 8 -> 12, 1 -> 14, 8 -> 10, 5 -> 10}]
Out[22]= {28, 3, 77, 4, 40, 1, 3, 3, 6, 5, 4, 2, 20, 3}
In[23]:= ListRestruct[{b, {j, n}, c + f[t], d/(h + d)}, {4 -> 1, 3 -> 2}]
Out[23]= {d/(d + h), c + f[t], {j, n}, b}
```

Means of operating with levels of the nested list are of a special interest. In this context the following tools can be rather useful. As one of such means the ***MaxLevel*** procedure can be presented whose call ***MaxLevel*[x]** returns the *maximum* nesting level of a list *x (at that, the nesting level of a simple* ***x*** *list is supposed equal to one)*. In addition, ***MaxLevel1*** procedure is an equivalent version of the previous procedure. Whereas the call ***ListLevels*[*x*]** returns the list of nesting levels of a list *x;* for the simple list *x* or empty list the procedure call returns {*1*}. The following fragment represents source codes of the above *three* procedures including typical examples of their applications.

```
In[1333]:= L = {a, b, a, {d, c, s}, a, b, {b, c, {x, y, {v, g, z,
                              {90, {500, {}, 77}}, a, k, a}}, b}, c, b};
In[1334]:= MaxLevel[L_/; ListQ[L]] := Module[{k},
            For[k = 1, k <= Infinity, k++, If[Level[L, {k}] == {},
                                            Break[], Continue[]]]; k]
In[1335]:= MaxLevel1[x_/; ListQ[x]] := Module[{a = x, k = 1},
```

```
While[NestListQ1[a], k++; a = Flatten[a, 1]; Continue[]]; k]

In[1336]:= Map[#[L] &, {MaxLevel, MaxLevel1}]
Out[1336]= {7, 7}

In[52]:= ListLevels[x_/; ListQ[x]] := Module[{a = x, b, c = {}, k = 1},
   If[! NestListQ1[x], {1}, While[NestListQ1[a], b = Flatten[a, 1];
   If[Length[b] >= Length[a], AppendTo[c, k++],
  AppendTo[c, k++]]; a = b; Continue[]]; c = AppendTo[c, k++]]]

In[53]:= Map[ListLevels[#] &, {L, {{{{}}}}, {}}]
Out[53]= {{1, 2, 3, 4, 5, 6, 7}, {1, 2, 3, 4}, {1}}
```

Between the above procedures the defining relations take place:

***Flatten*[x] ≡ *Flatten*[x, *MaxLevel*[x]]; *MaxLevel*[x] ≡ *ListLevels*[x][[-1]]**

The ***AllElemsMaxLevels*** procedure extends the procedure ***ElemsMaxLevels*** onto all expressions composing the analyzed list [8,16]. The call ***AllElemsMaxLevels*[*x*]** returns the list of the *ListList* type whose **2**–element sublists have all *possible* elements of a list ***x*** as the first elements, and their maximal nesting levels in the ***x*** list as the second elements.

```
In[67]:= AllElemsMaxLevels[x_/; ListQ[x]] :=
                              Module[{g = ToString1[x], c, Agn},
                           If[x == {}, {}, Agn[z_/; ListQ[x], y_] :=
                         Module[{a = MaxLevelList[z], d = {}, h},
                     h = Map[{#, Level[z, {#}]} &, Range[1, a]];
   Do[Do[AppendTo[d, If[FreeQ[h[[j]][[2]], y[[k]]], Nothing,
                          {y[[k]], j}]], {k, 1, Length[y]}], {j, 1, a}];
  d = Gather[d, #1[[1]] == #2[[1]] &];
  d = Map[Sort[#, #1[[2]] >= #2[[2]] &] &, d]; Map[#[[1]] &, d]];
           c = AllSubStrings[g, 0, ExprQ[#] &];
       g = DeleteDuplicates[ToExpression[c]]; g = Agn[x, g];
                                   If[Length[g] == 1, g[[1]], g]]]

In[68]:= L := {a, b, {{a, b}, {{m, n, {p, {{{f[t]}}}}}}}, c, {}, m, n, p,
                           {{{{a + b}, g}}}}; AllElemsMaxLevels[L]
Out[69]= {{a, 6}, {b, 6}, {m, 4}, {n, 4}, {p, 5}, {f, 8}, {t, 9}, {c, 1}, {g, 4},
{{}, 1}, {f[t], 8}, {a + b, 5}, {{a, b}, 2}, {{f[t]}, 8}, {{a + b}, 4}, {{{f[t]}}, 7},
{{{{f[t]}}}, 5}, {{{a + b}, g}, 3}, {{{{a + b}, g}}, 2}, {{p, {{{f[t]}}}}, 4},
{{{{{a + b}, g}}}, 1}, {{m, n, {p, {{{f[t]}}}}}, 3}, {{{m, n, {p, {{{f[t]}}}}}}, 2},
{{{a, b}, {{m, n, {p, {{{f[t]}}}}}}}, 1}, {{a, b, {{a, b}, {{m, n, {p, {{{f[t]}}}}}}},
c, {}, m, n, p, {{{{a + b}, g}}}}, 1}}
```

The procedure call ***ElemsOnLevelList*[*x*]** returns the nested list whose elements – the nested two-element lists, whose the first elements are nesting levels of a list *x*, whereas the second elements – the lists of elements at these nesting levels. If list *x* is empty, then the list {} is returned. Below, the source code of the procedure with an example of its application are represented.

```
In[2370]:= ElemsOnLevelList[x_/; ListQ[x]] :=
                    Module[{a, b, c = {}, d = {}, k = 1, t, f, h, g},
  f = ReplaceAll[x, {{} -> Set[g, FromCharacterCode[3]], 2 -> h}];
                                          a = LevelsOfList[f];
    Do[AppendTo[c, {a[[t = k++]], Flatten[f][[t]]}], {Length[a]}];
      c = Map[Flatten, Gather[c, #1[[1]] == #2[[1]] &]]; k = 1;
                Do[AppendTo[d, {c[[t = k++]][[1]], Select[c[[t]],
     EvenQ[Flatten[Position[c[[t]], #]][[1]]] &]}], {Length[c]}];
                 c = ReplaceAll[d, {Null -> Nothing, h -> 2}];
        ReplaceAll[Sort[c, #1[[1]] < #2[[1]] &], g -> Nothing]]
In[2371]:= ElemsOnLevelList[L]
Out[2371]= {{1, {a, b, c, m, n, p}}, {3, {a, b}}, {4, {m, n, g}},
           {5, {p, a + b}}, {8, {f[t]}}}
```

The following procedure represents a rather useful version of the above procedure. The procedure call ***ElemsOnLevel1*[*x*, *y*]** returns the result of distribution of elements on nesting levels of a list ***x***. In addition, at a nesting level ***n*** of form ...***{a, b, ..., {c}, ..., d}***... only ***{a, b, ..., d}*** elements other than lists are considered as elements, whereas the elements of more higher nesting level ***p*>*n***, such as ***{c}***, are ignored. The source code of the procedure ***ElemsOnLevel1*** and examples of its use are represented below.

```
In[2221]:= ElemsOnLevel1[x_/; ListQ[x], y___] :=
                  Module[{a = ElemsOnLevel[x], b, c = {}, d = {}},
  b[t_] := AppendTo[c, t]; SetAttributes[b, Listable]; Map[b, a];
               c = Gather[Partition[c, 3], #1[[3]] == #2[[3]] &];
                                           c = Map[Flatten, c];
            Do[AppendTo[d, {c[[j]][[3]], Map[c[[j]][[#]] &,
               Range[1, Length[c[[j]]], 3]]}], {j, Length[c]}];
                           c = Sort[d, #1[[1]] < #2[[1]] &];
                                If[{y} != {} && ! HowAct[y],
                 y = Map[{#[[1]], Length[#[[2]]]} &, c], 77]; c]
```

```
In[2222]:= t := {{p, b, x^2 + z^2, c^b, 7.7, 78, m/n}, u, c^2,
                {{{n, {"h", f, {m, n, p}, c}, np^2}}}, {77, "x"}}
In[2223]:= ElemsOnLevel1[t]
Out[2223]= {{1, {u, c^2}}, {2, {p, b, x^2 + z^2, c^b, 7.7, 78, m/n,
            77, "x"}}, {4, {n, np^2}}, {5, {"h", f, c}}, {6, {m, n, p}}}
In[2224]:= ElemsOnLevel1[t, agn]
Out[2224]= {{1, {u, c^2}}, {2, {p, b, x^2 + z^2, c^b, 7.7, 78, m/n,
            77, "x"}}, {4, {n, np^2}}, {5, {"h", f, c}}, {6, {m, n, p}}}
In[2225]:= agn
Out[2225]= {{1, 2}, {2, 9}, {4, 2}, {5, 3}, {6, 3}}
```

The procedure call returns the result as the nested list of the form *{{la, {a1,…,an}}, {lb, {b1,…,bm}},…,{lc, {c1,…,cp}}}* that defines the distribution of elements *{q1,…,qt}* on a nesting level *lq,* while thru the optional argument ***y*** – *an indefinite variable* – is returned the nested list of the *ListList* type of the form *{{la, na}, {lb, ba},…, {lc, ca}},* where *lj* – a nesting level and *nj* – number of elements on this level. The ***ElemsOnLevel1*** procedure is of certain interest as in determining the structural organization of nested lists and at programming of a number tasks connected with nested lists.

Using the ***ElemsOnLevelList*** procedure, we can determine a tool of converting of any list into so-called *canonical* form, i.e. in the list of form ***{Level1, {Level2, {Level3, {Level4,…,Leveln}…}}}};*** at the same time, all elements of a ***Levelj*** level are sorted *{j=1..n}*. The problem is solved by a tool, whose call ***RestructLevelsList[x]*** returns a list *x* in the above canonical form. The fragment below represents source code of the tool and an example of its use.

```
In[376]:= RestructLevelsList[x_/; ListQ[x]] :=
  Module[{a, b = FromCharacterCode[3], g = FromCharacterCode[4],
 c, d, h = {}}, d = b; a = ElemsOnLevelList[ReplaceAll[x, {} -> {g}]];
 c = Map[{AppendTo[h, #[[1]]]; #[[1]], Join[Sort[#[[2]]], {b}]} &, a];
                                    h = Flatten[{1, Differences[h]}];
         Do[d = ReplaceAll[d, b -> If[c[[j]][[1]] - j == 1, c[[j]][[2]],
                  Nest[List, c[[j]][[2]], h[[j]] - 1]]], {j, 1, Length[h]}];
                          ReplaceAll[d, {b -> Nothing, g -> {}}]]

In[377]:= RestructLevelsList[L]
Out[377]= {a, b, c, m, n, p, {{}, {a, b, {g, m, n, {a + b, p, {{{f[t]}}}}}}}}
```

The following procedure has algorithm different from the previous procedure and defines a tool of converting of any list into the above canonical form; all elements of a ***Levelj*** level are sorted *{j = 1..n}*. The procedure call ***CanonListForm[x]*** returns a list *x* in the above canonical form. The fragment presents source code of the procedure and typical examples of its application.

```
In[7]:= CanonListForm[x_/; ListQ[x]] :=
Module[{a = Map[{#[[1]], Sort[#[[2]]]} &, ElemsOnLevelList[x]],
         b, c, h = {}, p, m, s, f, n = 2, d = FromCharacterCode[3]},
  b = Max[Map[#[[1]] &, a]]; AppendTo[h, c = "{" <> d <> "1,"];
                     Do[Set[c, "{" <> d <> ToString[n++] <> ","];
                                        AppendTo[h, c], {j, 2, b}];
                     p = StringJoin[h] <> StringMultiple["}", b];
                             m = Map[Rule[d <> ToString[#[[1]]],
                     StringTake[ToString1[#[[2]]], {2, -2}]] &, a];
           m = Map[If[#[[2]] == "", Rule[#[[1]], "{}"], #] &, m];
                                        s = StringReplace[p, m];
           f[t_] := If[! StringFreeQ[ToString[t], d], Nothing, t];
                                      SetAttributes[f, Listable];
           Map[f, ToExpression[StringReplace[s, ",}" -> "}"]]]]
In[8]:= L = {s, "a", g, {{{{{m}}}}}, m, {{{77}}}, m, c, m, {f, d, {{72, s}},
  h, m, {m + p, {{p}}, n, 52, p, a}}, {7, {90, 500}}}; CanonListForm[L]
Out[8]= {"a", c, g, m, m, m, s, {7, d, f, h, m, {52, 90, 500, a, n, p,
                                          m + p, {72, 77, s, {p, {m}}}}}}
```

The ***CanonListForm*** uses a number of receptions useful in practical programming of the problems dealt of lists of various type. Whereas the following simple function allows to obtain a representation of a list *x* in a slightly different canonical format: {{*L1*}, {{*L2*}}, {{{*L3*}}},…,{{{… {*Ln*}… }}}} where *Lj* present the sorted list elements at appropriate nesting *j* level of the *x* list *(j = 1..n):*

```
In[4331]:= CanonListForm1[x_/; ListQ[x]] :=
  Map[Nest[List, #[[2]], #[[1]] - 1] &, Map[{#[[1]], Sort[#[[2]]]} &,
                                                ElemsOnLevelList[x]]]
In[4332]:= CanonListForm1[L = {a, b, {c, d, {g, h, {x, {y, {z}}}}}}]
Out[4332]= {{a, b}, {{c, d}}, {{{g, h}}}, {{{{x}}}}, {{{{{y}}}}}, {{{{{{z}}}}}}}
In[4333]:= Map[LevelsList[#] &, CanonListForm1[L]]
Out[4333]= {1, 2, 3, 4, 5, 6}
```

At the same time, the nesting of elements of a list returned by the ***CanonListForm1*** function can be defined, for example, by ***LevelsList*** procedure calls as illustrates the last example of the previous fragment. Incidentally, the list of elements on each level of the nested list, which in turn are different from the lists, is of a certain interest. This problem is solved by means of the procedure whose call ***ElemsOnLevels4*[*x*]** returns the list of **2**–element sub–lists in ascending order of the nesting levels of a list ***x;*** the *first* element of each sublist defines the list of elements *(which are different from the list)* of the ***j***–th nesting level, whereas the *second* element defines the ***j***–level.

```
In[7]:= ElemsOnLevels4[x_/; ListQ[x]] := Module[{a = {}, b = 77},
    Do[b = Level[x, {j}]; If[b != {}, AppendTo[a, {Map[If[ListQ[#],
                         Nothing, #] &, b], j}], Return[a]], {j, 1, Infinity}]]
In[8]:= ElemsOnLevels4[{a, b, {c, d, {g, h, {x, {y, {z, g}}}}}}]
Out[8]= {{{a, b}, 1}, {{c, d}, 2}, {{g, h}, 3}, {{x}, 4}, {{y}, 5}, {{z, g}, 6}}
```

On the basis of the above procedure the ***NumElemsOnLevels*** function useful enough in a number of appendices can be quite easily programmed. The call ***NumElemsOnLevels*[*x*]** returns the list of *ListList* type, whose two–element sublists define nesting levels and quantity of elements on them respectively. While the function call ***NumElemsOnLevel*[*x, p*]** returns the quantity of elements of a list ***x*** on its nesting level ***p***. In a case of absence of the ***p*** level the function call returns **$***Failed* with printing of the appropriate message. The source codes of both functions with examples of their application are represented in [8-16]. Whereas the problem of by-level sorting of elements of the nested list is solved by the procedure whose call ***SortOnLevels1*[*x, y*]** returns the default sort result of each nesting level of a list ***x***, if optional ***y*** argument is missing, or according to a set ordering function ***y***.

```
In[7]:= SortOnLevels1[x_/; ListQ[x], y___] := Module[{a, b = x, c},
                                  a = MaxLevel[x]; Do[c = Level[b, {j}];
b = ReplaceAll[b, c -> Sort[c, If[{y} != {}, y, Nothing]]], {j, a, 1, -1}]; b]
In[8]:= g = {3, 2, 1, {5, 77, 6, 8, {72, 8, 9, {0, 5, 6, 1}}, 78, 12, 67, 78}};
In[9]:= SortOnLevels1[g, #1 <= #2 &]
Out[9]= {1, 2, 3, {5, 6, 8, 77, {8, 9, 72, {0, 1, 5, 6}}, 12, 67, 78, 78}}
```

The procedure call ***LevelsOfList*[x]** returns the list of levels of elements of a list ***Flatten*[x]** of a source ***x*** list. In addition, in a case of the empty ***x*** list, {} is returned; in a case of a simple ***x*** list the single list of length ***Length*[*Flatten*[x]]**, i.e. ***{1,1,...,1,1}*** will be returned, i.e. level of all elements of a simple list is equal ***1***. On lists of the kind {{...{{}}...}} the procedure call returns the empty list, i.e. {}. The following fragment represents source code of the procedure with a typical example of its application.

```
In[10]:= LevelsOfList[x_/; ListQ[x]] := Module[{L, L1, t, p, k, h,
         g, j, s, w = ReplaceAll[x, {} -> {FromCharacterCode[2]}]},
                  {j, s} = ReduceLevelsList[w]; j = Prepend[j, 1];
Delete[If[j == {}, {}, If[! NestListQ1[j], Map[#^0 &, Range[1, Length[j]]],
If[FullNestListQ[j], Map[#^0 &, Range[1, Length[Flatten[j]]]], {p, h,
L, L1, g} = {1, FromCharacterCode[1], j, {}, {}}; ClearAll[t];
                                   Do[For[k = 1, k <= Length[L], k++,
          If[! ListQ[L[[k]]] && ! SuffPref[ToString[L[[k]]], h, 1],
    AppendTo[g, 0]; AppendTo[L1, h <> ToString[p]],
          If[! ListQ[L[[k]]] && ! SuffPref[ToString[L[[k]]], h, 1],
    AppendTo[g, 0]; AppendTo[L1, L[[k]]], AppendTo[g, 1];
    AppendTo[L1, L[[k]]]]]];
    If[! MemberQ[g, 1], L1, L = Flatten[L1, 1]; L1 = {}; g = {}; p++],
                                                    {Levels[j, t]; t}];
      ToExpression[Map[StringDrop[#, 1] &, L]]]]] + s - 1, 1]]
In[11]:= L = {a, m, n, {{b}, {c}, {{m, {{{gv}}}, n, {{{{{gs}}}}}}}}, d};
In[12]:= LevelsOfList[L]
Out[12]= {1, 1, 1, 3, 3, 4, 7, 4, 9, 1}
In[13]:= LevelsOfList[Flatten[L]]
Out[13]= {1, 1, 1, 1, 1, 1, 1, 1, 1, 1}
In[14]:= ElemsAtLevels[x_/; ListQ[x]] :=
                 Module[{a = Flatten[x], b}, b = LevelsOfList[x];
                     Map[{a[[#]], b[[#]]} &, Range[1, Length[a]]]]
In[15]:= ElemsAtLevels[L]
Out[15]= {{a, 1}, {m, 1}, {n, 1}, {b, 3}, {c, 3}, {m, 4}, {gv, 7}, {n, 4},
                                                          {gs, 9}, {d, 1}}
```

Using the previous procedure, it is easy to program simple procedure whose call ***ElemsAtLevels*[x]** returns the list of *ListList* type, whose two-element sub-lists determine the elements of a ***Flatten*[x]** list and the nesting levels at which they are in ***x***.

To illustrate a number of techniques that are rather useful in solving problems related to the nested lists, you can refer to the ***RestNestList*** procedure algorithm, which is as follows: the calling ***RestNestList***[*x, y*] procedure returns the original nested list *x*, while through second argument *y* – *an indefinite variable* – the ***Flatten***[*x*] list is returned. The procedure forms a *distribution* vector of brackets ("{", "}") in the *x* list in the form of a *W* list of the *ListList* type on the basis of which the initial list *x* is restored from the ***Flatten***[*x*] list. The source code of the above procedure illustrates this quite clearly.

```
In[325]:= RestNestList[x_ /; NestListQ1[x], y_ /; SymbolQ[y]] :=
   Module[{a = ToString1[x], b, W = {}, d}, b = StringLength[a];
     Do[d = StringTake[a, {j}]; If[d == "{", AppendTo[W, {1, j}],
If[d == "}", AppendTo[W, {2, j}], AppendTo[W, Nothing]]], {j, b}];
                    d = ToString1[Flatten[x]]; y = ToExpression[d];
Do[d = StringInsert[d, If[W[[j]][[1]] == 1, "{", "}"], W[[j]][[2]] + 1],
                        {j, 1, Length[W]}]; ToExpression[d][[1]]]
In[326]:= L = {a, m, n, {{b}, {c}, {{m, {{{"g"}}}, n, {{{{{gs}}}}}}}}, d};
In[327]:= RestNestList[L, gsv]
Out[327]= {a, m, n, {{b}, {c}, {{m, {{{"g"}}}, n, {{{{{gs}}}}}}}}, d}
In[328]:= gsv
Out[328]= {a, m, n, b, c, m, "g", n, gs, d}
```

Using the ***ElemsOnLevels2*** procedure [8,16], it is possible to program a procedure allowing to process by the set symbol the list elements which are determined by their arrangements on nesting levels and their location at the nested levels. The call ***SymbToElemList***[*x*, {*m*, *n*}, *s*] returns the result of application of a symbol **s** to an element of a list *x* which is located on a nesting level ***m***, and be ***n–th*** element at this nesting level. The nested list {{*m1*, *n1*}, …, {*mp*, *np*}} can be as the second argument of the ***SymbToElemList***, allowing to execute processing by means of **s** symbol the elements of the *x* list whose locations are defined by pairs {*mj*, *nj*} (*j* = *1..p*) of the above format. At that, the structure of the initial *x* list is preserved. The fragment below represents source code of the procedure and examples of its application.

```
In[1118]:= Lst = {s, "a", g, {{{{{}}}}}, b, 72, m, c, m, {f, d, 77, s, h, m,
                                     {m + p, {{}}, n, 50, p, a}}};
```

```
In[1119]:= SymbToElemList[x_/; ListQ[x],
              y_/; NonNegativeIntListQ[y] && Length[y] == 2 ||
                ListListQ[y] && And1[Map[Length[#] == 2 &&
                  NonNegativeIntListQ[#] &, y]], G_Symbol] :=
  Module[{a, b, c, d, h, g = If[ListListQ[y], y, {y}], f, n = 1, u},
                                      SetAttributes[d, Listable];
    f = ReplaceAll[x, {} -> Set[u, {FromCharacterCode[6]}]];
                        h = Flatten[f]; a = ElemsOnLevels2[f];
         d[t_] := "g" <> ToString[n++]; c = Map[d[#] &, f];
  h = GenRules[Map["g" <> ToString[#] &, Range[1, Length[h]]], h];
           SetAttributes[b, Listable]; a = ElemsOnLevels2[c];
    Do[b[t_] := If[MemberQ[a, {t, g[[j]][[1]], g[[j]][[2]]}], G[t], t];
                    Set[c, Map[b[#] &, c]], {j, 1, Length[g]}];
       ReplaceAll[ReplaceAll[c, h], {G[u[[1]]] -> G[], u -> {}}]]
In[1120]:= SymbToElemList[Lst, {{4, 1}, {6, 1}, {3, 1}, {1, 1}, {5, 1},
                                               {1, 6}, {2, 3}}, S]
Out[1120]= {S[s], "a", g, {{{{{S[]}}}}}, b, 72, S[m], c, m, {f, d, S[77], s,
                          h, m, {S[m + p], {{S[]}}, n, 50, p, a}}}
In[1121]:= SymbToElemList[{{}, {{{}}, {{{}}}}}, {{2, 1}, {4, 1}, {5, 1}}, G]
Out[1121]= {{G[]}, {{{G[]}}, {{{G[]}}}}}
```

Unlike the previous tool, the ***SymbToLevelsList*** procedure provides processing by a symbol of all elements of a list which are located at the set nesting levels [12-16]. Using the procedure ***ElemsOnLevels2,*** it is possible to program the ***ExpandLevelsList*** procedure allowing to expand a list by means of inserting into the set positions *(nestings levels and sequential numbers on them)* of a certain list. Using the ***ElemOfLevels*** procedure the useful testing procedure can be programmed, namely. The procedure call ***DispElemInListQ[x,y,n,j]*** returns *True* if an ***y*** element – ***j-th*** on ***n*** nesting level of a nonempty ***x*** list, and *False* otherwise. In addition to the above tools of processing of the nested lists the following function is an useful enough tool. The function call ***ElemOnLevelListQ[x, y, n]*** returns *True,* if an element ***y*** belongs to the ***n–th*** nesting level of a list ***x,*** and *False* otherwise. When processing of sublists in the lists is often need of check of the existence fact of sublists overlaping that entere to the lists. The procedure call ***SubListOverlapQ[x, y, z]*** returns *True,* if a list ***x*** on a nesting level *z* contains overlapping sublists *y*, and *False* otherwise. Whereas the call ***SubStrOverlapQ***[*x, y, z, n*] through optional *n* argument – *an indefinite symbol* – additionally returns the list of consecutive quantities of overlapings of the *y* sublist on the *z* nesting level of the *x* list. In a case of the nesting level *z* nonexisting for the *x* list, the procedure call returns $*Failed* with printing of the appropriate message [7,9,10-16].

In some programming problems that use the list structures arises a quite urgent need of replacement of values of a list that are located at the set nesting levels. The standard functions of the ***Mathematica*** don't give this opportunity. In this regard the procedure has been created whose call ***ReplaceLevelList***[*x,n,y,z*] returns the result of the replacement of *y* element of a list *x* that is located at a nesting level *n* onto a value *z*. The lists that have identical length also can act as arguments *y, n* and *z*. In a case of violation of the set condition the procedure call returns $*Failed*. In a case of lack of the **4*th*** optional *z* argument the procedure call ***ReplaceLevelList***[*x, n, y*] returns the result of removal of *y* elements which are located on a nesting level *n* of the *x* list. The following fragment represent source code of the procedure and some typical examples of its application.

```
In[7]:= ReplaceLevelList[x_/; ListQ[x], n_/; IntegerQ[n] &&
                    n > 0 || IntegerListQ[n], y_, z___] :=
 Module[{a, c = Flatten[x], d, b = SetAttributes[ToString4, Listable],
  h = FromCharacterCode[2], k, p = {}, g = FromCharacterCode[3],
        u = FromCharacterCode[4], m, n1 = Flatten[{n}],
                              y1 = Flatten[{y}], z1},
                    If[{z} != {}, z1 = Flatten[{z}], z1 = y1];
   If[Length[DeleteDuplicates[Map[Length, {n1, y1, z1}]]] != 1,
  $Failed, a = ToString4[x]; SetAttributes[StringJoin, Listable];
        b = ToExpression[ToString4[StringJoin[u, a, g <> h]]];
  b = ToString[b]; m = StringPosition[b, h]; d = LevelsOfList[x];
     b = StringReplacePart[ToString[b], Map[ToString, d], m];
         For[k = 1, k <= Length[n1], k++, AppendTo[p, u <>
    Map[ToString4, y1][[k]] <> g <> Map[ToString, n1][[k]] ->
              If[{z} == {}, "", Map[ToString, z1][[k]]]]];
  b = StringReplace[b, p]; d = Map[g <> # &, Map[ToString, d]];
```

```
Map[ClearAttributes[#, Listable] &, {StringJoin, ToString4}];
  ToExpression[StringReplace[b, Flatten[{u -> "", ", }" -> "}",
"{," -> "{", ",," -> ",", ",," -> "", ", " -> "", GenRules[d, ""]}]]]]]
In[8]:= p := {a, j, n, {{b + d}, {c}, {{m, {{{g}}}, n, {{{{{gsv, vgs}}}}}}}}, d};
In[9]:= ReplaceLevelList[p, {3, 9}, {b + d, gsv}, {Art, Kr}]
Out[9]= {a, j, n, {{Art}, {c}, {{m, {{{g}}}, n, {{{{{Kr, vgs}}}}}}}}, d}
In[10]:= ReplaceLevelList[p, 9, gsv, Art]
Out[10]= {a, j, n, {{b + d}, {c}, {{m, {{{g}}}, n, {{{{{Art, vgs}}}}}}}}, d}
```

The call ***MapAt[f,e,n]*** of the built-in *MapAt* function applies *f* to an element at position ***n*** in an ***e*** expression; whereas other its formats allow to apply *f* to the elements at the set positions in the ***e*** expression. At the same time, the following procedure allows to apply *f* to elements located on the set nesting levels with the set sequential numbers on the these nesting levels in a list. The procedure call ***MapAtLevelsList[f,x,y]*** returns the result of applying of *f* to the elements of a list ***x*** that are located on the set nesting levels ***L1,…,Lk*** with the set sequential numbers ***p1, …, pk*** on these nesting levels; at that, the second argument is a ***y*** *ListList*-list of the format {{***L1, p1***}, …, {***Lk, pk***}}, as examples below a rather visually illustrate. Whereas the procedure call ***MapAtLevelsList[f, x, y, z]*** with third optional ***z*** argument – *an indefined symbol* – through it additionally returns the *ListList* list whose elements are three-elements sublists for which the first elements define elements of the list ***Flatten[x]***, the *2nd* elements define their positions in the ***Flatten[x]*** list, and the *3rd* elements define their nesting levels in the ***x*** list. On a list ***x*** of the format {{{...{{...}}...}}} the procedure call returns {{{...{{f[]}}...}}}. Whereas the call ***MapAtLevelsList[f, x, y, z]*** additionally thru the optional ***z*** argument returns the list of format {{{}, ***1, MaxLevel[x]***}}. This procedure is of interest in the problems of the lists processing. The fragment below represents source code of the procedure along with typical examples of its application.

```
In[27]:= MapAtLevelsList[f_ /; SymbolQ[f], x_ /; ListQ[x],
                                        y_ /; ListListQ[y], z___] :=
  Module[{a, b, c = FromCharacterCode[2], d, g, p, n = 1, s},
s = ReplaceAll[x, {} -> {c}]; a = LevelsOfList[s]; d = ClusterList[a];
                              b = Map[c <> # &, Map[ToString, y]];
```

```
f[t_] := {"(" <> If[t === Null, "f[]", ToString1[t]] <> ")" <> c <>
           ToString[d[[n++]]]}[[1]]; d = MapListAll[f, s]; Clear[f];
                       g[t_] := If[MemberQ[b, StringTake[t,
             {Set[p, Flatten[StringPosition[t, c]][[-1]]], -1}]],
         ToString[f] <> "[" <> StringTake[t, {1, p - 1}] <> "]",
         StringTake[t, {1, p - 1}]]; SetAttributes[g, Listable];
If[{z} != {} && NullQ[z], z = ReplaceAll[Map[{Flatten[s][[#]], #,
             a[[#]]} &, Range[1, Length[a]]], "\.02" -> {}], 77];
n = ToExpression[Map[g, d]]; n = ReplaceAll[n, "\.02" -> Null];
                ReplaceAll[n, {f[Null] -> f[], {Null} -> {}}]]

In[28]:= MapAtLevelsList[f, {a, b, c, {{x, y, z}, {{m, n*t, p}}}, c, d},
                                  {{1, 1}, {1, 5}, {3, 3}, {4, 2}}]
Out[28]= {f[a], b, c, {{x, y, f[z]}, {{m, f[n t], p}}}, c, f[d]}
In[29]:= MapAtLevelsList[f, {{{{{a, b, c}, {x, y, z}}}}}, {{5, 1}, {5, 5},
                                                      {5, 3}}, g72]
Out[29]= {{{{{f[a], b, f[c]}, {x, f[y], z}}}}}
In[30]:= g72
Out[30]= {{a, 1, 5}, {b, 2, 5}, {c, 3, 5}, {x, 4, 5}, {y, 5, 5}, {z, 6, 5}}
```

Unlike the ***MapAtLevelsList*** the ***MapAtLevelsList1*** allows to apply a set of functions to the specified elements of a list that are depended on a nesting level at which they are located. The call ***MapAtLevelsList1***[*x, y, z*] returns the result of applying of a function from a list *z* to the elements of a list *x* that are located on a set nesting levels *L1,…,Lk* with the set sequential numbers ***p1,…,pk*** on these nesting levels; in addition, the *2nd* argument is a list *y* of the form {{*L1, p1*},…,{*Lk, pk*}}. While the *3rd* argument is a list *z* of the form {{***F1, L1***},…,{***Fp, Lp***}} where a sublist {***Fj, Lj***} defines applying of a ***Fj*** function on a nesting level ***Lj***. In a case if in the list *z* there are different functions at the same level, then only the first of them is used. The given procedure is of a certain interest in problems of the lists processing [6,8,10-16]. At last, the ***SymbolToLevelsList*** procedure gives possibility to apply a function to all elements of the set nesting levels of a list ***x***. The call ***SymbolToLevelsList***[***x, m, Sf***] returns the list structurally similar to a list *x* and to its elements at the nesting levels ***m*** *(list or separate integer)* function *Sf* is applied. In a case of absence of real nesting levels in ***m*** *(i.e. nonexisting levels in the **x** list)* the call returns $*Failed* with printing of the appropriate message [8,16].

The standard ***ReplaceList*** function attempts to transform an expression by applying a rule or list of rules in all possible ways, and returns the list of the results obtained. The following procedure is an useful enough modification of the ***ReplaceList*** function. The call ***ReplaceList1[x, y, z, p]*** returns the list that is the result of replacement in a list ***x*** of elements whose positions are determined by a list ***y*** at a nesting level ***p*** onto appropriate expressions that are defined by a list ***z***. In addition, if a certain element should be deleted, in the ***z*** list the key word *"Nothing"* is coded in the appropriate position. The procedure processes the main espesial situations. The following fragment represents source code of the procedure and examples of its application.

```
In[7]:= ReplaceList1[x_/; ListQ[x], y_/; IntegerListQ[y],
                                z_/; ListQ[z], p_/; IntegerQ[p]] :=
                          Module[{a = MaxLevelList[x], b, c = {}},
  If[Length[y] != Length[z], Print["The 2nd and 3rd arguments
                                  have different lengths"]; $Failed,
  If[p > a, Print["The given nesting level is more than maximal"];
                                    $Failed, b = Level[x, {p}];
  Do[AppendTo[c, If[y[[j]] <= Length[b], b[[y[[j]]]] -> If[z[[j]] ===
          "Nothing", Nothing, z[[j]]], Nothing]], {j, 1, Length[y]}];
                                  If[c == {}, x, Replace[x, c, {p}]]]]]
In[8]:= L := {a,b, {{a,b}, {{m,n, {p, {{{}}}}}}}, c, {}, m,n,p, {{{{a*b}, g}}}}
In[9]:= ReplaceList1[L, {1, 2, 5}, {Avz, Agn, Vsv}, 4]
Out[9]= {a,b,{{a,b},{{Avz,Agn,{p,{{{}}}}}}},c,{},m,n,p,{{{{a*b},Vsv}}}}
In[10]:= ReplaceList1[L, {1, 2}, {{Avz, Agn}, {77, 72}}, 2]
Out[10]= {a, b, {{Avz, Agn}, {77, 72}}, c, {}, m, n, p, {{{{a*b}, g}}}}
```

The ***InsertToList*** procedure is based on the above procedure ***ReplaceList1*** and ***Sequences*** [8,16] and attempts to transform a list by including of expressions in the tuples of its elements that are located on the set nesting level. The ***InsertToList*** procedure is a rather useful modification of the built-in ***Insert*** function. The procedure call ***InsertToList[x, y, z, h, p]*** returns the list that is the result of inserting into ***x*** list on a nesting level ***p*** of expressions from a list ***z;*** the positions for inserting are defined by means of the appropriate ***y*** list which defines the positions of elements of the ***x*** list on the ***p–th*** nesting level [7,10-16].

Using the ***ElemsOnLevels2*** procedure [16], it is possible to program the procedure allowing to expand a list by means of inserting into the given positions *(nestings levels and sequential numbers on them)* of the list. The call ***ExpandLevelsList*[*x, y, z*]** returns the result of inserting of the ***z*** list to a nesting level ***m*** relative to ***n–th*** position at this nesting level; at that, the second ***y*** argument in common case is a nested list **{{*m, n*}, *p*},...,{*mt, nt*}, *pt*}}**, allowing to execute inserting to positions, whose locations are defined by pairs **{*mj, nj*} {*j=1..t*}** *(nestings levels and sequential numbers on them)*, whereas ***pt*∈{*1, –1, 0*}** defines insertion at the right, at the left and at situ relative to the set position. Thus, the argument ***y*** has the format **{{*m, n*}, *p*}**, or the kind of the above nested list **{{*m, n*}, *p*},...,{*mt, nt*}, *pt*}}**. At that, the structure of an initial ***x*** list is preserved.

```
In[2385]:= ExpandLevelsList[x_/; ListQ[x], y_, z_/; ListQ[z]] :=
      Module[{a, b, c, d, h, g = If[Length[Flatten[y]] == 3, {y}, y], f,
         n = 1, u, p = ToString[z]}, SetAttributes[d, Listable];
      f = ReplaceAll[x, {} -> Set[u, {FromCharacterCode[2]}]];
         h = Flatten[f]; a = ElemsOnLevels2[f];
      d[t_] := "g" <> ToString[n++]; c = Map[d[#] &, f];
h = GenRules[Map["g" <> ToString[#] &, Range[1, Length[h]]], h];
      SetAttributes[b, Listable]; a = ElemsOnLevels2[c];
   Do[b[t_] := If[MemberQ[a, {t, g[[j]][[1]][[1]], g[[j]][[1]][[2]]}],
If[g[[j]][[2]] == -1, p <> "," <> t, If[g[[j]][[2]] == 1, t <> "," <> p, p, 7]], t];
         Set[c, Map[b[#] &, c]], {j, 1, Length[g]}];
         c = ToExpression[ToString[c]];
   ReplaceAll[ReplaceAll[c, Map[ToExpression[#[[1]]] ->
         #[[2]] &, h]], u[[1]] -> {}]]
In[2386]:= ExpandLevelsList[{a, d, {b, h, {c, d}}}, {{{1, 1}, 1},
            {{2, 1}, 0}, {{3, 1}, -1}}, {{x, y, z}}]
Out[2386]= {a, {{x, y, z}}, d, {{{x, y, z}}, h, {{{x, y, z}}, c, d}}}
In[2387]:= ExpandLevelsList[{a, d, {b, h, {c, d}}}, {{{1, 1}, 1},
            {{2, 1}, 0}, {{3, 1}, -1}}, {{}}]
Out[2387]= {a, {{}}, d, {{{}}, h, {{{}}, c, d}}}
In[2388]:= ExpandLevelsList[{}, {{1, 1}, 0}, MultiEmptyList[7]]
Out[2388]= {{{{{{{{}}}}}}}}
```

The procedure is widely used by tools processing list structures.

The following rather simple procedure is intended for the grouping of elements of a list according to their multiplicities. The procedure call ***GroupIdentMult*[x]** returns the nested list of the following format:

$$\{\{\{n_1\}, \{x_1, x_2, ..., x_a\}\}, \{\{n_2\}, \{y_1, y_2, ..., y_b\}\}, ..., \{\{n_k\}, \{z_1, z_2, ..., z_c\}\}\}$$

where $\{x_i, y_j, ..., z_p\}$ are elements of a list ***x*** and $\{n_1, n_2, ..., n_k\}$ – multiplicities corresponding to them $\{i = 1..a, j = 1..b, ..., p = 1..c\}$. The fragment below represents the source code of the procedure along with typical examples of its application.

```
In[1287]:= GroupIdentMult[x_ /; ListQ[x]] :=
                                   Module[{a = Gather[x], b},
        b = Map[{DeleteDuplicates[#][[1]], Length[#]} &, a];
                          b = Map[DeleteDuplicates[#] &,
        Map[Flatten, Gather[b, SameQ[#1[[2]], #2[[2]]] &]]];
        b = Map[{{#[[1]]}, Sort[#[[2 ;; -1]]]} &, Map[Reverse,
   Map[If[Length[#] > 2, Delete[Append[#, #[[2]]], 2], #] &, b]]];
                       b = Sort[b, #1[[1]][[1]] > #2[[1]][[1]] &];
                           If[Length[b] == 1, Flatten[b, 1], b]]
In[1288]:= L = {a, c, b, a, a, c, g, d, a, d, c, a, c, c, h, h, h, h, h, g, g};
In[1289]:= GroupIdentMult[L]
Out[1289]= {{{5}, {a, c, h}}, {{3}, {g}}, {{2}, {d}}, {{1}, {b}}}
In[1290]:= GroupIdentMult[{a, a, a, a, a, a, a, a, a, a, a, a, a, a, a}]
Out[1290]= {{15}, {a}}
In[1291]:= GroupIdentMult[RandomInteger[2, 47]]
Out[1291]= {{{19}, {2}}, {{16}, {0}}, {{12}, {1}}}
In[1292]:= GroupIdentMult[RandomInteger[42, 77]]
Out[1292]= {{{4}, {9, 20, 24, 32, 34}}, {{3}, {0, 2, 5, 12, 17, 18}},
            {{2}, {3, 4, 8, 15, 16, 19, 21, 22, 25, 31, 35, 40, 41}},
            {{1}, {6, 7, 10, 11, 14, 26, 28, 29, 30, 37, 38, 39, 42}}}
In[1293]:= Sum[%[[k]][[1]]*Length[%[[k]][[2]]], {k, 1, Length[%]}][[1]]
Out[1293]= 77
```

In addition, elements of the returned nested list are sorted in decreasing order of multiplicities of elements groups of the initial ***x*** list. In a number of problems dealing with structures of list type the procedure is of a certain interest. That procedure is used in a number of tools of the ***MathToolBox*** package [16].

Note, along with above means we have programmed a lot of other means for processing lists, which are intended both for mass application and in special cases. Some are original, while others to varying degrees extend the functionality of the built-in means or extend their applicability. All these tools are included in the attached package ***MathToolBox*** [16].

3.6. *Additional tools for the Mathematica*

Here we will present some of the additional tools created at using of ***Mathematica*** for the programming of applications and in preparation of a series of books on computer algebra systems.

The following procedure expands the standard ***MemberQ*** function onto the nested lists, its call ***MemberQL[x, y]*** returns *True* if an expression ***y*** belongs to any nesting level of list ***x***, and *False* otherwise. While the call with the *3rd* optional ***z*** argument – *an indefinite variable* – in addition through ***z*** returns the list of the *ListList* type, the first element of each its sublist determines a level of the ***x*** list, whereas the second determines quantity of ***y*** elements on this level provided that the main output is *True*, otherwise ***z*** remains undefinite. The fragment below represents source code of the procedure with typical example of its use.

```
In[2144]:= MemberQL1[x_ /; ListQ[x], y_, z___] :=
                    Module[{a = MaxLevel[x], b = {}, c = {}, k = 0},
               Do[AppendTo[b, Count[Level[x, {j}], y]], {j, a}];
        If[Plus[Sequences[b]] >= 1, If[SymbolQ[z], Map[{k++,
   If[# != 0, AppendTo[c, {k, #}], 72]} &, b], 77]; z = c; True, False]]
In[2145]:= MemberQL1[{a, b, {c, d, {f, d, h, d}, s, {p, w, {n, m, d,
           d, r, u, d, {x, d, {d, m, n, d}, d, y}}, t}}, x, y, z}, d, agn]
Out[2145]= True
In[2146]:= agn
Out[2146]= {{2, 1}, {3, 2}, {4, 3}, {5, 2}, {6, 2}}
In[2147]:= MemberQL1[Flatten[{a, b, {c, d, {f, d, h, d}, s, {p, w,
                  {n, m, d, d, r, u, d}, t}}, x, y, z}], d, avz]
Out[2147]= True
In[2148]:= avz
Out[2148]= {{1, 6}}
```

At programming of certain procedures of access to files has been detected the expediency of creation of a procedure useful also in other appendices. Therefore, the procedure ***PosSubList*** has been created, whose call ***PosSubList*[*x, y*]** returns the nested list of initial and final elements for entrance into a simple ***x*** list of the tuple of elements set by a list ***y***. The fragment represents the source code of the procedure and an example of its use.

```
In[7]:= PosSubList[x_/; ListQ[x], y_/; ListQ[y]] :=
          Module[{d, a = ToString1[x], b = ToString1[y],
      c = FromCharacterCode[16]}, d = StringTake[b, {2, -2}];
   If[! StringFreeQ[a, d], b = StringReplace[a, d -> c <> "," <>
            StringTake[ToString1[y[[2 ;; -1]]], {2, -2}]];
                    Map[{#, # + Length[y] - 1} &,
     Flatten[Position[ToExpression[b], ToExpression[c]]]], {}]]
In[8]:= PosSubList[{a, a, b, a, a, a, b, a, x, a, b, a, y, z, a, b, a}, {a, b, a}]
Out[8]= {{2, 4}, {6, 8}, {10, 12}, {15, 17}}
```

The above approach once again illustrates *incentive* motives and prerequisites for programming of the user tools expanding the ***Mathematica*** software. Many of tools of our ***MathToolBox*** package appeared exactly in this way. So, the both procedures ***Gather1*** and ***Gather2*** a little extend the built-in function ***Gather***, being an useful in a number of applications [8,12-16].

The following group of means serves for sorting of lists of various type. Among them can be noted such as ***SortNL, SortLS, SortNL1, SortLpos, SortNestList.*** For example, the procedure call ***SortNestList*[*x,p,y*]** returns the sorting result of a nested *numeric* or *symbolic* list ***x*** by ***p–th*** element of its sub-lists according to the sorting functions *Less, Greater* for numeric lists, and *SymbolLess, SymbolGreater* for symbolic lists. In both cases a nested list with the nesting level **<3** as actual ***x*** argument is supposed, otherwise an initial ***x*** list is returned. In addition, in a case of *symbolic* lists the comparison of elements is carried out on the basis of their character codes. The following fragment represents source code of the procedure with typical example of its application.

```
In[76]:= SortNestList[x_/; NestListQ[x], p_/; PosIntQ[p], y_] :=
           Module[{a = DeleteDuplicates[Map[Length, x]], b},
```

```
b = If[AllTrue[Map[ListNumericQ, x], TrueQ] &&
                  MemberQ[{Greater, Less}, y], y,
      If[AllTrue[Map[ListSymbolQ, x], TrueQ] &&
      MemberQ[{SymbolGreater, SymbolLess}, y], y],
            Return[Defer[SortNestList[x, p, y]]]];
   If[Min[a] <= p <= Max[a], Sort[x, b[#1[[p]], #2[[p]]] &],
                       Defer[SortNestList[x, p, y]]]]

In[77]:= SortNestList[{{42, 47, 72}, {77, 72, 52}, {30, 23}}, 2, Less]
Out[77]= {{30, 23}, {42, 47, 72}, {77, 72, 52}}
```

Sorting of a nested list at the nesting levels composing it is of quite certain interest. In this regard the following procedure can be a rather useful tool. The call ***SortOnLevel*[*x, m*]** returns the sorting result of a list ***x*** at its nesting level ***m*** [16]. Whereas the ***SortOnLevels*** procedure is a rather natural generalization of the previous procedure. The call ***SortOnLevels*[*x,m,sf*]** where optional ***sf*** argument – a sorting pure function analogously to the previous procedure returns the sorting result of ***x*** list at its nesting levels ***m***. Furthermore, as an argument ***m*** can be used a single level, the levels list or ***"All"*** word which determines all nesting levels of the ***x*** list which are subject to sorting. If all ***m*** levels are absent then the call returns ***$****Failed* with printing of the appropriate message, otherwise the call prints the message concerning only levels absent in the ***x*** list. It must be kept in mind, that by default the sorting is made in symbolic mode, i.e. all elements of the sorted ***x*** list before sorting by means of the built-in ***Sort*** function are presented in the string format. While the call ***SortOnLevels*[*x, m, sf*]** returns the sorting result of a list ***x*** at its nesting levels ***m*** depending on a sorting pure ***sf*** function that is the *optional* argument. The following fragment represents source code of the procedure and examples of its application.

```
In[75]:= SortOnLevels[x_/; ListQ[x], m_/; IntegerQ[m] ||
                  IntegerListQ[m] || m === All, sf___] :=
  Module[{a, b, c = ReplaceAll[x, {} -> {Null}], d, h, t, g, s},
    a = LevelsOfList[c]; d = Sort[DeleteDuplicates[a]];
                      If[m === All || SameQ[d, Set[h,
         Sort[DeleteDuplicates[Flatten[{m}]]]]], t = d,
                        If[Set[g, Intersection[h, d]] == {},
```

```
Print["Levels " <> ToString[h] <> " are absent in the list; " <>
  "nesting levels must belong to " <> ToString[Range[1, Max[d]]]];
        Return[$Failed], t = g; s = Select[h, ! MemberQ[d, #] &];
          If[s == {}, Null, Print["Levels " <> ToString[s] <>
  " are absent in the list; " <> "nesting levels must belong to " <>
                              ToString[Range[1, Max[d]]]]]]]];
                    Map[Set[c, SortOnLevel[c, #, sf]] &, t];
                              ReplaceAll[c, Null -> Nothing]]

In[76]:= SortOnLevels[{b, t, "c", {{3, 2, 1, {g, s*t, a}, k, 0}, 2, 3, 1},
              1, 2, {{m, n, f}}, {{2, 3, 6, {{{g, f, d, s, m}}}}}}, 7, 8]
      Levels {7} are absent in the list;
      nesting levels must belong to {1, 2, 3, 4, 5, 6}
Out[76]= $Failed
In[77]:= SortOnLevels[{b, t, "c", {{3, 2, 1, {g, s*t, a}, k, 0}, 2, 3, 1},
              1, 2, {{m, n, f}}, {{2, 3, 6, {{{g, f, d, s, m}}}}}}, 6]
Out[77]= {b, t, "c", {{3, 2, 1, {g, s*t, a}, k, 0}, 2, 3, 1}, 1, 2, {{m, n, f}},
                                       {{2, 3, 6, {{{d, f, g, m, s}}}}}}
```

The procedure call ***SortOnLevel***[*x, m*] returns the sorting result of a list *x* at its nesting level *m*. If the *m* level is absent, the procedure call returns $*Failed,* printing the appropriate message. It must be kept in mind that by default the sorting is made in the symbolic format, i.e. all elements of the sorted *x* list will be represented in the string format. Whereas the procedure call ***SortOnLevel***[*x, m, Sf*] returns the sorting result of the *x* list at its nesting level *m* depending on the sorting pure *Sf* function that is the optional argument. In addition, the cross-cutting sorting at the set nesting level is made. The fragment below represents source code of the procedure and an example of its application.

```
In[10]:= SortOnLevel[x_ /; ListQ[x], m_ /; IntegerQ[m], Sf___] :=
  Module[{a, b = ReplaceAll[x, {} -> {Null}], c, d, f, g, h = {}, n = 1,
          p, v}, a = LevelsOfList[b]; d = DeleteDuplicates[a];
                                            If[! MemberQ[d, m],
   Print["Level " <> ToString[m] <> " is absent in the list; " <>
   "nesting level must belong to " <> ToString[Range[1, Max[d]]]];
          $Failed,  f[t_] := "(" <> ToString1[t] <> ")" <> "_" <>
  ToString1[a[[n++]]]; SetAttributes[f, Listable]; c = Map[f, b];
  g[t_] := If[SuffPref[t, "_" <> ToString[m], 2], AppendTo[h, t], Null];
                          SetAttributes[g, Listable]; Map[g, c];
```

```
p = Sort[Map[StringTake[#, {1, Flatten[StringPosition[#, "_"]]
                                        [[-1]] - 1}] &, h], Sf]; n = 1;
v[t_] := If[ToExpression[StringTake[t, {Flatten[StringPosition[t,
                     "_"]][[-1]] + 1, -1}]] == m, p[[n++]],
      StringTake[t, {1, Flatten[StringPosition[t, "_"]][[-1]] - 1}]];
         SetAttributes[v, Listable]; c = ToExpression[Map[v, c]];
                                   ReplaceAll[c, Null -> Nothing]]]
In[11]:= SortOnLevel[{p, b, a, u, c, {{{n, {h, f, c}, m}}}, 3, 2, 1}, 1]
Out[11]= {1, 2, 3, a, b, {{{n, {h, f, c}, m}}}, c, p, u}
```

Along with the above and other similar means [8-16,22], a procedure whose call ***ElemsOnLevel***[*x*] returns the format of a list *x* with its internal structure preserved is of great interest but instead of its elements there are **3**–element lists, where as their *1st* element - element of the *x* list, the *2nd* element - its position in the ***Flatten***[*x*] list and the third element - its nesting level in the *x* list *(see fragment below)*.

```
In[7]:= ElemsOnLevel[x_ /; ListQ[x]] := Module[{d, f, f1, f2, n = 1,
                                    p, z = "\[InvisibleComma]"},
                    f[t_] := ToString1[t] <> z <> ToString[n++];
                f1[t_] := ToString[t] <> z <> ToString[p[[n++]]];
                          f2[t_] := ToExpression[StringSplit[t, z]];
                 Map[SetAttributes[#, Listable] &, {f, f1, f2}];
p = LevelsOfList[x]; d = Map[f,x]; n=1; d = Map[f1,d]; Map[f2,d]]
In[8]:= ElemsOnLevel[{{{{a, b}}}, {c, d, m, {{n, d}}}, s, g, {a, k}}]
Out[8]= {{{{{a, 1, 4}, {b, 2, 4}}}}, {{c, 3, 2}, {d, 4, 2}, {m, 5, 2},
          {{{n, 6, 4}, {d, 7, 4}}}}, {s, 8, 1}, {g, 9, 1}, {{a, 10, 2}, {k, 11, 2}}}
```

The procedure is quite useful in solving of the number the problems of processing nested lists and in combination with the above–mentioned tools it extends the functional component of ***Mathematica*** in this direction. In particular, the procedure is useful in solving the task of testing the continuous distribution of elements at a set nesting level of a list. The problem is solved by means of ***SolidLevelQ*** procedure, represented below.

```
In[432]:= SolidLevelQ[x_ /; ListQ[x], n_ /; IntegerQ[n], y___] :=
                          Module[{a = ElemsOnLevel[x], b, c, p, t = 0},
                           If[MemberQ[Range[1, c = MaxLevel[x]], n],
               b = Partition[Flatten[a], 3]; b = Select[b, #[[3]] == n &];
```

```
If[b == {}, Goto[j], b = Map[#[[2]] &, b]; a = Range[b[[1]], b[[-1]]];
  Do[If[b[[p]] + 1 == b[[p + 1]], Nothing, t++], {p, Length[b] - 1}];
                                    If[a == b, p = True, p = False];
   If[p === False && {y} != {} && ! HowAct[y], y = t + 1, 77]; p],
  Label[j]; Print["The second argument should be in range " <>
                                        ToString[{1, c}]]; $Failed]]
In[433]:= SolidLevelQ[{3, 2, 1, {{g, s + t, a}, k, 0, 2, 3, 1}, 1, 2, {a, b},
                                   m, n, {c, {d}, t}, g, {d}, f}, 1]
Out[433]= False
In[434]:= SolidLevelQ[{3, 2, 1, {{g, s + t, a}, k, 0, 2, 3, 1}, 1, 2, {a, b},
                                 m, n, {c, {d}, t}, g, {d}, f}, 1, g]
Out[434]= False
In[435]:= g
Out[435]= 5
In[436]:= SolidLevelQ[{5, 6, 7, 8, {9, 11}, 10, 1}, 3]
          "The second argument should be in diapazon {1, 2}"
Out[436]= $Failed
In[437]:= SolidLevelQ[{5, 6, 7, 8, {9, {c}, 11}, 10, 1}, 2, svg]
Out[437]= False
In[438]:= svg
Out[438]= 2
In[439]:= SolidLevelQ[{5, 6, 7, 8, 9, 11, 10, 1}, 2]
          "The second argument should be in diapazon {1, 1}"
Out[439]= $Failed
In[440]:= SolidLevelQ[{5, 6, 7, 8, 9, 11, 10, 1}, 1]
Out[440]= True
```

Calling the ***SolidLevelQ*[*x, n*]** procedure returns *True* if the elements of a level ***n*** of a list ***x*** are arranged sequentially, i.e. not separated by other nesting levels, and *False* otherwise. Whereas through optional *3rd* argument ***y*** – *an indefinite variable* – the call ***SolidLevelQ*[*x, n, y*]** returns the number of solid segments of the elements of the ***n–th*** nesting level if the main result is *False*. The procedure processes the erroneous situation in a case of invalid nesting level ***n*** with returning value *$Failed* and printing of the appropriate message. The previous fragment represents source code of procedure and the typical examples of its application.

The following procedure should be preceded by a *procedure* that allows to do that a list of an arbitrary structure and nesting whose all elements are of the form {*h*}, is result in the list of the same structure, but with elements of the form ***h***. The procedure call ***IntSimplList***[*x*] returns the result of the above restructuring of a list *x* of an arbitrary structure and nesting.

```
In[7]:= IntSimplList[x_/; ListQ[x]] := Module[{a = ToString1[x],
                    b = {}, c = {}, d, k, j, p = ""}, d = StringLength[a];
  Do[If[StringTake[a, {j}] == "{" && StringTake[a, {j + 1}] != "{",
                                          AppendTo[b, j], 77], {j, d - 1}];
 For[k = 1, k <= Length[b], k++, For[j = b[[k]], j <= Infinity, j++,
      p = p <> StringTake[a, {j}]; If[SyntaxQ[p], AppendTo[c, j];
                                              Break[], Continue[]]; p = ""]];
ToExpression[StringReplacePart[a, "", Map[{#, #} &, Join[b, c]]]]]

In[8]:= sv := {{{p}, {F[b]}, {a + b}}, {u^3}, {c}, {{{{n/m}, {{"h"}, {c^2},
                                       {g[f]}}, {n^2 + t}}}}, {{y}, {"x"}}}
In[9]:= IntSimplList[sv]
Out[9]= {{p, F[b], a + b}, u^3, c, {{{n/m, {"h", c^2, g[f]}, n^2 + t}}},
                                                                   {y, "x"}}
```

By substantially using now the previous procedure, we can more easily program a procedure that applies a certain symbol to the desired element of the nested list at a set nesting level.

```
In[7]:= SymbolToElemOnLevel[F_/; SymbolQ[F], x_/; ListQ[x],
                                            n_Integer, m_Integer] :=
  Module[{a = ToString1[ElemsOnLevel[x]], b, c, d, g, t, u, s, z},
  s[t_] := If[IntegerQ[t], ToString[t], t]; SetAttributes[s, Listable];
        z[t_] := If[StringQ[t] && IntegerQ[ToExpression[t]],
  ToExpression[t], If[Quiet[Check[Part[t, 0] === F, False]] &&
 StringQ[Part[t, 1]] && IntegerQ[Set[u, ToExpression[Part[t, 1]]]],
             F[u], t]]; d = Map[s, x]; SetAttributes[z, Listable];
                                  a = ToString1[ElemsOnLevel[d]];
 If[n <= MaxLevel[x] - 1 && n > 0, If[Length[Level[x, {n}]] >= m,
    b = ReduceAdjacentStr[ReduceAdjacentStr[a, "{", 1], "}", 1];
                              b = ToExpression["{" <> b <> "}"];
  g[t_] := If[IntegerQ[t], Nothing, t]; SetAttributes[g, Listable];
             b = Quiet[Check[Select[b, #[[3]] == n &][[m]][[1]],
  Return[{Print["No element with number " <> ToString[m] <>
                     " at level " <> ToString[n]]; $Failed}[[1]]]]];
              c = ToString1[b]; b = F @@ {b}; b = ToString1[b];
```

```
                              t = ToExpression[StringReplace[a, c -> b]];
                                   t = IntSimplList[Map[g, t]]; Map[z, t],
  Print["No element with number " <> ToString[m] <> " at level "
                                          <> ToString[n]]; $Failed],
      Print["No level with number " <> ToString[n]]; $Failed]]
In[8]:= t := {{p, b, x^2 + y^2, c + b, 7.7, 78, m/n}, u, c^2,
                         {{{n, {"h", f, {m, n, p}, c}, n + p^2}}}, {y, "x"}}
In[9]:= SymbolToElemOnLevel[F, t, 2, 3]
Out[9]= {{p, b, F[x^2 + y^2], b + c, 7.7, 78, m/n}, u, c^2,
                         {{{n, {"h", f, {m, n, p}, c}, n + p^2}}}, {y, "x"}}
In[10]:= SymbolToElemOnLevel[F, t, 4, 2]
Out[10]= {{p, b, x^2 + y^2, b + c, 7.7, 78, m/n}, u, c^2,
                    {{{n, {"h", f, {m, n, p}, c}, F[n + p^2]}}}, {y, "x"}}}
In[11]:= SymbolToElemOnLevel[F, t, 2, 12]
       "No element with number 12 at level 2"
Out[11]= $Failed
In[12]:= SymbolToElemOnLevel[F, t, 7, 6]
       "No level with number 7"
Out[12]= $Failed
```

The procedure call ***SymbolToElemOnLevel*[*F,x,n,m*]** returns the result of applying of a symbol ***F*** to an element with number ***m*** of nesting level ***n*** of the nested list ***x.*** The procedure handles the erroneous situations due to using of incorrect nesting levels and elements numbers at nesting levels with return **$***Failed* and printing of appropriate message. Meantime, at a nesting level ***n*** of form **...**{***a, b,..., {c},..., d***}**...** only {***a, b,..., d***} elements other than lists are considered as elements, and elements of more higher nesting level ***p > n,*** such as {***c***}, are ignored. The above fragment represents the source code of the procedure along with typical examples of its application.

The following procedure is a rather useful generalization of the previous procedure. The call ***SymbolToElemOnLevel1*[*F,x,n*]** returns the result of applying of a symbol ***F*** to elements of the nested list ***x*** that are defined by a nested list ***n,*** coded in the form of integer nested list {{l_1, {p_1 ,..., p_n}}, ..., {l_t, {q_1, ..., q_m}}}. In this list for elements in form {l_1, {p_1 ,..., p_n}} as the first element l_1 is a nesting level whereas the ***2nd*** element-list are numbers elements on the set nesting level. In addition, elements of the *Integer* type in the list *x* are coded in the string format. At the same time, the procedure handles the erroneous situations which are caused by the using of incorrect nesting levels and elements numbers at nesting levels with return *$Failed* and printing of appropriate messages. The fragment below represents the source code of the ***SymbolToElemOnLevel1*** procedure with examples of its use.

```
In[5]:= SymbolToElemOnLevel1[F_/; SymbolQ[F],
                                        x_/; ListQ[x], n_/; ListQ[n]] :=
  Module[{a = x, b, d, m = If[IntegerQ[n[[1]]], {n}, n], t = {}, h = {},
                                                   s = {}, v = {}, u, k, j},
  d = Gather[LevelsOfList[x]]; d = Map[{#[[1]], Length[#]} &, d];
                              Map[{s = Flatten[Append[s, d[[#]][[1]]]],
     v = Flatten[Append[v, d[[#]][[2]]]]} &, Range[1, Length[d]]];
 Map[{AppendTo[t, m[[#]][[1]]], AppendTo[h, Max[m[[#]][[2]]]]} &,
                                                      Range[1, Length[m]]];
                                         If[Set[u, Complement[t, s]] != {},
                        Return[{Print["Levels " <> ToString[u] <>
                                         " are absent"]; $Failed}[[1]]],
    For[k = 1, k <= Length[d], k++, For[j = 1, j <= Length[m], j++,
      If[d[[k]][[1]] == m[[j]][[1]] && d[[k]][[2]] < Max[m[[j]][[2]]],
   Return[{Print["The element numbers greater than the number
 of elements on level " <> ToString[d[[k]][[1]]]]; $Failed}[[1]]], 7]]];
Do[Do[a = SymbolToElemOnLevel[F, a, k[[1]], j], {j, k[[2]]}], {k, m}]; a]]
In[6]:= h := {{a, b, c}, c, d, {{{g, v, {m, n, p}, f}}}, {x, y, z}}
In[7]:= SymbolToElemOnLevel1[F, h, {{2, {1, 2, 3, 6}}, {4, {1, 2}},
                                                 {5, {1, 2, 3}, {4, {1, 2}}}}]
Out[7]= {{F[a],F[b],F[c]}, F[c], d, {{{F[g], F[v], {F[m], F[n], F[p]}, f}}},
                                                                  {x, y, F[z]}}
In[8]:= SymbolToElemOnLevel1[F, h, {{2, {1, 4, 6}}, {5, {1, 2, 3}}}]
Out[8]= {{F[a], b, c}, c, d, {{{g, v, {F[m], F[n], F[p]}, f}}},
                                                               {F[x], y, F[z]}}
In[9]:= SymbolToElemOnLevel1[F, h, {{2, {1, 4, 6, 7}}, {6, {1, 2, 3}},
                                                              {7, {1, 2, 3}}}]
          "Levels {6, 7} are absent"
Out[9]= $Failed
In[10]:= SymbolToElemOnLevel1[F, h, {{2, {1, 6, 7}}, {5, {1, 2}}}]
          "The element numbers greater than the number of
          elements on level 2"
Out[10]= $Failed
```

Finally, the simple ***SymbolToListAll*** procedure returns the result of applying of the given ***S*** symbol to each element at all nesting levels of a list ***x***. The following fragment represents the source code of the procedure with an example of its application.

```
In[147]:= SymbolToListAll[x_/; ListQ[x], S_/; SymbolQ[S]] :=
 Module[{a}, SetAttributes[a, Listable]; a[t_] := S @@ {x}; Map[a, x]]
In[148]:= t := {{a, b}, c, m + n, 77, {{{m, {{c + d, n/p}}}}}, {h, "g"}}
In[149]:= SymbolToListAll[t, F]
Out[149]= {{F[a], F[b]}, F[c], F[m + n], F[77], {{{F[m], {{F[c + d],
                                        F[n/p]}}}}}, {F[h], F["g"]}}
```

The above procedures ***LevelsOfList, IntSimplList, SolidLevelQ, SymbolToElemOnLevel, SymbolToElemOnLevel1, SymbolToListAll*** are of a certain interest in programming problems related to the nested lists of an arbitrary structure, extending ***Mathematica's*** built-in means. These means admit a number of modifications, representing an independent interest too [6-15].

The possibility of exchange by elements of the nested lists which are located at the different nesting levels is of a certain interest. The problem is successfully solved by the procedure ***SwapOnLevels***. The procedure call ***SwapOnLevels[x, y]*** returns the result of *exchange* of elements of a list ***x***, being at the nesting levels and with their sequential numbers at these levels that are defined by the nested list ***y*** of the format {{{***s1, p1***}, {***s2, p2***}}, ..., {{***sk1, pk1***}, {***sk2, pk2***}}} where a pair {{***sj1, pj1***}, {***sj2, pj2***}} defines replacement of an element which is at the nesting level ***sj1*** with a sequential number ***pj1*** at this level by an element that is at the nesting level ***sj2*** with a sequential number ***pj2*** at this level, and vice versa. In a case of impossibility of such exchange because of lack of a nesting level ***sj*** or/and a sequential number ***pj*** the procedure call prints the appropriate message. In addition, in a case of absence in the ***y*** list of the acceptable pairs for exchange the procedure call returns *$Failed* and prints the above message. The next fragment represents source code of the ***SortOnLevels*** procedure along with typical examples of its application.

```
In[229]:= L := {b, t, c, {{3, 2, 1, {g, s, a}, k, 0}, 2, 3, 1}, 1, 2, {m, n, f}}
In[230]:= SwapOnLevels[L, {{{1, 5}, {4, 3}}, {{1, 1}, {3, 3}}}]
```

```
Out[230]= {1, t, c, {{3, 2, b, {g, s, 2}, k, 0}, 2, 3, 1}, 1, a, {m, n, f}}

In[231]:= SwapOnLevels[x_/; ListQ[x], y_/; ListListQ[y]] :=
  Module[{a = ElemsOnLevels2[x], b, c, d, f, g, h, p, n, s, z, u = 0,
                                        w = ReplaceAll[x, {} -> Null]},
   g[t_] := "(" <> ToString1[t] <> ")"; SetAttributes[g, Listable];
                        f[t_] := h[[n++]]; SetAttributes[f, Listable];
          s[t_] := ToExpression[t][[1]]; SetAttributes[s, Listable];
  Do[z = y[[j]]; n = 1; If[MemberQ5[a, #[[2 ;; 3]] == z[[1]] &] &&
                                 MemberQ5[a, #[[2 ;; 3]] == z[[2]] &],
                               b = Select[a, #[[2 ;; 3]] == z[[1]] &][[1]];
                               c = Select[a, #[[2 ;; 3]] == z[[2]] &][[1]];
              a = ReplaceAll[a, b -> d]; a = ReplaceAll[a, c -> h];
              a = ReplaceAll[a, d -> c]; a = ReplaceAll[a, h -> b];
  p = Map[g, w]; h = Map[ToString1, a]; h = Map[s, Map[f, p]], u++;
                                      Print["Pairs " <> ToString[z] <>
                 " are incorrect for elements swap"]], {j, 1, Length[y]}];
   If[u == Length[y], $Failed, ReplaceAll[h, Null -> Nothing]]]

In[232]:= SwapOnLevels[L, {{{{7, 1}, {2, 3}}, {{8, 1}, {3, 3}}}}]
Pairs {{{7, 1}, {2, 3}}, {{8, 1}, {3, 3}}} are incorrect for elements swap
Out[232]= $Failed
```

A certain interest is the *conditional sorting* of lists when some elements in a list are not involved in the sorting, that is, they are defined as unmovable. The immobility of the elements of the sorted list is determined by some condition *(position, type, etc.)*. The ***SortLcond*** procedure is one of means solving this problem. The procedure call ***SortLcond*[*x, y, z*]** returns the sorting result of a list ***x*** according to a sorting function defined by the *optional* argument **z** – *a pure function (at absence of z argument the canonical sorting order is used)*, provided that the elements of the initial ***x*** list that are defined by a position or their list ***y*** are unmovable. The procedure processes the erroneous positions situation with returning **$***Failed* with printing of the appropriate messages.

```
In[14]:= SortLcond[x_/; ListQ[x], y_/; IntegerQ[y] | |
                               IntegerListQ[y], z___/; PureFuncQ[z]] :=
                     Module[{a = Flatten[{x}], b = {}, c = Length[x]},
                       Map[If[# < 1 | | # > c, AppendTo[b, #], 7] &, y];
 If[b != {}, Print["Positions " <> ToString[b] <> " are invalid"]; $Failed,
```

```
b = Map[{#, a[[#]]} &, y]; Map[{a[[#]] = Nothing} &, y];
                                                    a = Sort[a, z];
Do[a = Insert[a, b[[j]][[2]], b[[j]][[1]]], {j, Length[b]}]; a]]
In[15]:= SortLcond[Range[1, 19], {1, 5, 9, 13, 17}, #1 > #2 &]
Out[15]= {1, 19, 18, 16, 5, 15, 14, 12, 9, 11, 10, 8, 13, 7, 6, 4, 17, 3, 2}
In[16]:= SortLcond[Range[1, 19], {0, 5, 21, 27}, #1 > #2 &]
         Positions {0, 21, 27} are invalid
Out[16]= $Failed
```

The natural version of the previous procedure is when the immobility of the elements of the sorted list is determined by their type. The ***SortLcond1*** procedure is one of means solving this problem. The procedure call ***SortLcond1[x, y, z]*** returns the sorting result of a list ***x*** according to a sorting function defined by the optional argument ***z*** – a pure function *(in a case of absence of z argument the canonical sorting order is used)*, provided that the elements of the initial ***x*** list that satisfy a testing pure function ***y*** are unmovable. The following fragment represents source code of the ***SortLcond1*** procedure with an example of its application.

```
In[15]:= SortLcond1[x_ /; ListQ[x], y_ /; PureFuncQ[y],
                                          z___ /; PureFuncQ[z]] :=
     Module[{a = Flatten[{x}], b = {}, c = Length[x], k = 0},
   Map[If[{k++, y @@ {#}}[[2]], AppendTo[b, {k, #}], 77] &, a];
   Map[{a[[#]] = Nothing} &, Map[#[[1]] &, b]]; a = Sort[a, z];
      Do[a = Insert[a, b[[j]][[2]], b[[j]][[1]]], {j, Length[b]}]; a]
In[16]:= SortLcond1[Range[1, 19], PrimeQ[#] &, #1 > #2 &]
Out[16]= {18, 2, 3, 16, 5, 15, 7, 14, 12, 10, 11, 9, 13, 8, 6, 4, 17, 1, 19}
```

Conditional sorting of types determined by ***SortLcond*** and ***SortLcond1*** procedures it is simple to extend on the nested lists, both as a whole and relative to the set nesting levels. We leave this to the interested reader as a rather useful exercise.

An example is the ***SortOnLevels*** procedure, being a rather natural generalization of the ***SortOnLevel*** procedure [8,16]. The procedure call ***SortOnLevels[x, m, Sf]*** where the optional ***Sf*** argument determines a sorting pure function analogously to the ***SortOnLevel*** procedure returns the sorting result of a list ***x*** at its nesting levels ***m***. Furthermore, as an argument ***m*** can be used a single level, the levels list or the "***All***" word that defines all nesting levels of the ***x*** list which are subject to sorting. If all ***m*** levels are absent then the procedure call returns *$Failed* with printing of appropriate message, otherwise the procedure call prints the message concerning only levels absent in the ***x*** list. It must be kept in mind, by default the sorting is made in *symbolic* format, i.e. all elements of a sorted ***x*** list before *sorting* by means of the standard ***Sort*** function are presented in the string format. Whereas the procedure call ***SortOnLevels[x, m, Sf]*** returns the sorting result of the ***x*** list at its nesting levels ***m*** depending on a sorting pure ***Sf*** function that is the optional argument. Fragment represents source code of the ***SortOnLevels*** procedure with an example of its typical application.

```
In[7]:= SortOnLevels[x_/; ListQ[x], m_/; IntegerQ[m] ||
                          IntegerListQ[m] || m === All, Sf___] :=
        Module[{a, b, c = ReplaceAll[x, {} -> {Null}], d, h, t, g, s},
          a = LevelsOfList[c]; d = Sort[DeleteDuplicates[a]];
                                                    If[m === All ||
   SameQ[d, Set[h, Sort[DeleteDuplicates[Flatten[{m}]]]]], t = d,
 If[Set[g, Intersection[h, d]] == {}, Print["Levels " <> ToString[h] <>
   " are absent in the list; " <> "nesting levels must belong to " <>
                                  ToString[Range[1, Max[d]]]];
      Return[$Failed], t = g; s = Select[h, ! MemberQ[d, #] &];
          If[s == {}, Null, Print["Levels " <> ToString[s] <>
   " are absent in the list; " <> "nesting levels must belong to " <>
                               ToString[Range[1, Max[d]]]]]]]];
                     Map[Set[c, SortOnLevel[c, #, Sf]] &, t];
                                ReplaceAll[c, Null -> Nothing]]

In[8]:= SortOnLevels[{{{3, 4, 5, 0, 8, 7, 9, 1}}, 9, 8, 7, {t, b, c, a, t},
                              {{6, 3, 3, 5, 2, 9, 8}}}, {1, 2, 3}]
Out[8]= {{{0, 1, 2, 3, 3, 3, 4, 5}}, 7, 8, 9, {a, b, c, t, t}, {{5, 6, 7, 8, 8, 9, 9}}}
```

The call ***Replace[e, r, lev]*** of the built-in function applies the rules ***r*** to parts of a list ***e*** specified by the nesting levels ***lev***. In addition, all rules are applied to all identical ***e*** elements of the ***lev***. An useful enough addition to the ***Replace*** function is the procedure, whose procedure call ***ReplaceOnLevels[x, y]*** returns the result of replacement of elements of a list ***x***, that are at the nesting levels and with their sequential numbers at these levels which are defined by the nested list *y* of the format {{*s1, p1, e1*}, {*s2, p2, e2*},…,{*sk, pk, ek*}} where sublist {*sj, pj, ej*} *(j = 1..k)* defines replacement of an element that is located at nesting level *sj* with sequential number *pj* at this level by an *ej* element. If some such substitution is not possible because of lack of a nesting level *sj* or/and a sequential number *pj* then the procedure call prints the appropriate message. At the same time, in a case of absence in the *y* list of the acceptable values {*sj, pj, ej*} for replacement the procedure call returns $*Failed* with printing of appropriate message. The fragment represents source code of the procedure with typical examples of its application.

```
In[2242]:= ReplaceOnLevels[x_/; ListQ[x], y_/; ListQ[y]] :=
                    Module[{a, b, d = {}, f, g, h, p, n, s, z, u = 0,
       w = ReplaceAll[x, {} -> Null], r = If[ListListQ[y], y, {y}]},
          a = ElemsOnLevels2[w]; b = Map[#[[2 ;; 3]] &, a];
  g[t_] := "(" <> ToString1[t] <> ")"; SetAttributes[g, Listable];
                f[t_] := h[[n++]]; SetAttributes[f, Listable];
    s[t_] := ToExpression[t][[1]]; SetAttributes[s, Listable];
            Do[z = r[[j]]; n = 1; If[MemberQ[b, z[[1 ;; 2]]],
                   Do[If[a[[k]][[2 ;; 3]] == z[[1 ;; 2]],
          AppendTo[d, PrependTo[a[[k]][[2 ;; 3]], z[[3]]]],
        AppendTo[d, a[[k]]]], {k, 1, Length[a]}]; a = d; d = {};
p = Map[g, w]; h = Map[ToString1, a]; h = Map[s, Map[f, p]], u++;
         Print["Data " <> ToString[z] <> " for replacement are
                            incorrect"]], {j, 1, Length[r]}];
  If[u == Length[r], $Failed, ReplaceAll[h, Null -> Nothing]]]

In[2243]:= ReplaceOnLevels[{t, c, {{{a + b, h}}}, {m, n, f},
                 {{{{c/d, g}}}}}, {{4, 1, m + n}, {5, 1, Sin[x]}}]
Out[2243]= {t, c, {{{m + n, h}}}, {m, n, f}, {{{{Sin[x], g}}}}}
In[2244]:= ReplaceOnLevels[{t, c, {{{}}}, {m, n, f}, {{{{}}}}},
                           {{4, 1, m + n}, {3, 1, Sin[x]}}]
Out[2244]= {t, c, {{Sin[x]}}, {m, n, f}, {{{m + n}}}}
```

In turn, the ***ReplaceOnLevels1*** procedure [16] works similar to the previous ***ReplaceOnLevels*** procedure with an important difference. The call ***ReplaceOnLevels1[x, y]*** returns the result of replacement of elements of a list ***x***, that are at the nesting levels and satisfying set conditions that are defined by the nested list *y* of the format {{*s1, c1, e1*}, {*s2, c2, e2*},…,{*sk, ck, ek*}}, where sublist {*sj, cj, ej*} *(j = 1..k)* determines replacement of an element that is located at nesting level ***sj*** and satisfies set condition ***cj*** by an ***ej*** element. If substitution is not possible because of absence of a nesting level ***sj*** or/and falsity of testing condition ***cj*** the call prints the appropriate message. At the same time, in a case of lack in *y* list of any acceptable values {*sj, cj, ej*} for replacement the call returns $*Failed* with print of the appropriate messages.

A rather useful addition to the ***ReplaceOnLevels*** procedure is the procedure whose call ***ExchangeListsElems***[*x, y, z*] returns the result of exchange by elements of a list *x* and a list *y* that are located at the nesting levels and with their sequential numbers at these levels. The receptions that were used at programming of the procedures ***LevelsOfList, ElemsOnLevels ÷ ElemsOnLevels2, SortOnLevel, SwapOnLevels, ReplaceOnLevels, ReplaceOnLevels1*** and ***ExchangeListsElems*** that are of independent interest are of a certain interest to the problems dealing with the nested lists [8].

Unlike the built-in ***Insert*** function the following procedure is a rather convenient means for inserting of expressions to the given place of any nesting level of the list. The procedure call ***InsertInLevels***[*x, y, z*] returns the result of inserting in a list *x* of ***expj*** expressions that are defined by the second *y* argument of the form {{***lev1, ps1, exp1***},…,{***levk, psk, expk***}} where ***levj*** defines the nesting level of *x*, ***psj*** defines the sequential number of this element on the level and ***expj*** defines an expression that will be inserted before *(z = 1)* or after *(z = 2)* this element *(j = 1..k)*. At that, on inadmissible pairs {***levj, psj***} the procedure call prints the appropriate messages. Whereas, in a case of lack in the *y* list of any acceptable {***levj, psj***} for inserting, the call returns $*Failed* with print of the appropriate messages. At the same time, the ***4th*** optional ***g*** argument – *an indefinite symbol* – allows to insert in the list the required sublists, increasing nesting level of *x* list in general. In this case, the expression ***expj*** is coded in the form *g*[*a, b, c, …*] which admits different useful compositions as the examples of the fragment below along with source code of the

InsertInLevels procedure very visually illustrate.

```
In[5]:= InsertInLevels[x_/; ListQ[x], y_/; ListQ[y],
                          z_/; MemberQ[{1, 2}, z], g___] :=
  Module[{a, b, c, d, h, f = ReplaceAll[x, {} -> Null], p, u = 0,
          r = If[ListListQ[y], y, {y}]}, a = ElemsOnLevels2[f];
                                         b = Map[#[[2 ;; 3]] &, a];
    d[t_] := If[StringQ[t] && SuffPref[t, "Sequences[", 1],
              ToExpression[t], t]; SetAttributes[d, Listable];
  Do[p = r[[j]]; If[Set[h, Select[a, #[[2 ;; 3]] == p[[1 ;; 2]] &]] == {},
  u++; Print["Level and/or position " <> ToString[p[[1 ;; 2]]] <>
                                   " are incorrect"], c = If[z == 2,
       "Sequences[" <> ToString[{h[[1]][[1]], p[[3]]}] <> "]",
       "Sequences[" <> ToString[{p[[3]], h[[1]][[1]]}] <> "]"];
    f = Map[d, ReplaceOnLevels[f, {Flatten[{p[[1 ;; 2]], c}]}]]],
                                                  {j, 1, Length[r]}];
    If[u == Length[r], $Failed, ReplaceAll[f, {If[{g} != {} &&
          NullQ[g], g -> List, Nothing], Null -> Nothing}]]]]
In[6]:= InsertInLevels[L = {t, c, {{{a + b, h}}}, {m, n, f}, {{{{77, g}}}},
                          77, 72}, {{4, 1, avz}, {5, 2, agn}}, 1]
Out[6]= {t, c, {{{avz, a + b, h}}}, {m, n, f}, {{{{77, agn, g}}}}, 77, 72}
In[7]:= InsertInLevels[L, {{7, 1, avz}, {5, 2, agn}}, 2]
   Level and/or position {7, 1} are incorrect
Out[7]= {t, c, {{{a + b, h}}}, {m, n, f}, {{{{77, g, agn}}}}, 77, 72}
In[8]:= InsertInLevels[{1, 2, 3, 4, 5, 6, 7, 8, 9}, {{1, 3, F[{avz, a, b, c}]},
                          {1, 7, F[{agn, art, kr}]}}, 2, F]
Out[8]= {1, 2, 3, {avz, a, b, c}, 4, 5, 7, {agn, art, kr}, 7, 8, 9}
```

Unlike the built-in ***Delete*** function the following procedure is a rather convenient means for deleting of expressions on the given place of any nesting level of the list. The procedure call ***DeleteAtLevels[x, y]*** returns the result of deleting in a list ***x*** of its elements that are determined by the second ***y*** argument of the format ***{{lev1, ps1}, ..., {levk, psk}}***, where ***levj*** determines the nesting level of ***x*** and ***psj*** defines the sequential number of this element on the level ***(j = 1..k)***. On inadmissible pairs ***{levj, psj}*** the procedure call prints the appropriate messages. Whereas in a case of lack in the ***y*** list of any acceptable ***{levj, psj}*** pair for the deleting, the procedure call returns ***$Failed*** with printing of the appropriate message. The following fragment represents source code of the procedure with typical examples of its application.

```
In[7]:= DeleteAtLevels[x_/; ListQ[x], y_/; ListQ[y]] :=
          Module[{a, b, c = 0, d, h, f = ReplaceAll[x, {} -> Null],
                                         r = If[ListListQ[y], y, {y}]},
           a = ElemsOnLevels2[f]; b = Map[#[[2 ;; 3]] &, a];
           d[t_] := If[t === "Nothing", ToExpression[t], t];
                                         SetAttributes[d, Listable];
           Do[h = r[[j]]; If[Select[b, # == h &] == {}, c++;
  Print["Level and/or position " <> ToString[h] <> " are incorrect"],
  f = ReplaceOnLevels[f, {Flatten[{h, "Nothing"}]}]], {j, 1, Length[r]}];
                                                      f = Map[d, f];
      If[c == Length[r], $Failed, ReplaceAll[f, Null -> Nothing]]]
In[8]:= DeleteAtLevels[{1, 2, 3, 4, 5, 6, 7, 8, 9, 10}, {{1, 5}, {1, 8}, {1, 3}}]
Out[8]= {1, 2, 4, 6, 7, 9, 10}
In[9]:= DeleteAtLevels[{t, c, {{{a*b, h}}}, {m, n, f}, {{{{77, g}}}},
                        77, 72}, {{4, 1}, {4, 2}, {5, 2}, {2, 1}, {2, 3}}]
Out[9]= {t, c, {{{}}}, {n}, {{{{77}}}}, 77, 72}
```

In a number of cases exists a need of generation of the list of variables in the form ***Vk (k* = *1..n)***, where ***V*** – a name and ***n*** – a positive integer. The standard functions ***CharacterRange*** and ***Range*** of the ***Mathematica*** don't solve the problem, therefore for these purposes it is rather successfully possible to use the procedures ***Range1*** ÷ ***Range5***, whose source codes with typical examples of their use can be found in [8,16]. The above tools of so-called ***Range*** group are useful at processing of the lists. So, the coder–decoder ***CodeEncode***, operating on the principle of switch, uses 2 functions ***Range5*** and ***Prime***. The procedure call ***CodeEncode***[***x***] returns the result of coding of a string ***x*** of *Latin* printable *ASCII*–symbols, and vice versa. The ***CodeEncode1*** tool is a rather useful extension of the above ***CodeEncode*** procedure in the event of datafiles of *ASCII* format [8,16].

The next group of tools serves for expansion of the built-in ***MemberQ*** function, and its tools are quite useful in work with list structures. This group is based on procedures ***MemberQ1*** ÷ ***MemberQ5*** which along with procedures ***MemberT***, ***MemberLN***, ***MemberQL*** and ***MemberQL1*** are useful in the lists processing. In principle, these means allow interesting enough modifications significantly broadening the sphere of their application. Source codes of the above tools of so–called ***Member–***group along with examples of their application can be found in [8,10-16].

On a basis of the ***Intersection2*** and ***ElemsOnLevelList*** [6,12] procedures the next procedure can be programmed that allows to receive intersection of the elements of nesting levels of a list. The procedure call ***ElemsLevelsIntersect***[***x***] returns the nested list whose two–element sublists has the format {{***n, m***}, {{***e1, p1***}, {***e2, p2***}, ... }}, where {***n, m***} – the nesting levels of a list ***x*** *(**n ÷ m**)* and {***ej, pj***} determines common ***ej*** element for the nesting levels {***n, m***}, whereas ***pj*** is its common minimal multiplicity for both nesting levels. In a case of the only list as an argument ***x*** the call returns the empty list, i.e. {}. The following fragment represents source codes of the ***Intersection2*** and ***ElemsOnLevelList*** along with examples of their application.

```
In[7]:= Intersection2[x__List] := Module[{a = Intersection[x], b = {}},
         Do[AppendTo[b, DeleteDuplicates[Flatten[Map[{a[[j]],
                    Count[#, a[[j]]]} &, {x}]]]], {j, Length[a]}]; b]
In[8]:= Intersection2[{a + b, a, b, a + b}, {a, a + b, d, b, a + b},
                                          {a + b, b, a, d, a + b}]
Out[8]= {{a, 1}, {b, 1}, {a + b, 2}}
In[9]:= ElemsLevelsIntersect[x_ /; ListQ[x]] :=
           Module[{a = ElemsOnLevelList[x], b, c = {}, d, h = {}},
                   d = Length[a]; Do[Do[If[k == j, Null,
          If[Set[b, Intersection2[a[[k]][[2]], a[[j]][[2]]]] != {},
  AppendTo[c, {{a[[k]][[1]], a[[j]][[1]]}, b}], Null]], {j, k, d}], {k, d}];
    Do[AppendTo[h, {c[[j]][[1]], Map[{#[[1]], Min[#[[2 ;; -1]]]} &,
                               c[[j]][[2]]]}], {j, Length[c]}]; h]
In[9]:= ElemsLevelsIntersect[{a, c, b, b, c, {b, b, b, c, {c, c, b, b}}}]
Out[9]= {{{1, 2}, {{b, 2}, {c, 1}}}, {{1, 3}, {{b, 2}, {c, 2}}}, {{2, 3}, {{b, 2}, {c, 1}}}}
```

The procedure call ***ToCanonicList***[***x***] converts a list ***x*** of the *ListList* type whose sub-lists have form {***a, hj***} and/or {{***a1,…,ap***}, ***hj***}, into equivalent nested classical list where ***a, ak*** are elements of list *(**k = 1..p**)* and ***hj*** – the nesting levels on which they have to be in the resultant list. The nested list with any combination of sub-lists of the above forms is allowed as the *x* argument. The following fragment represents source code of the ***ToClassicList*** procedure with 2 examples of its use which well illustrates the procedure essence.

```
In[15]:= ToCanonicList[x_ /; ListQ[x] && ListListQ[x] &&
                                         Length[x[[1]]] == 2] :=
  Module[{a, b, c, d, y, v, h, f, m, g = FromCharacterCode[6]},
                       v[t_] := Join[Map[{{#, t[[2]]}} &, t[[1]]]];
           h[t_] := If[ListQ[t[[1]]], Map[{#, t[[2]]} &, t[[1]]], t];
  f[t_] := Module[{n = 1}, Map[If[OddQ[n++], #, Nothing] &, t]];
 y = Partition[Flatten[Join[Map[If[ListQ[#[[1]]], v[#], {#}] &, x]]], 2];
                                   a = Sort[y, #1[[2]] <= #2[[2]] &];
 a = Map[{#[[1]][[-1]], Flatten[#]} &, Gather[a, #1[[2]] == #2[[2]] &]];
          a = Map[{#[[1]], Sort[f[#[[2]]]]} &, a]; m = Length[a];
      d = Map[#[[1]] &, a]; d = Flatten[{d[[1]], Differences[d]}];
              a = Map[{#[[1]], b = #[[2]]; AppendTo[b, g]} &, a];
                            c = MultiList[a[[1]][[2]], d[[1]] - 1];
 Do[c = Quiet[ReplaceAll[c, g -> MultiList[a[[j]][[2]], d[[j]] - 1]]],
                          {j, 2, m}]; ReplaceAll[c, g -> Nothing]]

In[16]:= ToCanonicList[{{a*b, 2}, {b, 2}, {{z, m, n}, 12}, {c, 4}, {d, 4},
  {{n, y, w, z}, 5}, {b, 2}, {m*x, 5}, {n, 5}, {t, 7}, {g, 7}, {x, 12}, {y, 12}}]
Out[16]= {{b, b, a*b, {{c, d, {n, n, w, m*x, y, z, {{g, t,
                                           {{{{{m, n, x, y, z}}}}}}}}}}}}
In[17]:= ToCanonicList[{{a, 1}, {b, 2}, {c, 3}, {d, 4}, {g, 5}, {h, 6}}]
Out[17]= {a, {b, {c, {d, {g, {h}}}}}}
```

A useful addition to the built-in ***Level*** function is procedure whose call ***DispLevels*[*x*]** returns the list of *ListList* type from **2**-element sub-lists whose the first element defines the level of the *x* list, while the second element determines the level itself of the *x* list. The following fragment represents the source code of the ***DispLevels*** procedure with examples of its application.

```
In[29]:= DispLevels[x_List] := Module[{a = {{1, x}}, b = x, k = 2},
Do[b = Level[b, {1}]; b = Flatten[Map[If[! ListQ[#], Nothing, #] &, b], 1];
                     AppendTo[a, {k++, b}], MaxLevel[x] - 2]; a]

In[30]:= DispLevels[{a, b, c, {m, {h, g}}, m}]
Out[30]= {{1, {a, b, c, {m, {h, g}}, m}}, {2, {m, {h, g}}}, {3, {h, g}}}
```

Using the ***DispLevels*** procedure, it is easy to obtain function whose call ***ReplaceLL[x, n, y]*** returns the result of replacing the *n–th* level of a list ***x*** with an expression ***y,*** whereas at using the word *"Nothing"* instead of ***y*** removes the *n–th* level of the ***x*** list. The function processes the erroneous situation associated with an incorrect list nesting level with output of the corresponding message. The fragment below represents the source code of the ***ReplaceLL*** function with examples of its typical application.

```
In[27]:= ReplaceLL[x_/; ListQ[x], n_Integer, y_] :=
                              If[0 < n && n <= MaxLevel[x],
                     ReplaceAll[x, DispLevels[x][[n]][[2]] -> y],
                  Print["Level " <> ToString[n] <> " is invalid"]]
In[28]:= g := {{a, b}, c, d, {{{m, {p, t}, n}}}, x, y}
In[29]:= ReplaceLL[g, 4, {a, b}]
Out[29]= {{a, b}, c, d, {{{a, b}}}, x, y}
In[30]:= ReplaceLL[g, 5, {a, b}]
Out[30]= {{a, b}, c, d, {{{m, {a, b}, n}}}, x, y}
In[31]:= ReplaceLL[g, 5, Nothing]
Out[31]= {{a, b}, c, d, {{{m, n}}}, x, y}
In[32]:= ReplaceLL[g, 7, Nothing]
         Level 7 is invalid
```

A natural extension of the previous ***ReplaceLL*** function is the ***InsDelRepList*** procedure, that allows to remove elements, replace, and insert an element at a set nesting level and in a set position of the specified nested level of a list. The ***InsDelRepList*** procedure calls define the following:

InsDelRepList[x, n, m, "Del"] – returns the result of deleting of the ***m–th*** element at the ***n–th*** nesting level of a list ***x;***

InsDelRepList[x, n, m, "Ins", y] – returns the result of inserting of an expression ***y*** into ***m–th*** position at the ***n–th*** nesting level of a list ***x;*** at the same time, if ***m<0*** then the inserting is done to the beginning of the ***x*** list, whereas at ***m >*** length of a nesting level ***n*** the inserting is done into the end of the level ***n;***

InsDelRepList[x, n, m, "Rep", y] – returns the result of replacing of an element at ***m–th*** position at the ***n–th*** nesting level of a list ***x*** with an expression ***y.*** The procedure processes the erroneous situation that is associated with the inadmissible nesting level with return *$Failed* and printing of the corresponding message. The fragment represents the source code of the procedure with examples of its application.

```
In[1942]:= InsDelRepList[x_ /; ListQ[x], n_Integer, m_Integer,
                h_ /; MemberQ[{"Ins", "Del", "Rep"}, h], y___] :=
                              Module[{a = DispLevels[x], b, c, d},
                                          If[n <= 0 | | n > MaxLevel[x],
         Print["Level " <> ToString[n] <> " is invalid"]; $Failed,
       b = a[[n]][[2]]; d = ToString[m] <> "-th element is lack";
            If[h === "Del", If[Length[b] < m, Print[d]; $Failed,
                               ReplaceAll[x, b -> Delete[b, m]]],
            If[h === "Rep", If[Length[b] < m, Print[d]; $Failed,
                          ReplaceAll[x, b -> ListAssign2[b, m, y]]],
  If[m < 1, c = Prepend[b, y], If[m > Length[b], c = Append[b, y],
                      c = Insert[b, y, m]]]; ReplaceAll[x, b -> c]]]]]
In[1943]:= g47 := {{a, b}, c, d, {{{m, {p, t}, n}}}, x, y, z}
In[1944]:= InsDelRepList[g47, 5, 1, "Del"]
Out[1944]= {{a, b}, c, d, {{{m, {t}, n}}}, x, y, z}
In[1945]:= InsDelRepList[g47, 5, 2, "Ins", agn]
Out[1945]= {{a, b}, c, d, {{{m, {p, agn, t}, n}}}, x, y, z}
In[1946]:= InsDelRepList[g47, 5, 2, "Rep", avz]
Out[1946]= {{a, b}, c, d, {{{m, {p, avz}, n}}}, x, y, z}
In[1947]:= InsDelRepList[g47, 7, 2, "Rep", avz]
          Level 7 is invalid
Out[1947]= $Failed
In[1948]:= InsDelRepList[g47, 5, 0, "Ins", avz]
Out[1948]= {{a, b}, c, d, {{{m, {avz, p, t}, n}}}, x, y, z}
```

Due to the canonical representation of lists, the procedure ***ExchangeLevels*** is of a certain interest [8,16], returning a list in *canonical* form on condition of exchange of its nesting levels. At that, the procedure below is a useful version of the above tool.

```
In[47]:= ExchangeLevels1[x_ /; ListQ[x], i_Integer, j_Integer] :=
                                          Module[{a = DispLevels[x]},
  If[MemberQ[Map[(# <= 0 | | # > MaxLevel[x]) &, {i, j}], True],
    Print["Levels " <> ToString[{i, j}] <> " are invalid"]; $Failed,
          ReplaceAll[ReplaceAll[x, a[[i]][[2]] -> a[[j]][[2]]],
                                      a[[j]][[2]] -> a[[i]][[2]]]]]
In[48]:= ExchangeLevels1[g47, 2, 5]
Out[48]= {{a, b}, c, d, {{{m, {a, b, {{m, {p, t}, n}}}, n}}}, x, y, z}
```

The procedure call ***ExchangeLevels1[x,i,j]*** returns the result of *exchange* of the nesting levels ***i*** and ***j*** of a nested list ***x***. A quite naturally there is the problem of exchange of the nesting levels of **2** various lists that is solved by means of the ***ListsExchLevels*** procedure. Using the method on which the last procedures are based, it is simple to program the means focused on the typical manipulations with the nested lists, in particular, removing and adding of the nesting levels. On the basis of the method used in the last procedures it is possible to do different manipulations with the nested lists including also their subsequent converting in lists of the canonical form [8-10,16]. For example, it is easy to program a function whose call ***PosElemOnLevel[x, n, y]*** returns positions of an element ***y*** on the ***n–th*** nesting level of a nested ***x*** list. The function processes the erroneous situation, associated with the inadmissible nesting level with return $*Failed* and print of the corresponding message. Fragment below represents the source code of the function with examples of its application.

```
In[3342]:= PosElemOnLevel[x_ /; ListQ[x], n_Integer, y_] :=
                              If[n <= 0 | | n > MaxLevel[x],
        Print["Level " <> ToString[n] <> " is invalid"]; $Failed,
                 Flatten[Position[DispLevels[x][[n]][[2]], y]]]
In[3343]:= g47 := {{a, b}, c, d, {{{m, {g, t, h, g, t, g}, n}}}, x, y, z, q}
In[3344]:= PosElemOnLevel[g47, 5, g]
Out[3344]= {1, 4, 6}
In[3345]:= PosElemOnLevel[g47, 7, g]
           Level 7 is invalid
Out[3345]= $Failed

In[3346]:= NumberOnLevels[x_ /; ListQ[x]] :=
   Map[{#[[1]], Map[#[[1]] &, Length[#[[2]]]]} &, DispLevels[x]]
In[3347]:= NumberOnLevels[g47]
Out[3347]= {{1, 8}, {2, 3}, {3, 1}, {4, 3}, {5, 6}}
```

That fragment is ended with a simple function whose call ***NumberOnLevels[x]*** returns the list of *ListList* type whose first sub-lists elements define the nesting levels of a list ***x***, while the second elements define the number of elements at each of these nesting levels. Means are of interest when working with lists.

The following procedure provides the sorting of elements of a list that are located on the set nesting level. The procedure call ***SortListOnLevel[x, n, y]*** returns the result of sorting of elements of a list ***x*** on its nesting level ***n*** according to an *ordering* function ***y*** *(an optional argument);* in the absence of ***y*** argument by default the sorting according in the standard order is done.

```
In[7]:= SortListOnLevel[x_ /; ListQ[x], n_Integer, y___] :=
                                          Module[{a = DispLevels[x]},
   If[MemberQ[Map[(# <= 0 | | # > MaxLevel[x]) &, {n}], True],
         Print["Level " <> ToString[n] <> " is invalid"]; $Failed,
                  ReplaceAll[x, a[[n]][[2]] -> Sort[a[[n]][[2]], y]]]]
In[8]:= SortListOnLevel[g47, 5, ToCharacterCode[ToString[#1]][[1]] >
                                  ToCharacterCode[ToString[#2]][[1]] &]
Out[8]= {{a, b}, c, d, {{{m, {t, t, h, g, g, g}, n}}}, x, y, z, q}
```

Unlike the standard functions ***Split, SplitBy*** the procedure call ***Split1[x, y]*** splits a list ***x*** on sub-lists consisting of elements that are located between occurrences of an element or elements of list ***y***. If ***y*** elements don't belong to the ***x*** list, the initial ***x*** list is returned. The following fragment represents source code of the ***Split1*** procedure with the typical example of its application.

```
In[7]:= Split1[x_ /; ListQ[x], y_] := Module[{a, b, c = {}, d, h, k = 1},
                                    If[MemberQ3[x, y] | | MemberQ[x, y],
         a = If[ListQ[y], Sort[Flatten[Map[Position[x, #] &, y]]],
    Flatten[Position[x, y]]]; h = a; If[a[[1]] != 1, PrependTo[a, 1]];
  If[a[[-1]] != Length[x], AppendTo[a, Length[x]]]; d = Length[a];
  While[k <= d - 1, AppendTo[c, x[[a[[k]] ;; If[k == d - 1, a[[k + 1]],
                                         a[[k + 1]] - 1]]]]; k++];
          If[h[[-1]] == Length[x], AppendTo[c, {x[[-1]]}]]; c, x]]
In[8]:= Split1[{a, b, a, b, c, d, a, b, a, b, c, d, a, b, d}, {a, c, d}]
Out[8]= {{a, b}, {a, b}, {c}, {d}, {a, b}, {a, b}, {c}, {d}, {a, b, d}, {d}}
```

At operating with the nested lists, a procedure whose call ***Lie[w]*** returns the result of converting of a source list ***w*** into a structurally similar list whose elements are in the string format and have length equal to the maximum length of all elements in the ***w*** list at all its nesting levels is of a certain interest. The following fragment represents the source code of the procedure with an example of its typical application.

```
In[369]:= Lie[x_ /; ListQ[x]] := Module[{a, b = Flatten[x], c, d, f},
            SetAttributes[ToString1, Listable]; a = ToString1[b];
                                        c = StringLength[a[[1]]];
                  Map[If[c < Set[d, StringLength[#]], c = d, 7] &, a];
                        f[t_, s_] := ToString1[t] <> StringRepeat[" ",
         s - StringLength[ToString1[t]]]; SetAttributes[f, Listable];
                        ClearAttributes[ToString1, Listable]; f[x, c]]
In[370]:= t := {{m, bbbb, g}, {{{n, m, ddd}}}, n, mmmmmm}; Lie[t]
Out[370]= {{"m     ", "bbbb  ", "g     "}, {{{"n     ", "m     ", "ddd   "}}},
                                                       "n     ", "mmmmmm"}
```

Using the ***Lie*** procedure, in particular, it is possible to easily program a procedure whose call ***ContinuousSL[x, y]*** returns the result of a continuous sort of all the elements of the nested list ***x*** *(i.e. ignoring its nesting levels)* with *retention* its internal structure. The sorting is done either by accepted conventions for the ***Sort*** function or on a basis of the optional ***y*** argument defining the *ordering* function. The following fragment represents the source code of the ***ContinuousSL*** procedure with examples of its use.

```
In[2430]:= ContinuousSL[x_ /; ListQ[x], y___] :=
                        Module[{a = ToString1[Lie[x]], b, c = {}, d},
                  b = StringLength[a]; Do[d = StringTake[a, {j}];
       If[MemberQ[{"{", "}"}, d], AppendTo[c, {d, j}], 7], {j, b}];
                           d = ToString1[Lie[Sort[Flatten[x], y]]];
 Do[d = StringInsert[d, c[[j]][[1]], c[[j]][[2]] + 1], {j, 1, Length[c]}];
                        Map[ToExpression, ToExpression[d]][[1]]]
In[2431]:= g47 := {{7, 122}, 14, 8, {{{500, {0, 90}, 6}}}, {47, 77, 42}}
In[2432]:= ContinuousSL[g47, #1 > #2 &]
Out[2432]= {{500, 122}, 90, 77, {{{47, {42, 14}, 8}}}, {7, 6, 0}}
In[2433]:= L = {c, 5, 9, {{sv}, {34}, {{agn, {{{500}}}, b, {{{90}}}}}}, a};
In[2434]:= ContinuousSL[L]
Out[2434]= {5, 9, 34, {{90}, {500}, {{a, {{{agn}}}, b, {{{c}}}}}}, sv}
```

The technique used in the continuous sorting algorithm of nested lists can be a rather useful in solving other types of work with nested lists. This is especially true for problems involving different permutations of elements of a file ***Flatten[x]*** with next restoring the internal structure of the nested ***x*** list. At the same time, it should be borne in mind that such technique implies the *standartization* of list elements along the length of their elements having a maximum length. As that is done in the ***ContinuousSL*** procedure by means of use the ***Lie*** procedure.

In a number of problems of processing of simple ***x*** lists on which the call ***SimpleListQ[x]*** returns *True,* the next procedure is of a certain interest. The procedure call ***ClusterList[x]*** returns the nested list of *ListList* type whose **2**–element sublists by the first element determine element of the simple nonempty ***x*** list whereas by the second element define its sequential number in a cluster of identical elements to which this element belongs. In the following fragment source code of the ***ClusterList*** procedure with typical examples of its application are represented.

```
In[2273]:= ClusterList[x_/; x != {} && SimpleListQ[x]] :=
  Module[{a = {}, b = {}, c = Join[x, {x[[-1]]}], d = Map[{#, 1} &,
                                         DeleteDuplicates[x]], n},
    Do[n = d[[Flatten[Position[d, Flatten[Select[d, #[[1]] ==
                                  c[[j]] &]]]][[1]]]][[2]]++;
                Flatten[Select[d, #[[1]] == c[[j]] &]][[2]];
 If[c[[j]] === c[[j + 1]], AppendTo[a, {c[[j]], n}], AppendTo[b, a];
            AppendTo[b, {c[[j]], n}]; a = {}], {j, 1, Length[c] - 1}];
          AppendTo[b, a]; b = ToString1[Select[b, # != {} &]];
                          b = If[SuffPref[b, "{{{", 1], b, "{" <> b];
   b = ToExpression[StringReplace[b, {"{{" -> "{", "}}" -> "}"}]]]
In[2274]:= ClusterList[{1, 1, 1, 3, 3, 3, 4, 4, 5, 5, 5, 4, 1, 1, 1}]
Out[2274]= {{1, 1}, {1, 2}, {1, 3}, {3, 1}, {3, 2}, {3, 3}, {4, 1},
               {4, 2}, {5, 1}, {5, 2}, {5, 3}, {4, 3}, {1, 4}, {1, 5}, {1, 6}}
In[2275]:= ClusterList[{1, 1, 1, 3, 3, t + p, 3, 4, 4, 5, a, 5, 5, 4,
                                              1, 1, a, 1, (a + b) + c^c}]
Out[2275]= {{1, 1}, {1, 2}, {1, 3}, {3, 1}, {3, 2}, {p + t, 1}, {3, 3},
          {4, 1}, {4, 2}, {5, 1}, {a, 1}, {5, 2}, {5, 3}, {4, 3}, {1, 4}, {1, 5},
                                                 {a, 2}, {1, 6}, {a + b + c^c, 1}}
In[2276]:= ClusterList[{6, 6, 6, 6, 6, 6, 6, 6, 6, 6, 6, 6}]
Out[2276]= {{6, 1}, {6, 2}, {6, 3}, {6, 4}, {6, 5}, {6, 6}, {6, 7},
                             {6, 8}, {6, 9}, {6, 10}, {6, 11}, {6, 12}}
In[2277]:= ClusterList[{1, 1, 1, 2, 2, 2, 3, 3, 3, 4, 4, 4}]
Out[2277]= {{1, 1}, {1, 2}, {1, 3}, {2, 1}, {2, 2}, {2, 3}, {3, 1}, {3, 2},
                                       {3, 3}, {4, 1}, {4, 2}, {4, 3}}
```

In order to simplify of algorithm of a number of tools that are oriented on solving of processing of the contents of the user packages, in particular, the ***SubListsMin*** procedure can be a rather useful used, and also for lists processing as a whole. The call ***SubListsMin[L, x, y, t]*** returns the sublists of a list ***L*** which are limited by ***{x, y}*** elements and have the minimum length; at ***t = "r"*** selection is executed from left to right, and at ***t = "l"*** from right to left. While the procedure call ***SubListsMin[L, x, y, t, z]*** with optional fifth ***z*** argument – *an arbitrary expression* – returns sublists without the limiting ***{x, y}*** elements. The next fragment presents source code of the procedure and examples of its use.

```
In[1242]:= SubListsMin[L_/; ListQ[L], x_, y_,
                       t_/; MemberQ[{"r", "l"}, t], z___] :=
                       Module[{a, b, c, d = {}, k = 1, j},
         {a, b} = Map[Flatten, Map3[Position, L, {x, y}]];
   If[a == {} || b == {} || a == {} && b == {} || L == {}, {},
  b = Select[Map[If[If[t == "r", Greater, Less][#, a[[1]]], #] &, b],
                                    ! SameQ[#, Null] &];
   For[k, k <= Length[a], k++, j = 1; While[j <= Length[b],
   If[If[t == "r", Greater, Less][b[[j]], a[[k]]], AppendTo[d,
   If[t == "r", a[[k]] ;; b[[j]], b[[j]] ;; a[[k]]]]; Break[]]; j++]];
 d = Sort[d, Part[#1, 2] - Part[#1, 1] <= Part[#2, 2] - Part[#2, 1] &];
 d = Select[d, Part[#, 2] - Part[#, 1] == Part[d[[1]], 2] - Part[d[[1]], 1] &];
  d = Map[L[[#]] &, d]; d = If[{z} != {}, Map[#[[2 ;; -2]] &, d], d];
                           If[Length[d] == 1, Flatten[d], d]]]

In[1243]:= SubListsMin[{a, b, a, c, d, q, v, d, w, j, k, d, h, f, d, h},
                                                   a, h, "r", 90]
Out[1243]= {c, d, q, v, d, w, j, k, d}
```

A useful addition to built-in functions ***Replace, ReplaceList*** and our tools ***ReplaceList1, ReplaceList2, ReplaceListCond,*** is a procedure whose call ***RepInsList[I, x, y, z, n, r]*** returns the result as follows, namely:

At ***I = "Ins"*** the result is inserting of an argument ***z*** *(may be a list or nested list)* before *(**r = "l"**)* or after *(**r = "r"**)* of occurrences of a sub-list ***y*** into a list ***x;*** whereas at argument ***I = "Rep"*** the result is replacement in a list ***x*** of occurrences of a sub-list ***y*** on argument ***z*** *(may be a list or nested list);* at that, if ***n*** is an integer, then ***n*** first replacements in the ***x*** are done, if ***n*** is ***Infinity,*** then replacements in the list ***x*** of all occurrences of a sub-list ***y*** onto argument ***z*** are done; at last, if ***n*** – an integer list then it defines sequentional numbers of the occurrences of ***y*** in the list ***x*** that are exposed to the above replacements. What is said about the argument ***n*** also fully applies to the call mode at ***I = "Rep".*** The procedure call on unacceptable arguments returns *$Failed* with appropriate *diagnostic* messages or is returned unevaluated. The following fragment represents the source code of the ***RepInsList*** procedure with examples of its typical application.

```
In[25]:= RepInsList[I_/; MemberQ[{"Rep", "Ins"}, I],
                    x_/; ListQ[x], y_/; ListQ[y], z_, n_, r___] :=
                                              Module[{a, b, c, d, t},
        {a, b, c} = Map[StringTake[ToString1[#], {2, -2}] &,
                                        {x, y, If[ListQ[z], z, {z}]}];
    If[I == "Ins", If[{r} != {}, If[r === "l", c = c <> "," <> b,
    If[r === "r", c = b <> "," <> c, Return[Print["Sixth optional
                  argument should be \"r\" or \"l\""]; $Failed]]]]];
If[IntegerQ[n] || n === Infinity, t = StringReplace[a, b -> c, n],
If[PosIntListQ[n] === True, t = StringSplit2[a, b]; d = Length[t];
                          t = StringJoin[Map[If[MemberQ[n, #],
       StringReplace[t[[#]], b -> c], t[[#]]] &, Range[1, d]]],
 Return[Print["Fourth argument n should be an integer, integer
                                    list or Infinity"]; $Failed]]],
If[IntegerQ[n] || n === Infinity, t = StringReplace[a, b -> c, n],
If[PosIntListQ[n] === True, t = StringSplit2[a, b]; d = Length[t];
                          t = StringJoin[Map[If[MemberQ[n, #],
       StringReplace[t[[#]], b -> c], t[[#]]] &, Range[1, d]]],
 Return[Print["Fourth argument n should be an integer, integer
     list or Infinity"]; $Failed]]]]; ToExpression["{" <> t <> "}"]]
In[22]:= x:= {a, b, c, 1, 2, a, b, c, 3, a, b, c, 4, 5, 6, a, b, c, h, a, b, c, g};
                                                  y:= {a, b, c}; z:= {m, n, p};
In[27]:= RepInsList["Rep", x, y, z, {1, 3}]
Out[27]= {m, n, p, 1, 2, a, b, c, 3, m, n, p, 4, 5, 6, a, b, c, h, a, b, c, g}
In[28]:= RepInsList["Rep", {aa, bb, aa, cc}, {aa}, {{m, n}}, {2}]
Out[28]= {aa, bb, {m, n}, cc}
In[30]:= RepInsList["Rep", x, y, G + S, 3]
Out[30]= {G + S, 1, 2, G + S, 3, G + S, 4, 5, 6, a, b, c, h, a, b, c, g}
```

```
In[31]:= RepInsList["Ins", {aa, bb, aa, cc, aa}, {aa}, gsv, {1, 2}, "r"]
Out[31]= {aa, gsv, bb, aa, cc, aa, gsv}
In[31]:= RepInsList["Ins", {aa, bb, aa, cc, aa}, {aa}, H, Infinity, "l"]
Out[31]= {H, aa, bb, H, aa, cc, H, aa}
```

A useful addition to built-in functions ***Split, SplitBy*** along with our tools ***Split1, Split2, SplitIntegerList, SplitList, SplitList1*** is a procedure *(based on the above* ***RepInsList*** *procedure)* whose call ***Split2[x, y, n]*** returns the result of splitting of a list ***x*** by sub-lists ***y;*** in addition, if ***n*** is an integer then ***n*** first splittings of the ***x*** are done, if ***n*** is *Infinity* then splittings of the list ***x*** by all occurrences of a sub-list ***y*** are done; at last, if ***n*** - an integer list then it defines *sequention* numbers of the occurrences of ***y*** in the list ***x*** by which the list ***x*** is exposed by the above splittings. The ***Split2*** handles the main errors with printing of diagnostic messages. Fragment represents source code of the procedure and examples of it use.

```
In[90]:= Split2[x_/; ListQ[x], y_/; ListQ[y], n_] :=
                                Module[{a = ToString[Unique[g]], b, c},
                                    b = RepInsList["Rep", x, y, a, n];
                              If[b === x, "Second argument is invalid",
                                        b = "{" <> ToString[b] <> "}";
c = StringReplace[b, {"{" <> a <> "," -> "{", ", " <> a <> "," -> "},{",
                         ", " <> a <> "}" -> "}"}]; ToExpression[c]]]
In[91]:= Split2[{a, b, c, v, g, a, b, c, h, a, b, g, j, a, b}, {a, b}, Infinity]
Out[91]= {{c, v, g}, {c, h}, {g, j}}
In[92]:= Split2[{a, b, c, v, g, a, b, c, h, a, b, g, j, a, b}, {a, b}, {1, 3}]
Out[92]= {{c, v, g, a, b, c, h}, {g, j, a, b}}
```

While the call ***StringReplace6[x, y -> z, n]*** returns the result of replacing in a list ***x*** of substrings ***y*** onto string ***z;*** at that, if ***n*** is an integer then ***n*** first replacements are done, if ***n*** is ***Infinity*** then replacements at all occurrences of a substring ***y*** are done; at last, if ***n*** - an integer list then it defines sequention numbers of the occurrences of ***y*** for which the replacements are done. In next fragment the source code of the procedure and an example of its typical application are represented.

```
In[95]:= StringReplace6[x_/; StringQ[x], y_/; RuleQ[y], n_] :=
                           Module[{a = StringSplit2[x, y[[1]]], b, c},
        If[a === x, "Second argument is invalid", b = Length[a]];
        If[IntegerQ[n] | | n === Infinity, StringReplace[x, y, n],
```

```
StringJoin[Map[If[MemberQ[n, #], StringReplace[a[[#]],
          y[[1]] -> y[[2]]], a[[#]]] &, Range[1, b]]]]]
In[96]:= StringReplace6["aabbccaahgaaffaa", "aa" -> "12", {2, 4}]
Out[96]= "aabbcc12hgaaff12"
```

At last, the following simple enough procedures ***MapList*** ÷ ***MapList2*** are a some kind of generalization of the built-in ***Map*** function to the lists of an arbitrary structure. The procedure call ***MapList[f, x]*** returns the result of applying of a symbol, block, function, module or pure function *f (except f symbol all remaining admissible objects shall have arity 1)* to each element of a list ***x*** with maintaining its internal structure. It is supposed that sub-lists of the list ***x*** have the unary nesting levels, otherwise the procedure call is returned unevaluated. The following fragment represents source code of the procedure and an example of its application.

```
In[7]:= MapList[f_ /; SymbolQ[f] || BlockFuncModQ[f] ||
                          PureFuncQ[f], x_ /; ListQ[x] &&
And1[Map[Length[DeleteDuplicates[LevelsOfList[#]]] == 1 &, x]]] :=
Module[{g}, SetAttributes[g, Listable]; g[t_] := (f) @@ {t}; Map[g, x]]
In[8]:= F[g_] := g^3; MapList[F, {{a, b, c}, {{m, n}}, {}, {{{h, p}}}}]
Out[8]= {{a^3, b^3, c^3}, {{m^3, n^3}}, {}, {{{h^3, p^3}}}}
```

MapList1 and ***MapList2*** are useful versions of the above tool [8].

In a number of nested lists processing tasks, it is of interest to distribute the same elements to the nesting levels of arbitrary list. The following ***AllonLevels*** procedure solves the problem in a certain sense. Calling ***AllonLevels[w]*** procedure returns the nested list of the following format

$$\{\{a, n_{a1}, ..., n_{ap}\}, \{b, n_{b1}, ..., n_{bp}\}, ..., \{z, n_{z1}, ..., n_{zp}\}\}$$

where elements ***{a, b, c, ..., z}*** represent all elements of a list ***w*** without their duplication whereas elements $\{n_{j1}, ..., n_{jp}\}$ submit nesting level numbers of the ***w*** list on which the corresponding elements $j \in \{a, b, c, ..., z\}$ are located. The following fragment represents the source code of the ***AllonLevels*** procedure along with typical examples of its application.

```
In[77]:= AllonLevels[x_ /; ListQ[x]] := Module[{a = {}, c = 1,
                                                b = MaxLevel1[x]},
```

```
While[c <= b, AppendTo[a, Map[{"_" <> ToString[c], #} &,
                                  Level[x, {c}]]]; c++];
   a = Map[If[IntegerQ[ToExpression[StringTake[#[[1]],
  {2, -1}]]] && ! ListQ[#[[2]]], #, Nothing] &, Flatten[a, 1]];
       a = Map[Flatten, Map[Reverse, a]];
       a = Gather[a, #1[[1]] == #2[[1]] &];
       a = Map[DeleteDuplicates, Map[Flatten, a]];
       a = Map[If[Length[#] == 2,
       {#[[1]], ToExpression[StringTake[#[[2]], {2, -1}]]},
 Join[{#[[1]]}, Map[ToExpression[StringTake[#, {2, -1}]] &,
                                  #[[2 ;; -1]]]]] &, a]]
In[78]:= X:= {a, b, m, c, b, {m, b, n, a, p}, {{x, y, a, n, b, c, z}}}
In[79]:= AllonLevels[X]
Out[79]= {{a, 1, 2, 3}, {b, 1, 2, 3}, {m, 1, 2}, {c, 1, 3}, {n, 2, 3},
         {p, 2}, {x, 3}, {y, 3}, {z, 3}}
In[80]:= AllonLevels[{a, b, c, d, f, g, h, s, d, r, t, u, u}]
Out[80]= {{a, 1}, {b, 1}, {c, 1}, {d, 1}, {f, 1}, {g, 1}, {h, 1}, {s, 1},
         {r, 1}, {t, 1}, {u, 1}}
```

The procedure rather successfully is used at problems solving related to the nested lists processing.

While unlike the previous procedure the ***CountOnLevelList*** procedure defines distributes the number of occurrences of list elements to the nesting levels based on their multiplicity. The procedure call ***CountOnLevelList***[*x*] returns the nested list which consists of **3**-element sublists whose the ***1st*** element - an element of the list *x*, the *2nd* – a nesting level contained it and the third – number of occurrences of the element on this nesting level.

```
In[2225]:= CountOnLevelList[x_ /; ListQ[x]] := Module[{c = {},
       j = 1, a = DeleteDuplicates[Flatten[x]], b = MaxLevel1[x]},
            While[j <= Length[a], AppendTo[c, Map[{a[[j]], #,
                      Count[x, a[[j]], {#}]} &, Range[1, b]]]; j++];
                        Map[Partition[#, 3] &, Map[Flatten, c]]]
In[2226]:= X := {a, b, m, c, b, {m, b, n, a, p}, {{x, y, b, n, b, c, z}}}
In[2227]:= CountOnLevelList[X]
Out[2227]= {{{a, 1, 1}, {a, 2, 1}, {a, 3, 0}}, {{b, 1, 2}, {b, 2, 1}, {b, 3, 2}},
{{m, 1, 1}, {m, 2, 1}, {m, 3, 0}}, {{c, 1, 1}, {c, 2, 0}, {c, 3, 1}}, {{n, 1, 0}, {n, 2, 1},
```

{n, 3, 1}}, {{p, 1, 0}, {p, 2, 1}, {p, 3, 0}}, {{x, 1, 0}, {x, 2, 0}, {x, 3, 1}}, {{y, 1, 0}, {y, 2, 0}, {y, 3, 1}}, {{z, 1, 0}, {z, 2, 0}, {z, 3, 1}}}

In some cases, special cases occur when sorting lists, one of which the following procedure presents. So, the procedure call ***SSort[x, p, t, sf]*** returns the list – the result of a special sorting of a list ***x*** according to a *sorting* function ***sf*** *(optional argument; in its absence the default function* ***Order*** *is used)*, when the resulting list at ***t=0*** starts with sorted ***p*** list elements belonging to ***x*** and at ***t=1*** ends with ***p*** elements. If elements ***p*** are not in the ***x*** list, then the ***Sort[x, sf]*** list is returned.

```
In[2221]:= SSort[x_/; ListQ[x], p_/; ListQ[p],
      t_/; ! FreeQ[{0, 1}, t], sf___] := Module[{a = Sort[x, sf], b, c},
       b = Intersection[x, c = Sort[Select[x, ! FreeQ[p, #] &], sf]];
                If[b == {}, a, If[t == 0, Join[c, Complement[x, b]],
                                   Join[Complement[x, b], c]]]]
In[2222]:= SSort[{s, f, h, d, a, m, k, h, m, p, t, y, m},
                                                       {m, s, h}, 0]
Out[2222]= {h, h, m, m, m, s, a, d, f, k, p, t, y}
In[2223]:= SSort[{s, f, h, d, a, m, k, h, m, p, t, y, m},
                                                       {m, p, t}, 1]
Out[2223]= {a, d, f, h, k, s, y, m, m, m, p, t}
```

A lot of the additional tools expanding the ***Mathematica***, in particular, for effective programming of a number of problems of manipulation with the list structures of various organization are presented a quite in details in [1-16]. Being additional tools for work with lists – *basic structures in* ***Mathematica*** – they are rather useful in a number of applications of various purpose. A number of means were already considered, while others will be considered along with means which are directly not associated with lists, but quite accepted for work with separate formats of lists. Many means represented here and in [1-16], arose in the process of programming a lot of applications as tools wearing a rather mass character. Some of them use techniques which are rather useful in the practical programming in ***Mathematica***. In particular, the above relates to a computer study of the *Cellular Automata (**CA**; Homogeneous Structures – **HS**)*.

3.7. Attributes of procedures and functions

In addition to definition of procedures *(blocks, modules)* and functions, the ***Mathematica*** system allows you to define general properties that are inherent in them. The system provides a set of attributes that can be used to specify different properties of procedures and functions irrespectively their definitions. At the same time, attributes can be assigned not only to functions and procedures, but also to symbols.

***Attributes*[G]** – *returns the attributes ascribed to a* **G** *symbol;*

Attributes*[G] = {a1, a2,...}** – *the function call sets the attributes* ***a1, a2,... *for a* **G** *symbol;*

***Attributes*[G] = {}** – *the function call sets* **G** *to have no attributes;*

***SetAttributes*[G, atr]** – *the function call adds the* **atr** *attribute to the attributes of a* **G** *symbol;*

***ClearAttributes*[G, attr]** – *the function call removes a* **attr** *from the attributes of a* **G** *symbol.*

Here are the most used attributes with their descriptions:

Orderless – *attribute defines orderless, commutative tools (their formal arguments are sorted into standard order);*

Flat – *attribute defines flat, associative tools (their arguments are "flattened out");*

Listable – *this attribute defines automatical element-by-element application of a symbol over lists that appear as arguments;*

Constant – *this attribute defines that all derivatives of a symbol are zero;*

NumericFunction – *the attribute defines that a tool is assumed to have a numerical value when its arguments are numeric quantities;*

Protected – *this attribute defines that values of a symbol cannot be changed;*

Locked – *this attribute defines that attributes of a symbol cannot be changed;*

ReadProtected – *attribute defines that values of a symbol cannot be read;*

Temporary – *the attribute defines that a symbol is local variable, removed when no longer used;*

Stub – *this attribute defines that a symbol needs is automatically called if it is ever explicitly input.*

The remaining admissible attributes can be found in detail in [2-6,9,10,15], here some useful examples of the application of the attributes presented above are given. For example, we can use the attribute ***Flat*** to specify that a function is *"flat"*, so that nested invocations are automatically flattened, and it behaves as if it were associative:

```
In[2222]:= SetAttributes[F, Flat]
In[2223]:= F[F[x, y, z], F[p, F[m, n], t]]
Out[2223]= F[x, y, z, p, m, n, t]
```

The ***Listable*** attribute is of particular interest at operating with list structures, its use well illustrates the following rather simple example:

```
In[2224]:= Attributes[ToString]
Out[2224]= {Protected}
In[2225]:= L = {a, b, {c, d}, {{m, p, n}}};
In[2226]:= ToString[L]
Out[2226]= "{a, b, {c, d}, {{m, p, n}}}"
In[2227]:= SetAttributes[ToString, Listable]
In[2228]:= ToString[L]
Out[2228]= {"a", "b", {"c", "d"}, {{"m", "p", "n"}}}
```

In this regard, a procedure whose call ***ListableS[F, x]*** returns the result of in one step, element-by-element application of a ***F*** symbol to a list ***x*** that acts as the second argument *(wherein, after the procedure call, the attributes of the **F** symbol remain the same as before the procedure call):*

```
In[2229]:= ListableS[F_Symbol, x_] := Module[{s, t,
  g = Attributes[F]}, If[MemberQ[g, Listable], s = F[x]; t = 1,
                              SetAttributes[F, Listable]; s = F[x]];
                    If[t === 1, s, ClearAttributes[F, Listable]; s]]
In[2230]:= ListableS[ToString, L]
Out[2230]= {"a", "b", {"c", "d"}, {{"m", "p", "n"}}}
```

The ***ListableS*** procedure can be represented by equivalent function ***ListableS1*** of the list format as follows:

```
In[2231]:= ListableS1[F_Symbol, x_] := {Save["#", {g, s, t}],
  g = Attributes[F], If[MemberQ[g, Listable], s = F[x]; t = 1,
  SetAttributes[F, Listable]; s = F[x]]; If[t === 1, s,
ClearAttributes[F, Listable]; s], Get["#"], DeleteFile["#"]}[[3]]
In[2232]:= {g, s, t} = {42, 47, 67}; ListableS1[F, L]
Out[2232]= {F[a], F[b], {F[c], F[d]}, {{F[m], F[p], F[n]}}}
In[2233]:= {g, s, t}
Out[2233]= {42, 47, 67}
```

The ***Temporary*** attribute determines that a symbol has local character, removed when no longer used. For instance, the local procedure variables have the ***Temporary*** attribute.

```
In[90]:= A[x__] := Module[{a = 77}, {a*x, Attributes[a]}]
In[91]:= A[5]
Out[91]= {385, {Temporary}}
In[92]:= A1[x_] := Module[{a = 7}, a = {a*x, Attributes[a], a};
                          ClearAttributes[a, Temporary]; a]
In[93]:= A1[5]
Out[93]= {35, {Temporary}, 7}
```

By managing the ***Temporary*** attribute, it is possible make the values of the local variables of the procedures available in the current session outside of these procedures, as the previous example illustrates. At that, you can both save the ***Temporary*** attribute for them or selectively cancel it.

The ***ReadProtected*** attribute prevents expression associated with a ***W*** symbol from being seen. In addition, this expression cannot be obtained not only by the function call ***Definition*[W]**, but also be written to a file, for example, by the function ***Save***, for example:

```
In[2129]:= G[x_, y_, z_] := x^2 + y^2 + z^2;
In[2130]:= SetAttributes[G, ReadProtected]
In[2131]:= Definition[G]
Out[2131]= Attributes[G] = {ReadProtected}
In[2132]:= Save["###", G]
In[2133]:= Read["###"]
Out[2133]= {ReadProtected}
```

This attribute is typically used to hide the values of certain program objects, especially procedure and function definitions. While this attribute is cancelled by means of the ***ClearAttributes*** function, for example:

In[2141]:= **ClearAttributes[G, ReadProtected]**
In[2142]:= **Definition[G]**
Out[2142]= G[x_, y_, z_] := x^2 + y^2 + z^2

The ***Constant*** attribute defines all derivatives of a ***g*** symbol to be zero, for example:

In[2555]:= **SetAttributes[g, Constant]**
In[2556]:= **g[x_] := a*x^9 + b*x^10 + c**
In[2557]:= **Definition[g]**
Out[2557]= Attributes[g] = {Constant} + c
g[x_] := a*x^9 + b*x^10
In[2558]:= **Map[D[g, {x, #}] &, Range[10]]**
Out[2558]= {0, 0, 0, 0, 0, 0, 0, 0, 0, 0}

The ***Locked*** attribute prohibits attributes change of a symbol:

In[2654]:= **ClearAttributes[Vs, {Locked}]**
... Attributes: Symbol Vs is locked.
In[2655]:= **Attributes[Vs]**
Out[2655]= {Listable, Locked}
In[2656]:= **Clear[Vs]; Attributes[Vs]**
Out[2656]= {Listable, Locked}
In[2657]:= **ClearAll[Vs]; Attributes[Vs]**
... ClearAll: Symbol Vs is locked.
Out[2657]= {Listable, Locked}
In[2658]:= **ClearAll[Gs]**
... ClearAll: Symbol Gs is Protected.
In[2659]:= **Attributes[Gs]**
Out[2659]= {Protected}

Note, that unlike the declaration by the ***Mathematica*** the function ***ClearAll*** to override a symbol attributes, this method does not work if the symbol has {***Protected, Locked***} attributes, as illustrated by the fragment above. The ***Mathematica*** claims, the call ***ClearAll***[*g1, g2,...*] clears all values, definitions, defaults, attributes, messages, associated with {*g1, g2, ...*} symbols whereas in reality it is not quite so. In addition, the ***Remove*** function also does not affect symbols with the {***Protected, Locked***} attributes. On the other hand, a symbol ***x*** with attributes {***Protected, Locked***} is saved in a ***w*** file by means of the functions call ***Save*[*w*, *x*]** and ***Write*[*w*, *Definition*[*x*]]** with saving of all attributes ascribed to the ***x*** symbol. At the same time, attributes assigned to a symbol ***x*** are relevant only within the current session, being lost in the new session. Calling ***Unlocked*[*f*]** deletes the current document ***nb*** by returning the *updated* ***nb*** document *(by replacing the* ***Locked*** *attribute with the* ***Stub*** *attribute)* and saving it to a ***nb***-file *f.*

```
In[2759]:= Unlocked[fnb_] := Module[{a = NotebookGet[]},
                                  a = ReplaceAll[a, "Locked" -> "Stub"];
                                NotebookClose[]; NotebookSave[a, fnb]]
In[2760]:= Unlocked["C:\\Temp\\Exp.nb"]
```

The ***NumericFunction*** attribute of a procedure or function ***F*** indicates that ***F*[*x1*, *x2*, *x3*, ...]** should be considered a numerical quantity whenever all its arguments are numerical quantities:

```
In[2858]:= Attributes[Sin]
Out[2858]= {Listable, NumericFunction, Protected}
```

The ***Orderless*** attribute of a procedure or function indicates that its arguments are automatically sorted in canonical order. This property is accounted for in pattern matching.

```
In[2953]:= SetAttributes[F, Orderless]
In[2954]:= F[n, m, p, 3, t, 7, a]
Out[2954]= F[3, 7, a, m, n, p, t]
In[2955]:= F[z_, y_, x_] := x + y + z
In[2956]:= Definition[F]
Out[2956]= Attributes[F] = {Orderless}
              F[x_, y_, z_] := x + y + z
In[2957]:= SetAttributes[g, Orderless]
In[2958]:= L = {n, m, u, 3, t, 7, a, c, u, d, s, j, a, p}; v := g @@ L;
                        Map[Part[v, #] &, Range[Length[L]]]
Out[2958]= {3, 7, a, a, c, d, j, m, n, p, s, t, u, u}
```

The last example of the previous fragment illustrates using of the ***Orderless*** attribute to sort lists in lexicographical order.

3.8. Additional tools expanding the built-in Mathematica functions, or its software as a whole

The ***string*** and ***list*** structures are of the most important in the ***Mathematica***, they both are considered in the previous two chapters in the context of means, additional to the built-in tools, without regard to a large number of the standard functions of processing of structures of this type. Quite naturally, here it isn't possible to consider all range of standard functions of this type, sending the interested reader to the reference information on the ***Mathematica*** or to the appropriate numerous publications. It is possible to find many of these publications on the website ***http://www.wolfram.com/books***. Having presented the means expanding the built-in ***Mathematica*** software in the context of processing of string and list structures in the present item we will represent the means expanding the ***Mathematica*** that are oriented on processing of other types of objects. Above all, we will present some tools of bit-by-bit processing of symbols.

The ***Bits*** procedure significantly uses function ***BinaryListQ***, providing a number of useful operations during of operating with symbols. On the tuple of factual arguments ***<x, p>***, where ***x*** – a ***1***-symbol string *(character)* and ***p*** – an integer in the range ***0 .. 8***, the call ***Bits[x, p]*** returns binary representation of the ***x*** in the form of the list, if ***p = 0***, and ***p-th*** bit of such representation of a symbol ***x*** otherwise. While on a tuple of actual arguments ***<x, p>***, where ***x*** – a nonempty binary list of length no more than ***8*** and ***p = 0***, the procedure call returns a symbol corresponding to the set *binary* ***x*** list; in other cases the call ***Bits[x,p]*** is returned as unevaluated. The fragment below represents source code of the procedure ***Bits*** along with an example of its application.

```
In[7]:= Bits[x_, P_/; IntegerQ[P]] := Module[{a, k},
        If[StringQ[x] && StringLength[x] == 1, If[1 <= P <= 8,
      PadLeft[IntegerDigits[ToCharacterCode[x][[1]], 2], 8][[P]],
  If[P == 0, PadLeft[IntegerDigits[ToCharacterCode[x][[1]], 2], 8],
                                                   Defer[Bits[x, P]]]],
  If[BinaryListQ[x] && 1 <= Length[Flatten[x]] <= 8, a = Length[x];
FromCharacterCode[Sum[x[[k]]*2^(a - k), {k, a}]], Defer[Bits[x, P]]]]]
```

```
In[8]:= Map9[Bits, {"A", "A", {1, 0, 0, 0, 0, 0, 1}, "A", {1, 1, 1, 1, 0, 1}},
                                                          {0, 2, 0, 9, 0}]
Out[8]= {{0, 1, 0, 0, 0, 0, 0, 1}, 1, "A", Bits["A", 9], "="}
```

If the previous ***Bits*** procedure provides a simple enough processing of symbols, the two procedures ***BitSet1*** and ***BitGet1*** provide the expanded bit-by-bit information processing like our ***Maple*** procedures [16]. In the ***Maple*** we created a number of procedures *(**Bit, Bit1, xNB, xbyte1, xbyte**)* that provide bit-by-bit information processing [22-28,42]; the ***Mathematica*** has similar means too, in particular, the call ***BitSet[n, k]*** returns the result of setting of **1** to the ***k-th*** position of *binary* representation of an integer ***n***. The procedure call ***BitSet1[n,p]*** returns result of setting to positions of the binary representation of an integer ***n*** that are determined by the first elements of sub-lists of a nested ***p*** list, ***{0 | 1}*** **-** values; in addition, in a case of non-nested ***p*** list a value replacement only in a single position of ***n*** integer is made. Procedures ***BitSet1*** and ***BitGet1*** are included in our package [16].

It should be noted that the ***BitSet1*** procedure functionally expands both the standard function ***BitSet,*** and ***BitClear*** of the ***Mathematica*** while the procedure ***BitGet1*** functionally extands the standard functions ***BitGet*** and ***BitLength*** of the system. The call ***BitGet1[n, p]*** returns the list of bits in the positions of *binary* representation of an integer ***n*** that are defined by a ***p*** list; at the same time, in a case of an integer ***p*** the bit in position ***p*** of *binary* representation of ***n*** integer is returned. While the procedure call ***BitGet1[x, n, p]*** through a symbol ***x*** in addition returns number of bits in the binary representation of an integer ***n***. The above means rather wide are used at bit-by-bit processing.

In the ***Mathematica*** the transformation rules are generally determined by the ***Rule*** function, whose call ***Rule[a, b]*** returns the transformation rule in the form ***a -> b***. These rules are used in transformations of expressions by the functions ***ReplaceAll, Replace, ReplaceRepeated, StringReplace, StringReplaceList, ReplacePart, StringCases,*** that use either one rule, or their list as simple list, and a list of *ListList* type. For dynamic generation of such rules the ***GenRules*** procedure can be useful, whose call

GenRules[x, y] depending on a type of its arguments returns a single rule or list of rules; the procedure call ***GenRules[x, y, z]*** with the third optional z argument – *any expression* – returns the list with single transformation rule or the nested list of *ListList* type. Depending on the coding format, the call returns result in the following formats, namely:

(1) **GenRules[**{*x, y, z,*...}, *a*] ⇒ {*x* -> *a, y* -> *a, z* -> *a,*...}
(2) **GenRules[**{*x, y, z,*...}, *a, h*] ⇒ {{*x* -> *a*}, {*y* -> *a*}, {*z* -> *a*},...}
(3) **GenRules[**{*x, y, z,*...}, {*a, b, c,*...}] ⇒ {*x* -> *a, y* -> *b, z* -> *c,*...}
(4) **GenRules[**{*x, y, z,*...}, {*a, b, c,*...}, *h*] ⇒ {{*x* -> *a*}, {*y* -> *b*}, {*z* -> *c*},...}
(5) **GenRules[***x*, {*a, b, c,*...}] ⇒ {*x* -> *a*}
(6) **GenRules[***x*, {*a, b, c,*...}, *h*] ⇒ {*x* -> *a*}
(7) **GenRules[***x, a*] ⇒ {*x* -> *a*}
(8) **GenRules[***x, a, h*] ⇒ {*x* -> *a*}

The ***GenRules*** procedure is useful, in particular, when in a procedure or function it is necessary to dynamically generate the *transformation rules* depending on conditions. The following fragment represents source code of the ***GenRules*** procedure and the most typical examples of its application onto all above cases of coding of the procedure call.

```
In[7]:= GenRules[x_, y_, z___] := Module[{a, b = Flatten[{x}],
                        c = Flatten[If[ListQ /@ {x, y} == {True, False},
                                          PadLeft[{}, Length[x], y], {y}]]},
   a = Min[Length /@ {b, c}]; b = Map9[Rule, b[[1 ;; a]], c[[1 ;; a]]];
   If[{z} == {}, b, b = List /@ b; If[Length[b] == 1, Flatten[b], b]]]
In[8]:= {GenRules[{x, y, z}, {a, b, c}], GenRules[x, {a, b, c}],
   GenRules[{x, y}, {a, b, c}], GenRules[x, a], GenRules[{x, y}, a]}
Out[8]= {{x → a, y → b, z → c}, {x → a}, {x → a, y → b}, {x → a},
                                                              {x → a, y → a}}
In[9]:= {GenRules[{x, y, z}, {a, b, c}, 7], GenRules[x, {a, b, c}, 42],
GenRules[x, a, 6], GenRules[{x, y}, {a,b,c}, 7], GenRules[{x, y}, a, 72]}
Out[9]= {{{x → a}, {y → b}, {z → c}}, {x → a}, {x → a},
                                   {{x → a}, {y → b}}, {{x → a}, {y → a}}}
```

Modifications ***GenRules1÷GenRules3*** of the above procedure are quite useful in many applications [1-15]. A number of tools of the ***MathToolBox*** package essentially use means of so-called ***GenRules***-group [16].

Considering the importance of the ***map*** function, starting with ***Maple 10***, the option *`inplace`*, admissible only at use of the ***map*** function with rectangular *rtable*-objects at renewing these objects in situ was defined. While for objects of other type this mechanism isn't supported as certain examples from [18,21-42] illustrate. For the purpose of disposal of this shortcoming was offered a quite simple ***MapInSitu*** procedure [42]. Along with it the similar tools for ***Mathematica*** in the form of two functions ***MapInSitu, MapInSitu1*** and the ***MapInSitu2*** procedure have been offered. With mechanisms used by the ***Maple*** procedure ***MapInSitu*** and ***Math***-tools ***MapInSitu÷MapInSitu2*** the reader can familiarize in [6-16,27,42]. Tools of the ***MapInSitu-****group* for both systems are characterized by the prerequisite, the second argument at their call points out on an identifier in the string format to which a certain value has been ascribed earlier and that is updated ***"in situ"*** after its processing by the {***map*** | ***Map***} tool. Anyway, the calls of the tools return ***Map[x,y]*** as a result.

The following procedure makes grouping of expressions that are set by ***x*** argument according to their types defined by the ***Head2*** procedure; in addition, a separate expression or their list is coded as a ***x*** argument. The procedure call ***GroupNames[x]*** returns simple list or nested list whose elements are lists whose first element - an object type according to the ***Head2*** procedure, whereas the others - expressions of this type. The next fragment represents source code of the ***GroupNames*** procedure with an example of its typical application.

```
In[7]:= GroupNames[x_] := Module[{a = If[ListQ[x], x, {x}], c, d,
                              p, t, b = {{"Null", "Null"}}, k = 1},
          For[k, k <= Length[a], k++, c = a[[k]]; d = Head2[c];
                              t = Flatten[Select[b, #[[1]] === d &]];
   If[t == {} && (d === Symbol && Attributes[c] === {Temporary}),
                              AppendTo[b, {Temporary, c}],
    If[t == {}, AppendTo[b, {d, c}], p = Flatten[Position[b, t]][[1]];
                              AppendTo[b[[p]], c]]]]; b = b[[2 ;; -1]];
                              b = Gather[b, #1[[1]] == #2[[1]] &];
                     b = Map[DeleteDuplicates[Flatten[#]] &, b];
                              If[Length[b] == 1, Flatten[b], b]]
```

```
In[8]:= GroupNames[{Sin, Cos, ProcQ, Locals2, 90, Map1, StrStr,
                    72/77, Avz, Nvalue1, a + b, Avz, 77, Agn, If, Vsv}]
Out[8]= {{"System", Sin, Cos, If}, {"Module", ProcQ, Locals2,
         Nvalue1, Agn}, {Integer, 90, 77}, {"Function", Map1, StrStr},
           {Rational, 72/77}, {Temporary, Avz, Vsv}, {Plus, a + b}}
```

The procedure call ***RemoveNames***[] without any arguments provides removal from the current ***Mathematica*** session of the names, whose types are other than procedures and functions, and whose *definitions* have been *evaluated* in the current session; moreover, the names are removed so that aren't recognized by the ***Mathematica*** any more. The procedure call ***RemoveNames***[] along with *removal* of the above names from the current session returns the nested **2**-element list whose *first* element defines the list of names of procedures, while the second element – the list of names of functions whose definitions have been evaluated in the current session. The following fragment represents source code of the ***RemoveNames*** procedure and an example of its use.

```
In[7]:= RemoveNames[x___] := Module[{a = Select[Names["`*"],
                              ToString[Definition[#]] != "Null" &], b},
  ToExpression["Remove[" <> StringTake[ToString[MinusList[a,
    Select[a, ProcQ[#] || ! SameQ[ToString[Quiet[DefFunc[#]]],
  "Null"] || Quiet[Check[QFunction[#], False]] &]]], {2, -2}] <> "]"];
                    b = Select[a, ProcQ[#] &]; {b, MinusList[a, b]}]
In[8]:= RemoveNames[]
Out[8]= {{"Art", "Kr", "Rans"}, {"Ian"}}
```

The above procedure is an useful tool in some appendices connected with *cleaning* of the working ***Mathematica*** field from definitions of the non–used symbols. The procedure confirmed a certain efficiency in management of random access memory.

In the context of use of the built-in functions ***Nest*** and ***Map*** for definition of new pure functions on a basis of the available ones, we can offer the procedure as an useful generalization of the built-in ***Map*** function, whose call ***Mapp[F, E, x]*** returns the result of application of a function/procedure ***F*** to an expression ***E*** with transfer to it of the factual arguments defined by a tuple of ***x*** expressions which can be empty. In a case of the empty ***x*** tuple the identity ***Map[F, E] ≡ Mapp[F, E]*** takes place. As formal arguments of the built-in function ***Map[w, g]*** act the *f* name of a procedure/function while as the second argument – *an arbitrary g expression,* to whose operands of the ***1st*** level the *w* is applied. The following fragment represents the source code of the ***Mapp*** procedure and a typical example of its application.

```
In[308]:= Mapp[f_/; ProcQ[f] || SysFuncQ[f] ||
                                          SymbolQ[f], Ex_, x___] :=
  Module[{a = Level[Ex, 1], b = {x}, c = {}, h, g = Head[Ex], k = 1},
       If[b == {}, Map[f, Ex], h = Length[a]; For[k, k <= h, k++,
  AppendTo[c, ToString[f] <> "[" <> ToString1[a[[k]]] <> ", " <>
                       ListStrToStr[Map[ToString1, {x}]] <> "]"]];
                                      g @@ Map[ToExpression, c]]]
In[309]:= Mapp[F, {a, b, c}, x, y, z]
Out[309]= {F[a, "F", y, z], F[b, "F", y, z], F[c, "F", y, z]}
In[310]:= Mapp[ProcQ, {Sin, ProcQ, Mapp, Definition2, StrStr}]
Out[310]= {False, True, True, True, False}
```

Note that algorithm of the ***Mapp*** procedure is based on the following relation, namely:

Map[F, Exp] ≡ Head[Exp][Sequences[Map[F, Level[Exp, 1]]]]

whose rightness follows from definition of the standard ***Level, Map, Head*** functions and our ***Sequences*** procedure considered in [6,8-16]. The relation can be used and at realization of cyclic structures for the solution of problems of other directionality, including programming on a basis of use of mechanism of the pure functions. While the ***Mapp*** procedure in the definite cases rather significantly simplifies programming of various tasks. The *Listable* attribute for a function *f* determines that it will be automatically applied to elements of the list which acts as its argument. Such approach can be used rather successfully in a number of cases of programming of blocks, functions, modules. In this context a rather simple ***Mapp1*** procedure is of interest, whose call ***Mapp1[x,y]*** unlike the call ***Map[x,y]*** returns the result of applying of a block, function or module *x* to all elements of *y* list, regardless of their location on list levels. Meanwhile, for a number of functions and expressions the *Listable* attribute does not work, and in this case the system provides special functions ***Map*** and ***Thread*** that in a certain relation can quite be referred to the structural means that provide application of functions to parts of expressions. In this regard we programmed a group of a rather simple and at the same time useful enough procedures and functions, so-called ***Map***–group which rather significantly expand the built–in ***Map*** function. The ***Map***–group consists of ***24*** tools ***Map1÷Map24*** different complexity levels. These tools are considered in detail in [5-14], they included in our package ***MathToolBox*** [16]. The above means from ***Map***–group rather significantly expand functionality of the built–in ***Map*** function. In a number of cases the means allow to simplify programming of procedures and functions.

An useful enough modification of standard ***Map*** function is the ***MapEx*** function whose call returns the list of application of symbol *f* to those elements of a list that satisfy a *testing* function *w (block, function, pure function, or module from one argument)* or whose positions are defined by the list of positive integers ***w***. The built-in function call ***MapAll[f, exp]*** applies *f* symbol to all subexpressions of an ***exp*** expression which are on all its levels. Whereas the procedure call ***MapToExpr[f, y]*** returns the result of application of a symbol *f* or their list only to all symbols of ***y*** expression. Furthermore, from the list *f* are excluded symbols entering into the ***y*** expression. For example, in a case if *f* = {*G, S*} then applying of *f* to a symbol *w* gives ***G[S[w]]***. At absence of acceptable *f* symbols the call returns the initial ***y*** expression. The call ***MapToExpr[f,y,z]*** with the *3rd* optional *z* argument – *a symbol or their list* – allows to exclude the *z* symbols from applying to them *f* symbols. In certain cases the procedure is a rather useful means at expressions processing.

The procedure ***MapListAll*** substantially adjoins the above ***Map***–group. The call ***MapAt[F, expr, n]*** of the standard ***MapAt*** function provides applying ***F*** to the elements of an expression ***expr*** at its positions ***n***. While the procedure call ***MapListAll[F, j]*** returns the result of applying ***F*** to all elements of a list ***j***. At that, a simple analog of the above procedure, basing on mechanism of temporary change of attributes for factual ***F*** argument in the call ***MapListAll1[F,j]*** solves the problem similarly to ***MapListAll*** procedure. On the list ***j*** of a kind {{... {{...}}...}} both procedures returns {{... {{F[]}}...}}. The following useful procedure ***MapExpr*** also adjoins the above ***Map***–group.

Calling the ***MapExpr[x, y]*** procedure returns the result of applying a symbol ***x*** to each variable of an expression ***y***, while calling the ***MapExpr[x, y, z]*** through optional argument ***z*** – an undefined symbol – additionally returns the list of all variables of the ***y*** expression in the string format. The following fragment represents the source code of the ***MapExpr*** procedure along with examples of its typical application.

```
In[1942]:= MapExpr[x_/; SymbolQ[x], y_, z___] :=
                                          Module[{a, b, c, d, p, g},
  If[SameQ[Head[y], Symbol], ToExpression[ToString[x @@ {y}]],
                                   a = ToString[MathMLForm[y]];
                    b = StringSplit[a, "\n" -> ""]; g = ToString[x];
              b = Map[If[# == "", Nothing, StringTrim[#]] &, b];
                           c = Map[If[! StringFreeQ[#, "<mi>"] &&
                                       ! StringFreeQ[#, "</mi>"],
  StringReplace[#, {"<mi>" -> "", "</mi>" -> ""}], Nothing] &, b];
  c = Sort[Map[If[Quiet[SystemQ[Name1[#]]], Nothing, #] &, c]];
      If[{z} != {} && ! HowAct[z], z = DeleteDuplicates[c], 77];
    p = Flatten[Map[{"[" <> # <> "," -> "[" <> g <> "[" <> # <> "],",
               " " <> # <> "]" -> " " <> g <> "[" <> # <> "]]",
               " " <> # <> "," -> " " <> g <> "[" <> # <> "],",
               "," <> # <> " " -> "," <> g <> "[" <> # <> "] ",
               "[" <> # <> "]" -> "[" <> g <> "[" <> # <> "]]"} &, c]];
       ToExpression[StringReplace[ToString[FullForm[y]], p]]]]
In[1943]:= exp = (a*y/(m + n) + b^z)/(cg - d*Log[h])*Sin[d + bc];
In[1944]:= MapExpr["F", exp, avz]
Out[1944]= ((F[b]^F[z] + (F[a]*F[y])/(F[m] + F[n]))*
                Sin[F[bc] + F[d]])/(F[cg] - F[d]*Log[F[h]])
In[1945]:= avz
Out[1945]= {"a", "b", "bc", "cg", "d", "h", "m", "n", "y", "z"}
In[1946]:= MapExpr[F, {a, b, {m, n, p}, g, s, Sin[y], c}, vsv]
Out[1946]= {F[a], F[b], {F[m], F[n], F[p]}, F[g], F[s], Sin[F[y]], F[c]}
```

```
In[1947]:= vsv
Out[1947]= {"a", "b", "c", "g", "m", "n", "p", "s", "y"}
In[1948]:= MapExpr[F, {a/b + c/d, n, {{h}}, Sin[p]}, avz]
Out[1948]= {F[a]/F[b] + F[c]/F[d], F[n], {{F[h]}}, Sin[F[p]]}
In[1949]:= avz
Out[1949]= {"a", "b", "c", "d", "h", "n", "p"}
```

In the context of structural analysis of the expressions, the ***VarsExpr*** procedure whose call ***VarsExpr[x]*** returns the five-element list, the ***1st*** element of which defines the list of standard tool names in the string format, the ***2nd*** element defines the list of the user tools names in the string format, the ***3rd*** element defines the list of the built-in operators in the string format, the fourth element defines the list of the variables in the string format, at last the firth element defines the list of the arithmetic operations in the string format which compose an expression x is a rather useful tool. The following fragment represents the source code of the ***VarsExpr*** procedure with an example of its typical use.

```
In[21]:= VarsExpr[x_] := Module[{a, b, d = {}, d1 = {}, d2 = {},
                                          d3 = {}, d4 = {}, f},
  a = PressStr[StringReplace[ToString[MathMLForm[x]], "\n" -> ""]];
                                    b = Map[SubsString[a, #, 7] &,
                      {{"<mi>", "</mi>"}, {"<mo>", "</mo>"}}];
        If[! StringFreeQ[a, "</msqrt>"], AppendTo[b, "sqrt"], 7];
                          b = Sort[DeleteDuplicates[Flatten[b]]];
  Map[If[Quiet[SystemQ[Name1[#]]], AppendTo[d, Name1[#]],
     If[Quiet[BlockFuncModQ[Name1[#]]], AppendTo[d1, #],
     If[PrefixQ["&#", #], AppendTo[d2, FromCharacterCode[
   ToExpression[StringTrim[SubsString[#, {"&#", ";"}, 7][[1]]]]]],
     If[SymbolQ[#], AppendTo[d3, #], AppendTo[d4, #]]]]] &, b];
            Map[Select[#, ! NullStrQ[#] &] &, {d, d1, d2, d3, d4}]]

In[22]:= VarsExpr[(f[1/b] -> Cos[a + Sqrt[c + d]])/(Tan[1/b] <-> 1/c^2)];
Out[22]= {{"Cos", "Sqrt", "Tan"}, {"f"}, {"<->", "->"},
                             {"a", "b", "c", "d"}, {"(", ")", "+"}}
```

Meantime, one point should be highlighted. In some cases, in the ***Mathematica's*** procedures and functions, the result may contain a special *space character* that has *Unicode F360* or appears as "\[*InvisibleSpace*]" in text format. That character by default is not visible on display, but is interpreted on input as an *ordinary* space. The space character can be used as an invisible separator between variables that are being multiplied together, as in ***A*B***. In connection with the above character, when programming a number of tasks, it is necessary to distinguish between ordinary strings and strings containing the above space characters. This task is solved by means of function whose call ***StringIsItFreeQ[x]*** returns *True* if ***x*** don't contain the characters "\[*InvisibleSpace*]" and "\[*InvisibleTimes*]", and *False* otherwise. The next fragment represents the source codes of some useful tools, processing the strings that contain the above characters along with a number of exemplifying examples.

```
In[7]:= {a = "aaaaa", b = "a\[InvisibleSpace]\[InvisibleSpace]aa
                                        \[InvisibleSpace]aa"}
Out[7]= {"aaaaa", "aaaaa"}
In[8]:= Map[StringLength[#] &, {a, b}]
Out[8]= {5, 8}
In[9]:= Map[StringFreeQ[#, "\[InvisibleSpace]"] &, {a, b}]
Out[9]= {True, False}
In[10]:= Map[Characters[#] &, {a, b}]
Out[10]= {{"a", "a", "a", "a", "a"}, {"a", "\[InvisibleSpace]",
        "\[InvisibleSpace]", "a", "a", "\[InvisibleSpace]", "a", "a"}}
In[11]:= StringIsItFreeQ[x_] := If[StringQ[x], StringFreeQ[x,
            {"\[InvisibleSpace]", "\[InvisibleTimes]"}], False]
In[12]:= StringIsFreeQ[b]
Out[12]= False
In[13]:= NullStrQ[x_/; StringQ[x]] := SameQ[x, ""] | |
    MemberQ[{"\[InvisibleSpace]", "\[InvisibleTimes]", "  "},
                              DeleteDuplicates[Characters[x]][[1]]]
In[14]:= NullStrQ["\[InvisibleSpace]\[InvisibleTimes]"]
Out[14]= True
In[15]:= PackStr[x_String] := StringReplace[x, {" " -> "",
        "\[InvisibleSpace]" -> "", "\[InvisibleTimes]" -> ""}]
In[16]:= a = "aaa\[InvisibleTimes]\[InvisibleSpace]a aa \
                  \[InvisibleSpace] aa\[InvisibleTimes]aa";
In[17]:= StringLength[a]
Out[17]= 16
In[18]:= a = PackStr[a]
```

Out[18]= "aaaaaaaaaa"
In[19]:= **StringLength[a]**
Out[19]= 10

The function call ***PackStr*[*x*]** returns the result of packing of a string ***x*** by deleting from it of all characters occurrences of the form {" ", "\[InvisibleSpace]", "\[InvisibleTimes]"} to character "". The function call ***NullStrQ*[*x*]** returns *True* if a string ***x*** has the form "" or is composed of an arbitrary number of characters {"\[InvisibleSpace]", "\[InvisibleTimes]"} in any combinations, and *False* otherwise. The examples represented above, certain features that should be taken into account when programming tasks involving the using of such symbols are illustrated quite clearly. Indeed, Indeed, processing of visually identical strings and containing characters with *Unicode* ***F360,760, 765, 2082*** and like them, and not containing them, by means of some built-in means can cause unpredictable and even unexpected results, which requires increased attention.

Similarly to ***Maple, Mathematica*** doesn't give any possibility to test inadmissibility of all actual arguments in block, function or module in a point of its call, interrupting its call already on the first inadmissible actual argument. Meanwhile, in view of importance of revealing of all inadmissible actual arguments only for one pass, the three procedures group ***TestArgsTypes ÷ TestArgsTypes2*** solving this important enough problem and presented in our ***MathToolBox*** package [16] has been created. In contrast to the above ***TestArgsTypes*** procedures that provide the *differentiated* testing of actual arguments received by a tested object for their admissibility, a rather simple function ***TrueCallQ*** provides testing of the call correctness of an object of type {*block, function, module*} as a whole; the function call ***TrueCallQ*[*x, args*]** returns *True* if the call ***x*[*args*]** is correct, and *False* otherwise.

To the ***TestArgsTypes ÷ TestArgsTypes2*** and ***TrueCallQ*** in a certain degree the ***TestArgsCall*** and ***TestFactArgs*** procedures adjoins whose call allows to allocate definitions of a function, block or module on which the call on the set actual arguments is quite correct. The source codes of the above tools are in [16].

```
In[7]:= TestActualArgs[x_/; BlockFuncModQ[x], a_/; ListQ[a]] :=
                    Module[{a = ArgsBFM1[x], b = 0, c, d, d1, t},
               c = Map[{b++; If[#[[2]] == "Arbitrary", True,
        ToExpression["ReplaceAll[" <> "Hold[" <> #[[2]] <> "]" <>
        "," <> #[[1]] <> "->" <> ToString1[args[[b]]] <> "]"]]} &, a];
        d = Map[ReleaseHold, Flatten[c]]; d1 = AllTrue[d, TrueQ];
                                          If[d1, d1, b = 1; t = {};
             Map[If[#, b++, AppendTo[t, b++]] &, d]; {False, t}]]
In[8]:= G[x_, y_/; StringQ[y], z__/; IntegerQ[z],
                                 t_/; RationalQ[t]] := {x, y, z, t}
In[9]:= TestActualArgs[G, {a, bs, 77.78, 90}]
Out[9]= {False, {2, 3, 4}}
In[10]:= TestActualArgs[G, {a, "avz", 90, 77/78}]
Out[10]= True
```

The call ***TestActualArgs**[x, y]* of the above procedure returns *True* if *actual* arguments tuple ***y*** for an object ***x*** is admissible and {*False*, ***d***} where ***d*** – the positions list of nonadmissible actual ***y*** arguments. Supposed that only *test* functions and patterns types {"_","__","___"} are used in the ***x*** header *(block, function, module).*

In a number of cases exists an urgent need of determination of the program objects along with their types activated directly in the current session. That problem is solved by means of the ***TypeActObj*** procedure whose call ***TypeActObj***[] without any arguments returns the nested list, whose sub-lists in the string format by the first element contain types of active objects of the current session, while other elements of the sub-lists are names corresponding to this type; in addition, the types recognized by the ***Mathematica***, or types defined by us, in particular, {*Function, Procedure*} can protrude as a type. In some sense the ***TypeActObj*** procedure supplements the ***ObjType*** procedure [8,16]. The next fragment represents the source code of the ***TypeActObj*** with a typical example of its application.

```
In[2227]:= TypeActObj[] := Module[{a = Names["`*"], b = {}, c,
                                                  d, h, p, k = 1},
   Quiet[For[k, k <= Length[a], k++, h = a[[k]]; c = ToExpression[h];
                             p = StringJoin["0", ToString[Head[c]]];
                      If[! StringFreeQ[h, "$"] || (p === Symbol &&
```

```
"Definition"[c] === Null), Continue[],
b = Append[b, {h, If[ProcQ[c], "0Procedure",
If[Head1[c] === Function, "0Function", p]]}]]]];
a = Quiet[Gather1[Select[b, ! #1[[2]] === Symbol &], 2]];
a = ToExpression[StringReplace[ToString1[DeleteDuplicates /@
Sort /@ Flatten /@ a], "AladjevProcedures`TypeActObj`" -> ""]];
Append[{}, Do[a[[k]][[1]] = StringTake[a[[k]][[1]], {2, -1}],
{k, Length[a]}]]; a]
```

```
In[2228]:= TypeActObj[]
Out[2228]= {{"Symbol", "args", "bc", "Bc", "cg", "Cg", "dims", "h",
"tan", "u", "v"}, {"List", "avz", "avz4"}, {"Times", "exp"},
{"Function", "F", "G"}, {"Procedure", "Sv", "VarsExpr"}}
```

The *TypeActObj* procedure is quite interesting in terms of analyzing of software and other objects activated in the current ***Mathematica*** session. The above procedure uses the ***Gather1*** and ***Gather2*** procedures; the second a little extend the function ***Gather1***, being an useful in a number of applications. The call ***Gather1[L, n]*** returns the nested list formed on a basis of a list ***L*** of the *ListList* type by means of grouping of sublists of the ***L*** by its ***n–th*** element. Whereas the call ***Gather2[L]*** returns either the simple list, or the list of *ListList* type that defines only multiple elements of the ***L*** list with their multiplicities. At absence of the multiple elements in ***L*** the procedure call returns the empty list, i.e. {} [7,8,16]. In general, we have programmed many software which extend, complement, or correct some aspects of the built-in ***Mathematica*** functions, or its software as a whole. Because of the aforesaid the above means along with numerous means represented by us in [8-16] can be considered as useful enough tools at processing of the objects of various type in the current session at procedural–functional programming of the various problems. At that, in our opinion, the detailed analysis of their source codes can be a rather effective remedy on the path of the deeper mastering of programming in ***Mathematica.*** Experience of holding of the master classes on ***Mathematica*** system with all evidence confirms expediency of joint use of both standard tools, and the user tools that have been created in the course of programming of various appendices.

On one very significant point, it makes sense to stop our attention. When working with ***Mathematica,*** it is quite real that there is a lack of memory in its workspace. In such cases, it is quite real that the evaluation of new procedures and functions in the current session becomes impossible in the absence of any diagnosis by the system. Let us give one fairly simple example in this regard. In the current session an attempt of the *evaluation* of the definition of a rather simple procedure whose source code is presented below had been done.

```
In[3347]:= NamesInMfile[x_/; FileExistsQ[x] &&
                            FileExtension[x] == "m"] :=
                         Module[{a = ReadString[x], b, c},
                 b = StringReplace[a, {"\n" -> "", "\r" -> ""}];
                                          c = StringCases[b,
                 Shortest["(*Begin[\"`" ~~ __ ~~ "`\"]*)"]];
                        a = Map[StringTake[#, {11, -6}] &, c];
                 b = Map[If[SymbolQ[#], #, Nothing] &, a]]
```

Calling *NamesInMfile*[*x*] procedure returns a list of names in string format that are contained in a file ***x*** of ***m***–format which contains the user package in the format described above. At the same time, the names of the package means, without assigned usages, are also returned. In order to resolve the given situation without leaving the current session, we can propose an useful approach that is based on the list format of the procedures and functions. We represent a similar approach on the basis of the previous procedure. The procedure, together with the factual argument – a ***m***–format file – is presented in the form of a list, whose elements separator is semicolons, as the next fragment easily illustrates.

```
In[3377]:= {x = "C:\\Mathematica\\MathToolBox.m";
          b = StringReplace[ReadString[x], {"\n" -> "", "\r" -> ""}];
     b = StringCases[b, Shortest["(*Begin[\"`" ~~ __ ~~ "`\"]*)"]];
                           b = Map[StringTake[#, {11, -6}] &, b];
                 Sort[Map[If[SymbolQ[#], #, Nothing] &, b]]}[[1]]
Out[3377]:= {"AcNb", "ActBFM", ..., "$Version1", "$Version2"}
In[3378]:= Length[%]
Out[3378]= 1322
```

The procedure call ***NamesInMBfiles*[*x*]** returns a list of the names in string format that are contained in a file ***x*** of format ***"nb"*** which contains the user package in the format described above. In addition, the names of the package means, without assigned usages, are also returned. The fragment represent the source code of the procedure with an example of its application.

```
In[3388]:= NamesInNBfiles[x_ /; FileExistsQ[x]] :=
  Module[{c = FileConvert[x -> "#.m"], b, h, g = {}, s = {}, k},
                                  a = ReadString[c]; DeleteFile[c];
   b = "`" <> StringReplace[a, {"RowBox[{" -> "", "\n" -> "",
                                               "\r" -> ""}] <> "`";
                          c = Map[#[[1]] &, StringPosition[b, "`"]];
                                 For[k = 1, k <= Length[c] - 1, k++,
                              h = StringTake[b, {c[[k]], c[[k + 1]]}];
                                     h = StringReplace[h, "`" -> ""];
  If[SymbolQ[h], AppendTo[g, h], 7]]; g = DeleteDuplicates[g];
  Map[If[NameQ[#] && ! SystemQ[#] && StringLength[#] > 1,
                                  AppendTo[s, #], 7] &, g]; Sort[s]]

In[3389]:= NamesInNBfiles["C:\\math\\mathtoolbox.nb"]
Out[3389]= {"AcNb", "ActBFM", "ActBFMuserQ", ..., "$Version2"}
In[3390]:= Length[%]
Out[3390]= 1317
```

The above mentioned procedure for solving a task uses the ***FileConvert*** function, whose call ***FileConvert*[*F1* -> *"File2.ext"*]** converts the contents of source file ***F1*** to the format defined by the extension ***ext*** and saves the result to the file ***"File2.ext"***. In addition, files can be converted from formats supported by the function ***Import*** to formats supported by ***Export.*** Given that the internal content of a certain file plays a rather significant role in solving programming problems related to the structure of the file, the question of converting the file into a more acceptable format seems to be quite important. In particular, the above procedure uses the ***FileConvert*** function for converting of the ***nb***-files to ***m***-files, facilitating the task solution. This approach has been used in a number of applications [8-15].

3.9. Certain additional tools of expressions processing in the Mathematica software

Analogously to the most software systems the ***Mathematica*** understands everything with what it manipulates as ***expression*** *(graphics, lists, formulas, strings, modules, functions, numbers, etc.)*. And although all these expressions, at first sight, significantly differ, ***Mathematica*** presents them in so–called *full format*. And only the postponed assignment ":=" has no full format. For the purpose of definition of the ***heading*** of an ***e*** expression *(the type defining it)* the built-in ***Head*** function is used whose call ***Head*[*e*]** returns the heading of an ***e*** expression:

```
In[3331]:= G := S; Z[x_] := Block[{}, x]; F[x_] := x; M[x_] := x;
  M[x_, y_] := x + y; Map[Head, {ProcQ, Sin, 77, a + b, # &, G, Z,
                                  Function[{x}, x], x*y, x^y, F, M}]
Out[3332]= {Symbol, Symbol, Integer, Plus, Function, Symbol,
                      Symbol, Function, Times, Power, Symbol, Symbol}
```

For more exact definition of headings we created an useful modification of built-in ***Head*** function in the form of the ***Head1*** procedure expanding its opportunities, for example, it concerns testing of blocks, system functions, the user functions, modules, etc. Thus, the call ***Head1*[*x*]** returns the heading of an expression ***x*** in the context {*Block, Function, Module, System, Symbol, Head*[*x*], *PureFunction*}. In addition, on the objects of the same name that have one name with several definitions the procedure call will return $*Failed*. The fragment below represents source code of the ***Head1*** procedure with examples of its use comparatively with the ***Head*** function as it is illustrated by certain examples of the following fragment on which the functional distinctions of both tools are rather evident.

```
In[3333]:= Head1[x_] := Module[{a = PureDefinition[x]},
                   If[ListQ[a], $Failed, If[a === "System", System,
                   If[BlockQ[x], Block, If[ModuleQ2[x], Module,
  f[PureFuncQ[x], PureFunction, If[Quiet[Check[FunctionQ[x],
                                  False]], Function, Head[x]]]]]]]]
In[3334]:= G := S; Z[x_] := Block[{}, x]; F[x_] := x; M[x_] := x;
  M[x_, y_] := x + y; Map[Head, {ProcQ, Sin, 6, a + b, # &, G, Z,
```

```
                              Function[{x}, x], x*y, x^y, F, M}]
Out[3334]= {Symbol, Symbol, Integer, Plus, Function, Symbol,
          Symbol, Function, Times, Power, Symbol, Symbol}
In[3335]:= Map[Head1, {ProcQ, Sin, 6, a + b, # &, G, Z,
                              Function[{x}, x], x*y, x^y, F, M}]
Out[3335]= {Module, System, Integer, Plus, PureFunction,
  Symbol, Block, PureFunction, Times, Power, Function, $Failed}
```

The ***Head1*** procedure has a quite certain meaning for more exact *(relatively to system standard)* classification of expressions according to their headings. On many expressions the calls of ***Head1*** procedure and ***Head*** function are identical, whereas on certain their calls significantly differ. In [2,4-6,8-16], two useful modifications of the ***Head1: Head2*** and ***Head3*** are represented. The expression concept is the important unifying principle in the system having identical internal structure which allows to confine a rather small amount of the *basic operations*. Meantime, despite identical basic structure of expressions, ***Mathematica*** provides a set of various functions for work as with expression, and its separate components.

Tools of testing of correctness of expressions. The system ***Mathematica*** has a number of the means providing the testing of correctness of syntax of expressions among which only two functions are available to the user, namely:

SyntaxQ["x"] *– returns True, if* **x** *– a syntactic correct expression; otherwise False is returned;*

SyntaxLength["x"] *– returns the quontity w of symbols, since the beginning of a "x" string that determines syntactic correct expression* ***StringTake["x", {1, w}]****; in a case w>****StringLength["x"]*** *the system declares that whole "x" string is correct, demanding continuation.*

In our opinion, it isn't very conveniently in case of software processing of the expressions. Therefore extension in the form of ***SyntaxLength1*** procedure is of certain interest.

```
In[4447]:= SyntaxLength1[x_ /; StringQ[x], y___] :=
                Module[{a = "", b = 1, d, h = {}, c = StringLength[x]},
          While[b <= c, d = SyntaxQ[a = a <> StringTake[x, {b}]];
        If[d, AppendTo[h, StringTrim2[a, {"+", "-", " "}, 3]]]; b++];
```

```
h = DeleteDuplicates[h];
If[{y} != {} && ! HowAct[{y}[[1]]], {y} = {h}];
If[h == {}, 0, StringLength[h[[-1]]]]]
```

```
In[4448]:= {SyntaxLength1["d[a[1]] + b[2]", g], g}
Out[4448]= {14, {"d", "d[a[1]]", "d[a[1]] + b", "d[a[1]] + b[2]"}}
```

The call ***SyntaxLength1[x]*** returns the maximum number *w* of position in a string ***x*** such that the next condition is carried out ***ToExpression[StringTake[x, {1, w}]]*** – a syntactically correct expression, otherwise ***0*** *(zero)* is will be returned; whereas the **call *SyntaxLength1[x, y]*** through the *2nd* optional *y* argument – *an indefinite variable* – additionally returns the list of substrings of the string ***x*** representing correct expressions.

Unlike the ***SyntaxLength1*** procedure, the procedure call ***SyntaxLength2[j]*** gathers correct subexpressions extracted from a string ***j*** into lists of expressions identical on the length. The function call ***ExtrVarsOfStr1[j]*** returns the sorted list of possible symbols in string format successfully extracted from a string ***j;*** if symbols are absent, the empty list – {} is returned. Unlike the ***ExtrVarsOfStr*** procedure the ***ExtrVarsOfStr1*** function provides the more exhaustive extraction of all possible symbols from the strings. Whereas, the procedure call ***FactualVarsStr1[j]*** returns the list of all factual variables extracted from a string ***j;*** source code of the last tool with an example are represented below.

```
In[6]:= FactualVarsStr1[x_/; StringQ[x]] := Module[{b = "",
  c = {}, h, t, k, a = StringLength[x] + 1, d = x <> "[", j = 1},
  While[j <= a, For[k = j, k <= a, k++,
  If[SymbolQ[t = StringTake[d, {k, k}]] | | t == "`", b = b <> t,
  If[! MemberQ[{"", "`"}, b],
  AppendTo[c, {b, If[MemberQ[CNames["AladjevProcedures`"],
  b], "AladjevProcedures`", h = If[ContextQ[b], "contexts",
  Quiet[ToExpression["Context[" <> b <> "]"]]];
  If[h == "AladjevProcedures`", $Context, h]]}], 7]; b = ""]; j = k + 1]];
  c = Map[DeleteDuplicates,
  Map[Flatten, Gather[c, #1[[2]] == #2[[2]] &]]];
  c = Map[Sort[#, ContextQ[#1] &] &, c];
  c = Map[If[MemberQ[#, "contexts"] &&
  ! MemberQ[#, "Global`"], Flatten[{"contexts",
```

```
ReplaceAll[#, "contexts" -> Nothing]}], #] &, c];
c = Map[Flatten[{#[[1]], Sort[#[[2 ;; -1]]]}] &, c];
Map[If[#[[1]] != "Global`" && MemberQ[#, "contexts"],
Flatten[{"contexts", ReplaceAll[#, "contexts" -> Nothing]}], #] &, c]]
In[7]:= FactualVarsStr1[PureDefinition[StrStr]]
Out[7]= {{"AladjevProcedures`", "StrStr"}, {"Global`", "x"},
{"System`", "If", "StringJoin", "StringQ", "ToString"}}
```

The procedure call ***FactualVarsStr1*[*x*]** on the whole returns the nested list whose sublists have contexts as the first element whereas the others define the symbols extracted from a string ***x*** which have these contexts. If the string ***x*** contains contexts then ***"contexts"*** element precedes their sorted tuple in sublist. The above means is useful enough in practical programming in the ***Mathematica*** and their codes contain a number of rather useful programming receptions [16].

Call ***SyntaxQ*[*x*]** of standard ***Mathematica*** function returns *True* if a string ***x*** corresponds to syntactically correct input for a single expression, and returns *False* otherwise. In addition, the function tests only syntax of expression, ignoring its semantics at its evaluation. Whereas the tools ***ExpressionQ, ExprQ, Expr1Q*** along with the *syntax* provide testing of expressions regarding their semantic correctness. The calls of all these tools on a string ***x*** returns *True* if string ***x*** contains a *syntactically* and *semantically* correct single expression, and *False* otherwise. Fragment below represents source code of the ***ExprQ1*** function and examples of its use in comparison with the built-in ***SyntaxQ*** function.

```
In[2214]:= Expr1Q[x_/; StringQ[x]] :=
Quiet[Check[SameQ[ToExpression[x], ToExpression[x]], False]]
In[2215]:= {z, a, c, d} = {500, 90, 77, 42}; SyntaxQ["z=(c+d)*a/0"]
Out[2215]= True
In[2216]:= Expr1Q["z=(c+d)*a/0"]
Out[2216]= False
In[2217]:= {SyntaxQ["77 = 72"], Expr1Q["77 = 72"]}
Out[2217]= {True, False}
```

Thus, the function call ***Expr1Q*[*x*]** returns *False* only if the call ***ToExpression*[*x*]** causes an erroneous situation for a string ***x*** that contains some expression.

It is possible to apply the ***Cases*** function for definition of the expressions coinciding with a given pattern, however not all problems of expressions comparison with *patterns* are solved by the standard means. For solution of the problem in broader aspect the ***EquExprPatt*** procedure can be rather useful whose call ***EquExprPatt[x, p]*** returns *True* if expression ***x*** corresponds to the given ***p*** pattern, and *False* otherwise. The fragment below presents source code of the procedure and an example of its use.

```
In[1395]:= EquExprPatt[x_, y_/; ExprPatternQ[y]] :=
            Module[{c, d = {}, j, t, v = {}, k = 1, p, g = {}, s = {},
                    a = Map[FullForm, Map[Expand, {x, y}]],
              b = Mapp[MinusList, Map[OP, Map[Expand, {x, y}]],
              {FullForm}], z = SetAttributes[ToString, Listable], w},
   {b, c} = ToString[{b, a}]; p = StringPosition[c[[2]], {"Pattern[",
                                                          "Blank[]]"}];
 While[k = 2*k-1; k <= Length[p], AppendTo[d, StringTake[c[[2]],
   {p[[k]][[1]], p[[k + 1]][[2]]}]]; k++]; {t, k} = {ToExpression[d], 1};
 While[k <= Length[t], AppendTo[v, StringJoin[ToString[Op[t[[k]]]]]];
                     k++]; v = ToString[v]; v = Map13[Rule, {d, v}];
 v = StringReplace[c[[2]], v]; b = Quiet[Mapp[Select, b, ! SystemQ[#] | |
                                   BlockFuncModQ[ToString[#]] &]];
                                   {b, k, j} = {ToString[b], 1, 1};
                        While[k <= Length[b[[1]]], z = b[[1]][[k]];
   AppendTo[g, {"[" <> z <> "," -> "[w", " " <> z <> "," -> " w",
         "[" <> z <> "]" -> "[w]", " " <> z <> "]" -> " w]"}]; k++];
                         While[j <= Length[b[[2]]], z = b[[2]][[j]];
   AppendTo[s, {"[" <> z <> "," -> "[w", " " <> z <> "," -> " w",
         "[" <> z <> "]" -> "[w]", " " <> z <> "]" -> " w]"}]; j++];
                               ClearAttributes[ToString, Listable];
       z = Map9[StringReplace, {c[[1]], v}, Map[Flatten, {g, s}]];
 SameQ[z[[1]], StringReplace[z[[2]], Join[GenRules[Flatten[Map[# <>
 "," &, Map[ToString, t]]], "w"], GenRules[Flatten[Map[# <> "]" &,
     Map[ToString, t]]], "w]"], GenRules[Flatten[Map[# <> ")" &,
                                 Map[ToString, t]]], "w)"]]]]]

In[1396]:= Mapp[EquExprPatt, {a + b*c^5, 5 + 6*y^7, a + b*p^m,
                                    a + b*m^p}, a + b*x_^n_]
Out[1396]= {True, True, True, True}
```

Expressions processing at level of their components. Means of this group provide a quite effective differentiated processing of expressions. Because of combined *symbolical* architecture the ***Mathematica*** gives a possibility of direct generalization of the element-oriented list operations to arbitrary expressions, that allows to support operations as on separate terms, and on sets of terms at the given levels in trees of the expressions. Without going into details to all tools supporting work with *components* of expressions, we will give only the main from them that have been complemented by our means. Whereas with more detailed description of built-in tools of this group, including admissible formats of coding, it is possible to get acquainted in the *Help,* or in the corresponding literature on the ***Mathematica*** system.

The call ***Variables[p]*** of built-in function returns the list of all independent variables of a polynomial ***p,*** at the same time, its application to an arbitrary expression has some limitations. Meantime for receiving all independent variables of a certain expression ***x*** it is quite possible to use a simple function whose call ***UnDefVars[x]*** returns the list of all independent variables of an expression ***x.*** Unlike the ***UnDefVars*** the call ***UnDefVars1[x]*** returns the list of all independent variables in string format of an expression ***x.*** In certain cases the mentioned functions have certain preferences relative to the built-in ***Variables*** function.

The call ***Replace[x, r {, j}]*** of built-in function returns result of application of a rule ***r*** of the form ***a → b*** or list of such rules for transformation of ***x*** expression as a whole; application of the *3rd* optional ***j*** argument defines application of ***r*** rules to parts of ***j*** level of a ***x*** expression. Meantime, the built-in ***Replace*** function has a number of restrictions some of which a simple procedure considerably obviates, whose call ***Replace1[x, r]*** returns result of application of ***r*** rules to all or selective independent variables of ***x*** expression. In a case of detection by the procedure ***Replace1*** of empty rules the appropriate message will be printed with the indication of the list of those ***r*** rules that were empty, i.e. whose left parts aren't entered into the list of independent variables of ***x*** expression. Fragment below presents source code of ***Replace1*** with examples of its use; in addition, comparison with result of use of the ***Replace*** function on the same expression is done.

```
In[33]:= Replace1[x_, y_ /; ListQ[y] &&
DeleteDuplicates[Map[Head, y]] == {Rule} || Head[y] == Rule] :=
   Module[{a = x // FullForm // ToString, b = UnDefVars[x], c, p, l,
   h = {}, r, k = 1, d = ToStringRule[DeleteDuplicates[Flatten[{y}]]]},
                                           p = Map14[RhsLhs, d, "Lhs"];
                      c = Select[p, ! MemberQ[Map[ToString, b], #] &];
   If[c != {}, Print["Rules " <> ToString[Flatten[Select[d, MemberQ[c,
                              RhsLhs[#, "Lhs"]] &]]] <> " are vacuous"]];
                    While[k <= Length[d], l = RhsLhs[d[[k]], "Lhs"];
                                           r = RhsLhs[d[[k]], "Rhs"];
                h = Append[h, {"[" <> l -> "[" <> r, " " <> l -> " " <> r,
                                        l <> "]" -> r <> "]"}]; k++];
               Simplify[ToExpression[StringReplace[a, Flatten[h]]]]]]
In[34]:= X = (x^2 - y^2)/(Sin[x] + Cos[y]) + a*Log[x + y];
         Replace[X, {x -> a + b, a -> 90, y -> Cos[a], z -> Log[t]}]
Out[34]= a*Log[x + y] + (x^2 - y^2)/(Cos[y] + Sin[x])
In[35]:= Replace1[X, {x -> a + b, a -> 90, y -> Cos[a], z -> Log[t],
                                                           t -> c + d}]
      Rules {ComplexInfinity -> (Log[t]), t -> (c + d)} are vacuous
Out[35]= 90*Log[a + b + Cos[a]] + ((a + b)^2 - Cos[a]^2)/
                                             (Cos[Cos[a]] + Sin[a + b])
```

Due to quite admissible impossibility of performance of the *replacements* of subexpressions of an expression at the required its levels, there are questions as of belonging of subexpressions of expression to its levels, and of belonging of subexpression to the given expression level. The following two procedures in a certain extent solve these problems. A call ***SubExprOnLevels*[*x*]** returns the nested list whose **2**–element sublists contain levels numbers as the first elements, and lists of subexpressions on these levels as the second elements of an expression ***x***. Whereas the call ***ExprOnLevelQ*[*x, y, z*]** returns *True* if a ***y*** subexpression belongs to the ***z–th*** level of ***x*** expression, and *False* otherwise. In addition, in a case of *False* return, the call ***ExprOnLevelQ*[*x, y, z, t*]** through the optional ***t*** argument – *an indefinite symbol* – returns additionally the list of levels numbers of the ***x*** expression which contain the *y* as a subexpression. The fragment below represents the source codes of both procedures with examples of their use.

```
In[1137]:= SubExprOnLevels[x_] := Module[{a, b, c = {}},
   Do[If[Set[a, DeleteDuplicates[Level[x, {j}]]] ===
     Set[b, DeleteDuplicates[Level[x, {j + 1}]]], Return[c],
       AppendTo[c, {j, a}]], {j, Infinity}]]
In[1138]:= SubExprOnLevels[(x^2 + y^2)/(x + y)]
Out[1138]= {{1, {1/(x + y), x^2 + y^2}}, {2, {x + y, -1, x^2, y^2}},
   {3, {x, y, 2}}}
In[1140]:= ExprOnLevelQ[x_, y_, z_Integer, t___] :=
   Module[{a = SubExprOnLevels[x], b = {}, c = {}},
     If[! MemberQ[Map[#[[1]] &, a], z], False,
   If[MemberQ[a[[z]][[2]], y], True, If[{t} != {} && NullQ[t],
   Do[If[MemberQ[a[[j]][[2]], y], AppendTo[b, a[[j]][[1]]], 7],
     {j, Length[a]}]; t = b; False, 7]]]]
In[1141]:= ExprOnLevelQ[(x + y)/(x + a*x^2/b^2), x^2, 1, agn]
Out[1141]= False
In[1142]:= agn
Out[1142]= {4}
```

At structural analysis of expressions, a quite certain interest is the ***CompOfExpr*** procedure, which allows to determine the component composition of an algebraical expression.

```
In[7]:= CompOfExpr[x_] :=
     Module[{a = ToString[FullForm[x]],
       b = Map[ToString, FullFormF[]],
   Num = {}, Str = {}, Sys = {}, Vars = {}, User = {}, av},
  ClearAll[av]; a = StringReplace4[a, GenRules[b, ""], av];
   a = "{" <> StringReplace[a, {"[" -> ",", "]" -> ","}] <> "}";
   a = Select[ToExpression[a], ! SameQ[#, Null] &];
   a = Sort[DeleteDuplicates[a]];
 Map[If[StringQ[#], AppendTo[Str, #],
   If[NumericQ[#], AppendTo[Num, #],
    If[SystemQ[#], AppendTo[Sys, #],
     If[BlockFuncModQ[#], AppendTo[User, #],
       AppendTo[Vars, #]]]]] &, a];
   {{"Sys", Sys}, {"User", User}, {"Vars", Vars}, {"Str", Str},
 {"Num", Num}, {"Op", ToExpression[Complement[b, av[[2]]]]}}]
```

```
In[8]:= X = {(x^2 - y^2)/(Sin[x]+Cos[y])/a^Log[x+y], {"a", "b", "c"},
    ToExpression["ToString1"], ToExpression["CompOfExpr"]};
In[9]:= CompOfExpr[X]
Out[9]= {{"Sys", {Cos, List, Log, Sin}}, {"User", {CompOfExpr,
               ToString1}}, {"Vars", {a, x, y}}, {"Str", {"a", "b", "c"}},
                    {"Num", {-1, 2}}, {"Op", {Plus, Power, Times}}}
In[10]:= CompOfExpr[{(Sin[x] + b)/(Cos[y] + c), ToString1,
                                          ProcQ, {73, 78}, "agn"}]
Out[10]= {{"Sys", {Cos, List, Sin}}, {"User", {ProcQ, ToString1}},
         {"Vars", {b, c, x, y}}, {"Str", {"agn"}}, {"Num", {-1, 73, 78}},
                                        {"Op", {Plus, Power, Times}}}
```

Calling ***CompOfExpr*[*x*]** procedure returns the nested list of two-element sub-lists; each sub-list contains one of the words *"Sys" (system tools), "User" (the user tools), "Vars" (variables), "Str" (strings), "Num" (numbers), "Op" (operations)* as the first element, while the second element represents the list of components *(type of which is defined by the corresponding first word)* of an algebraical ***x*** expression.

In the certain cases exists necessity to execute the exchange of values of variables with the corresponding exchange of all their attributes. So, variables ***x*** and ***y*** having values ***77*** and ***72*** should receive the values **42** and ***47*** accordingly along with the appropriate exchange of all their attributes. The procedure call ***VarExch*[*x, y*]** solves this problem, returning *Null,* i.e. nothing. The list of two names of variables in string format for exchange by values and attributes or the nested list of *ListList* type acts as the actual argument; anyway all elements of pairs of the list have to be definite, otherwise the call returns *Null* with printing of the appropriate diagnostic message, for example:

```
In[7]:= x = a + b; y = m - n; SetAttributes[x, {Protected, Listable}]
In[8]:= {x, y}
Out[8]= {a + b, m - n}
In[9]:= VarExch[{"x", "y"}]
In[10]:= Definition[x]
Out[10]= x = m - n
In[11]:= Definition[y]
Out[11]= Attributes[y] = {Listable, Protected}
         y = a + b
```

On the other hand, the procedure call ***Rename***[*x, y*] in the regular mode returns *Null,* providing replacement of *x* name of some defined object on *y* name with saving of all attributes of this object. In addition, the *x* name is removed from the current session by the ***Remove*** function. But if *y* argument defines the name of a defined object or an undefined name with attributes, the call is returned unevaluated. If the first *x* argument is illegal for renaming, the procedure call returns *Null;* in addition, the ***Rename*** procedure successfully processes also objects of the same name of type *"Block", "Function", "Module".* The ***Rename1*** procedure is an useful version of the above procedure, being based on our procedure ***Definition2.*** The call ***Rename1***[*x, y*] is similar to the call ***Rename***[*x, y*] whereas the call ***Rename1***[*x, y, z*] with the third optional *z* argument - an arbitrary expression - performs the same functions as the call ***Rename1***[*x, y*] without change of an initial *x* object.

The ***VarExch1*** procedure is a version of the above ***VarExch*** procedure and is based on use of the ***Rename*** procedure with *global* variables; it admits the same type of actual argument, but unlike the second procedure the call ***VarExch1***[*w*] in a case of detection of indefinite elements of a list *w* or its sublists will be returned unevaluated without print of any diagnostic message. In the fragment below, source code of the ***Rename1*** procedure along with typical examples of its application is represented.

```
In[7]:= Rename1[x_String /; HowAct[x], y_ /; ! HowAct[y], z___] :=
        Module[{a = Attributes[x], b = Definition2[x][[1 ;; -2]],
                                                  c = ToString[y]},
   b = Map[StringReplacePart[#, c, {1, StringLength[x]}] &, b];
                                                  ToExpression[b];
 ToExpression["SetAttributes[" <> c <> ", " <> ToString[a] <> "]"];
    If[{z} == {}, ToExpression["ClearAttributes[" <> x <> ", " <>
                     ToString[a] <> "]; Remove[" <> x <> "]"], Null]]

In[8]:= x := 500; y = 500; SetAttributes[x, {Listable, Protected}]
In[9]:= Rename1["x", Trg42]
In[10]:= {x, Trg42, Attributes["Trg42"]}
Out[10]= {x, 500, {Listable, Protected}}
```

```
In[11]:= Rename1["y", Trg47, 90]
In[12]:= {y, Trg47, Attributes["Trg47"]}
Out[12]= {500, 500, {}}
```

Use in procedures of global variables, in a lot of cases will allow to simplify programming, sometimes significantly. This mechanism sufficient in detail is considered in [15]. Meanwhile, mechanism of global variables in ***Mathematica*** isn't universal, quite correctly working in a case of evaluation of definitions of procedures containing global variables in the current session in the ***Input***-paragraph; whereas in general case it isn't supported when the loading in the current session of the procedures that contain global variables, in particular, from ***nb***-files with the subsequent activation of their contents.

For the purpose of exclusion of similar situation a tool has been offered, whose call ***NbCallProc[x]*** reactivates a block, a function or a module ***x*** in the current session, whose definition was in a ***nb***-file loaded into the current session with returning of *Null*, i.e. nothing. The call ***NbCallProc[x]*** reactivates in the current session all definitions of blocks, functions and modules with the same name ***x*** and with different headings. All these definitions have to be loaded previously from some ***nb***-file into the current session and activated by means of function *"Evaluate Notebook"* of the ***GUI***. The following fragment represents source code of the ***NbCallProc*** procedure with example of its use for the above ***VarExch1*** procedure that uses the global variables.

```
In[2442]:= NbCallProc[x_/; BlockFuncModQ[x]] :=
   Module[{a = SubsDel[StringReplace[ToString1[DefFunc[x]],
  "\n \n" -> ";"], "`" <> ToString[x] <> "`", {"[", ","}, -1]}, Clear[x];
                                                            ToExpression[a]]
In[2443]:= NbCallProc[VarExch1]
```

The performed verification convincingly demonstrates, that the ***VarExch1*** that contains the global variables and uploaded from the ***nb***-file with subsequent its activation *(by the "Evaluate Notebook")*, is carried out absolutely correctly and with correct functioning of mechanism of global variables restoring values after an exit from the ***VarExch1*** procedure. The ***NbCallProc*** has a number of rather interesting appendices above all if necessity of aplication of procedures activated in the *Input*-paragraph of the current session arises.

Maple has 2 useful tools of manipulation with expressions of the type {***range, equation, inequality, relation***}, whose calls ***lhs(Exp)*** and ***rhs(Exp)*** return the left and the right parts of an expression ***Exp*** respectively. More precisely, the call ***lhs(Exp), rhs(Exp)*** returns a value ***op(1, Exp)*** and ***op(2, Exp)*** respectively. Whereas ***Mathematica*** has no similar useful means. The given deficiency is compensated by the ***RhsLhs*** procedure, whose the source code with examples of application are given below. The call ***RhsLhs[w, y]*** depending on a value {***"Rhs", "Lhs"***} of the second ***y*** argument returns right or left part of ***w*** expressions respectively relatively to operator ***Head[w]***, whereas the call ***RhsLhs[x,y,t]*** in addition through an indefined ***t*** variable returns operator ***Head[x]*** concerning whom splitting of the ***x*** expression onto left and right parts was made. ***RhsLhs*** procedure can be rather easily modified in the light of expansion of the analyzed operators ***Head[x]***. ***RhsLhs1*** procedure is a certain functional equivalent to the previous procedure [8-16].

```
In[7]:= RhsLhs[x__] := Module[{a = Head[{x}[[1]]],
        b = ToString[InputForm[{x}[[1]]]], d, h = {x},
   c = {{Greater, ">"}, {Or, "||"}, {GreaterEqual, ">="}, {Span, ";;"},
    {And, "&&"}, {LessEqual, "<="}, {Unequal, "!="}, {Rule, "->"},
     {Less, "<"}, {Plus, {"+", "-"}}, {Power, "^"}, {Equal, "=="},
      {NonCommutativeMultiply, "**"}, {Times, {"*", "/"}}}},
      If[Length[h] < 2 || ! MemberQ[{"Lhs", "Rhs"}, h[[2]]],
        Return[Defer[RhsLhs[x]]], Null];
      If[! MemberQ[Select[Flatten[c], ! StringQ[#] &], a] ||
        a == Symbol, Return[Defer[RhsLhs[x]]], Null];
   d = StringPosition[b, Flatten[Select[c, #[[1]] == a &], 1][[2]]];
        a = Flatten[Select[c, #[[1]] == a &]];
        If[Length[h] >= 3 && ! HowAct[h[[3]]],
   ToExpression[ToString[h[[3]]] <> "=" <> ToString1[a]], Null];
        ToExpression[If[h[[2]] == "Lhs",
        StringTrim[StringTake[b, {1, d[[1]][[1]] - 1}]],
      StringTrim[StringTake[b, {d[[1]][[2]] + 1, -1}]]]]]
```

```
In[8]:= Mapp[RhsLhs, {a^b, a*b, a -> b, a <= b, a || b, a && b}, "Rhs"]
Out[8]= {b, b, b, b, b, b}
In[9]:= {{RhsLhs[7 ;; 42, "Rhs", s], s}, {RhsLhs[a && b, "Lhs", v], v}}
Out[9]= {{42, {Span, ";;"}}, {a, {And, "&&"}}}
```

In a number of appendices the undoubted interest presents an analog of the ***Maple***-procedure ***whattype(x)*** that returns the type of an expression ***x*** which is one of basic ***Maple***-types. The procedure of the same name acts as a similar analog in system ***Mathematica*** whose call ***WhatType[x]*** returns type of an object ***x*** of one of basic types {*"Module"*, *"DynamicModule"*, *"Complex"*, *"Block"*, *"Real"*, *"Integer"*, *"Rational"*, *"Times"*, *"Rule"*, *"Power"*, *"And"*, *"Alternatives"*, *"List"*, *"Plus"*, *"Condition"*, *"StringJoin"*, *"UndirectedEdge"*, **...**}. The fragment represents source code of the procedure and examples of its application for identification of the types of various objects.

```
In[7]:= WhatType[x_/; StringQ[x]] := Module[{b = t, d,
              c = $Packages, a = Quiet[Head[ToExpression[x]]]},
          If[a === Symbol, Clear[t]; d = Context[x];
          If[d == "Global`", d = Quiet[ProcFuncBlQ[x, t]];
          If[d === True, Return[{t, t = b}[[1]]],
                              Return[{"Undefined", t = b}[[1]]]],
          If[d == "System`", Return[{d, t = b}[[1]]], Null]],
                              Return[{ToString[a], t = b}[[1]]]];
          If[Quiet[ProcFuncBlQ[x, t]],
       If[MemberQ[{"Module", "DynamicModule", "Block"}, t],
                                    Return[{t, t = b}[[1]]], t = b;
  ToString[Quiet[Head[ToExpression[x]]]]], t = b; "Undefined"]]
In[8]:= Map[WhatType, {"a^b", "a**b", "3+7*I", "{42, 47}", "a&&b"}]
Out[8]= {"Power", "NonCommutativeMultiply", "Complex",
                                                   "List", "And"}
In[9]:= Map[WhatType, {"a_/; b", "a <> b", "a <-> b", "a | b"}]
Out[9]= {"Condition", "StringJoin", "TwoWayRule", "Alternatives"}
```

However, it should be noted that the ***WhatType*** procedure don`t support exhaustive testing of types, meantime on its basis it is simple to expand the class of the tested types.

The functions ***Replace*** and ***ReplaceAll*** of ***Mathematica*** have essential restrictions in relation to *replacement* of subexpressions relatively of very simple expressions as it will illustrated below.

The reason of it can be explained by the following *circumstance,* using the procedure useful enough also as independent means. The call ***ExpOnLevels*[*x, y, z*]** returns the list of an expression ***x*** levels on which an subexpression ***y*** is located. While procedure call with the third optional ***z*** argument – *an undefinite symbol* – through it additionally returns the nested list of *ListList* type of all subexpressions of expression ***x*** on all its levels. In addition, the first element of each sublist of such *ListList* list determines a level of the ***x*** expression while the second element defines the list of subexpressions located on this level. If subexpression ***y*** is absent on the levels identified by ***Level*** function, the procedure call returns the appropriate diagnostic message. The fragment below presents source code of the ***ExpOnLevels*** procedure with typical examples of its application.

```
In[7]:= ExpOnLevels[x_, y_, z___] := Module[{a = {}, b},
                Do[AppendTo[a, {j, Set[b, Level[x, {j}]]}];
             If[b == {}, Break[], Continue[]], {j, 1, Infinity}];
          a = a[[1 ;; -2]]; If[{z} != {} && NullQ[z], z = a, 77];
     b = Map[If[MemberQ[#[[2]], y], #[[1]], Nothing] &, a];
             If[b == {}, "Subexpression " <> ToString1[y] <>
                              " can't be identified", b]]
In[8]:= ExpOnLevels[a + b^3 + 1/x^(3/(a + 2)) + b[t] + 1/x^2, x^2]
Out[8]= "Subexpression x^2 can't be identified"
In[9]:= ExpOnLevels[a + b^3 + 1/x^(3/(a + 2)) + b[t] + a/x^2, x^2, g]
Out[9]= "Subexpression x^2 can't be identified"
In[10]:= g
Out[10]= {{1, {a, b^3, a/x^2, x^(-(3/(2 + a))), b[t]}},
     {2, {b, 3, a, 1/x^2, x, -(3/(2 + a)), t}}, {3, {x, -2, -3, 1/2 + a}},
                                   {4, {2 + a, -1}}, {5, {2, a}}}
```

Replacement subexpressions in expressions. The procedure ***ExpOnLevels*** can determine admissible replacements carring out by means of the standard functions ***Replace*** and ***ReplaceAll*** as they are based on the ***Level*** function that evaluates the list of all subexpressions of an expression on the set levels. The call of the built–in ***Replace*** function on unused rules don`t return any diagnostical information, at the same time, if all rules were not used, then the function call is returned as unevaluated. In turn, the procedure below that is based on the previous ***ExpOnLevels*** procedure gives full diagnostics concerning the unused rules. The procedure call ***ReplaceInExpr*[*x, y, z*]** is analogous to the call ***Replace*[*x, y, All*]** where *y* is a rule or their list whereas thru the *3rd* optional *z* argument – *an undefined symbol* – additionally is returned the message identifying the list of the unused rules.

The procedure call ***ReplaceInExpr1*[*x, y, z*]** is analogous to the call ***ReplaceInExpr*[*x, y, z*]** but not its result where *y* is a rule or their list whereas through the third optional *z* argument – *an undefined symbol* – additionally the message is returned which identifies a list of the unused rules. If unused rules are absent, then the *z* symbol remains undefined. The following fragment represents source code of the ***ReplaceInExpr1*** procedure with typical examples of its application. Of the presented examples one can clearly see the difference between both procedures.

```
In[7]:= ReplaceInExpr1[x_, r_/; RuleQ[r] || ListRulesQ[r], y___] :=
                    Module[{a = ToString1 @@ {ToBoxes @@ {x}}, b,
                                   c = If[RuleQ[r], {r}, r], d, h = {}},
                    Do[b = ToString1 @@ {ToBoxes @@ {c[[j]][[1]]}};
                        d = ToString1 @@ {ToBoxes @@ {c[[j]][[2]]}};
                                   If[StringFreeQ[a, b], AppendTo[h, j],
                    a = StringReplace[a, b -> d]], {j, 1, Length[c]}];
          a = ToExpression[a]; If[{y} != {} && NullQ[y], y = h, 77];
                    ReleaseHold[MakeExpression[a, StandardForm]]]
In[8]:= ReplaceInExpr1[x^2 + 1/x^2 + c[t], {x^2 -> m^3, t -> j[x]}]
Out[8]= 1/m^3 + m^3 + c[2[x]]
In[9]:= ReplaceInExpr1[(a + b[t]) + 1/x^(3/(b[t] + 2)) + b[t] +
              a/x^2, {x^2 -> mp, b[t] -> gsv, x^3 -> tag, a -> 77}, gs]
Out[9]= 77 + 2*gsv + 77/mp + x^(-(3/(2 + gsv)))
In[10]:= gs
Out[10]= {3}
In[11]:= ReplaceInExpr[(a + b[t]) + 1/x^(3/(b[t] + 2)) + b[t] +
              a/x^2, {x^2 -> mp, b[t] -> gsv, x^3 -> tag, a -> 77}, gs1]
Out[11]= 77 + 2*gsv + 77/x^2 + x^(-(3/(2 + gsv)))
In[12]:= gs1
Out[12]= "Rules {1, 3} were not used"
```

Using the built-in ***ToBoxes*** function that creates the boxes corresponding to the printed form of expressions in the form

StandardForm, we can allocate the subexpressions composing an expression. The procedure call ***SubExpressions[x]*** returns the list of subexpressions composing an expression ***x***, in a case of impossibility the empty list is returned, i.e. {}. The fragment below represents source code of the ***SubExpressions*** procedure with a typical example of its application.

```
In[12]:= SubExpressions[x_] := Module[{b, c = {}, d, h, t,
                                      a = ToString1[ToBoxes[x]]},
    b = Select[ExtrVarsOfStr[a, 2], SystemQ[#] || UserQ[#] &];
                          Do[h = b[[j]]; d = StringPosition[a, h];
    Do[t = "["; Do[If[StringCount[t, "["] == StringCount[t, "]"],
                                     AppendTo[c, h <> t]; Break[],
    t = t <> StringTake[a, {d[[p]][[2]] + k + 1}]], {k, 1, Infinity}],
                            {p, 1, Length[d]}], {j, 1, Length[b]}];
    c = Map[Quiet[Check[ToExpression[#], Nothing]] &, c];
  Map[ReleaseHold[MakeExpression[#, StandardForm]] &, c]]

In[13]:= SubExpressions[a*b + 1/x^(3/(b[t] + 2)) + J[t] + d/x^2]
Out[13]= {d/x^2, 3/(2 + b[t]), a*b + d/x^2 + x^(-(3/(2 + b[t]))) + J[t],
   a*b, -(3/(2 + b[t])), 2 + b[t], b[t], Sin[t], x^2, x^(-(3/(2 + b[t])))}
```

Unlike the above ***SubExpressions*** procedure, the procedure ***SubExpressions1*** is based on the standard ***FullForm*** function. The call ***SubExpressions1[x]*** returns the list of sub-expressions that compose an expression ***x***, while in a case of impossibility the empty list is returned, i.e. {}. The system ***Level*** function and our ***SubExpressions ÷ SubExpressions2*** means allow to outline possibilities of the ***Mathematica*** concerning the replacements of the sub-expressions in expressions [8,12-16].

As an alternative to the above tools can be offered the ***Subs*** procedure that is functionally equivalent to the above standard ***ReplaceAll*** function, however which is relieved of a number of its shortcomings. Procedure call ***Subs[x, y, z]*** returns the result of substitutions to an expression ***x*** of all occurrences of ***y*** sub-expressions onto ***z*** expressions. In addition, if ***x*** - an arbitrary correct expression, then as the *2nd* and *3rd* arguments defining substitutions of format ***y -> z***, an unary substitution or their list coded in form ***y*** ≡ {*y1, y2, ..., yn*} and ***z*** ≡ {*z1, z2, ..., zn*} act, defining the list of substitutions {*y1 -> z1, y2 -> z2, ..., yn -> zn*} which are carried out consistently in the order defined at the ***Subs*** call. A number of bright examples of its use on those expressions and with those types of substitutions where the ***Subs*** surpasses the standard ***ReplaceAll*** function is represented, in particular, in [8-15]. These examples rather clearly illustrate advantages of the ***Subs*** procedure before the similar system software.

At last, ***Substitution*** is an integrated procedure of the tools ***Subs ÷ Subs2***. The procedure call ***Substitution***[*x, y, z*] returns the result of substitutions into an arbitrary *x* expression of an expression *z* instead of occurrences in it of all *y* subexpressions. In addition, if as *x* expression any correct expression admitted in ***Math***–language is used, whereas as a single substitution or their set are coded *y* ≡ {*y1,y2,...,yn*} and *z* ≡ {*z1,z2,...,zn*} as the *2nd* and *3rd* arguments defining substitutions of the format *y -> z* by defining the set of substitutions {*y1 -> z1, y2 -> z2, ..., yn -> zn*} carried out consistently. The ***Substitution*** allows essentially to extend possibilities of expressions processing. The following fragment represents source code of the ***Substitution*** procedure and examples of its application, well illustrating its advantages over the standard means.

```
In[7]:= Substitution[x_, y_, z_] := Module[{d, k = 2, subs, subs1},
   subs[m_, n_, p_] := Module[{a, b, c, h, t},
   If[! HowAct[n], m /. n -> p, {a, b, c, h} =
   First[{Map[ToString, Map[InputForm, {m, n, p, 1/n}]]}];
   Simplify[ToExpression[StringReplace[StringReplace[a,
   b -> "(" <> c <> ")"], h -> "1/" <> "(" <> c <> ")"]]];
   If[t === m, m /. n -> p, t]]];
   subs1[m_, n_, p_] := ToExpression[StringReplace[ToString[
   FullForm[m]],
   ToString[FullForm[n]] -> ToString[FullForm[p]]]];
   If[! ListQ[y] && ! ListQ[z], If[Numerator[y] == 1 &&
   ! SameQ[Denominator[y], 1], subs1[x, y, z],
   subs[x, y, z]], If[ListQ[y] && ListQ[z] && Length[y] ==
   Length[z], If[Numerator[y[[1]]] == 1 &&
   ! SameQ[Denominator[y[[1]]], 1],
   d = subs1[x, y[[1]], z[[1]]], d = subs[x, y[[1]], z[[1]]]];
```

```
        For[k, k <= Length[y], k++, If[Numerator[y[[k]]] == 1 &&
     ! SameQ[Denominator[y[[k]]], 1], d = subs1[d, y[[k]], z[[k]]],
      d = subs[d, y[[k]], z[[k]]]]]; d, Defer[Substitution[x, y, z]]]]]
In[8]:= Replace[1/x^2 + 1/y^3, {{x^2 -> a + b}, {y^3 -> c + d}}]
Out[8]= {1/x^2 + 1/y^3, 1/x^2 + 1/y^3}
In[9]:= Substitution[1/x^2 + 1/y^3, {x^2, y^3}, {a + b, c + d}]
Out[9]= 1/(a + b) + 1/(c + d)
In[10]:= Replace[1/x^2*1/y^3, {{1/x^2 -> a + b}, {1/y^3 -> c + d}}]
Out[10]= {1/(x^2 y^3), 1/(x^2 y^3)}
In[11]:= Substitution[1/x^2*1/y^3, {x^2, y^3}, {a + b, c + d}]
Out[11]= 1/((a + b)*(c + d))
```

It should be noted that the ***Substitution*** procedure rather significantly extends the standard tools intended for ensuring replacements of subexpressions in expressions as the following examples rather visually illustrate. The ***Substitution1*** procedure can be considered as an analog of the ***Substitution*** procedure. Syntax of the procedure call ***Substitution1[x, y, z]*** is identical to the procedure call ***Substitution[x, y, z]***, returning the result of substitutions into arbitrary ***x*** expression of ***z*** subexpression*(s)* instead of all occurences of ***y*** subexpression*(s)*. A quite simple ***Substitution2*** function is the simplified version of the previous ***Substitution*** procedure, its call ***Substitution2[x, y, z]*** returns the result of substitutions into an expression ***x*** of a subexpression ***z*** instead of all occurences of a subexpression ***y***. The ***Substitution2*** function significantly uses expressions in the ***FullForm*** form and supports a rather wide range of substitutions.

```
In[2211]:= Substitution2[x_, y_, z_] :=
           ToExpression[StringReplace[ToString[FullForm[x]],
             ToString[FullForm[y]] -> ToString[FullForm[z]]]]
In[2212]:= Substitution2[Sin[x^2]*Cos[1/b^3], 1/b^3, x^2]
Out[2212]= Cos[x^2]*Sin[x^2]
In[2213]:= Substitution2[1 + 1/x^2, x^2, a + b]
Out[2213]= 1 + 1/x^2
```

Meantime, already the second example of application of the function reveals its shortcomings, forcing on the same basis to complicate its algorithm. The following version in the procedure form somewhat enhances the function`s possibilities.

```
In[2242]:= Substitution3[x_, y_, z_] := Module[{c,
 a = ToString[FullForm[Simplify[x]]], b = ToString[FullForm[z]]},
              c = Map[ToString[FullForm[#]] &, {y, 1/y}];
       c = GenRules[c, b]; ToExpression[StringReplace[a, c]]]
In[2243]:= Substitution3[1 + 1/x^2, x^2, a + b]
Out[2243]= 1 + a + b
In[2244]:= Substitution3[x^2 + 1/(a + 1/x^2), x^2, a + b]
Out[2244]= a + b + 1/(2*a + b)
In[2245]:= Substitution3[x^2 + 1/(1/x^2 + x^2), x^2, a + b]
Out[2245]= a + b + 1/(2*a + 2*b)
In[2246]:= Substitution[x^2 + 1/(1/x^2 + x^2), x^2, a + b]
Out[2246]= a + b + 1/(a + b + 1/(a + b))
```

Meantime, and the above version of the ***Substitution2*** don`t fully solve the problem, as illustrated by the *3rd* example of the previous fragment, making it impractical to further complicate such ***FullForm***-based means. And only the above ***Substitution*** procedure solves the set problem.

The following procedure allows to eliminate restrictions inherent in means of the above so-called ***Subs***-group. The call ***SubsInExpr***[*x,r*] returns the result of substitution in an arbitrary expression ***x*** set in the form ***Hold***[*x*] of the rigth parts of a rule or their list ***r*** instead of occurences of the left parts *corresponding* them. In addition, all the left an the rigth parts of ***r*** rules should be coded in the ***Hold***-form, otherwise the procedure call returns *$Failed* with printing of the appropriate message. The fragment below represents source code of the ***SubsInExpr*** procedure with typical examples of its application.

```
In[2261]:= SubsInExpr[x_/; Head[x] == Hold, r_/; RuleQ[r] ||
                        ListRulesQ[r]] := Module[{a, b, c, f},
 c = Map[Head[(#)[[1]]] === Hold && Head[(#)[[2]]] === Hold &,
                        Set[b, Flatten[{r}]]]; If[! And @@ c,
     Print["Incorrect tuple of factual arguments"]; $Failed,
          f[t_] := StringTake[ToString1[t], {6, -2}]; a = f[x];
     c = Map[Rule[f[#[[1]]], "(" <> f[#[[2]]] <> ")"] &, b];
                ToExpression[StringReplaceVars[a, c]]]]
In[2262]:= SubsInExpr[Hold[(a + b^3)/(c + d^(-2))],
                          Hold[d^-2] -> Hold[Sin[t]]]
```

```
Out[2262]= (a + b^3)/(c + Sin[t])
In[2263]:= SubsInExpr[Hold[1/(a + 1/x^2)],
                              Hold[1/x^2] -> Hold[Sin[t]]]
Out[2263]= 1/(a + Sin[t])
```

The function call ***SubsInExpr1**[x,r]* analogously to the above ***SubsInExpr*** procedure also returns the substitution result in an expression ***x*** set in the string format of the rigth parts of a rule or their list ***r*** instead of occurences of the left parts *corresponding* them. At that, in contrast to the the above ***SubsInExpr*** procedure all the left an the rigth parts of the rules ***r*** should be also coded in string format like its first argument, otherwise the function call is returned unevaluated. Fragment below represents source code of the function ***SubsInExpr1*** with examples of its use.

```
In[7]:= SubsInExpr1[x_/; StringQ[x], r_/; (RuleQ[r] | |
        ListRulesQ[r]) && (And @@ Map[StringQ[(#)[[1]]] &&
                     StringQ[(#)[[2]]] &, Flatten[{r}]])] :=
                   ToExpression[StringReplaceVars[x, r]]
In[8]:= SubsInExpr1["1/x^2", "1/x^2" -> "Sin[t]"]
Out[8]= Sin[t]
In[9]:= SubsInExpr1["(a + b^3)/(c + d^(-2))", "d^(-2)" -> "Sin[t]"]
Out[9]= (a + b^3)/(c + Sin[t])
```

On a basis of our means of replacement of subexpressions in expressions, the means of differentiation and integration of expressions are programmed. For example, the ***Subs*** procedure is used in realization of the ***Df*** procedure [8] whose call ***Df**[x, y]* provides differentiation of an expression ***x*** on its arbitrary ***y*** subexpression, and rather significantly extends the built-in function ***D***. Our ***ReplaceAll1*** procedure is functionally equivalent to the built-in ***ReplaceAll*** function by relieving a number of shortages of the second. Based on the ***ReplaceAll1*** procedure a number of variants of the ***Df*** procedure, namely the ***Df1*** and ***Df2***, using a number of useful methods of programming were programmed. The ***Df1*** and ***Df2*** procedures in some cases are more useful than the ***Df*** procedure what rather visually illustrate examples given in [7-12,14]. In addition, the ***Df, Df1*** and ***Df2*** rather significantly extend the built-in ***D*** function.

The receiving of similar expansion as well for the standard ***Integrate*** function which has rather essential restrictions on use of arbitrary expressions as integration variables is presented an quite natural to us. Two variants of such expansion in the form of the simple procedures ***Int*** and ***Int1*** which are based on the above ***Subs*** procedure have been proposed for the set purpose, whose source codes and examples of application can be found in [6-16]. Meanwhile, a simple enough ***Subs1*** procedure, being as a certain extension and complement of the ***Subs*** procedure, can be used for realization of procedures ***Integrate2*** and ***Diff1*** of integration and differentiation accordingly.

```
In[3331]:= Integrate2[x_, y__] := Module[{a, b, d,
                   c = Map[Unique["gs"] &, Range[1, Length[{y}]]]},
        a = Riffle[{y}, c]; a = If[Length[{y}] == 1, a, Partition[a, 2]];
                              d = Integrate[Subs1[x, a], Sequences[c]];
              {Simplify[Subs1[d, If[ListListQ[a], Map[Reverse, a],
                                  Reverse[a]]]], Map[Remove, c]}[[1]]]
In[3332]:= Integrate2[(a/b + d)/(c/b + h/b), 1/b, d]
Out[3332]= (d*((2*a)/b + d*Log[1/b]))/(2*(c + h))
In[3333]:= Integrate2[Sqrt[a + Sqrt[c + d]*b], Sqrt[c + d]]
Out[3333]= (2*(a + b*Sqrt[c + d])^(3/2))/(3*b)
In[3334]:= Diff1[x_, y__] := Module[{a, b, d,
                   c = Map[Unique["s"] &, Range[1, Length[{y}]]]},
        a = Riffle[{y}, c]; a = If[Length[{y}] == 1, a, Partition[a, 2]];
                                     d = D[Subs1[x, a], Sequences[c]];
              {Simplify[Subs1[d, If[ListListQ[a], Map[Reverse, a],
                                  Reverse[a]]]], Map[Remove, c]}[[1]]]
In[3335]:= Diff1[(c + a/b)*Sin[b + 1/x^2], a/b, 1/x^2]
Out[3335]= Cos[b + 1/x^2]
In[3336]:= Diff1[(c + a/b)*Sin[d/c + 1/x^2], 1/c, a/b, 1/x^2]
Out[3336]= -d*Sin[d/c + 1/x^2]
```

The procedure call ***Integrate2[x, y]*** provides integrating of an expression ***x*** on the subexpressions defined by a sequence ***y***. In addition, the procedure with the returned result by means of ***Simplify*** function performs a sequence of algebraical and other transformations and returns the simplest form it finds. While the procedure call ***Diff1[x, y]*** which is also realized on a basis of the ***Subs1*** returns the differentiation result of an expression ***x*** on the generalized {*y, z, g...*} variables which can be as arbitrary expressions. The result is returned in the simplified form on the basis of the ***Simplify*** function. The above fragment represents source codes of the ***Diff1*** and ***Integrate2*** procedures along with examples of their application. The variants of realization of the means ***Df ÷ Df2, Diff1, Diff2, Int, Int1, Integrate2, ReplaceAll1, Subs, Subs1, SubsInExpr*** and ***SubsInExpr1*** illustrate different receptions enough useful in a lot of problems of programming in the ***Mathematica*** and, first of all, in problems of the system character. Moreover, the above means essentially extend the appropriate system means [7-16].

The previous means, expanding similar built-in tools, at the same time have certain restrictions. The next means eliminate the defects inherent in the above and built-in means, being the most *universal* in this class for today. As a basis of the following means is the ***ToStringRational*** procedure. The procedure call ***ToStringRational***[*x*] returns an expression *x* in the string format that is rather convenient for expressions processing, including replacements of subexpressions, integrating and differentiation on the subexpressions other than simple symbols. Whereas the procedure call ***SubsExpr***[*x, y*] returns the result of substitutions in an expression *x* of right parts instead of *occurences* of left parts defined by a rule or their list *y* into the *x* expression. Fragment below represents source codes of the above two procedures and typical examples of their application.

```
In[7]:= ToStringRational[x_] := Module[{b, c = {}, h, p, t = "", n,
    a = "(" <> StringReplace[ToString1[x] <> ")", " " -> ""]},
    b = Map[#[[1]] - 1 &, StringPosition[a, "^(-"]];
    Do[h = ""; p = SyntaxQ[StringTake[a, {b[[j]]}]];
    If[p, Do[h = StringTake[a, {j}];
  If[! SyntaxQ[h], AppendTo[c, j + 1]; Break[], 7], {j, b[[j]], 1, -1}],
    Do[h = StringTake[a, {j}]; t = h <> t;
  If[SyntaxQ[t], AppendTo[c, j]; Break[], 7], {j, b[[j]], 1, -1}]],
    {j, 1, Length[b]}]; h = StringInsert[a, "1/", c];
  h = StringTake[StringReplace[h, "^(-" -> "^("], {2, -2}];
```

```
                     h = StringReplace[h, "1/" -> ToString[n] <> "/"];
                                     h = ToString1[ToExpression[h]];
                              h = StringReplace[h, ToString[n] -> "1"]]
In[8]:= ToStringRational[1/x^2 + 1/(1 + 1/(a + b)^2) + 1/x^3]
Out[8]= "1/(1 + 1/(a + b)^2) + 1/x^3 + 1/x^2"
In[13]:= SubsExpr[x_, y_/; RuleQ[y] || ListRulesQ[y]] :=
   Module[{a = If[RuleQ[y], {y}, y], b = ToStringRational[x], c},
    c = Map[Rule[#[[1]], #[[2]]] &, Map[Map[ToStringRational,
       {#[[1]], #[[2]]}] &, a]]; ToExpression[StringReplace[b, c]]]
In[14]:= SubsExpr[a*b/x^3 + 1/x^(3/(b[t] + 2)) +
  1/f[a + 1/x^3]^2 + 1/(x^2 + m) - 1/x^3, {x^2 -> av, x^3 -> gs}]
Out[14]= -(1/gs) + (a*b)/gs + 1/(av + m) + x^(-(3/(2 + b[t]))) +
                                                      1/f[a + 1/gs]^2
```

Unlike the ***ToString1*** tool the ***ToStringRational*** procedure provides convenient representation of rational expressions in the string format, that allows to process the expressions more effectively by means of strings processing tools. The procedures ***ToStringRational*** and ***SubsExpr,*** generalizing tools of the same orientation, meanwhile, don`t belittle them illustrating different useful enough methods of programming with their advantages and shortcomings.

At last, the following two procedures ***Differentiation*** and ***Integrate3*** provide the differentiation and integrating on the variables as which can be subexpressions different from simple symbols. The call ***Differentiation*[*x, y, z, t, ...*]** returns result of differentiation of an expression ***x*** on subexpressions which can be difer from simple symbols defined by the *{y, z, t, ...}* tuple of arguments starting from the second. Whereas the procedure call ***Integrate3*[*x, y, z, t, ...*]** returns the result of integraiting of an expression ***x*** on subexpressions that can be difer from simple symbols defined by the *{y, z, t, ...}* tuple of arguments starting from the second. It should be noted that the ***Differentiation*** and ***Integrate3*** procedures return the result processed by means of built-in ***Simplify*** function that performs a sequence of algebraic and other transformations returning the simplest form it finds. The fragment below represents source codes of the above two procedures with typical examples of their application.

```
In[7]:= Differentiation[x_, y__] := Module[{a = {y}, b = x, c},
          c = Map[Unique["g"] &, Range[1, Length[a]]];
        Do[b = SubsExpr[b, a[[j]] -> c[[j]]], {j, 1, Length[a]}];
    b = D[b, Sequences[c]]; Simplify[SubsExpr[b, Map[c[[#]] ->
                          a[[#]] &, Range[1, Length[a]]]]]]
In[8]:= Differentiation[1/(1 + 1/x^2 + 1/x^3) + 1/(1 + 1/(a + b +
               1/x^3)^2) + 1/(1 + 1/x^3), 1/x^3, x^2]
Out[8]= -((2*x^5)/(1 + x + x^3)^3)
In[15]:= Integrate3[x_, y__] := Module[{a = {y}, b = x, c},
          c = Map[Unique["g"] &, Range[1, Length[a]]];
        Do[b = SubsExpr[b, a[[j]] -> c[[j]]], {j, 1, Length[a]}];
                          b = Integrate[b, Sequences[c]];
Simplify[SubsExpr[b, Map[c[[#]] -> a[[#]] &, Range[1, Length[a]]]]]]
In[16]:= Integrate3[1/x^2 + 1/(x^2 + x^3), x^2, x^3]
Out[16]= x^2*(-1 + x*Log[x^2] + (1 + x)*Log[x^2*(1 + x)])
```

The procedures ***Diff*** and ***Integral1*** have certain limitations that at use demand corresponding wariness; some idea of such restrictions is illustrated by the following very simple example:

```
In[2221]:= Diff[(a + b*m)/(c + d*n), a + b, c + d]
Out[2221]= -(m/((c + d)^2*n))
In[2222]:= Integral1[(a + b*m)/(c + d*n), a + b, c + d]
Out[2222]= ((a + b)^2 m*Log[c + d])/(2*n)
```

For the purpose of an exception of these shortcomings two modifications of the built-in ***Replace*** and ***ReplaceAll*** functions in the form of the procedures ***Replace4*** and ***ReplaceAll2*** have been programmed accordingly. These procedures expand the standard means and allow to code the previous two procedures ***Integral1*** and ***Diff*** with wider range of correct applications in the context of use of the generalized variables of differentiation and integrating. The call ***Replace4[x, a -> b]*** returns the result of application to an expression ***x*** of a substitution ***a -> b***, when as its left part an arbitrary expression is allowed. At absence in the ***x*** expression of occurrences of the subexpression ***a*** an initial ***x*** expression is returned. Unlike previous the call ***ReplaceAll2[x,r]*** returns the result of application to an expression x of a rule ***r*** or consecutive application of rules from the ***r*** list; as the left parts of rules any expressions are allowed.

Fragment below presents source codes of both procedures with typical examples of their application.

```
In[2358]:= Replace4[x_, r_ /; RuleQ[r]] := Module[{a, b, c, h},
                    {a, b} = {ToString[x // InputForm],
                    Map[ToString, Map[InputForm, r]]};
                    c = StringPosition[a, Part[b, 1]];
          If[c == {}, x, If[Head[Part[r, 1]] === Plus,
     h = Map[If[(#[[1]] === 1 || MemberQ[{" ", "(", "[", "{"},
       StringTake[a, {#[[1]] - 1, #[[1]] - 1}]]) && (#[[2]] ===
         StringLength[a] || MemberQ[{" ", ")", "]", "}", ","},
            StringTake[a, {#[[2]] + 1, #[[2]] + 1}]]), #] &, c],
            h = Map[If[(#[[1]] === 1 || ! Quiet[SymbolQ[
       StringTake[a, {#[[1]] - 1, #[[1]] - 1}]]]) && (#[[2]] ===
                    StringLength[a] || ! Quiet[SymbolQ[
            StringTake[a, {#[[2]] + 1, #[[2]] + 1}]]]), #] &, c]];
                    h = Select[h, ! SameQ[#, Null] &];
   ToExpression[StringReplacePart[a, "(" <> Part[b, 2] <> ")", h]]]]
In[2359]:= Replace4[(c + d*x)/(c + d + x), c + d -> a + b]
Out[2359]= (c + d*x)/(a + b + x)
In[2360]:= Replace4[Sqrt[a + b*x^2*d + c], x^2 -> a + b]
Out[2360]= Sqrt[a + c + b*(a + b)*d]
In[2364]:= ReplaceAll2[x_, r_ /; RuleQ[r] || ListRulesQ[r]] :=
            Module[{a = x, k = 1}, If[RuleQ[r], Replace4[x, r],
         While[k <= Length[r], a = Replace4[a, r[[k]]]; k++]; a]]
In[2365]:= ReplaceAll2[Sin[a + b*x^2*d + c*x^2], x^2 -> a + b]
Out[2365]= Sin[a + (a + b)*c + b*(a + b)*d]
```

On the basis of the ***Replace4*** procedure the procedures ***Diff*** and ***Integral1*** can be expanded in the form of procedures ***Difff*** and ***Integral2***. The procedure call ***Difff**[x,y,z,t,...]* returns result of *differentiation* of an expression ***x*** on the generalized variables *{y, z, t,...}* which are any expressions. The result is returned in the simplified form on a basis of the built-in ***Simplify*** function. While the procedure call ***Integral2**[x, y, z, ...]* returns the result of integrating of an expression ***x*** on the generalized variables *{y, z, t, ...}* that are arbitrary expressions. The result is returned in the simplified form on the basis of the ***Simplify*** function. The fragment below represents the source codes of the above means with typical examples of their application.

```
In[53]:= Difff[x_, y__] := Module[{a = x, a1, a2, a3, c = {}, d, k = 1,
                                n = g, b = Length[{y}]}, Clear[g];
               While[k <= b, d = {y}[[k]]; AppendTo[c, Unique[g]];
                     a1 = Replace4[a, d -> c[[k]]]; a2 = D[a1, c[[k]]];
   a3 = Replace4[a2, c[[k]] -> d]; a = a3; k++]; g = n; Simplify[a3]]
In[54]:= Difff[(a + b)/(c + d + x), a + b, c + d]
Out[54]= -(1/(c + d + x)^2)
In[65]:= Integral2[x_, y__] := Module[{a = x, a1, a2, a3, c = {}, d,
                              k = 1, n = g, b = Length[{y}]},  Clear[g];
               While[k <= b, d = {y}[[k]]; AppendTo[c, Unique[g]];
             a1 = Replace4[a, d -> c[[k]]]; a2 = Integrate[a1, c[[k]]];
   a3 = Replace4[a2, c[[k]] -> d]; a = a3; k++]; g = n; Simplify[a3]]
In[66]:= Integral2[(a + c + h*g + b*d)/(c + h), c + h, b*d]
Out[66]= 1/2*b*d*(2*a + 2*c + b*d + 2*g*h)*Log[c + h]
```

Along with the above tools of so-called ***Replace***-group, the ***Replace5*** function *(basing on the built-in **InputString** function)* can be mentioned, providing wide possibilities on replacement of subexpressions in expressions in interactive mode. At last, the ***Replace6*** procedure is intended for replacement of elements of a list that are located on the set nesting levels and meet certain conditions [8,16]. The above means are useful in many cases of processing of algebraic expressions that are based on a set of rules, including symbolic differentiation and integrating on the generalized variables that are arbitrary algebraic expressions.

Expressions in strings. The tools that highlight expressions from strings are of unquestionable interest. Meanwhile, in this direction, ***Mathematica*** has quite limited facilities and we have programmed a number of facilities of this type [8-16]. Above all, the procedure call ***ExprsInStrQ[w, y]*** returns *True*, if a string ***w*** contains *correct* expressions, and *False* otherwise; while through the second optional ***y*** argument – *an indefinite variable* – a list of expressions which are in ***x*** is returned. The fragment represents source code of the ***ExprsInStrQ*** procedure along with a typical example of its application.

```
In[77]:= ExprsInStrQ[x_ /; StringQ[x], y___] := Module[{a = {}, d,
                              c = 1, d, j, b = StringLength[x], k = 1},
                    For[k = c, k <= b, k++, For[j = k, j <= b, j++,
                                          d = StringTake[x, {k, j}];
          If[! SymbolQ[d] && SyntaxQ[d], AppendTo[a, d]]]; c++];
                     a = Select[Map[StringTrim, Map[StringTrim2[#,
                        {"-", "+", " "}, 3] &, a]], ExpressionQ[#] &];
              If[a == {}, False, If[{y} != {} && ! HowAct[{y}[[1]]],
                                    y = DeleteDuplicates[a]]; True]]
In[78]:= {ExprsInStrQ["a (c + d) - b^2 = Sin[x] h*/+", t], t}
Out[78]= {True, {"a*(c + d)", "a*(c + d) - b", "a*(c + d) - b^2",
     "(c + d)", "(c + d) - b", "(c + d) - b^2", "c + d", "d", "b", "b^2",
       "2", "Sin[x]", "Sin[x]*h", "in[x]", "in[x]*h", "n[x]", "n[x]*h"}}
```

In a number of problems of manipulation with expressions, including differentiation and integrating on the generalized variables, the question of definition of structure of expression through subexpressions entering in it including any variables is topical enough. The given problem is solved by the ***ExprComp*** procedure, whose the call ***ExprComp*[*x*]** returns the list of all subexpressions composing *x* expression, while the procedure call ***ExprComp*[*x, z*]**, where the second optional *z* argument – *an indefined variable* – through *z* additionally returns the nested list of subexpressions of an arbitrary expression *x* on nesting levels, since the first level. Fragment below represents source code of the ***ExprComp*** procedure and an example of its application.

```
In[7]:= ExprComp[x_, z___] := Module[{a = {x}, b, h = {}, F, q, t=1},
                      F[y_ /; ListQ[y]] := Module[{c = {}, d, p, k, j = 1},
                                For[j = 1, j <= Length[y], j++, k = 1;
                                        While[k < Infinity, p = y[[j]];
                                a = Quiet[Check[Part[p, k], $Failed]];
     If[a === $Failed, Break[], If[! SameQ[a, {}], AppendTo[c, a]]];
                                                  k++]]; c]; q = F[a];
    While[q != {}, AppendTo[h, q]; q = Flatten[Map[F[{#}] &, q]]];
                                         If[{z} != {} && ! HowAct[z],
                              z = Map[Select[#, ! NumberQ[#] &] &, h]];
                           Sort[Select[DeleteDuplicates[Flatten[h],
                        Abs[#1] === Abs[#2] &], ! NumberQ[#] &]]]
```

```
In[8]:= ExprComp[(1/b Cos[a+Sqrt[c+d]])/(Tan[1/b] - 1/c^2), g]
Out[8]= {a, 1/b, b, -(1/c^2), c, d, Sqrt[c + d], c + d, a + Sqrt[c + d],
        Cos[a + Sqrt[c + d]], 1/b + Cos[a + Sqrt[c + d]], Tan[1/b],
                     1/(-(1/c^2) + Tan[1/b]), -(1/c^2) + Tan[1/b]}
In[9]:= g
Out[9]= {{1/b + Cos[a + Sqrt[c + d]], 1/(-(1/c^2) + Tan[1/b])},
{1/b, Cos[a + Sqrt[c + d]], -(1/c^2) + Tan[1/b]}, {b, a + Sqrt[c + d],
-(1/c^2), Tan[1/b]}, {a, Sqrt[c + d], 1/c^2, 1/b}, {c + d, c, b}, {c, d}}
```

The procedure below is of a certain interest and completes this chapter. The procedure call ***FuncToExpr[f, x]*** returns the result of applying of a symbol, block, function *(including pure functions)* or module *f* *(except the f symbol all remaining admissible objects shall have arity* **1***)* to each variable *(excluding the standard symbols)* of an expression ***x***. While the call ***FuncToExpr[f, x, y]*** with the *3rd* optional ***y*** argument – *a list of symbols* – returns the result of applying of a symbol, block, function *(including a pure function)* or a module *f* *(excepting f symbol all remaining admissible objects shall have arity* **1***)* to each variable *(excluding the standard symbols and symbols from* ***y*** *list)* of an expression ***x***. The following fragment represents source code of the ***FuncToExpr*** procedure along with typical examples of its application.

```
In[7]:= FuncToExpr[f_/; SymbolQ[f] || BlockFuncModQ[f] ||
  PureFuncQ[f], x_, y___List] := Module[{a = ToString1[x], b, c},
                                             b = ExtrVarsOfStr[a, 2];
    b = Select[b, If[{y} == {}, ! SystemQ[#] &, (! SystemQ[#] &&
                              ! MemberQ[Map[ToString, y], #]) &]];
          c = Map[# -> ToString[(f)] <> "@@{" <> # <> "}" &, b];
                       ReplaceAll[x, Map[ToExpressionRule, c]]]
In[8]:= FuncToExpr[f, Sin[m + n]/(x*G[x, y] + S[y, t])]
Out[8]= Sin[f[m] + f[n]]/(f[x] f[G][f[x], f[y]] + f[S][f[y], f[t]])
In[9]:= FuncToExpr[G, {a, b, c, d, 77*Sin[y + 72]}]
Out[9]= {G[a], G[b], G[c], G[d], 77*Sin[72 + G[y]]}
In[10]:= FuncToExpr[f, Sin[m + n]/(x*G[x, y] + S[y, t]), {G, S}]
Out[10]= Sin[f[m] + f[n]]/(f[x]*G[f[x], f[y]] + S[f[y], f[t]])
```

The means presented in the chapter along with other means from our package [8,16], extend, sometimes even substantially, the built-in ***Mathematica*** means.

Chapter 4: Software for input–output in Mathematica

The ***Mathematica*** language being the built-in programming language that first of all is oriented onto symbolic calculations and processing has rather limited facilities for data processing that first of all are located in external memory of the computer. In this regard the language significantly concedes to traditional programming languages. At the same time, being oriented, first of all, to solution of tasks in symbolic view, the ***Mathematica*** language provides a set of tools for access to files that can quite satisfy a wide range of the users of mathematical applications of the ***Mathematica.*** In this chapter the tools of access to files are considered on rather superficial level owing to the limited volume, extensiveness of this theme and purpose of the present book. The reader, interested in tools of access to datafiles of the ***Mathematica*** can appeal to documentation delivered with the system. At that, for the purpose of development of methods of *access* to file system of the computer we programmed a number of effective tools that are represented in the ***MathToolBox*** [16]. Whereas in the present chapter the attention is oriented on the means which expands standard tools of the ***Mathematica*** for ensuring of work with files of the computer. Some of them are useful to practical application in ***Mathematica.*** Here it is also appropriate to note that a number of tools of our ***MathToolBox*** package [16] subsequently served as analogues in subsequent versions of ***Mathematica;*** it applies *primarily* to file access tools.

4.1. Tools of the Mathematica for work with internal files

Means of ***Math***–language provide access of the user to files of several types that can be conditionally divided into two large groups, namely: internal and external files. During the routine work the system deals with three various types of internal files from which we will note the files having extensions {*"nb", "m", "mx"*}, their structure is distinguished by the standard system tools and that are important enough already on the first stages of work with system. Before further consideration we will note that the concept of *file qualifier* (***FQ***) defining the full path to the required file in file system of the computer or to its *subdirectory*, practically, completely coincides with similar concept for ***Maple*** system excepting that if in the ***Maple*** for ***FQ*** the format of type {*symbol, string*} is allowed whereas in the ***Mathematica*** for ***FQ*** the string format is admissible only.

The function call ***Directory***[] returns an active directory of the current session whereas the call ***SetDirectory***[*x*] returns a ***x*** directory, doing it active in the current session; in addition, as an active *(current)* directory is understood the directory whose datafiles are processed by means of tools of access if only their names, but not full paths to them are specified. Meanwhile, the ***SetDirectory*** function allows only real–life subdirectories as an argument, causing on nonexistent subdirectories an erroneous situation with returning $*Failed*. On the other hand, the ***SetDir2*** procedure allows to sets the current working directory; at that, as an argument can be also nonexistent subdirectories even on inactive *I/O* devices as the current subdirectories. The fragment represents source code of the procedure ***SetDir2*** and its use.

```
In[25]:= SetDir2[x_ /; StringQ[x]] := Module[{a, b, c, t, y},
                                 a = Map[# <> ":" &, Adrive[]];
              b = Map[ToUpperCase, StringCases[x, t_ ~~ ":"]];
  If[FreeQ[a, b], y = StringReplace[x, b -> a[[1]], 1], y = x];
  If[Set[c, Quiet[CreateDirectory[y]]] === $Failed, y,
                                              SetDirectory[c]]]
In[26]:= SetDirectory["F:\\Temp\\Grodno\\77"]
      ... SetDirectory: Cannot set current directory to
          F:\\Temp\\Grodno\\77.
Out[26]= $Failed
In[27]:= SetDir2["F:\\Temp\\Grodno\\77"]
Out[27]= "C:\\Temp\\Grodno\\77"
In[28]:= Adrive[] := Module[{a, b, c, d}, {b, a} = {{},
    CharacterRange["A", "Z"]}; Do[d = Directory[]; c = a[[k]];
AppendTo[b, If[Quiet[SetDirectory[c <> ":\\"]] === $Failed,
     Nothing, SetDirectory[d]; c]], {k, 1, Length[a]}]; Sort[b]]
```

In[29]:= **Adrive[]**
Out[29]= {"C", "D", "E", "F", "G"}

The ***SetDir2*** procedure essentially uses a procedure whose call ***Adrive***[] returns the list of the current active *I/O* devices of the computer. ***MathToolBox*** package [16] provides a number of means along with their certain modifications *(**SetDir, SetDir1, Adrive1, CopyDir, CopyFileToDir, etc.**)* that use different useful programming techniques in ***Mathematica*** and extending the built-in file access tools useful from a practical standpoint. At the same time, it should be borne in mind that for the reason that the ***MathToolBox*** package was developed *(truth, with rather considerable intervals)* from ***2013*** to ***May 2020,*** different versions of the ***Mathematica*** system were used, so in number of cases is necessary to *re-debugging* some package tools under the current version of the system. As a rule, this is not particularly difficult.

We programmed a number of rather interesting procedures for ensuring work with files of the ***Mathematica Input***-format whose names have extensions {***".nb", ".m", ".txt"***}, etc. All such tools are based on analysis of structure of the contents of files returned by access functions, in particular, ***ReadFullFile.*** Some of them give a possibility to create rather effective user libraries containing definitions of the ***Mathematica*** objects. These and certain other tools have been implemented as a part of a special package supporting the releases ***8 ÷ 12.1*** of ***Mathematica*** [16].

Some remarks should be made concerning the system ***Save*** function which saves the objects in a file in the *Append* mode; in addition, indefinite symbols in this file are not saved without of any messages, i.e. the ***Save*** call returns *Null*, i.e. nothing. At the same time, at saving of procedure or function with a name ***Avz*** in a file by means of the ***Save*** in the file all active objects of the same ***Avz*** name in the current session with different headings – *the identifiers of their originality* – are saved too. For elimination of this situation a generalization of the ***Save*** function concerning the saving of ***Mathematica*** objects with concrete headings is offered. The ***Save1*** procedure solves the problem whose source code with typical examples of its application are represented by means of the following fragment.

```
In[1326]:= Save1[x_String, y_/; DeleteDuplicates[Map[StringQ,
          Flatten[{y}]]][[1]]] := Module[{Rs, t = Flatten[{y}], k = 1},
            Rs[n_, m_] := Module[{b, c = ToString[Unique[b]],
  a = If[SymbolQ[m], Save[n, m], If[StringFreeQ[m, "["], $Failed,
     StringTake[m, {1, Flatten[StringPosition[m, "["]][[1]] - 1}]]]},
      If[a === Null, Return[], If[a === $Failed, Return[$Failed],
      If[SymbolQ[a], b = DefFunc3[a], Return[$Failed]]]];
  If[Length[b] == 1, Save[n, a], b = Select[b, SuffPref[#, m, 1] &]];
  If[b != {}, b = c <> b[[1]], Return[$Failed]]; ToExpression[b];
       a = c <> a; ToExpression["Save[" <> ToString1[n] <> "," <>
           ToString1[a] <> "]"]; BinaryWrite[n, StringReplace[
           ToString[StringJoin[Map[FromCharacterCode,
                       BinaryReadList[n]]]], c -> ""]]; Close[n];];
          For[k, k <= Length[t], k++, Rs[x, t[[k]]]]]
In[1327]:= A[x_] := x^2; A[x_, y_] := x+y; A[x_, y_, z_] := x+y+z;
          A[x__] := {x}; DefFunc3[A]
Out[1327]= {"A[x_] := x^2", "A[x_, y_] := x + y",
              "A[x_, y_, z_] := x + y + z", "A[x__] := {x}"}
In[1328]:= Save1["rans.m", {"A[x_, y_, z_]", "A[x__]"}]
In[1329]:= Clear[A]; << "rans.m"
In[1330]:= DefFunc3[A]
Out[1330]= {"A[x_, y_, z_] := x + y + z", "A[x__] := {x}"}
```

The call ***Save1[x, y]*** saves in a file ***x*** the definitions of the objects defined by the second factual ***y*** argument – *the name of an active object in the current session or its heading in string format, or their combinations in the list format.* The ***Save1*** procedure can be used as built-in ***Save*** function, and solving a saving problem of the chosen objects activated in the current session in the file differentially on the basis of their headings. A successful call returns *Null*, doing the demanded savings; otherwise, *$Failed* or unevaluated call are returned. The previous fragment presents the result of application of the ***Save1*** procedure for a selective saving of the objects activated in the current session in file. In a number of cases the procedure ***Save1*** has undoubted interest.

The function call ***Save2[x, y]***, where ***Save2*** – a modification of the ***Save*** function, appends to a file ***x*** the definitions of the means set by a name or by their list *y* in the format convenient for subsequent processing by a number of means, particularly, by the ***CallSave*** procedure. Thus, the function is a rather useful extension of the built-in ***Save*** function [7,11-16].

In a number of cases there is an urgent need of saving in a file of state of the current session with subsequent restoration by means of loading of the file to the current session different from the previous session. In this context, ***SaveCurrentSession*** and ***RestoreCS*** procedures are useful for saving and restoration of state of the current session respectively. Thus, the procedure call ***SaveCurrentSession*[]** saves the state of the ***Mathematica*** current session in the ***m***–file **"*SaveCS.m*"** with returning of the name of the target file. Whereas the call ***SaveCurrentSession*[*x*]** saves the state of the ***Mathematica*** current session in a ***m***–file ***x*** with returning of the name of the target ***x*** file; in addition, if a ***x*** file has not **"*m*"** extension then the extension is added to the ***x*** string. The call ***RestoreCS*[]** restores the ***Mathematica*** current session that has been previously stored by means of procedure ***SaveCurrentSession*** in **"*SaveCS.m*"** file with returning *Null*, i.e. nothing. While the **call *RestoreCS*[*x*]** restores the ***Mathematica*** current session that has been previously stored by means of the procedure ***SaveCurrentSession*** in a ***m***-file ***x*** with returning *Null*. In absence of the above ***m***-file the procedure call returns **$***Failed*. The fragment represents source codes of the above procedures along with typical examples of their application.

```
In[47]:= SaveCurrentSession[x___String] :=
      Module[{a = Names["*"], b = If[{x} == {}, "SaveCS.m",
        If[SuffPref[x, ".m", 2], x, x <> ".m"]]}, Save1[b, a]; b]
In[48]:= RestoreCS[x___String] := Module[{a = If[{x} == {},
"SaveCS.m", If[FileExistsQ[x] && FileExtension[x] == "m",
        x, $Failed]]}, If[a === $Failed, $Failed, On[General];
                              Quiet[Get[a]]; Off[General]]]
In[49]:= SaveCurrentSession["C:\\temp\\SaveCS.m"]
Out[49]= "C:\\Temp\\SaveCS.m"
In[50]:= RestoreCS["C:\\Temp\\SaveCS.m"]
```

So, the represented means are rather useful in a case when is required to create copies of the current ***Mathematica*** sessions at certain moments of operating with the system.

4.2. Tools of the Mathematica for work with external files

According to such a quite important indicator as means of access to files, the ***Mathematica,*** in our opinion, possesses a number of advantages in comparison with ***Maple.*** First of all, ***Mathematica*** does automatic processing of hundreds of data formats and their subformats on the basis of the unified use of *symbolic* expressions. For each specific format the *correspondence* between *internal* and *external* presentation of a format is defined using the general mechanism of data elements of ***Mathematica.*** For today ***Mathematica*** supports many various formats of files for various purposes, their list can be received by means of the variables **$*ImportFormats*** *(the imported files)* and **$*ExportFormats*** *(the exported files)* in quantities *226* and *188* respectively *(version* ***Mathematica 12.1****),* while the basic formats of files for versions ***8–12.1*** are considered rather in details in [1-15].

By the function call ***FileFormat*[*x*]** an attempt to define an input format for a file given by a name ***x*** in the string format is made. In a case of existence for the file ***x*** of name extension the ***FileFormat*** function is, as a whole, similar to the ***FileExtension*** function, returning the available extension, except for a case of packages ***(m–****datafiles)* when instead of extension the file type **"*Package*"** is returned. In addition, in certain cases the format identification is done incorrectly, in particular, the attempt to test a ***doc–***file without an extension returns **"*XLS*",** ascribing it to the files created by means of *Excel 95/97/2000/XP/2003* that is generally incorrect. The ***FileFormat*** function also incorrectly tests *I/O* device base directories, for example:

In[3331]:= **Map[FileFormat, {"C:/", "C:\\"}]**

... **General:** Further output of General::cdir will be suppressed during this calculation.

... **General:** Cannot get deeper in directory tree: C:\\Documents and Settings.

... General: Cannot get deeper in directory tree: C:\\ProgramData\\Application Data.
... General: Cannot get deeper in directory tree: C:\\ProgramData\\Desktop.
... General: Further output of General::dirdep will be suppressed during this calculation.
Out[3331]= {"KML", "KML"}
In[3332]:= **FileFormat["C:/Temp\\Burthday"]**
Out[3332]= "XLS"

In this regard, the procedures ***FileFormat1*** ÷ ***FileFormat3*** have been programmed that extend the capabilities of the built-in ***FileFormat*** function and eliminate the above disadvantages. A version of the ***FileFormat*** function attempts to identify file type without its extension, being based on information of the creator of file that is contained in the contents of the file. The ***FileFormat3*** procedure rather accurately identifies datafiles of the following often used types {***DOC, DOCX, PDF, ODT, TXT, HTML***}. In addition, concerning the ***TXT*** type the verification of a datafile is made in the latter case, believing that the datafile of this type has to consist only of symbols with the decimal codes:

0 ÷ 127 – *ASCII symbols*
1 ÷ 31 – *the control ASCII symbols*
32 ÷ 126 – *the printed ASCII symbols*
97 ÷ 122 – *letters of the Latin alphabet in the lower register*
129 ÷ 255 – *Latin–1 symbols of ISO*
192 ÷ 255 – *letters of the European languages*

The procedure call ***FileFormat3*[*x*]** returns the type of a file given by a name or a classifier ***x;*** in addition, if the datafile has an extension, it relies as the extension of the datafile. Whereas the call ***FileFormat3*[*x, y*]** with the second optional argument – an arbitrary ***y*** expression – in a case of file without extension returns its full name with extension defined for it, at the same time renaming the ***x*** datafile, taking into account the calculated format. The following fragment represents source code of the ***FileFormat3*** procedure and the most typical examples of its use.

In[3332]:= **FileFormat3[x_/; FileExistsQ[x], t___] := Module[{b, c, a = FileExtension[x]}, If[a != "", ToUpperCase[a],**

```
c = If[Quiet[StringTake[Read[x, String], {1, 5}]] === "%PDF-",
        {Close[x], "PDF"}[[-1]], Close[x]; b = ReadFullFile[x];
c = If[! StringFreeQ[b, {"MSWordDoc", "Microsoft Office Word"}], "DOC",
   If[! StringFreeQ[b, "docProps"], "DOCX"],
   If[! StringFreeQ[b, ".opendocument.textPK"], "ODT",
   If[! StringFreeQ[b, {"!DOCTYPE HTML", "text/html"}], "HTML",
   If[MemberQ3[Range[0, 255], DeleteDuplicates[Flatten[
     Map[ToCharacterCode[#] &, DeleteDuplicates[Characters[b]]]]]],
                                        "TXT", Undefined]]]]];
      If[{t} != {}, Quiet[Close[x]]; RenameFile[x, x <> "." <> c], c]]]

In[3333]:= Map[FileFormat2, {"C:/", "C:\\", "E:\\", "E:/",
                                        "C:/Temp", "C:\\Temp"}]
Out[3333]= {"Directory", "Directory", "Directory",
                        "Directory", "Directory", "Directory"}
In[3334]:= FileFormat3["C:/Temp/Kiri"]
Out[3334]= "DOCX"
In[3335]:= FileFormat3["C:/Temp/Kiri", Agn]
Out[3335]= "C:\\Temp\\Kiri.DOCX"
In[3336]:= Map[FileFormat3, {"C:\\Temp.Burthday",
                  "c:\\Temp/cinema", "c:/Temp/ransian",
              "c:/Temp/Grodno", "c:/Temp/Math_Trials"}]
Out[3336]= {"DOC", "TXT", "HTML", "PDF", "DOCX"}
```

Now, using the algorithm implemented by ***FileFormat3*** it is rather simple to modify it for testing of other types of datafiles whose full names have no extension. That can be rather useful in the processing problems of datafiles. In a certain relation the ***FileFormat3*** procedure complements the built-in ***FileFormat*** function along with procedures ***FileFormat1*** and ***FileFormat2.***

The ***Mathematica*** provides effective system-independent access to all aspects of datafiles of any size. At that, the opening and closing of files the following built-in functions of access are used: ***Close, OpenRead, OpenWrite, OpenAppend.*** Moreover, a name or full path to a file in the string format acts as a formal argument of the first three functions; at that, the function call ***OpenWrite*[]** without factual arguments is allowed, opening a new file located in a subdirectory intended for temporary files for writing. Whereas the ***Close*** function closes a file given by its name, full path or a *Stream*–object. In attempt to close a closed or nonexistent file the system causes an erroneous situation. For elimination of such situation, undesirable in many cases, it is possible to use the simple ***Closes*** function doing the closing of any file including a closed or nonexistent file without output of any erroneous messages with returning *Null,* i.e. nothing, but, perhaps, the name or full path to the closed file:

```
In[2331]:= Close["C:/Temp/Math/test77.txt"]
        ... General: C:/Temp/Math/test77.txt is not open.
Out[2331]= Close["C:/Temp/Math/test77.txt"]
In[2332]:= Closes[x_] := Quiet[Check[Close[x], Null]]
In[2333]:= Closes["C:/Temp/Math/test77.txt"]
```

An object of the following format is understood as a *Stream* object of the functions of access such as ***OpenRead, OpenWrite, OpenAppend, Read, BinaryWrite, Write, WriteString,*** etc:

{***OutputStream* | *InputStream***}**[*<File>*, *<Logical IO channel>*]**

The function call ***Streams*[]** returns the list of *Stream* objects of files opened in the current session including system files. For obtaining the list of all *Stream* objects of files different from the system files it is possible to use the function call ***StreamsU*[]:**

```
In[2214]:= StreamsU[] := Streams[][[3 ;; –1]]
In[2215]:= StreamsU[]
Out[2215]= {OutputStream["C:/temp/galina.txt", 3]}
In[2216]:= CloseAll[] := Map[Close, StreamsU[]]
In[2217]:= CloseAll[]; StreamsU[]
Out[2217]= {}
```

It must be kept in mind that after the termination of work with an opened file, it remains opened up to its explicit closing by means of the ***Close*** function. For closing of all channels and files opened in the current session, excepting system files, it is possible to apply a quite simple ***CloseAll*** function, whose call ***CloseAll*[]** closes all open both files and channels with return of the list of the closed files.

Similar to the ***Maple*** the ***Mathematica*** also has opportunity to open the same file on different *streams* and in various *modes,* using different coding of its name or path by using alternative registers for letters or/and replacement of "\\" separators of the subdirectories on "/", and vice versa at opening of files. The fragment below illustrates application of a similar approach for opening of the same file on two different channels on reading with the subsequent alternating reading of records from it.

```
In[2222]:= g = "C:\\temp\\cinema_2019.txt"; {S, S1} =
{OpenRead[g], OpenRead[If[UpperCaseQ[StringTake[g, 1]],
ToLowerCase[g], ToUpperCase[g]]]}
Out[2222]= {InputStream["C:/temp/cinema_2019.doc", 3],
            InputStream["c:\\temp\\cinema_2019.txt", 4]}
In[2223]:= t = {}; For[k = 1, k <= 3, k++,
                       AppendTo[t, {Read[S], Read[S1]}]]
Out[2223]= {"ran1", "ran1", "ran2", "ran2", "ran3", "ran3"}
```

Meantime it must be kept in mind that the special attention at opening of the same file on different channels is necessary and, above all, at various modes of access to the file in order to avoid of the possible especial situations, including distortion of data in a file. Whereas in certain cases this approach at operating with large enough files can give a quite notable temporal effect with simplification of certain algorithms of data processing that are in files. The interesting enough examples of application of such approach can be found in our books [1-15].

The ***Mathematica*** has useful tools for operating with the ***pointer*** defining the current position of scanning of a file. The following functions provide such work: ***StreamPosition, Skip, SetStreamPosition*** and ***Find.*** So, functions ***StreamPosition*** and ***SetStreamPosition*** allow to monitor of the current position of the pointer of an open file and to establish for it a new position respectively. Moreover, on the closed or nonexistent datafiles the calls of these functions cause erroneous situations.

Reaction of the ***Skip*** function to the status of a file is similar, whereas the function call ***Find*** opens a stream to reading from a file. The sense of the presented functions is a rather transparent and in more detail it is possible to familiarize oneself with them, for instance, in books [12-14]. In connection with these tools the question of definition of the status of a file – opened, closed or doesn't exist – arises. In this regard ***FileOpenQ*** procedure can be as a rather useful tool [16], whose call ***FileOpenQ[F]*** returns the nested list {{***R, F, Channel***},...} if a ***F*** file is open on reading/ writing (***R*** = {*"read"* | *"write"*}), ***F*** defines actually the ***F*** file in the stylized format *(LowerCase + all "\\" are replaced on "/")* whereas *Channel* defines the logical channel on which the ***F*** file in the mode specified by the first element of the ***R*** list was open; if ***F*** file is closed, the empty list is returned, i.e. {}, if ***F*** file is absent, then $*Failed* is returned. At that, the nested list is used with the purpose, that the ***F*** file can be opened according to syntactically various file specifiers, for example, *"Agn47"* and *"AGN47"*, that allows to do its processing in the various modes simultaneously.

The ***FileOpenQ1*** is a useful extension of ***FileOpenQ*** that was considered above. The call ***FileOpenQ1[f]*** returns the nested list of the format {{***R, x, y,...,z***}, {{***R, x1, y1,...,z1***}} if a ***f*** file is open for reading or writing *(**R** = {"in" | "out"})*, and ***f*** determines the file in any format *(Register + "/" and/or "\\")*; if the ***f*** file is closed or is absent, the empty list is returned, i.e. {}. Moreover, sublists {***x, y,...,z***} and {***x1, y1,...,z1***} define files or full paths to them that are open for reading and writing respectively. Moreover, if in the current session all user files are closed, except system files, the call ***FileOPenQ1[x]*** on an arbitrary ***x*** string returns $*Failed*. The files and paths to them are returned in formats which are determined in the list returned by the function call ***Streams[]***, irrespective of format of ***f*** file.

At last, the procedure call ***FileOpenQ2[x]*** returns *True* if a ***x*** file is open, and *False* otherwise *(file is closed or absent)*. Whereas the call ***FileOpenQ2[x, y]*** also returns *True* or *False* depending on the openness of the file ***x***, returning thru the second optional argument – a symbol ***y*** – the list in the string format of the file mode of ***x*** {*"in"*, *"out"*} where ***x*** file is open for reading *("in")* or writing *("out")* accordingly. In addition, the ***x*** file can be opened in both modes at the same time. The fragment below represents source code of the ***FileOpenQ2*** procedure and the most typical examples of its application.

```
In[2186]:= FileOpenQ2[x_String, y___Symbol] :=
           Module[{a, b, c}, a = FileExistsQ[b = Stilized[x]];
  If[a, c = Map[Stilized, Map[ToString, Streams[][[3 ;; -1]]]];
       c = Select[c, ! StringFreeQ[#, b] &];
       c = Map[StringCases[#, ("o" | "i") ~~ __ ~~ "["] &, c];
       c = Flatten[Map[StringTrim[#, "["] &, c]];
       c = DeleteDuplicates[Map[StringReplace[#,
                          "putstream" -> ""] &, Flatten[c]]];
             If[{y} == {}, If[c != {}, True, False],
             If[c == {}, y = c; False, y = c; True]], False]]
In[2197]:= Write["c:\\temp/cinema_2019.doc", 424767];
                          Read["C:/temp/cinema_2019.doc"];
In[2198]:= FileOpenQ2["C:\\temp\\cinemA_2019.DOC"]
Out[2198]= True
In[2199]:= {FileOpenQ2["c:/temp/cinema_2019.doc", g], g}
Out[2199]= {True, {"in", "out"}}
In[2200]:= Stilized[x_String] :=
               ToLowerCase[StringReplace[x, "/" -> "\\"]]
In[2201]:= Stilized["outputstream[C:/Temp/aAa.txt, 3]"]
Out[2201]= "outputstream[c:\\temp\\aaa.txt, 3]"
```

The fragment also represents a simple ***Stilized*** function that styles an arbitrary character string by replacing all instances of letters to the lower case and "/" to "\\". The function is used by the ***FileOpenQ2*** procedure, making it easier to operate with files that use the same *ID* in different encoding.

Functions ***Skip, Find, StreamPosition, SetStreamPosition*** provide rather effective means for a rather thin manipulation with files and in combination with a number of other functions of access they provide the user with a standard set of functions for files processing, and give opportunity on their base to create own tools allowing how to solve specific problems of operating with files, and in a certain degree to extend standard means of the system. A number of similar means is presented and in our books [1-15], and in our ***MathToolBox*** package [16]. In addition to the presented standard operations of files processing, some other tools of the package rather significantly facilitates *effective* programming of higher level at the solution of many problems of files processing and management of ***Mathematica.*** Naturally, the consideration rather in details of earlier represented tools of access to files and the subsequent tools doesn't enter purposes of the present book therefore we will represent relatively them only short excursus in the form of brief information along with some comments on the represented means *(see also books on the **Mathematica** system in* [15]).

Among means of processing, the following functions can be noted**:** ***FileNames –*** depending on the coding format returns the list of full paths to the files and/or directories contained in the given directory onto arbitrary nesting depth in file system of the computer. Whereas the functions ***CopyFile, RenameFile, DeleteFile*** serve for copying, renaming and removal of the files accordingly. Except the listed means for work with datafiles the ***Mathematica*** has a number of rather useful functions that here aren't considered however with them the reader can familiarize in reference base of the ***Mathematica*** or in the corresponding literature [8]. Along with the above functions ***OpenRead, Read, OpenWrite, Read, Write, Skip*** and ***Streams*** of the lowest level of access to files, the functions ***Get, Put, Export, Import, ReadList, BinaryReadList, BinaryWrite, BinaryRead*** are too important in problems of access to files which support operations of reading and writing of data of the required formats. With these means along with a number of quite interesting examples and features of their use, at last with certain critical remarks to their address the reader can familiarize in [1-15]. Meanwhile, these means of access together with the considered means and tools remaining without our attention form a rather developed basis of effective processing of files of various formats.

On the other hand, along with actually processing of the internal contents of files, ***Mathematica*** has a number of means for search of files, their testing, work with their names, etc. We will list only some of them, namely**:** ***FindFile, FileNameDepth, FileExistsQ, FileBaseName, FileNameSplit, ExpandFileName,***

FileNameJoin, FileNameTake. With the these means along with a number of interesting enough examples and features of their use, at last with critical remarks to their address the reader can familiarize oneself in our books [1-15].

In particular, as it was noted earlier [1-15], the ***FileExistsQ*** function like certain other functions of access during the search is limited only to the directories defined in the predetermined **$*Path*** variable. For the purpose of elimination of the deficiency a rather simple ***FileExistsQ1*** procedure has been offered. The following fragment represents source code of the ***FileExistsQ1*** procedure along with a typical example of its application.

```
In[2226]:= FileExistsQ1[x__/; StringQ[{x}[[1]]]] :=
                          Module[{b = {x}, a = SearchFile[{x}[[1]]]},
      If[a == {}, False, If[Length[b] == 2 && ! HowAct[b[[2]]],
 ToExpression[ToString[b[[2]]] <> " = " <> ToString1[a]], 1]; True]]
In[2227]:= FileExistsQ1["Book_2020.doc", t42]
Out[2227]= True
In[2228]:= t42
Out[2228]= {"C:\\Mathematica\\Book_2020.doc",
                           "E:\\Mathematica\\Book_2020.doc"}
```

The procedure call ***FileExistsQ1[x]*** returns *True* if ***x*** defines a real datafile in system of directories of the computer and *False* otherwise; whereas the call ***FileExistsQ1[x, y]***, in addition thru the second actual argument – *an indefinite variable* – returns the list of full paths to the found datafile ***x*** if the basic result of the call is *True*. That procedure substantially uses the procedure ***SearchFile,*** whose call ***SearchFile[F]*** returns the list containing full paths to a datafile ***F*** found in file system of the computer; if the datafile ***F*** has not been found, the empty list is returned. We will note, the procedure ***SearchFile*** uses the ***Run*** function that is used by a number of tools of our ***MathToolBox*** package [16]. The following fragment presents source code of the ***SearchFile*** procedure along with a typical example of its application.

```
In[2322]:= SearchFile[F_/; StringQ[F]] :=
                          Module[{a, b, f, dir, h = Stilized[F], k},
{a, b, f} = {Map[ToUpperCase[#] <> ":\\" &, Adrive[]], {}, "###.txt"};
```

```
dir[y_/; StringQ[y]] := Module[{a, b, c, v},
Run["Dir " <> "/A/B/S " <> y <> " > " <> f];
c = {}; Label[b]; a = Stilized[ToString[v = Read[f, String]]];
If[a == "endoffile", Close[f]; DeleteFile[f]; Return[c],
If[SuffPref[a, h, 2], If[FileExistsQ[v], AppendTo[c, v]];
Goto[b], Goto[b]]]]];
For[k = 1, k <= Length[a], k++, AppendTo[b, dir[a[[k]]]]]; Flatten[b]]
```

```
In[2323]:= SearchFile["Book_2020.doc"]
Out[2323]= {"C:\\Mathematica\\Book_2020.doc",
"E:\\Mathematica\\Book_2020.doc"}
```

The ***SearchFile1*** procedure is a functional analogue of the above ***SearchFile*** procedure. Unlike the previous procedure the ***SearchFile1*** seeks out a file in *three* stages: *(1)* if the required file is set by a full path only existence of the concrete file is checked, at detection the full path to it is returned, *(2)* search is done in the list of directories determined by the predetermined ***$Path*** variable, *(3)* a search is done within file system of the computer. Note, that speed of both procedures essentially depends on the sizes of file system of the computer, first of all, if a required file isn't defined by the full path and isn't in the directories defined by the ***$Path*** variable. In addition, in this case the search is done if possible even in directory *"c:\\$recycle.bin"* of the *Windows* **7.**

Along with tools of processing of external files the system has also the set of useful enough means for manipulation with directories of the ***Mathematica,*** and file system of the computer in general. We will list only some of these important functions:

DirectoryQ[j] – *the call returns True if a **j** string determines an existing directory, and False otherwise; unfortunately, the standard function at coding "/" at the end of **j** string returns False irrespective of existence of the tested directory; a quite simple **DirQ** procedure* [8] *eliminates that defect of the standard function;*

DirectoryName[d] – *the call returns the path to a directory that contains a **d** file; if **d** is a real subdirectory then chain of subdirectories to it is returned; in addition, taking into account the file concept that identifies files and subdirectories, and the circumstance that the call **DirectoryName[d]** doesn't consider actual existence of **d**, the similar* *approach in a certain measure could be considered justified, however on condition of taking into account of reality of the tested **d** path such approach causes certain questions. Therefore, from this standpoint a rather simple **DirName** procedure [6] which returns "None" if **d** is a subdirectory, the path to a subdirectory containing **d** file, and $Failed otherwise is offered. At that, the search is done within full file system of the computer, but only not within system of subdirectories defined by means of the predetermined **$Path** variable;*

***CreateDirectory[d]** – the call creates the given **d** directory with return of the path to it; meanwhile, such means doesn't work in a case of designation of the nonexistent device of external memory (flash card, disk, etc.) therefore we created a rather simple **CDir** procedure [7] that resolves this problem: the procedure call **CDir[d]** creates the given **d** directory with return of the full path to it; in the absence or inactivity of the device of external memory the directory is created on a device from the list of all active devices of external memory that has maximal volume of available memory with returning of the full path to it;*

***CopyDirectory[j1, j2]** – the call completely copies a **j1** directory into a **j2** directory, but in the presence of the accepting **j2** directory the call **CopyDirectory[j1, j2]** causes an erroneous situation with return of $Failed that in a number of cases is undesirable. For the purpose of elimination of such situation a rather simple **CopyDir** procedure can be offered, which in general is similar to the standard **CopyDirectory** function, but with the difference that in the presence of the accepting **j2** directory the **j1** directory is copied as a subdirectory of the **j2** with returning of the full path to it;*

***DeleteDirectory[d]** – the function call deletes from file system of the computer the given **d** directory with returning Null, i.e. nothing, regardless of attributes of the directory (Archive, Read-only, Hidden, and System). Meanwhile, such approach, in our opinion, is not quite justified, relying only on the circumstance that the user is precisely sure what he does. While in general there has to be an insurance from removal, in particular, of files and directories having such attributes as read-only (**R**), hidden (**H**) and system (**S**). To this end, particularly, it is possible before removing of an element of file system to previously check up its attributes what the useful **Attrib** procedure considered in the following section provides.*

4.3. *Tools of Mathematica for attributes processing of directories and datafiles*

The ***Mathematica*** has no tools of operating with attributes of files and directories what, in our opinion, is a rather essential shortcoming at creation on its basis of various data processing systems. By the way, the similar means are absent in the ***Maple*** also, therefore we created for it a set of procedures {***Atr, F_atr, F_atr1, F_atr2***} that have solved this problem [41]. These tools presented below solve this problem for the ***Mathematica***. The fragment below represents the ***Attrib*** procedure that provides processing of attributes of files and directories.

```
In[3327]:= Attrib[F_/; StringQ[F], x_/; ListQ[x] &&
   AllTrue[Map3[MemberQ, {"-A", "-H", "-S", "-R", "+A", "+H",
              "+S", "+R"}, x], TrueQ] || x == {} || x == "Attr"] :=
   Module[{a, b = "attrib ", c, d = " > ", h = "attrib.exe", p, f, g, t, v},
                              a = ToString[v = Unique["ArtKr"]];
        If[Set[t, LoadExtProg["attrib.exe"]] === $Failed,
                                        Return[$Failed], Null];
        If[StringLength[F] == 3 && DirQ[F] &&
            StringTake[F, {2, 2}] == ":", Return["Drive " <> F],
        If[StringLength[F] == 3 && DirQ[F], f = StandPath[F],
        If[FileExistsQ1[StrDelEnds[F, "\\", 2], v], g = v;
   f = StandPath[g[[1]]]; Clear[v], Return["<" <> F <> "> is not a
                                      directory or a datafile"]]]];
        If[x === "Attr", Run[b <> f <> d <> a],
        If[x === {}, Run[b <> " -A -H -S -R " <> f <> d <> a],
          Run[b <> StringReplace[StringJoin[x], {"+" -> " +",
                                "-" -> " -"}] <> " " <> f <> d <> a]]];
        If[FileByteCount[a] == 0, Return[DeleteFile[a]],
                    d = Read[a, String]; DeleteFile[Close[a]]];
  h = StringSplit[StringTrim[StringTake[d, {1, StringLength[d] -
                        StringLength[f]}]]]; Quiet[DeleteFile[t]];
       h = Flatten[h /. {"HR" -> {"H", "R"}, "SH" -> {"S", "H"},
          "SHR" -> {"S", "H", "R"}, "SRH" -> {"S", "R", "H"},
          "HSR" -> {"H", "S", "R"}, "HRS" -> {"H", "R", "S"},
          "RSH" -> {"R", "S", "H"}, "RHS" -> {"R", "H", "S"}}];
                       If[h === {"File", "not", "found", "-"} ||
    MemberQ[h, "C:\\Documents"], "Drive " <> f, {h, g[[1]]}]]
```

```
In[3328]:= Attrib["C:\\Mathematica", "Attr"]
Out[3328]= {{}, "C:\\Mathematica"}
In[3329]:= Attrib["c:/temp\\", {"+A", "+R"}]
In[3330]:= Attrib["c:/temp\\", "Attr"]
Out[3330]= {{"A", "R"}, "C:\\Temp"}
In[3331]:= Attrib["c:/temp\\", {"-R"}]
In[3332]:= Attrib["c:/temp\\", "Attr"]
Out[3332]= {{"A"}, "C:\\Temp"}
```

The successful procedure call ***Attrib[w, "Attr"]*** returns the list of attributes of a file or directory *w* in the context *Archive ("**A**"), Read-only ("**R**"), Hidden ("**H**")* and *System ("**S**")*. At that, also other attributes inherent to the system files and directories are possible; in particular, on the main directories of devices of external memory *"Drive w"* whereas on a nonexistent directory or file the message ***"w isn't a directory or file"*** is returned. At that, the call is returned in the form of list of the format ***{x, y, ..., z, Pt}*** where the last element determines a full path to a file or directory *w;* the files and subdirectories of the same name can be in various directories, however processing of attributes is made only concerning the first file/directory from the list of objects of the same name. If the full path to a file or directory *w* is defined as the first argument of the ***Attrib*** procedure, only this object is processed. The elements of the returned list that precede its last element define attributes of a processed file or directory.

The procedure call ***Attrib[w, {}]*** returns *Null,* i.e. nothing, cancelling all attributes for a processed file or directory *w* while the call ***Attrib[w, {"x","y",...,"z"}]*** where *x,y,z*∈*{"-A","-H","-S", "-R", "+A", "+H", "+S", "+R"},* also returns *Null,* i.e. nothing, setting/cancelling the attributes of the processed directory or file *w* determined by the second argument. At impossibility to execute processing of attributes the call ***Attrib[w, x]*** returns the corresponding messages. Procedure ***Attrib*** allows to carry out processing of attributes of a file or a directory that is located in any place of file system of the computer. The ***Attrib*** procedure is represented to us as a rather useful means for operating with file system of the computer.

In turn, the ***Attrib1*** procedure in many respects is similar to the ***Attrib*** procedure both in the functional, and in descriptive relation, but the ***Attrib1*** procedure has also certain differences. The successful procedure call ***Attrib1[w, "Attr"]*** returns the list of attributes in the string format of a directory or a file ***w*** in the context *Archive ("**A**"), Hidden ("**H**"), System ("**S**"), Read-only ("**R**")*. The call ***Attrib1[w, {}]*** returns *Null,* cancelling all attributes for the processed file/directory ***w*** whereas the call ***Attrib1[w, {"x", "y",…,"z"}]*** where *x, y, z*∈*{"-A", "-H", "-S", "-R", "+A", "+H", "+S", "+R"}*, also returns *Null,* i.e. nothing, setting/cancelling the attributes of the processed file or directory ***w*** defined by the second argument, whereas the call ***Attrib1[w, x, y]*** with the *3rd* optional ***y*** argument – *any expression* – in addition deletes the program file ***"attrib.exe"*** from the directory determined by the call ***Directory[]***. The source code of the ***Attrib1*** procedure with the most typical examples of its use can be found in [8,10,16].

At the same time, the possible message ***"cmd.exe** – Corrupt File"* that arises at operating of the above procedures ***Attrib*** and ***Attrib1*** should be ignored. Both procedures essentially use our procedures ***LoadExtProg, StrDelEnds, StandPath, FileExistsQ1*** and ***DirQ*** along with use of the standard ***Run*** function and the ***Attrib*** command of the *MS DOS*. In addition, the possibility of removal of the ***"attrib.exe"*** program file from the directory that is determined by the call ***Directory[]*** after the call of the ***Attrib1*** leaves the ***Mathematica*** unchanged. So, in implementation of both procedures the ***Run*** function was enough essentially used, which has the following coding format:

Run[s1,…,sn] – in the basic operational system *(for example, MS DOS)* executes a command that is formed from expressions ***sj** (**j=1..n**)* that are parted by blank symbols with return of code of success of the command completion in the form of an integer. As a rule, the ***Run*** function does not demand of an interactive input, however on some operational platforms it generates text messages. In [1-15] rather interesting examples of application of the ***Run*** function at programming in the ***Mathematica*** with the *MS DOS* commands are represented.

Note that use of the ***Run*** function illustrates one of a rather useful methods of interface with the basic operational platform, but here two very essential moments take place. Above all, the ***Run*** function on some operational platforms *(e.g., Windows **XP** Professional)* demands certain external reaction of the user at an exit from the ***Mathematica*** into the operational platform, and secondly, the call by means of the ***Run*** function of functions or *MS DOS* commands assumes their existence in the directories system determined by the ***$Path*** variable since, otherwise the ***Mathematica*** doesn't recognize them.

For instance, similar situation takes place in the case of use of the external *DOS* commands, for this reason in realization of the procedures ***Attrib, Attrib1*** which through the ***Run*** use the external command "***attrib***" of *DOS*, the connection to system of directories of ***$Path*** of the directories containing the "***attrib.exe***" utility has been provided whereas for internal commands of the *DOS* it isn't required. Once again, possible messages "***cmd.exe – Corrupt File***" which can arise at execution of the ***Run*** function should be ignored.

Thus, at using of the internal command ***Dir*** of *MS DOS* of an extension of the list of directories defined by the ***$Path*** is not required. At the same time, on the basis of standard reception on the basis of extension of a list defined by the ***$Path*** variable the ***Mathematica*** doesn't recognize the external commands of *MS DOS*. In this regard we programmed procedure whose call ***LoadExtProg[x]*** provides search in file system of the computer of a program ***x*** set by the full name with its subsequent copying into a directory defined by the call ***Directory[]***. The procedure call ***LoadExtProg[x]*** searches out ***x*** datafile in file system of the computer and copies it to the directory determined by the call ***Directory[]***, returning ***Directory[]*** <> "\\" <> ***x*** if the file already was in this directory or has been copied into this directory.

The first directory containing the found ***x*** file supplements the list of the directories defined by the predetermined ***$Path*** variable. Whereas the procedure call ***LoadExtProg[x, y]*** with the second optional ***y*** argument – *an undefinite variable* – in addition through ***y*** returns the list of all full paths to the found ***x*** datafile without a modification of the directories list determined by the predetermined **$*Path*** variable. In case of absence of a possibility to find the required ***x*** file *$Failed* is returned. The next fragment presents source code of the ***LoadExtProg*** procedure along with an example of its application, in particular, for loading into the directory determined by the call ***Directory*[]** of a copy of *external* command ***"attrib.exe"*** of *MS DOS* with check of the result.

```
In[2232]:= LoadExtProg[x_/; StringQ[x], y___] :=
             Module[{a = Directory[], b = Unique["agn"], c, d, h},
                       If[PathToFileQ[x] && FileExistsQ[x],
           CopyFileToDir[x, Directory[]], If[PathToFileQ[x] &&
                 ! FileExistsQ[x], $Failed, d = a <> "\\" <> x;
                 If[FileExistsQ[d], d, h = FileExistsQ1[x, b];
                 If[h, CopyFileToDir[b[[1]], a];
                 If[{y} == {}, AppendTo[$Path, FileNameJoin[
           FileNameSplit[ b[[1]]][[1 ;; -2]]]], y = b]; d, $Failed]]]]]
In[2233]:= LoadExtProg["C:\\attrib.exe"]
Out[2233]= $Failed
In[2234]:= LoadExtProg["attrib.exe"]
Out[2234]= "c:\\users\\aladjev\\documents\\attrib.exe"
In[2235]:= FileExistsQ[Directory[] <> "\\" <> "attrib.exe"]
Out[2235]= True
In[2236]:= Attrib1["c:\\Mathem\\book_2020.doc", "Attr"]
Out[2236]= {"A", "S", "R"}
```

Therefore, in advance by means of the call ***LoadExtProg*[*x*]** it is possible to provide access to a necessary ***x*** file if of course it exists in file system of the computer. So, using the ***LoadExtProg*** in total with the system ***Run*** function, it is possible to execute a number of very useful {*.exe* | *.com*} programs in the ***Mathematica*** software – the programs of different purpose that are absent in file system of the ***Mathematica*** thereby significantly extending the functionality of ***Mathematica*** that is demanded by a rather wide range of various appendices.

The above ***LoadExtProg*** and ***FileExistsQ1*** procedures use the ***CopyFileToDir*** procedure whose call ***CopyFileToDir*[*x, y*]** provides copying of a file or directory ***x*** into a ***y*** directory with return of the full path to the copied file/directory. If the copied file already exists, it isn't updated if the target directory already exists, the *x* directory is copied into its subdirectory of the same name. The fragment presents source code of the ***CopyFileToDir*** procedure with typical examples of its application:

```
In[5]:= CopyFileToDir[x_/; PathToFileQ[x], y_/; DirQ[y]] :=
    Module[{a, b}, If[DirQ[x], CopyDir[x, y], If[FileExistsQ[x],
                                        a = FileNameSplit[x][[-1]];
  If[FileExistsQ[b = y <> "\\" <> a], b, CopyFile[x, b]], $Failed]]]
In[6]:= CopyFileToDir["c:/math/book_2020.doc", Directory[]]
Out[6]= "C:\\Users\\Aladjev\\Documents\\book_2020.doc"
In[7]:= CopyFileToDir["C:\\Temp", "E:\\Temp"]
Out[7]= "E:\\Temp\\Temp"
```

The ***CopyFileToDir*** procedure has a variety of appendices in processing problems of file system of the computer.

In conclusion of the section an useful enough procedure is represented which provides only two functions – *(1)* obtaining of the list of attributes ascribed to a file or directory, and *(2)* the removal of all ascribed attributes. The call ***Attribs[x]*** returns the list of attributes in string format which are ascribed to a file or a directory ***x***. On the main directories of volumes of direct access the procedure call ***Attribs*** returns *$Failed,* while the procedure call ***Attribs[x, y]*** with the 2nd optional ***y*** argument – *an arbitrary expression* – deletes all attributes which are ascribed to a file or a directory ***x*** with returning ***0*** at a successful call. The following fragment represents source code of the ***Attribs*** procedure with the most typical examples of its application:

```
In[3330]:= Attribs[x_/; FileExistsQ[x] || DirectoryQ[x], y___] :=
         Module[{b, a = StandPath[x], d = ToString[Unique["g"]],
                                          c = "attrib.exe", g},
              If[DirQ[x] && StringLength[x] == 3 &&
                              StringTake[x, {2, 2}] == ":", $Failed,
            g[] := Quiet[DeleteFile[Directory[] <> "\\" <> c]];
              If[! FileExistsQ[c], LoadExtProg[c]];
              If[{y} == {}, Run[c <> " " <> a <> " > ", d]; g[];
    b = Characters[StringReplace[StringTake[Read[d, String],
   {1, -StringLength[a] - 1}], " " -> ""]]; DeleteFile[Close[d]]; b,
```

```
a = Run[c <> " -A -H -R -S " <> a]; g[]; a]]]
In[3331]:= Map[Attribs, {"c:\\", "e:/", "c:/tm", "c:/tm/bu.doc"}]
Out[3331]= {$Failed, $Failed, {"A"}, {"A", "R", "S"}}
In[3332]:= Attribs["c:/tm/bu.doc", 77]
Out[3332]= 0
In[3333]:= Attribs["c:/tm/bu.doc"]
Out[3333]= {}
```

Note, that as *x* argument the usage of an existing file, full path to a file or a directory is supposed. At the same time, the file ***"attrib.exe"*** is removed from the directory defined by the call ***Directory***[] after a procedure call. The ***Attribs*** procedure is rather fast-acting, supplementing procedures ***Attrib, Attrib1.*** The ***Attribs*** procedure is effectively applied in programming of means of access to elements of file system of the computer at processing their attributes. Thus, it should be noted once again that the ***Mathematica*** has no means for processing of attributes of files and directories therefore the offered procedures ***Attrib, Attrib1*** and ***Attribs*** in a certain measure fill this niche.

So, the declared possibility of extension of the ***Mathematica*** directories that is determined by the **$*Path*** variable, generally doesn't operate already concerning the external commands of *MS DOS* what well illustrates both consideration of the above procedures ***Attrib, LoadExtProg*** and ***Attrib1,*** and an example with the external *"tasklist"* command which is provided display of all active processes of the current session with *Windows* ***7:***

```
In[2565]:= Run["tasklist", " > ", "C:\\Temp\\tasklist.txt"]
Out[2565]= 1
In[2566]:= LoadExtProg["tasklist.exe"];
Run["tasklist" <> " > " <> "C:\\Temp\\tasklist.txt"]
Out[2566]= 0
: System Idle Process
: 0
: Services
: 0
===============
: Skype.exe
: 2396
```

```
: Console
: 1
===============
: Mathematica.exe
: 4120
: Console
: 1
: WolframKernel.exe
: 5888
: Console
: 1
===============
```

The first example of the previous fragment illustrates that attempt by means of the ***Run*** to execute the external command *"tasklist"* of *DOS* completes unsuccessfully *(return code **1**)*, while result of the call ***LoadExtProg["tasklist.exe"]*** with search and upload into the directory defined by the call ***Directory[]*** of the *"tasklist.exe"* file, allows to successfully execute by means of the ***Run*** function the external command *"tasklist"* with preserving of result of its performance in file of ***txt***-format whose contents is represented by the shaded area. Meanwhile, use of external software on the basis of the ***Run*** function along with possibility of extension of functionality of the ***Mathematica*** causes a rather serious portability question. So, the means developed by means of this method with use of the external commands of *MS DOS* are subject to influence of variability of the commands of *DOS* depending on version of basic operating system. In a number of cases it demands a certain adaptation of the software according to the basic operating system.

4.4. Additional tools for files and directories processing of file system of the computer

This item presents tools of files and directories processing of file system of the computer which supplement and in certain cases also extend the above means. Unlike the ***DeleteDirectory*** and ***DeleteFile*** functions the ***DelDirFile1*** procedure removes a directory or file from file system of the computer.

Similarly to functions ***DeleteFile*** and ***DeleteDirectory***, the call ***DelDirFile***[*w*] removes from file system of the computer a file or directory *w*, returning *Null*, i.e. nothing. Whereas the call ***DelDirFile***[*w, y*] with the *2nd* optional argument ***y*** – *an arbitrary expression* – removes from file system of the computer a file or a directory *w*, irrespectively from existence of attribute *Read-only* for it. The ***DelDirFile1*** procedure is a rather useful extension of the ***DelDirFile*** procedure [2] on a case of open files in addition to the *Read-only* attribute of both the separate files, and the files being in the deleted directory. The procedure call ***DelDirFile1***[*x*] is equivalent to the call ***DelDirFile***[*w, y*], providing removal of a file or directory *x* irrespective of openness of a separate *w* file and the *Read-only* attribute ascribed to it, or existence of similar files in *w* directory. The fragment represents source code of the ***DelDirFile1*** procedure along with typical examples of its use.

```
In[2242]:= DelDirFile1[x_/; StringQ[x] && FileExistsQ[x] | |
                        DirQ[x] && If[StringLength[x] == 3 &&
                        StringTake[x, {2, 2}] == ":", False, True]] :=
    Module[{a = {}, b = "", c = Stilized[x], d, f = "#$#", k = 1},
  If[DirQ[x], Run["Dir " <> c <> " /A/B/OG/S > " <> f]; Attribs[c, 7];
        For[k, k < Infinity, k++, b = Read[f, String];
        If[SameQ[b, EndOfFile], DeleteFile[Close[f]]; Break[],
                                       Attribs[b, 7]; Close2[b]]];
        DeleteDirectory[x, DeleteContents -> True], Close2[x];
                                    Attribs[x, 7]; DeleteFile[x]]]
In[2243]:= Attribs["c:\\temp\\paper_201119.docx"]
Out[2243]= {"A", "S", "H", "R"}
In[2244]:= DelDirFile1["c:\\temp\\paper_201119.docx"]
In[2245]:= FileExistsQ["c:\\temp\\paper_201119.docx"]
Out[2245]= False
In[2246]:= DirectoryQ["c:\\temp\\Rans_IAN"]
Out[2246]= True
In[2247]:= Attribs["c:\\temp\\Rans_IAN"]
Out[2247]= {"A", "S", "H", "R"}
In[2248]:= DelDirFile1["c:\\temp\\Rans_IAN"]
In[2249]:= DirectoryQ["c:\\temp\\Rans_IAN"]
Out[2249]= False
```

Meanwhile, before representation of the following means it is expedient to determine one a rather useful procedure whose essence is as follows. As noted above, the file qualifier depends both on register of symbols, and the used *dividers* of directories. So, the same file with different qualifiers *"c:\\Tmp\\cinem.txt"* and *"c:/tmp/cinem.txt"* opens in **2** various streams. Therefore its closing by means of the built-in ***Close*** function doesn't close the *"cinem.txt"* file, demanding closing of all streams on which it was earlier open. For solution of this problem the ***Close1*** and ***Close2*** procedures have been programmed.

```
In[3]:= Read["C:/Temp\\paper_201119.docx"];
        Read["C:/Temp/paper_201119.docx"];
        Read["C:/Temp\\Paper_201119.docx"];
        Read["c:/temp/paper_201119.Docx"]; StreamsU[]
Out[3]= {InputStream["C:/Temp\\paper_201119.docx", 3],
         InputStream["C:/Temp/paper_201119.docx", 4],
         InputStream["C:/Temp\\Paper_201119.docx", 5],
         InputStream["c:/temp/paper_201119.Docx", 6]}
In[4]:= Close["C:\\Temp\\paper_201119.docx"]
    ... General: C:\Temp\paper_201119.docx is not open.
Out[4]= Close["C:\\Temp\\paper_201119.docx"]
In[5]:= StreamsU[]
Out[5]= {InputStream["C:/Temp\\paper_201119.docx", 3],
         InputStream["C:/Temp/paper_201119.docx", 4],
         InputStream["C:/Temp\\Paper_201119.docx", 5],
         InputStream["c:/temp/paper_201119.Docx", 6]}
In[5]:= Close1[x___String] := Module[{a = Streams[][[3 ;; -1]],
                              b = {x}, c = {}, k = 1, j},
    If[a == {} || b == {}, {}, b = Select[{x}, FileExistsQ[#] &];
      While[k <= Length[a], j = 1; While[j <= Length[b],
        If[Stilized[a[[k]][[1]]] == Stilized[b[[j]]],
        AppendTo[c, a[[k]]]]; j++]; k++];
      Map[Close, c]; If[Length[b] == 1, b[[1]], b]]]
In[7]:= Close1["C:\\Temp\paper_201119.docx"]
Out[7]= "C:\\Temp\\paper_201119.docx"
In[13]:= StreamsU[]
Out[13]= {}
```

```
In[21]:= Close2[x___String] := Module[{a = Streams[][[3 ;; -1]],
                               b = {}, c, d = Select[{x}, StringQ[#] &]},
                                  If[d == {}, {}, c[y_] := Stilized[y];
                               Map[AppendTo[b, Part[#, 1]] &, a];
                            d = DeleteDuplicates[Map[c[#] &, d]];
                     Map[Close, Select[b, MemberQ[d, c[#]] &]]]]
In[22]:= Close["C:\\Temp\\paper_201119.docx"]
      ... General: C:\Temp\paper_201119.docx is not open.
Out[22]= Close["C:\\Temp\\paper_201119.docx"]
In[23]:= Close2["C:\\Temp\\paper_201119.docx"]
Out[23]= {"C:/Temp\\paper_201119.docx",
                              "C:/Temp/paper_201119.docx",
                              "C:/Temp\\Paper_201119.docx",
                              "c:/temp/paper_201119.Docx"}
In[24]:= StreamsU[]
Out[24]= {}
```

The call ***Close1***[*x, y, z, ...*] closes all off really-existing files in a {*x, y, z, ...*} list irrespective of quantity of streams on which they have been opened by means of various files qualifiers with returning their list. In other cases the call on admissible factual arguments returns the empty list, while on inadmissible factual arguments a call is returned unevaluated. The procedure ***Close2*** is a functional analogue of the above procedure ***Close1.*** The call ***Close2***[*x, y, z,...*] closes all off really-existing files in a {*x, y, z,...*} list irrespective of quantity of streams on which they have been opened by various files qualifiers with returning their list. The call on any admissible factual arguments returns the empty list, whereas on inadmissible actual arguments the call is returned unevaluated. The previous fragment represents source codes of both procedures along with examples of their use. In a number of appendices ***Close1*** and ***Close2*** are quite useful means.

The tools representing a quite certain interest at operating with file system of the computer as independently and as a part of tools of files processing and directories complete the section. They are used and by a number of means of our ***MathToolBox*** package [16]. In particular, at operating with files the ***OpenFiles*** procedure can be rather useful, whose call ***OpenFiles***[] returns the two–element nested list, whose the first sublist with the ***1st*** "*read*" element contains full paths to the files opened on reading whereas the ***2nd*** sublist with the first "*write*" element contains full paths to files opened on writing in the current session. In a case of absence of such files the call returns the *empty* list, i.e. {}. Whereas the call ***OpenFiles***[*x*] with one factual ***x*** argument – *a file classifier* – returns the result of the above format relative to an open ***x*** file irrespective of a format of coding of its qualifier. If ***x*** defines a closed or a nonexistent file then the procedure call returns the empty list, i.e. {}. The following fragment represents source code of the procedure with a typical example of its use.

```
In[333]:= OpenFiles[x___String] := Module[{a = StreamsU[],
                              b, c, d, h1 = {"read"}, h2 = {"write"}},
        If[a == {}, {}, d = Map[{Part[#, 0], Part[#, 1]} &, a];
              b = Select[d, #[[1]] == InputStream &];
              c = Select[d, #[[1]] == OutputStream &];
              b = Map[DeleteDuplicates,
      Map[Flatten, Gather[Join[b, c], #1[[1]] == #2[[1]] &]]];
      b = Map[Flatten, Map[If[SameQ[#[[1]], InputStream],
  AppendTo[h1, #[[2 ;; -1]]], AppendTo[h2, #[[2 ;; -1]]]] &, b]];
  If[{x} == {}, b, If[SameQ[FileExistsQ[x], True], c = Map[Flatten,
    Map[{#[[1]], Select[#, Stilized[#] === Stilized[x] &]} &, b]];
    If[c == {{"read"}, {"write"}}, {}, c = Select[c, Length[#] > 1 &];
                              If[Length[c] > 1, c, c[[1]]], {}]]]]]
In[334]:= Write["c:/temp\\paper_201119.docx", 211119];
                              Read["C:/Temp/paper_201119.docx"];
In[335]:= OpenFiles["C:\\temp\\paper_201119.docx"]
Out[335]= {{"read", "C:/Temp/paper_201119.docx"},
          {"write", "c:/temp\\paper_201119.docx"}}
```

As a procedure similar to the ***OpenFiles***, the procedure can be used, whose call ***StreamFiles***[] returns the nested list from 2 sublists, the first sublist with the first "***in***" element contains full paths/names of the files opened on the reading whereas the ***2nd*** sublist with the first "***out***" element contains full paths/names of the files opened on the recording. Whereas in the absence of the open files the call ***StreamFiles***[] returns "*AllFilesClosed*".

```
In[2336]:= StreamFiles[]
Out[2336]= {{"in", "C:/Temp/paper_201119.docx"},
           {"out", "c:/temp\\paper_201119.docx"}}
In[2337]:= CloseAll[]; StreamFiles[]
Out[2337]= "AllFilesClosed"
```

The following procedure is represented as a rather useful tool at operating with file system of the computer, whose call ***DirEmptyQ[w]*** returns *True* if ***w*** directory is empty, otherwise *False* is returned. At that, the procedure call ***DirEmptyQ[w]*** is returned unevaluated, if ***w*** isn't a real directory. At the same time, the call ***DirEmptyQ[w, y]*** with optional argument ***y*** – *an indefinite variable* – through ***y*** returns the contents of ***w*** directory in format of ***Dir*** command of *MS DOS*. The following fragment presents source code of the ***DirEmptyQ*** procedure with typical enough examples of its application.

```
In[3128]:= DirEmptyQ[d_/; DirQ[d], y___] :=
        Module[{a, b = {"$$1", "$$2"}, c, p = Stilized[d], t = 1},
  Map[Run["Dir " <> p <> If[SuffPref[p, "\\", 2], "", "\\"] <> # <>
                       " > " <> b[[t++]]] &, {" /S/B ", " /S "}];
       c = If[ReadString[b[[1]]] === EndOfFile, True, False];
        If[{y} != {} && SymbolQ[y],
        y = StringReplace[ReadString[b[[2]]], "\n" -> ""], 7];
                                                 DeleteFile[b]; c]
In[3129]:= DirEmptyQ["c:\\Galina47"]
Out3[129]= DirEmptyQ["c:\\Galina47"]
In[3130]:= DirEmptyQ["c:\\Galina", gs]
Out[3130]= False
In[3131]:= gs
Out[3131]= "Volume in drive C is OS
           Volume Serial Number is E22E-D2C5
           Directory of c:\\galina
           21.11.2019  15:27    <DIR>        .
           21.11.2019  15:27    <DIR>        ..
           21.11.2019  17:46    <DIR>        Victor
                      0 File(s)          0 bytes
          Directory of c:\\galina\\Victor
```

```
21.11.2019  17:46    <DIR>          .
21.11.2019  17:46    <DIR>          ..
               0 File(s)              0 bytes
     Total Files Listed:
               0 File(s)              0 bytes
               5 Dir(s)  288 095 285 248 bytes free"
```

In addition to the previous ***DirEmptyQ*** procedure the call ***DirFD[j]*** returns the **2**-element nested list whose the ***1st*** element determines the list of subdirectories of the first nesting level of a ***j*** directory whereas the second element – the list of files of a ***j*** directory; if the ***j*** directory is empty, the procedure call returns the empty list, i.e. {}. The fragment below presents source code of the ***DirFD*** procedure with an example of its application.

```
In[320]:= DirFD[d_/; DirQ[d]] := Module[{a = "$#$", b = {{}, {}},
          c, h, t, p = StandPath[StringReplace[d, "/" -> "\\"]]},
               If[DirEmptyQ[p], Return[{}], Null];
  c = Run["Dir " <> p <> " /B " <> If[SuffPref[p, "\\", 2], "", "\\"]
                                          <> "*.* > " <> a];
       t = Map[ToString, ReadList[a, String]]; DeleteFile[a];
  Map[{h = d <> "\\" <> #; If[DirectoryQ[h], AppendTo[b[[1]], #],
       If[FileExistsQ[h], AppendTo[b[[2]], #], Null]]} &, t]; b]

In[321]:= DirFD["C:\\Program Files\\Wolfram Research\\
Mathematica\\12.1\\Documentation\\English\\Packages"]
Out[321]= {{"ANOVA", "Audio", "AuthorTools", ..., {}}}
In[322]:= Length[%[[1]]]
Out[322]= 48
```

In particular, in the previous example the list of directories with records on the packages delivered with the ***Mathematica 12.1*** is returned. So, with ***Mathematica 48*** packages of different purpose that is simply seen from the name of the subdirectories containing them are being delivered.

In addition to the ***DirFD*** procedure, the ***DirFull*** procedure presents a certain interest whose call ***DirFull[j]*** returns list of all full paths to subdirectories and files contained in a ***j*** directory and its subdirectories; the ***1st*** element of the list is the ***j*** directory. Whereas on an empty ***j*** directory the call returns the empty list.

At last, the procedure call ***TypeFilesD[d]*** returns the sorted list of types of files located in a ***d*** directory with returning word *"undefined"* on files without of name extension. In addition, the files located in the ***d*** directory and in all its subdirectories of an arbitrary nesting level are considered. Moreover, on the empty ***d*** directory the call ***TypeFilesD[d]*** returns the empty list, i.e. {}.

The ***FindFile1*** procedure serves as a useful extension of the standard ***FindFile*** function, providing search of a file within file system of the computer. The call ***FindFile1[x]*** returns a full path to the found file ***x***, or the list of full paths (*if the **x** file is located in different directories of file system of the computer)*, otherwise the call returns the empty list. Whereas the call ***FindFile1[x, y]*** with the *2nd* optional ***y*** argument – *full path to directory* – returns full path to the found ***x*** file, or list of full paths located in the ***y*** directory and its subdirectories. At the same time, the ***FindFile2*** function serves as other useful extension of standard ***FindFile*** function, providing search of a ***y*** file within a ***x*** directory. The function call ***FindFile2[w, y]*** returns the list of full paths to the found ***y*** file, otherwise the call returns the empty list. Search is done in the ***w*** directory and all its subdirectories. The fragment below presents source codes of the ***FindFile1*** procedure and ***FindFile2*** function with typical examples of their application.

```
In[7]:= FindFile1[x_/; StringQ[x], y___] := Module[{c, d = {}, k = 1,
                           a = If[{y} != {} && PathToFileQ[y], {y},
    Map[# <> ":\\" &, Adrive[]]], b = "\\" <> ToLowerCase[x]},
                                        For[k, k <= Length[a], k++,
  c = Map[ToLowerCase, Quiet[FileNames["*", a[[k]], Infinity]]];
   d = Join[d, Select[c, SuffPref[#, b, 2] && FileExistsQ[#] &]]];
                                       If[Length[d] == 1, d[[1]], d]]
In[8]:= FindFile1["Book_2020.doc"]
Out[8]= {"c:\\ma\\book_2020.doc", "e:\\ma\\book_2020.doc"}

In[9]:= FindFile2[x_/; DirectoryQ[x], y_/; StringQ[y]] :=
                          Select[FileNames["*.*", x, Infinity],
         Stilized[FileNameSplit[#][[-1]]] == Stilized[y] &]

In[10]:= FindFile2["e:\\", "book_2020.doc"]
Out[10]= {"e:\\Mathematica\\Book_2020.doc"}
```

The ***FindFile1*** in many respects is functionally similar to the ***FileExistsQ1*** procedure however in the time relation is partially less fast-acting in the same file system of the computer *(a number of rather interesting questions of files and directories processing can be found in the collection* [15]).

It is possible to represent the ***SearchDir*** procedure as one more indicative example, whose call ***SearchDir[d]*** returns the list of *all* paths in file system of the computer that are completed by a ***d*** subdirectory; in case of lack of such paths the procedure call ***SearchDir[d]*** returns the empty list. In a combination with the procedures ***FindFile1, FileExistsQ1*** the ***SearchDir*** procedure is a rather useful at operating with file system of the computer, that confirms their use for the solution of problems of similar type. The fragment below presents source code of the ***SearchDir*** procedure with typical examples of its application.

```
In[9]:= SearchDir[d_/; StringQ[d]] := Module[{a = Adrive[], c,
  t = {}, p, b = "\\" <> ToLowerCase[StringTrim[d, ("\\" | "/") ...]]
   <> "\\", g = {}, k = 1, v}, For[k, k <= Length[a], k++, p = a[[k]];
                    c = Map[ToLowerCase, Quiet[FileNames["*", p <>
                                                ":\\", Infinity]]];
                    Map[If[! StringFreeQ[#, b] || SuffPref[#, b, 2] &&
                           DirQ[#], AppendTo[t, #], Null] &, c]];
                    For[k = 1, k <= Length[t], k++, p = t[[k]] <> "\\";
                                       a = StringPosition[p, b];
                          If[a == {}, Continue[], a = Map[#[[2]] &, a];
                    Map[If[DirectoryQ[v = StringTake[p, {1, # - 1}]],
                    AppendTo[g, v], Null] &, a]]]; DeleteDuplicates[g]]

In[10]:= SearchDir["\\Temp/"]
Out[11]= {"c:\\temp", ..., "e:\\temp", "e:\\temp\\temp"}
```

By operating time these tools yield to our procedures ***isDir*** and ***isFile*** for the ***Maple*** system, providing testing of files and directories respectively [39]. So, the ***isFile*** procedure not only tests the existence of a file, but also the mode of its openness, what in certain cases is a rather important. There are also other rather interesting tools for testing of the state of directories and files, including their types [8-10,15,16].

The ***Mathematica*** has two standard functions ***RenameFile*** and ***RenameDirectory*** for renaming of files and directories of file system of the computer respectively. Meanwhile, from the point of view of the file concept these functions would be very expedient to be done by uniform tools because in this concept directories and files are in many respects are identical and their processing can be executed by the same tools. At the same time the mentioned standard functions and on restrictions are quite identical: for renaming of a name ***x*** of an element of file system of the computer onto a new ***y*** name the element with name ***y*** has to be absent in the system, otherwise $*Failed* with a certain diagnostic message are returned. Furthermore, if as a ***y*** only a new name without full path to a new ***y*** element is coded, then it copying to the current directory is done; in a case of directory ***x*** it with all contents is copied into the current directory under a new ***y*** name. Therefore, similar organization is inconvenient in many respects, what stimulated us to determine for renaming of the directories and files the uniform ***RenDirFile*** procedure that provides renaming of an element ***x*** *(directory or file)* in situ with preservation of its type and all its attributes; at that, as an argument ***y*** a new name of the ***x*** element is used. Therefore, the successful procedure call ***RenDirFile*[*x, y*]** returns the full path to the renamed ***x*** element. In a case of existence of an element ***y*** the message *"Directory/datafile <y> already exists"* is returned. In other unsuccessful cases the procedure call returns $*Failed* or is returned unevaluated. With source code of the ***RenDirFile*** the reader can familiarized, for example, in [10,15,16].

Meanwhile, at the same time to the means represented, we have created a whole series of means for computer file system access, that not only extend the capabilities of system functions focused on similar work, but also significantly complement the system capabilities, providing advanced facilities for processing elements of the computer file system. Note that ***MathToolBox*** tools [15,16] greatly enhance ***Mathematica***'s capabilities in the context of the computer file system access. Below, some special tools of files and directories processing are considered.

4.5. Special tools for files and directories processing

In this section some special means of processing of files and directories are represented; in certain cases they can be useful. Removal of a file in the current session is made by means of the standard ***DeleteFile*** function whose call ***DeleteFile***[{*x, y, z, ...*}] returns *Null*, i.e. nothing in a case of successful removal of the given file or their list, and $*Failed* otherwise. At the same time, in the list of files only those are deleted that have no *Protected*-attribute. Moreover, this operation doesn't save the deleted files in the system ***$Recycle.Bin*** directory that in a number of cases is extremely undesirable, first of all, in the light of possibility of their subsequent restoration. The fact that the system function ***DeleteFile*** is based on the *MS DOS* command ***Del*** that according to specifics of this operating system immediately deletes a file from file system of the computer without its preservation, that significantly differs from similar operation of ***Windows*** system that by default saves the deleted file in the special ***$Recycle.Bin*** directory. For elimination of this shortcoming the ***DeleteFile1*** procedure has been offered, whose source code with examples of its application are represented by the fragment below.

```
In[57]:= DeleteFile1[x_/; StringQ[x] || ListQ[x], t___] :=
                    Module[{a = Flatten[{x}], b, c, p = {}},
          b = SysDir[] <> If[! StringFreeQ[Ver[], " XP "],
                                   "recycler", "$recycle.bin"];
                        Map[{Quiet[Close[#]], c = Attribs[#],
                               If[{t} != {}, CopyFileToDir[#, b];
         If[MemberQ[c, "R"], Attribs[#, y]; DeleteFile[#],
                               AppendTo[p, #]; DeleteFile[#]],
                          If[MemberQ[c, "R"], AppendTo[p, #],
            CopyFileToDir[#, b]; DeleteFile[#]]]} &, a]; p]
In[58]:= DeleteFile1[{"c:/temp/CKA.doc", "c:/temp/rans_ian.txt",
         "c:/temp/description.doc", "c:/temp/Шишаков.doc"}, gs]
Out[58]= {"c:/temp/rans_ian.txt", "c:/temp/description.doc"}
In[59]:= DeleteFile1[{"c:/temp/CKA.doc", "c:/temp/rans_ian.txt",
         "c:/temp/description.doc", "c:/temp/Шишаков.doc"}]
Out[59]= {"c:/temp/CKA.doc", "c:/temp/Шишаков.doc"}
```

The procedure call ***DeleteFile1[x]*** where ***x*** – a separate file or their list, returns the list of files ***x*** that have *Protected* attribute with deleting files given by an argument ***x*** with saving them in the ***$Recycle.Bin*** directory of the *Windows* system if they have not *Protected* attribute. Meanwhile, the files removed by the call ***DeleteFile1[x]*** are saved in ***$Recycle.bin*** directory however they are invisible to viewing by the system tools, for example, by *Ms Explorer,* complicating cleaning of the given system directory. While the call ***DeleteFile1[x, t]*** with the *2nd* optional ***t*** argument – *an expression* – returns the list of files ***x*** that have not ***Protected*** attribute with deleting files set by the argument ***x*** regardless of whether they have ***Protected*** attribute with saving them in the ***$recycle.bin*** directory of the *Windows* system. At the same time, in the ***$recycle.bin*** directory a copy only of the last deleted file always turns out. This procedure is oriented to *Windows* ***XP, 7*** and above operational platforms however it can be spread and to other operational platforms.

Note, the procedure substantially uses our ***SysDir*** function, whose call ***SysDir[]*** returns the root directory of the DSS device on which *Windows* is installed:

```
In[17]:= SysDir[] := StringTake[GetEnvironment["windir"][[2]],
                                                    {1, 3}]; SysDir[]
Out[17]= "C:\\"
```

in combination with the ***Attribs*** and ***CopyFileToDir*** procedures. The first procedure was mentioned above, whereas the second procedure is used by our other files and directories processing tools too, extending the capabilities of the built-in access tools.

The procedure call ***CopyFileToDir[x, y]*** provides copying of a file or directory ***x*** into a ***y*** directory with return of the full path to the copied file or directory. In a case if the copied file ***x*** already exists, it isn't updated; if the target directory already exists, the ***x*** directory is copied into its subdirectory of the same name. This procedure has a variety of appendices in problems of processing of file system of the computer. The next fragment represents source code of the ***CopyFileToDir*** procedure with an example of its typical application.

```
In[361]:= CopyFileToDir[x_ /; PathToFileQ[x], y_ /; DirQ[y]] :=
                    Module[{a, b}, If[DirQ[x], CopyDir[x, y],
               If[FileExistsQ[x], a = FileNameSplit[x][[-1]];
  If[FileExistsQ[b = y <> "\\" <> a], b, CopyFile[x, b]], $Failed]]]

In[362]:= CopyFileToDir["c:/temp/CKA.doc", "c:/mathematica"]
Out[362]= "C:\\mathematica\\CKA.doc"
```

For restoration from the system directory ***$Recycler.Bin*** of the packages which were removed by means of the ***DeleteFile1*** procedure in ***Windows XP*** *Professional*, the ***RestoreDelPackage*** procedure providing restoration from ***$recycler.bin*** directory of such packages has been offered [1,8,12,16]. The successful call ***RestoreDelPackage*[*F, "Context'"*]**, where the first argument ***F*** defines the name of a file of the format {***"cdf", "m", "mx", "nb"***} that is subject to restoration whereas the second argument - the context associated with a package returns the list of *full* paths to the restored files, at the same time by deleting from directory ***$Recycler.Bin*** the restored files with the necessary package. At that, this tools is supported on the *Windows* **XP** platform, while on the *Windows* **7** platform the ***RestoreDelFile*** procedure is of a certain interest, restoring files from the directory ***$Recycler.Bin*** that earlier were removed by the call of ***DeleteFile1*** procedure.

The procedure call ***RestoreDelFile*[*f, r*]**, where the ***1st*** actual argument ***f*** defines the name of a file or their list that are subject to restoration, while the second ***r*** argument defines the name of a target directory or full path to it for the restored files, returns the directory for the restored files; at the same time the delete of the restored files from the ***$recycle.bin*** directory is made in any case. In a case of absence of the requested files in the ***$recycle.bin*** directory the procedure call returns the empty list, i.e. **{}**, with printing of the appropriate messages *(such messages are print for each file absent in the above Windows directory)*. It should be noted, that the nonempty files are restored too. If the ***2nd*** ***r*** argument defines a directory name in string format, but not the full path to it, a target ***r*** directory is created by means of call ***Directory*[];** i.e. the current work directory. The fragment below represents source code of the procedure with examples of its application.

```
In[2216]:= RestoreDelFile[f_/; StringQ[f] || ListQ[f],
      r_/; StringQ[r]] := Module[{a = Flatten[{f}], b, c, d, p, t = 0},
                         b = SysDir[] <> "$Recycle.bin";
                               Map[{c = b <> "\\" <> #,
   If[! FileExistsQ[c], Print["File " <> # <> " can`t be restored"];
           t++, CopyFileToDir[c, p = If[DirQ[r], r, Directory[]]];
                                       d = Attrib[c, "Attr"];
   If[MemberQ[d[[1]], "R"], Attrib[c, {}], 7]; DeleteFile[c]]} &, a];
                                       If[Length[a] == t, {}, b]]

In[2217]:= RestoreDelFile[{"description.doc", "Shishakov.doc",
                     "rans_ian.txt", "rans.txt"}, "c:\\restore"]
         File rans.txt can`t be restored
Out[2217]= "C:\\Users\\Aladjev\\Documents"
In[2218]:= RestoreDelFile[{"description7.doc", "Vaganov.doc",
                     "rans.txt", "ian2019.txt"}, "c:\\restore"]
         File description7.doc can`t be restored
         File Vaganov.doc can`t be restored
         File rans.txt can`t be restored
         File ian2019.txt can`t be restored
Out[2218]= {}
```

On the other hand, for removal from ***$Recycle.bin*** directory of the files saved by the ***DeleteFile1*** procedure on the *Windows* ***XP*** platform, the procedure is used whose call ***ClearRecycler*[]** returns ***0***, deleting files of specified type from the ***$Recycle.bin*** directory with saving in it of the files removed by of ***Windows XP*** or its appendices. In addition, the *Dick Cleanup* command in *Windows* ***XP*** in some cases completely does not clear ***$Recycler*** from files what successfully does the call ***ClearRecycler*[*"ALL"*]**, returning ***0*** and providing removal of all files from the system ***Recycler*** directory. In [8,10,15] it is possible to familiarize with source code of the ***ClearRecycler*** procedure and examples of its use. For ***Windows 7*** platform and above the ***ClearRecyclerBin*** procedure provides removal from the ***Recycler*** directory of all directories and files or only of those that are conditioned by the ***DeleteFile1*** procedure. The procedure call ***ClearRecyclerBin*[]** returns *Null*, and provides removal from the system directory ***$Recycle.Bin*** of directories and files which are deleted by the

DeleteFile1 procedure. Whereas the call ***ClearRecyclerBin[w]***, where *w – an arbitrary expression –* also returns *Null*, i.e. nothing, and removes from the ***$Recycle.Bin*** directory of all directories and files whatever the cause of their emergence in the directory. In addition, the procedure call on the empty ***Recycler*** directory returns *$Failed* or nothing, depending on the operating platform. The following fragment represents source code of the procedure with typical examples of its application.

```
In[88]:= ClearRecyclerBin[x___] := Module[{c, d = {}, p, b = "#$#"},
              c = SysDir[] <> If[! StringFreeQ[Ver[], " XP "],
                   "Recycler", "$Recycle.Bin"];
  Run["Dir " <> c <> "/A/B/S/L > " <> b]; p = ReadList[b, String];
        DeleteFile[b]; If[p == {}, Return[$Failed],
           Map[{If[{x} != {}, Attrib[#, {}];
        AppendTo[d, If[DirectoryQ[#], #, Nothing]];
                 Quiet[DeleteFile[#]],
        If[SuffPref[FileNameSplit[#][[-1]], "$", 1] ||
       SuffPref[#, "desktop.ini", 2], Null, Attrib[#, {}];
        AppendTo[d, If[DirectoryQ[#], #, Nothing]];
 Quiet[DeleteFile[#]]]]} &, p]]; Quiet[Map[DeleteDirectory, d]]; ]

In[89]:= ClearRecyclerBin[]
In[90]:= ClearRecyclerBin[All]
```

The following useful procedure has the general character at operating with the devices of direct access and is rather useful in a number of applications, above all, of the system character. The procedure below to a great extent is an analogue of ***Maple Vol_Free_Space*** procedure [41,42] that returns a volume of free memory on devices of direct access. The call ***FreeSpaceVol[w]*** depending on type of an actual *w* argument that should define the logical name in string format of a device, returns simple or the nested list; elements of its sublists determine a device name, volume of free memory for device of direct access, and unit of its measurement respectively. In a case of absence or inactivity of the *w* device the procedure call returns the message *"Device is not ready"*. The following fragment represents source code of the ***FreeSpaceVol*** procedure with a typical example of its use.

```
In[9]:= FreeSpaceVol[x_/; MemberQ3[Join[CharacterRange["a",
                    "z"], CharacterRange["A", "Z"]], Flatten[{x}]]] :=
                          Module[{a = "#$#", c, d = Flatten[{x}], f},
    f[y_] := Module[{n, b}, n = Run["Dir " <> y <> ":\\ > " <> a];
                  If[n != 0, {y, "Device is not ready"}, b = StringSplit[
               ReduceAdjacentStr[ReadFullFile[a], " ", 1]][[-3 ;; -2]];
         {y, ToExpression[StringReplace[b[[1]], "ÿ" -> ""]], b[[2]]}]];
            c = Map[f, d]; DeleteFile[a]; If[Length[c] == 1, c[[1]], c]]
In[9]:= FreeSpaceVol[{"a", "c", "d", "e"}]
Out[9]= {{"a", "Device is not ready"}, {"c", 270305714176, "bytes"},
                          {"d", 0, "bytes"}, {"e", 2568826880, "bytes"}}
```

The procedure below facilitates solution of the problem of use of external ***Mathematica*** programs or operational platform. The procedure call ***ExtProgExe[x, y, h]*** provides a search in file system of the computer of a *{**exe** | **com**}* file with program with its *subsequent* execution on ***y*** arguments of the command string. Both arguments ***x*** and ***y*** should be encoded in the string format. Successful performance of this procedure returns the full path to **"$*TempFile*$"** file of *ASCII* format that contains the result of execution of a ***x*** program, and this file can be processed by the standard tools on the basis of its structure. At that, in a case of absence of the file with the demanded ***x*** program the procedure call returns $*Failed* while using of the third ***h*** optional argument – *an arbitrary expression* – the file with the ***x*** program uploaded in the current directory defined by the function call ***Directory*[]**, is removed from this directory; also the **"$*TempFile*$"** datafile is removed if it is empty or implementation of the ***x*** program was terminated abnormally. The fragment below represents source code of the ***ExtProgExe*** procedure with examples of its use.

```
In[310]:= ExtProgExe[x_/; StringQ[x], y_/; StringQ[y], h___] :=
    Module[{a = "$TempFile$", b = Directory[] <> "\\" <> x, c, d},
                              d = x <> " " <> y <> " > " <> a;
Empty::file = "File $TempFile$ is empty; the file had been deleted.";
                If[FileExistsQ[b], c = Run[d], c = LoadExtProg[x];
                If[c === $Failed, Return[$Failed]]; c = Run[d];
                If[{h} != {}, DeleteFile[b]]];
   If[c != 0, DeleteFile[a]; $Failed, If[EmptyFileQ[a], DeleteFile[a];
```

```
                              Message[Empty::file], Directory[] <> "\\" <> a]]]
```

```
In[311]:= ExtProgExe["tasklist.exe", " /svc ", 1]
Out[311]= "C:\\Users\\Aladjev\\Documents\\$TempFile$"
In[312]:= ExtProgExe["systeminfo.exe", "", 1]
Out[312]= "C:\\Users\\Aladjev\\Documents\\$TempFile$"
In[313]:= ExtProgExe["Rans_Ian.com", "a", b]
Out[In[313]:= $Failed
```

The following procedure is a rather useful generalization of built-in ***CopyFile*** function whose call ***CopyFile[a, b]*** returns the full name of the file to it is copied and *$Failed* if it cannot do the copy; in addition, file ***a*** must already exist, whereas ***b*** file must not. Thus, in the program mode the standard ***CopyFile*** function is insufficiently convenient. The procedure call ***CopyFile1[a, b]*** returns the full path to the file that had been copied. In contrast to ***CopyFile*** function, the procedure call ***CopyFile1[a, b]*** returns the list of format **{*b, b**}** where ***b*** – the full path to the copied file and ***b**** – the full path to the previously existing copy of a *"xy.a"* file in the format *"xy.a"*, if the target directory for ***b*** already contained ***a*** file. In a case ***a ≡ b*** *(where identity is considered up to standardized paths of both files)* the call returns the standardized path to the ***a*** file, doing nothing. In other successful cases the call ***CopyFile1[a, b]*** returns the full path to the copied file. Even if the nonexistent path to the target directory for the copied file is defined, then such path taking into account available devices of direct access will be created. The fragment below represents source code of the ***CopyFile1*** procedure with typical examples of its application which illustrate quite clearly the aforesaid.

```
In[81]:= CopyFile1[x_/; FileExistsQ[x], y_/; StringQ[y]] :=
                    Module[{a, b, c, d, p = Stilized[x], j = Stilized[y]},
     b = Stilized[If[Set[a, DirectoryName[j]] === "", Directory[],
                                        If[DirectoryQ[a], a, CDir[a]]]];
                         If[p == j, p, If[FileExistsQ[j], Quiet[Close[j]];
                          Quiet[RenameFile[j, c = StringReplace[j,
                         Set[d, FileBaseName[j]] -> "$" <> d <> "$"]]];
                                                  CopyFileToDir[p, b];
                  {b <> "\\" <> FileNameTake[p], j = b <> "\\" <> c},
                                                  CopyFileToDir[p, b]]]]
```

```
In[82]:= CopyFile1["C:/temp/CKA.doc", "CKA.DOC"]
Out[82]= {"c:\\users\\aladjev\\documents\\cка.doc",
                    "c:\\users\\aladjev\\documents\\$cка$.doc"}
In[83]:= CopyFile1["c:/temp/cka.doc", "g:\\Grodno\\Cka.doc"]
Out[83]= "C:\\grodno\\cка.doc"
```

So, the tools represented in the chapter sometimes a rather significantly simplify programming of problems dealing with file system of the computer. Along with that, these tools extend built-in means of access, illustrating a number of useful enough methods of programming of tasks of similar type. These means in a number of cases significantly supplement the access tools supported by system, facilitating programming of a number of rather important appendices that deal with the files of various format. Our experience of programming of the access tools that extend the similar means of the ***Mathematica*** allows to notice that basic access tools of ***Mathematica*** in combination with its global variables allow to program more simply and effectively the user original access tools. Moreover, the created access tools possess sometimes by the significantly bigger performance in relation to the similar means developed in the ***Maple*** software. Thus, in the ***Mathematica*** it is possible to solve the tasks linked with rather complex algorithms of processing of files, while in the ***Maple***, first of all, in a case of rather large files the efficiency of such algorithms leaves much to be desired. In a number of appendices the means, represented in the present chapter along with other similar means from package [16] are represented as rather useful, by allowing, at times, to essentially simplify the programming. At that, it must be kept in mind, a lot of means which are based on the ***Run*** function and the *DOS* commands generally can be nonportable to other versions of the system and operational platform demanding the appropriate debugging to appropriate new conditions. In general, our access tools [1-16] are usefully expand and supplement the built-in ***Mathematica*** tools of the same purpose, making it easier to solve a number of tasks of processing elements of the computer's file system. At present our access tools [16] are used in various applications.

Chapter 5: Organization of the user software

The ***Mathematica*** no possess comfortable enough tools for organization of the user libraries similarly to the case of ***Maple,*** creating certain difficulties at organization of the user software developed in its environment. For saving of definitions objects and results of calculations ***Mathematica*** uses files of different organization. At that, files of text format that not only are easily loaded into the current session, in general are most often used, but also are convenient enough for processing by other known means, for example, the word processors. Moreover, the text format provides the portability on other computing platforms. One of the main prerequisites of saving in files is possibility of use of definitions along with their usage for the ***Mathematica*** objects in the subsequent sessions of the system. At that, with questions of standard saving of objects *(blocks, modules, functions etc.)* the interested reader can familiarize in details in [1-15,17], some of them were considered in this book in the context of organization of packages while here we present simple tools of organization of the user libraries in the ***Mathematica*** system.

Meanwhile, here it is expedient to make a number of very essential remarks on use of the above system means. First, the mechanism of processing of erroneous and especial situations represents a rather powerful mean of programming practically of each quite complex algorithm. However, in the ***Mathematica*** such mechanism is characterized by essential shortcomings, for example, successfully using in the *Input* mode the mechanism of messages print concerning erroneous {*Off, On*} situations, in body of procedures such mechanism generally doesn't work as illustrates the following a rather simple fragment:

```
In[1117]:= Import["C:\\Mat\\A.m"]
... Import::nffil: File C:\Mat\A.m not found during Import.
Out[17]= $Failed
In[1118]:= Off[Import::nffil]
In[1119]:= Import["D:\\Mat\\A.m"]
Out[1119]= $Failed
```

```
In[1123]:= On[Import::nffil]
In[24]:= F[x_] := Module[{a}, Off[Import::nffil];
                              a := Import[x]; On[Import::nffil]; a]
In[1125]:= F["C:\\Mat\\A.m"]
... Import::nffil: File C:\Mat\A.m not found during Import.
Out[1125]= $Failed
```

In a case of creation of rather complex procedures in which is required to solve questions of the suppressing of output of a number of erroneous messages, tools of ***Mathematica*** system are presented to us as insufficiently developed. The interested reader can familiarize with other peculiarities of the specified system tools in [1-15]. Now, we will present certain approaches concerning creation of the user libraries in ***Mathematica.*** Some of them can be useful in practical work with ***Mathematica.***

In view of the scheme of organization of library considered in ***Maple*** [26] with organization different from the main library, we will present realization of the similar user library for a case of the ***Mathematica.*** On the first step in a directory, let us say, "c:/Lib" the *txt*-files with definitions of the user tools with their usage are placed. In principle, you can to place any number of definitions in the *txt*-files, in this case it is previously necessary to read a *txt*-file whose name *coincides* with name of the required tool, whereupon in the current session tools whose definitions are located in the file with usage are available. It is convenient in a case when in a single file are located the main tools along with tools accompanying them, excluding system tools. On the second step the tools together with their usage are created and debugged with their subsequent saving in the required file of a library subdirectory "C:\\Lib".

To save the definitions and usage in *txt*-files perhaps in two ways, namely: *(1)* by the function call ***Save,*** saving previously evaluated definitions and their usage in a *txt*-file given by its first argument; at that, saving is made in the ***append***-mode, or *(2)* by creating *txt*-files with names of tools and usage whose contents are formed by means of a simple word processor, for example, ***Notepad.*** At that, by means of the ***Save*** function we have possibility to create libraries of the user tools, located in an arbitrary directory of file system of the computer.

For operating with *txt*-files of such *organization* was created the procedure ***CallSave*** whose call ***CallSave*[x,y,z]** returns the result of a call ***y*[z]** of a tool ***y*** on the ***z*** list of factual arguments passed to ***y*** provided that the tool definition ***y*** with usage are located in a ***x*** *txt*-file that has been earlier created by means of ***Save*** function. If a tool with the given ***y*** name is absent in the ***x*** file, the procedure call returns *$Failed*. If a ***x*** data-file contains definitions of several tools of the same name ***y***, the procedure call ***CallSave*[x,y,z]** is executed relative to their *definition* whose formal arguments correspond to a ***z*** list of actual arguments. If ***y*** determines the list, the call returns the names list of all tools located in the ***x*** file [1,16,24]. More detailed information on the capabilities of such organization of user libraries can be found in [5-10]. In our opinion, the represented approach quite can be used for the organization of simple and effective user libraries of traditional type.

As another an useful enough approach, based on the use of *mx*-format files to store tool definitions and their usage, we will introduce the ***CALLmx*** procedure whose the call serves to save means definitions in the library directory in files of *mx*-format with their subsequent uploading into the current session. The possibilities of the procedure can be found in [1,5,10,11,16]. It is possible to represent the ***UserLib*** procedure that supports some useful enough functions as one more rather simple example of maintaining the user libraries. The call ***UserLib*[W, g]** provides a number of important functions on maintaining of a simple user library located in a **W** file of *txt*-format. As the second actual ***g*** argument the **2**-element list acts that defines such functions as: *(**1**)* return of the list of tools names, contained in ***W***, *(**2**)* print to the screen of full contents of a library file ***W*** or a separate tool, *(**3**)* saving in the library file ***W*** in the *append*-mode of a tool with the given name, *(**4**)* loading into the current session of all tools whose definitions are in the ***W***, *(**5**)* uploading into the current session of a tool with the given name whose definition is in the

W library file. There is a rather good opportunity to extend the procedure with a number of useful enough functions such as deletion from a library of definitions of the specified means or their obsolete versions, etc. With the procedure the reader can familiarize more in details, for example, in [4-9,15,16].

The *list* structure of the ***Mathematica*** allows to rather easily simulate the operating with structures of a number of systems of computer mathematics, for example, ***Maple***. So, in ***Maple*** the *tabular* structure as one of the most important structures is used that is rather widely used both for the organization of structures of data, and for organization of the libraries of software. Similar tabular organization is widely used for organization of package modules of ***Maple*** along with a number of tools of our ***UserLib*** library [42]. For simulation of main operations with the tabular organization similar to the ***Maple,*** in ***Mathematica*** the ***Table1*** procedure can be used. On a basis of such tabular organization supported by the ***Table1*** procedure it is rather simply possible to determine the user libraries. As one of such approaches we presented an example of the library ***LibBase*** whose structural organization has format of the *ListList*–type [14,16]. The main operations with the library organized thus are supported by the procedure ***TabLib*** whose source code with examples of its use are represented in [8-10,12,15,16].

The interested reader can develop own means of the library organization in ***Mathematica,*** using approaches offered by us along with others. However, the problem of organization of convenient help bases for the user libraries exists. A number of approaches in this direction can be found in [14]. In particular, on a basis of the list structure supported by ***Mathematica,*** it is rather simply to define help bases for the user libraries. On this basis as one of possible approaches an example of the ***BaseHelp*** procedure has been represented, whose structural organization has the list format [10,16]. Meanwhile, it is possible to create the help bases on a basis of packages containing usage on means of the user library which are saved in files of ***mx***–format. At that, for complete library it is possible to create only *one* help ***mx***-file, uploading it as required into the current session by means of the ***Get*** function with receiving in the subsequent of access to all usage that are in the file. The ***Usage*** procedure can represent an quite certain interest for organization of a help database for the user libraries [8,9,12,16]. There too the interested reader can find and other useful tools for organizing user libraries.

5.1. MathToolBox package for Mathematica system

However, allowing the above approaches to organization of the user software, in our opinion the most convenient approach is the organization on the basis of packages. The ***packages*** are one of the main mechanisms of ***Mathematica*** extension which contain definitions of the new symbols with their usage that are intended for use both outside of package and in it. The symbols can correspond, in particular, to the definitions of new means defined in the package that extend the functional ***Mathematica*** possibilities. At that, according to the adopted system *agreement* all new symbols that entered in a certain package are placed in a context whose name is connected with name of the package.

At uploading of a package in the current session, the given context is added into the beginning of the list defined by global $*ContextPath* variable. As a rule, for ensuring of association of a package with context a construction ***BeginPackage*["*x*`"]** coded at its beginning is used. At uploading of package in the current session the ***"x`"*** context will update the current values of global variables $*Context* and $*ContextPath.* The closing bracket of the package is construction ***EndPackage*[].** The package body itself, as a rule, consists of 2 parts – reference information *(usage)* for all symbols included in the package and definitions of symbols constituting the package. So, the ***N*** symbol help is framed in the form ***N::usage*** = *"Description of N symbol"*. In turn, the symbols definitions are framed with constructs of the following format ***Begin*["`*N*`"]** and ***End*[],** for example, for the above symbol ***N***. So, as a matter of experience works with ***Mathematica*** system, as a basis of the organization of the user software we offer a scheme.

At the *first* stage, in a new ***nb***–document a program object of the following organization is formed, namely:

```
General information on a package
BeginPackage["Context`"]
N1::usage = "Description of N1 tool"
================================
Np::usage = "Description of Np tool"
Begin["`N1`"]
Definition of N1 tool
End[]
=================================
Begin["`Np`"]
Definition of Np tool
End[]
EndPackage[]
```

Before the main *body* of the object the *general* information about the package is placed, followed by the opening bracket of the package with a context assigned to it. The opening bracket is followed by a set of the ***usage***–sentences containing reference information for all package tools named ***N1, ..., Np.*** At the same time, it should be noted that each tool included in the package must have the appropriate ***usage***–sentence, otherwise, if you upload the package into the current session, you will not have access to such tool. The definition of each tool to be included in the given package is then placed in special block, for example, ***Begin*["\`*N1*\`"] ... *End*[],** ending all such blocks with the closing bracket ***EndPackage*[].** The definitions of means included in the package should be previously, whenever possible, are debugged including processing of the main special and error situations.

At the *second* stage by a chain of commands *"Evaluation → Evaluation Notebook"* of the graphic user interface *(**GUI**)* is made evaluation of the *Notebook,* i.e. actually the package with return of results of the following form:

```
In[3212]:= BeginPackage["Agn`"]
           Name::usage = "Description of Name tool"
           Begin["`Name`"]
           Name[x_] := x^2
           End[]
           Begin["`Name1`"]
           Name1[x_] := x^3
           End[]
           EndPackage[]
Out[3212]= "Agn`"
Out[3213]= "Description of Name tool"
Out[3214]= "Agn`Name`"
Out[3216]= "Agn`Name`"
Out[3217]= "Agn`Name1`"
Out[3219]= "Agn`Name1`"
In[3220]:= CNames["Agn`"]
Out[3220]= {"Name"}
```

The procedure call ***CNames*["*Agn*`"]** returns the name list in string format of all symbols whose definitions are located in the package with context "*Agn*`".

The evaluation of the above package with context *"Agn`"* in the current session activates all definitions and usage contained in the package. Therefore the following stage consists in saving of the package in files of formats {*nb, mx*}. The first saving is made by a chain of commands of ***GUI "File → Save"***, whereas by a call of the built-in system function ***DumpSave*** of the format

```
In[15]:= DumpSave["c:\\Math\\FileName.mx", "Agn`"]
Out[15]= {"Agn`"}
```

saving of this package in a file ***"FileName.mx"*** of the *Math* directory is provided *(names of directory and file to the discretion of the user)* with return of list of contexts ascribed to the package. All subsequent loadings of the ***mx***-file with the package to the current session are made at any time, when demanding use of the tools that are contained in it, by a call of the built-in system function ***Get*** of the format ***Get*[*"C:\ \Math\ \FileName.mx"*]**.

As noted above the built-in ***DumpSave*** function writes out definitions in a binary format that is optimized for input by the ***Mathematica.*** Meantime, at the call ***DumpSave[f, x]*** where *f* is a file of ***mx***–format a symbol, list of symbols or a context can be used as the *2nd* ***x*** argument. In order to enhance the call format of the ***DumpSave*** function some tools have been proposed [15].

In particular, the procedure call ***DumpSave1[x, y]*** returns the nested list whose first element defines the full path to a file ***x*** of ***mx***–format *(if necessary to the file is assigned the **mx**–extension)* whereas the second element defines the list of objects and/or contexts from the list defined by argument ***y*** whose definitions were unloaded into the ***x*** file of ***mx***–format.

Evaluation of definition of a symbol ***x*** in the current session it will associate with the context of ***"Global'"*** which remains at its unloading into a ***mx***–file by the ***DumpSave*** function. While in some cases there is a need of saving of symbols in the files of ***mx***–format with other contexts. This problem is solved by the procedure whose call ***DumpSave2[f, x, y]*** returns nothing, at the same time unloading into ***mx***–file ***f*** the definition of symbol or the list of symbols ***x*** that have context ***"Global'"***, with context ***y.*** Thus, in the current session the ***x*** symbol receive the ***y*** context.

Finally, a simple ***DumpSave3*** procedure allows an arbitrary expression to be used as the second argument of the procedure. Calling the ***DumpSave3[f, exp]*** procedure returns a variable in a string format while saving an ***exp*** expression in a ***mx***-file ***f.*** Then the subsequent call ***Get[f]*** returns nothing with activating the variable returned by the previous call ***DumpSave3[f, exp]*** with the ***exp*** value assigned to it. The fragment below represent the source code of the procedure with an example of it application.

```
In[2267]:= DumpSave3[f_/; StringQ[f], exp_] := Module[{a},
                    {ToString[a], a := exp, DumpSave[f, a]}[[1]]]
In[2268]:= DumpSave3["dump.mx", a*77 + b*78]
Out[2268]= "a$33218"
In[2269]:= Clear["a$33218"]
In[2270]:= Get["dump.mx"]; ToExpression["a$33218"]
Out[2270]= 77*a + 78*b
```

Fundamental differences between files of two formats ***mx*** and ***nb*** assume to save packages at least in files of these types, and that is why. Files of ***mx***–format are optimized for input in ***Mathematica,*** each such file has a plain text header identifying its type and contexts ascribed to it. In turn, the rest of a ***mx***–file containing definitions of tools is presented in the dump binary format that is not allowing to edit it. Files saved by ***DumpSave*** function can be load by ***Get*** function. Meantime, files of format *mx* can`t be exchanged between operating systems that differ in compliance with ***$SystemWordLength*** predefined variable.

Whereas files of the format ***nb (notebooks)*** are structured interactive documents that can contain calculations, text, typeset expressions, user interface elements, etc. Notebooks are typical method of interacting with ***Mathematica*** front end. Files of this format are automatically associated with the ***Mathematica*** on computers which have the ***Mathematica*** installed. In addition, *mx*–files contain only printable *ASCII* characters, are viewable and largely readable in any text editor. In addition, notebooks are cross–platform, meaning that a notebook created on any supported platform can be read by ***Mathematica*** on any other platform. Therefore to edit a package it is reasonable to do on the basis of the ***nb***–file containing it while most effective to do the current work with the package on the basis of its ***mx***–file.

It is this approach to software saving that we have chosen and implemented in the package ***MathToolBox***. Our package ***MathToolBox*** [16] that is attached to the present book can as a bright example of the above organization of the user software. Package contains more than ***1320*** tools eliminating restrictions of a number of standard tools of the ***Mathematica,*** and expand its software with new tools. In this context, ***MathToolBox*** can serve as a certain additional tool of procedural programming, especially useful in the numerous applications where certain non–standard evaluations have to accompany programming. In addition, tools presented in ***MathToolBox*** have a direct relation to principal questions of procedural–functional programming in ***Mathematica,*** not only for the decision of applied problems, but, above all, for creation of software that extends frequently used facilities of the system and/or eliminating their defects or extending the system with new facilities. Software presented in this package contains a number of rather useful and effective receptions of programming in the ***Mathematica,*** and extends its software which allows in the system to programme the tasks of various purpose more simply and effectively. Additional tools composing the above package embrace the following sections of the ***Mathematica*** system, namely:

- *additional tools in interactive mode of the system*
- *additional tools of processing of expressions*
- *additional tools of processing of symbols and strings*
- *additional tools of processing of sequences and lists*
- *additional tools expanding standard built-in functions or the system software as a whole (control structures branching and loop, etc.)*
- *determination of procedures in the* **Mathematica** *software*
- *determination of the user functions and pure functions*
- *means of testing of procedures and functions*
- *headings of procedures and function*
- *formal arguments of procedures and functions*
- *local variables of modules and blocks; means of their processing*
- *global variables of modules and blocks; means of their processing*
- *attributes, options and values by default for arguments of the user blocks, functions and modules; additional means of their processing*
- *useful additional means for processing of procedures and functions*
- *additional means of the processing of internal* ***Mathematica*** *files*
- *additional means of the processing of external* ***Mathematica*** *files*
- *additional tools of the processing of attributes of directories and files*
- *additional and special means of processing of directories and files*
- *additional tools of work with packages and contexts ascribed to them*
- *organization of the user software in the* ***Mathematica*** *system*

Archive ***Archive76.ZIP*** with this package *(Freeware license)* can be freely downloaded here [16]. Archive contains 5 files of formats {***nb, mx, cdf, m, txt***}. Such approach allows to satisfy the user on different operating platforms. Memory size demanded for the ***MathToolBox*** package in ***Mathematica*** of version ***12.1.0*** *(on platform Windows 7 Professional)* yields the following result:

```
In[1]:= MemoryInUse[]
Out[1]= 85042560
In[2]:= Get["C:\\Mathematica\\MathToolBox.mx"]
In[3]:= MemoryInUse[]
Out[3]= 96349800
In[4]:= N[(% - %%%)/1024^2]
Out[4]= 10.7834
```

i.e. in ***Mathematica 12.1.0*** the ***MathToolBox*** package demands a little more ***10.78*** *Mb* while amount of tools whose definitions are located in the package, at the moment of its load to the current session of the ***Mathematica*** system is available on the basis of the following simple evaluation:

```
In[5]:= Length[CNames["AladjevProcedures`"]]
Out[5]= 1325
```

where ***CNames*** – tool from the package, "***AladjevProcedures`***" – context ascribed to it. More detailed information on the means contained in the package can be found in [1-16].

Because the ***MathToolBox*** package contains definitions and usage for a large number of frequently used tools that often use each other, it is useful to define uploading of the package when you load ***Mathematica*** itself. To this end, you can to update the ***Init.m*** file of *txt*-format from ***$UserBaseDirectory*** <> "***kernel***" directory adding to it the entry ***Get["Dir\\MathToolBox.mx"]*** where ***Dir*** determines the full path to directory with ***mx***-file of the package. It's easy to do with a simple text editor or in the current session of ***Mathematica.*** Furthermore, for this purpose it is possible to use a simple ***Init*** procedure whose source code with a typical example of its application is represented below.

```
In[317]:= Init[x_/; StringQ[x]] := Module[{a, b, c},
                              a[d_] := StringReplace[d, "\\" -> "/"];
                    b = $UserBaseDirectory <> "\\kernel\\Init.m";
                                   c = ReadString[b]; OpenWrite[b];
WriteString[b, c, "\n", a["Get[" <> "\"" <> x <> "\"]"]]; Close[b]]
```

```
In[318]:= Init["C:\\Mathematica\\MathToolBox.mx"]
Out[318]= "C:\\Users\\Aladjev\\AppData\\Roaming\\
                              Mathematica\\kernel\\Init.m"
```

The procedure call ***Init*[*x*]** where actual argument ***x*** defines the full path to a file of format ***mx, nb*** or ***m*** with the user package in addition mode updates the above file ***"Init.m"*** which locates in the user directory defined by the predefined ***$UserBaseDirectory*** variable according to the corresponding condition. In particular, if ***"Init.m"*** file had content before the procedure call

(User Mathematica initialization file **),**

then as a result of the procedure call the file gets the content

```
(** User Mathematica initialization file **)
Get["C:/Mathematica/MathToolBox.mx"]
```

After that, as a result of uploading ***Mathematica*** all means of the package become available in the current session along with updating of the lists of contexts defined by predetermined variables ***$Packages*** and ***$ContextPath*** by the package context. While the function call ***Contexts*[]** returns the list of all contexts supplemented by contexts ***"AladjevProcedures'Name'"***, where ***Name*** is the name of a package tool. The above scheme of the organization of the user software provides access to means of a package on an equal basis with built–in system means at once after uploading of the ***Mathematica*** except for two moments: *(1)* help on a tool ***N*** is available by **?*N*** or by **??*N*** only, and *(2)* all source codes of the package means are open.

The above technique allows to program a simple function, whose call ***JoinTxtFiles*[*x, y*]** returns the path to a ***x*** file that is updated by adding of a file ***y*** to the contents of a text file ***x***.

```
In[35]:= JoinTxtFiles[x_String, y_String] := {WriteString[x,
            ReadString[x], "\n", ReadString[y]], Close[x]}[[2]]

In[36]:= JoinTxtFiles["C:/Temp/In.txt", "C:/Temp/In1.txt"]
Out[36]= "C:/Temp/In.txt"
```

The above fragment represents source code of the function ***JoinTxtFiles*** with a typical example of its application.

The above method loads the desired file at the beginning of the current session, while on the function call ***Needs[Context, f]*** the desired file *f (including the **mx-file**)* with the package can be loaded at any time of the current session and its context placed in ***$Packages*** and ***$ContextPath,*** if it was not already there.

Meanwhile, it is appropriate to make one very significant comment here. The ***MathToolBox*** package [16] was created for a rather long period of time, albeit with a number of intervals. Therefore, ***Mathematica*** releases ***8.0 - 12.1*** are responsible for creating the tools that make it possible additional debugging of tools to the current ***Mathematica*** release. The stability of built-in ***Math***-language of the ***Mathematica*** system is significantly higher than the corresponding component of the ***Maple*** system, but it is also not ***100%.*** That is why, in some cases the necessary additional debugging of some package tools is required, that in the vast majority of cases is not essentially difficult. Naturally, due to a rather large number of package means, such additional debugging was carried out by us in a limited enough amount, leaving it to the reader who uses certain package means in his activities. In most cases, the means features of the package are compatible with the ***Mathematica 12.1.0*** software environment. Note that some package tools are functionally fully or partially duplicate each other, illustrating different useful programming approaches and techniques, or certain undocumented *(hidden)* capabilities of the built-in the ***Mathematica*** language.

In any case, as demonstrated by many years of experience in teaching different courses in ***Mathematica*** at universities in ***Belarus*** and the ***Baltic States,*** this package not only represents the tools for applied and system programming in ***Mathematica,*** but also proved to be a rather useful collection of tasks aimed both at mastering programming in ***Mathematica*** system and at increasing its level as a whole. Being a rather useful reference and training material describing a lot of useful programming techniques in ***Mathematica,*** including the non-standard ones, the ***MathToolBox*** package is attached as an auxiliary material to our books [8-15].

5.2. Operating with the user packages in Mathematica

Similarly to the well-developed software the ***Mathematica*** is an extendable system, i.e. in addition to the built-in tools that quite cover requirements of quite wide range of the users, the system allows to program those tools that absent for the specific user of built-in language along with extending and correcting standard software. At that, the user can find the missing tools which are not built-in in numerous packages delivered with the ***Mathematica,*** and existing packages for various applied fields. The question consists only in finding of a package necessary for a concrete case containing definitions of functions, modules and other objects demanded for applications that are programmed in the ***Mathematica***. A package has standard organization and contains definitions of various objects, these or those functions, procedures, variables, etc., that solve well-defined problems.

Mathematica provides a standard set of packages whose list is defined by a concrete version of the system. For receiving of packages list which are delivered with the current release of the ***Mathematica*** it is possible to use the procedure, whose call ***MathPackages*[]** returns list of packages names with a certain confidence speaking about their basic purpose. While the call ***MathPackages*[*j*]** with optional *j* argument *(an indefinite variable)* returns through it in addition the three-element list whose the ***1st*** element defines the current release of ***Mathematica,*** the ***2nd*** element - the type of the license and the ***3rd*** element - deadline of action of the license [16]. The following fragment represents the typical examples of its application.

```
In[91]:= MathPackages[]
Out[91]= {"AbelianGroup", "AbortHandling", ..., "ZTransform"}
In[92]:= Length[%]
Out[92]= 3712
In[93]:= MathPackages[gs]; gs
Out[93]= {"12.1.0 for Microsoft Windows (64-bit)
          (March 14, 2020)", "Professional", "Sun31May"}
```

From the fragment follows that the ***Mathematica*** of version ***12.1.0*** contains *3712* packages oriented on different appendices, including the packages of strictly system purpose. Before use of means contained in an applied package, the package should be previously loaded to the current ***Mathematica*** session by means of the function call ***Get[Package]***.

<u>The concept of context in Mathematica</u>. In ***Mathematica*** this concept was entered for organization of work with symbols that present various objects *(modules, functions, variables, packages and so on)*, in particular, in order to avoid the possible conflicts with symbols of the same name. Main idea consists in that that full name of an arbitrary symbol consists of two parts, namely: a context and a short name, i.e. the full name of a certain object has format: *"context'short name"* where the sign <'> *(backquote)* carries out the role of some marker, identifying context in the system. For example, *Agn'Vs* represents a symbol with the *Agn* context and with short *Vs* name. At that, with such symbols it is possible to execute various operations as with usual names; furthermore, the system considers *aaa'xy* and *bbb'xy* as various symbols. So, the most widespread use of context consists in its assignment to functionally identical or semantically connected symbols. For example, *Agn`StandPath, Agn`MathPackages* define that procedures *StandPath* and *MathPackages* belong to the same group of the means which associate with *"Agn'"* context which is ascribed to a certain package. The current context of a session is in the global variable ***$Context:***

```
In[2223]:= $Context
Out[2223]= "Global`"
```

In the current ***Mathematica*** session the current context by default is determined as *"Global'"*. Whereas the global variable ***$ContextPath*** determines the list of contexts after the ***$Context*** variable for search of a symbol entered into the current session. It is possible to reffer to the symbols from the current context simply by their short names; thus, if this symbol intersects with a symbol from the list determined by the ***$ContextPath*** variable, the second symbol will be used instead of the symbol from the current context, for example:

```
In[2224]:= $ContextPath
```

Out[2224]= {"DocumentationSearch`", "ResourceLocator`", "URLUtilities`", "AladjevProcedures`", "PacletManager`", "System`", "Global`"}

While the calls ***Context*[*x*]** and ***Contexts*[]** return a context ascribed to a ***x*** symbol and the list of all contexts of the current session respectively:

In[2225]:= **Context[DeleteFile1]**
Out[2225]= "AladjevProcedures`"
In[2226]:= **Contexts[]**
Out[2226]= {"AladjevProcedures`", **...**, "$CellContext`"}

In addition, by analogy with file system of the computer, contexts quite can be compared with directories. It is possible to determine the path to a file, specifying a directory containing it and a name of the file. At the same time, the current context can be quite associated with the current directory to the files of which can be referenced simply by their names. Furthermore, like file system the contexts can have hierarchical structure, in particular, ***"Visualization`VectorFields`VectorFieldsDump`"***. So, the path of search of a context of symbols in the ***Mathematica*** is similar to a path of search of program files. At the beginning of the session the current context by default is *"Global`"*, and all symbols entered in the session are associated with this context, excepting the built-in symbols, e.g., ***Do***, that are associated with *"System`"* context. Path of search of contexts by default includes the contexts for system–defined symbols. While for the symbols removed by means of the ***Remove*** function, the context can not be determined. At using of contexts there is no guarantee that **2** symbols of the same name are available in different contexts. Therefore the ***Mathematica*** defines as a maximum priority the priority of choice of that symbol with this name, whose context is the first in the list which is determined by the global variable **$*ContextPath***. Therefore, for placement of such context at the beginning of the specified list you can use the construction:

In[30]:= **$ContextPath**
Out[30]= {"DocumentationSearch`", "ResourceLocator`", "URLUtilities`", "PacletManager`", "System`", "Global`"}

In[31]:= **PrependTo[$ContextPath, "Ian`"]**

Out[31]= {"Ian`", "DocumentationSearch`", "URLUtilities`", "ResourceLocator`", "PacletManager`", "System`", "Global`"}

In[32]:= **$ContextPath**

Out[32]= {"Ian`", "DocumentationSearch`", "URLUtilities`", "ResourceLocator`", "PacletManager`", "System`", "Global`"}

An useful procedure provides assignment of a context to a definite or indefinite symbol. The call ***ContextToSymbol1*[*x,y,z*]** returns *Null,* i.e. nothing, providing assignment of a ***y*** context to a ***x*** symbol while the third optional ***z*** argument – *the string* – defines for ***x*** an usage; at its absence for an undefinite ***x*** symbol the usage – *empty* string, i.e. "", whereas for a definite ***x*** symbol the usage has view *"Help on x"*. With the ***ContextToSymbol1*** procedure and examples of its use can familiarize in [8,15,16].

A rather useful procedure in a certain relation expands the above procedure and provides assignment of the set context to a definite symbol. The call ***ContextToSymbol2*[*x,y*]** returns two-element list of format {*x,y*} where ***x*** – the name of the processed definite ***x*** symbol and ***y*** – its new context, providing *assignment* of a ***y*** context to the definite ***x*** symbol; while the procedure call ***ContextToSymbol2*[*x, y, z*]** with the optional third ***z*** argument – *an arbitrary expression* – also returns **2**–element list of the above format {*x, y*}, providing assignment of a certain ***y*** context to the definite ***x*** symbol with saving of symbol definition ***x*** and all its attributes along with usage in file ***"x.mx"***.

Thence, before a procedure call ***ContextToSymbol2*[*x, y*]** for change of the existing context of a symbol ***x*** on a new ***y*** symbol in the current session it is necessary to evaluate definition of ***x*** symbol and its usage in the format *x::usage = "Help on x object."* *(if an usage exists, of course)* with assignment to the ***x*** symbol of necessary attributes.

In addition, along with possibility of assignment of the set context to symbols the procedure ***ContextToSymbol2*** is a rather useful means for extension by new means of the user package contained in a ***mx***-file. The technology of similar updating is as follows. On the first step the definition of a new ***x*** tool with its usage describing these tools is evaluated along with ascribing of the necessary attributes. On the second step, by means of the call ***ContextToSymbol2***[*x, y, j*] the assignment of a *y* context to *x* symbol along with its usage with saving of the updated *x* object in *"x.mx"* file is provided. At last, the call ***Get***[*w*] loads into the current session the revised user package located in a *mx*–file *w* with an *y* context, whereas the subsequent call ***DumpSave***[*p, y*] saves in the updated *mx*–file *w* all objects which have *y* context, including the objects that earlier have been obtained by means of the procedure call ***ContextToSymbol2***[*x, y*] or ***Get***[*"x.mx"*]. Such approach provides a rather effective method of updating of the user packages located in *mx*–files [8-10,12-16].

The ***ContextToSymbol3*** procedure is a useful modification of the above procedure ***ContextToSymbol2***. The procedure call ***ContextToSymbol3***[*x, y*] returns 2–element list of format {*x, y*}, where *x* – the name in string format of a definite *x* symbol, *y* – its new context, providing assignment of a certain *y* context to the definite *x* symbol; on the inadmissible arguments the call is returned as unevaluated. The fragment below represents source code of the ***ContextToSymbol3*** procedure with example its use.

```
In[2214]:= ContextToSymbol3[x_/; StringQ[x] &&
      SymbolQ[x] && ! NullQ[x] && ! SameQ[x, "System`"],
                                          y_/; ContextQ[y]] :=
         Module[{a = Flatten[{PureDefinition[x]}], b, c, d, h},
                 b = StringSplit[a[[1]], {"[", " = ", " := "}][[1]];
                   h = Help[Symbol[b]]; c = Attributes[x];
                  ToExpression["Unprotect[" <> b <> "]"];
            d = "BeginPackage[\"" <> y <> "\"]" <> "\n" <>
    If[NullQ[h], "", b <> "::usage=" <> ToString1[h]] <> "\n" <>
       StringJoin[Map[# <> "\n" &, a]] <> "EndPackage[]";
                         Remove[x]; Quiet[ToExpression[d]];
ToExpression["SetAttributes[" <> b <> "," <> ToString[c] <> "]"]; {b, y}]
In[2215]:= V77[x_] := Module[{a = 42}, a*x];
   V77[x_, y_] := Module[{}, x*y]; V77::usage = "Help on V77.";
                       SetAttributes[V77, {Listable, Protected}]
In[2216]:= ContextToSymbol3["V77", "AvzAgnVsv`"]
Out[2216]= {"V77", "AvzAgnVsv`"}
```

```
In[2217]:= Attributes[V77]
Out[2217]= {Listable, Protected}
In[2218]:= Definition[V77]
Out[2218]= Attributes[V77] = {Listable, Protected}
           V77[x_] := Module[{a = 42}, a*x]
           V77[x_, y_] := Module[{}, x*y]
In[2219]:= Context[V77]
Out[2219]= "AvzAgnVsv`"
In[2220]:= ?V77
Out[2220]= "Help on V77."
```

On the basis of the previous procedure, ***RenameMxContext*** procedure was programmed whose call ***RenameMxContext[x,y]*** returns the name of a ***mx***-file ***x*** with replacement of its context by a new ***y*** context; at that, the package located in the existing ***x*** file can be uploaded into current session or not, while at use of the third optional argument – *an arbitrary expression* – the call ***RenameMxContext[x, y, z]*** additionally removes the ***x*** package from the current session. The fragment presents source code of the ***RenameMxContext*** procedure with examples of its use.

```
In[3368]:= BeginPackage["RansIan`"]
           GSV::usage = "Help on GSV."
           ArtKr::usage = "Help on ArtKr."
           Begin["`ArtKr`"]
           ArtKr[x_, y_, z_] := Module[{a = 74}, a*x*y*z]
           End[]
           Begin["`GSV`"]
           GSV[x_, y_] := Module[{a = 69}, a*x*y]
           End[]
           EndPackage[];
In[3378]:= DumpSave["avzagn.mx", "RansIan`"]
Out[3378]= {"RansIan`"}
In[3379]:= CNames["RansIan`"]
Out[3379]= {"ArtKr", "GSV"}
In[3380]:= RenameMxContext[x_ /; FileExistsQ[x] &&
             FileExtension[x] == "mx", y_ /; ContextQ[y], z___] :=
Module[{a = ContextInMxFile[x], b = Quiet[Check[Get[x], "Er"]], c},
    If[b === "Er", "File " <> x <> " is corrupted", b = CNames[a];
                 c = Quiet[AppendTo[Map[a <> # <> "`" &, b], a]];
```

```
                    Map[Quiet[ContextToSymbol3[#, y]] &, b];
ToExpression["DumpSave[" <> ToString1[x] <> "," <> ToString1[y]
      <> "]"]; DeletePackage[a]; If[{z} != {}, x, DeletePackage[y]; x]]]
```

```
In[3381]:= RenameMxContext["avzagn.mx", "Tampere`", 77]
Out[3381]= "avzagn.mx"
In[3382]:= ContextInMxFile["avzagn.mx"]
Out[3382]= "Tampere`"
```

The ***ReplaceContextInMx1*** procedure – an extension of the ***ReplaceContextInMx*** procedure on a case of absence of context for a ***mx***-file *w*. The procedure call ***ReplaceContextInMx1***[*x, w*] returns the 3-element list of the form {*a, x, w*}, where ***a*** – an old context, ***x*** – a new context and *w* – updated *w* file with a new ***x*** context, if its previous version had context or did not have it *(in this case the absence of context is identified as* $Failed*)*. In a case if *w* file is corrupted, the message *"File w is corrupted"* is returned. Since as a result of its execution the procedure clears *all* symbols in the current session that have the ***"Global`"*** context, then it is desirable to make calling this procedure at the beginning of the current session to avoid possible misunderstandings. The next fragment represents source code of the procedure and examples of its typical application.

```
In[3312]:= ReplaceContextInMx1[x_ /; ContextQ[x],
                    f_ /; FileExistsQ[f] && FileExtension[f] == "mx"] :=
                                Module[{a = ContextInMxFile[f], b, c, d},
                    If[ContextQ[a], RenameMxContext[f, x]; {a, x, f},
    If[SameQ[a, $Failed], Map[ClearAll[#] &, CNames["Global`"]];
Get[f]; b = CNames["Global`"]; Map[ContextToSymbol3[#, x] &, b];
                                          DumpSave[f, x]; {a, x, f}, a]]]
In[3313]:= ReplaceContextInMx1["Tampere`", "agn47.mx"]
Out[3313]= {"Grodno`", "Tampere`", "agn42.mx"}
In[3314]:= ReplaceContextInMx1["Tallinn`", "rans.mx"]
Out[3314]= "File rans.mx is corrupted"
In[3315]:= ReplaceContextInMx1["Grodno`", "avzagn.mx"]
Out[3315]= {$Failed, "Grodno`", "avzagn.mx"}
```

Presently, using the above procedure ***ContextToSymbol2*** or ***ContextToSymbol3***, the procedure that executes replenishment of ***mx***-file *f* contained a package by new tools can be presented.

The procedure call ***AdjunctionToMx[y, f]*** returns full path to a ***mx***-file with a context updated by new ***y*** tools. At that, a single ***y*** symbol or their list can be as the first argument whereas their definitions and usage should be previously evaluated. Besides, if the ***mx***-file had been already uploaded, it remains, otherwise it will be unloaded of the current session. The procedure call on a ***mx***-file *f* without context returns $*Failed.*

```
In[2216]:= AdjunctionToMx[y_/; SymbolQ[y] || ListQ[y] &&
  DeleteDuplicates[Map[SymbolQ[#] &, Flatten[{y}]]] == {True},
        f_/; FileExistsQ[f] && FileExtension[f] == "mx"] :=
                          Module[{a = ContextInMxFile[f], b},
 If[a === $Failed, $Failed, If[! FreeQ[$Packages, a], b = 77, Get[f]];
          Map[Quiet[ContextToSymbol2[#, a]] &, Flatten[{y}]];
        ToExpression["DumpSave[" <> ToString1[f] <> "," <>
                                      ToString1[a] <> "]"];
                 If[! SameQ[b, 77], RemovePackage[a], 72]; f]]
In[2217]:= G72[x_, y_] := x^2 + y^2; G72::usage = "Help on G72
                      function."; V77[x_, y_] := x^3 + y^3;
     V77::usage = "Help on V77 function."; Get["avzagn.mx"]
In[2218]:= ContextInMxFile["avzagn.mx"]
Out[2218]= "Tampere`"
In[2219]:= CNames["Tampere`"]
Out[2219]= {"ArtKr", "GSV"}
In[2220]:= AdjunctionToMx[{G72, V77}, "avzagn.mx"]
Out[2220]= "avzagn.mx"
In[2221]:= ClearAll[ArtKr, GSV, G72, V77]
In[2222]:= Get["avzagn.mx"]; CNames["Tampere`"]
Out[2222]= {"ArtKr", "G72", "GSV", "V77"}
```

In addition to the previous procedure the procedure call ***CreationMx[x, y, f]*** creates a new ***mx***-file *f* with tools defined by the ***y*** argument *(a single symbol or their list)* and with a context ***x***, returning full path to the *f* file. At that, definitions and usage of the ***y*** symbols should be previously evaluated. Furthermore, if ***mx***-file *f* already exists, it remains, but instead of it a new ***mx***-file is created. The procedure call for a context ***x*** that exists in the ***$Packages*** variable returns $*Failed* [8-10,15,16].

Sometimes, it is expedient to replace a context of means of the user package uploaded into the current session. This task is solved by means of the ***RemoveContext*** procedure, whose call ***RemoveContext[j, x, y, z, h,…]*** returns nothing, replacing in the current session a context *j* ascribed to the means {*x, y, z, h,…*} of the user package by the ***"Global`"*** context. In the absence of the {*x, y, z, h,…*} means with the *j* context the procedure call returns *$Failed*. In addition, a ***mx***-file contained the means {*x, y, z, h,…*} remains without change. The fragment represents source code of the procedure ***RemoveContext*** with an example of its use.

```
In[18]:= RemoveContext[at_/; ContextQ[at], x__] :=
  Module[{a = {}, b, c = {}, d = Map[ToString, {x}], f = "$$$", Attr},
                                   d = Intersection[CNames[at], d];
                                 b = Flatten[Map[PureDefinition, d]];
          If[b == {}, $Failed, Attr := Map[{#, Attributes[#]} &, d];
                          Do[AppendTo[a, StringReplace[b[[k]], at <>
                                d[[k]] <> "`" -> ""]], {k, 1, Length[d]}];
                                                  Write[f, a]; Close[f];
  Do[AppendTo[c, at <> d[[k]]], {k, 1, Length[d]}]; c = Flatten[c];
          Map[{ClearAttributes[#, Protected], Remove[#]} &, d];
                         Map[ToExpression, Get[f]]; DeleteFile[f];
          Map[ToExpression["SetAttributes[" <> #[[1]] <> "," <>
                              ToString[#[[2]]] <> "]"] &, Attr]; ]]
In[19]:= Get["avzagn.mx"]
In[20]:= CNames["Tampere`"]
Out[20]= {"Art", "G72", "G721", "GSV", "V77"}
In[21]:= RemoveContext["Tampere`", Art, G72, G721, GSV, V77]
In[22]:= Map[Context, {Art, G72, G721, GSV, V77}]
Out[22]= {"Global`", "Global`", "Global`", "Global`", "Global`"}
```

In connection with the context processing means discussed above, it quite is reasonablly note a procedure for testing of the correctness of *mx*-files. Calling ***CorrectMxQ[f]*** procedure returns *True* if the existing a ***mx***-file is correctly loaded into the current session by means of the call ***Get[f]***, and *False* otherwise. While the call ***CorrectMxQ[f, t]*** additionally through the *2nd* optional ***t*** argument – *an indefined variable* – returns two-element list of the format {***c, "Yes"***} where ***c*** – a context of the *f* file if the *f* file was already loaded into the current session, {***c, "No"***} if *f* file is not loaded and the message *"File f is corrupted"* if *f* file is corrupted.

Following fragment represents source code of the ***CorrectMxQ*** procedure with examples of its typical application.

```
CorrectMxQ[f_/; FileExistsQ[f] && FileExtension[f] == "mx", t___] :=
                         Module[{a = ContextInMxFile[f], b, c, d},
                                                {If[ContextQ[a],
     If[FreeQ[$ContextPath, a], d = {a, "No"}, d = {a, "Yes"}]; True,
    If[! SameQ[a, $Failed], d = "File " <> f <> " is corrupted"; False,
                   b = CNames["Global`"]; DumpSave["##.mx", b];
                Map[ClearAll, b]; Get[f]; c = CNames["Global`"];
            If[MemberQ3[b, c], d = {a, "Yes"}; True, d = {a, "No"};
      Map[ClearAll, CNames["Global`"]]; Get["##.mx"]; True]]],
                                      Quiet[DeleteFile["##.mx"]],
                    If[{t} != {} && SymbolQ[t], t = d, Null]}[[1]]]

In[2331]:= CorrectMxQ["c:\\mathematica\\mathtoolbox.mx"]
Out[2331]= True
In[2332]:= CorrectMxQ["c:/mathematica/mathtoolbox.mx", h]
Out[2332]= True
In[2333]:= h
Out[2333]= {"AladjevProcedures`", "Yes"}
In[2334]:= CorrectMxQ["gsv.mx", g]
Out[2334]= False
In[2335]:= g
Out[2335]= "File gsv.mx is corrupted"
In[2336]:= CorrectMxQ["vsv.mx", t]
Out[2336]= True
In[2337]:= t
Out[2337]= {$Failed, "No"}
```

Interconnection of contexts and packages in Mathematica. Because of the importance of the relationships of contexts and packages, the necessity of defining of contexts of symbols arises. Meanwhile, in the current session, there may be symbols of the same name with different contexts whereas the built-in function ***Context*** returns only the ***1st*** context located in the *$ContextPath* list. Meantime the complete result is provided by the procedure whose call ***ContextDef[x]*** returns the list of contexts assigned to a symbol ***x***. Following fragment represents source code of the procedure with examples of its typical application.

```
In[1]:= BeginPackage["RansIan`"]
        GSV::usage = "help on GSV."
        Begin["`GSV`"]
        GSV[x_, y_, z_] := Module[{a = 72}, x*y*z*a]
        End[]
        EndPackage[];
In[7]:= BeginPackage["Tampere`"]
        GSV::usage = "help on GSV."
        Begin["`GSV`"]
        GSV[x_, y_, z_] := Module[{a = 77}, x*y*z*a]
        End[]
        EndPackage[];
```

... GSV: Symbol GSV appears in multiple contexts {Tampere`, RansIan`}; definitions in context Tampere` may shadow or be ... .

```
In[13]:= GSV[x_Integer, z_Integer] := Module[{a = 42}, (x + z)*a]
In[14]:= Context[GSV]
Out[14]= "Tampere`"
In[15]:= $ContextPath
Out[15]= {"Tampere`", "RansIan`", "DocumentationSearch`",
      "ResourceLocator`", "URLUtilities`", "AladjevProcedures`",
                          "PacletManager`", "System`", "Global`"}
In[16]:= ContextDef[x_ /; SymbolQ[x]] :=
              Module[{a = $ContextPath, b = ToString[x], c = {}},
           Do[If[! SameQ[ToString[Quiet[Check[ToExpression[
      "Definition1[" <> ToString1[a[[k]] <> b] <> "]"], "Null"]]],
  "Null"], AppendTo[c, {a[[k]] <> b, If[ToString[Definition[b]] !=
             "Null", "Global`" <> b, Nothing]}]], {k, 1, Length[a]}];
              Map[StringReplace[#, "`" <> ToString[x] -> "`"] &,
                                     DeleteDuplicates[Flatten[c]]]]
In[17]:= ContextDef[GSV]
Out[17]= {"Tampere`", "Global`", "RansIan`"}
In[78]:= DefContext[x_ /; ContextQ[x], y_Symbol] :=
                            Module[{a = $ContextPath, b, c, d},
  If[Set[d, ContextDef[y]] == {} || d == {"Global`"}, Definition[y],
      If[FreeQ[d, x] || FreeQ[a, x], $Failed, a = PrependTo[a, x];
                           b = ToExpression[c = x <> ToString[y]];
                        If[x == "Global`" && ContextDef[y] != {},
  Quiet[Definition2[y][[-2]]], StringReplace[Definition2[b][[1]],
                  {x -> "", ToString[y] <> "`" -> ""}]], $Failed]]]
```

```
In[79]:= DefContext["RansIan`", GSV]
Out[79]= "GSV[x_, y_, z_] := Module[{a = 72}, x*y*z*a]"
In[80]:= DefContext["Tampere`", GSV]
Out[80]= "GSV[x_, y_, z_] := Module[{a = 77}, x*y*z*a]"
In[81]:= DefContext["Global`", GSV]
Out[81]= "GSV[x_Integer, z_Integer] := Module[{a = 42}, (x+z)*a]"
```

Because of the multiplicity admissibility of contexts for a symbol, it is advantageous to have a means for determining the symbol depending on its context. The task is solved by means of a procedure whose source code is represented in the previous fragment and whose call ***DefContext*[*c, s*]** returns the definition of a symbol ***s*** having a context ***c***. If ***s*** is an undefined symbol, the procedure call returns *Null;* if ***c*** is not a context of the ***s*** symbol, then the procedure call returns *$Failed;* if ***s*** is not a symbol, then the procedure call is returned as unevaluated. Thus, at using of the objects of the same name, to avoid misunderstandings it is necessary, generally, to associate them with the contexts which have been ascribed to them.

For receiving access to the package tools it is necessary that a package containing them was uploaded to the current session, and the list defined by means of the ***$ContextPath*** variable has to include the context corresponding to the package. A package can be loaded in any place of the current document by means of the call ***Get*["*context`*"]** or by means of the call ***Needs*["*context`*"]** to define uploading of a package if the context associated with the package is absent in the list defined by ***$Packages*** variable. In a case if package begins with ***BeginPackage*["*Package`*"]**, at its uploading to the lists defined by the variables ***$ContextPath*** and ***$Packages*** only context ***"Package`"*** is placed, providing the access to exports of the package and system means.

If a package uses means of other packages, then the package should begin with the construction ***BeginPackage*["*Package`*", {"*Package1`*", ..., "*Package2`*"}]** with indication of the list of the contexts associated with such packages. It allows to include, in addition, in the system lists ***$ContextPath*** and ***$Packages*** the demanded contexts. With features of uploading of packages the reader can familiarize oneself, in particular, in [6-8,10-15].

When operating with contexts, the question often arises of testing a string expression as a potentially possible context. The system does not have such a tool and it is possible use a simple function whose call ***ContextQ[j]*** returns *True* if *j* is a potentially possible context and *False* otherwise.

```
In[78]:= ContextQ[j_] := StringQ[j] && StringLength[j] > 1 &&
  StringFreeQ[j, "``"] && SymbolQ[StringReplace[j, "`" -> ""]] &&
          StringTake[j, -1] == "`" && ! StringTake[j, 1] === "`"
In[79]:= ContextQ["a2a`b1bb`ccc1`"]
Out[79]= True
In[80]:= ContextQ["aa``bbb`ccc`"]
Out[80]= False
```

A package similarly the procedure allows a nesting; at that, in ***Mathematica*** all subpackages composing it are distinguished and registered. The means defined in the main package, and in its subpackages are fully accessible in the current session after uploading of the nested package as quite visually illustrates a number of simple examples [8-10]. Meanwhile, for performance of the aforesaid it is necessary to redefine system ***$ContextPath*** variable after uploading of the nested package, having added all contexts of subpackages of the main package to the list defined by the ***$ContextPath*** variable. In this context the ***ToContextPath*** procedure automatizes this task, whose call ***ToContextPath***[*x*] provides updating of contents of the current list determined by ***$ContextPath*** variable by adding to its end of all contexts of *m*-file *x* containing in a simple or nested package. Fragment below represents source code of the procedure with an example of use.

```
In[3333]:= ToContextPath[x_/; FileExistsQ[x] &&
    FileExtension[x] == "m"] := Module[{a = ReadString[x], b},
                              b = StringReplace[a, "\n" -> ""];
                      b = StringCases[b, "["~~ Shortest[__] ~~"]"];
                         b = Map[StringTrim[#, ("[" | "]")] &, b];
                 b = Select[b, ContextQ[Quiet[ToExpression[#]]] &];
                         b = ToExpression[DeleteDuplicates[b]];
                 $ContextPath = Flatten[Insert[$ContextPath, b, -3]];
                              DeleteDuplicates[$ContextPath]]
```

```
In[3334]:= ToContextPath[Directory[] <> "\\init.m"]
Out[3334]= {"DocumentationSearch`", "ResourceLocator`",
          "URLUtilities`", "AladjevProcedures`", "PacletManager`",
        "NeuralNetworks`", "NeuralNetworks`Bootstrap`Private`",
          "GeneralUtilities`", "MXNetLink`", "System`", "Global`"}
```

However, because of certain features the use of the nested packages doesn't make a special sense.

Thus, if the call ***Context***[*x*] of built-in function returns the context associated with a symbol *x*, then an interesting enough question of detecting of a *m*–file with a package containing the given context arises. The call ***FindFileContext***[*x*] returns the list of full paths to *m*–files with packages containing the *x* context; in a case of absence of such files the call returns the empty list. In addition, the call ***FindFileContext***[*x, y, z, ...*] with optional {*y, z, ...*} arguments – *the names in string format of devices of external memory of direct access* – provides search of required files on the specified devices instead of all file system of the computer in a case of the procedure call with one actual argument. The search of the required *m*-files is done also in the ***$Recycle.bin*** directory of *Windows* 7 system [12-16]. However, it must be kept in mind, that search within all file system of the computer can demand a rather essential temporal expenditure.

We have created a number of tools [8] for processing of the user packages located in files of type {*cdf, nb, m, mx*}. At that, of particular interest is the procedure for determining whether a file of type *mx* with user package contains the specified tools.

```
In[3332]:= ToolsInMxQ[x_, y_/; FileExistsQ[y] &&
                              FileExtension[y] == "mx", t___] :=
                          Module[{a = Map[ToString, Flatten[{x}]],
                                        b = ContextsInFiles[y], c, d},
  If[MemberQ[$ContextPath, b], MemberQ6[CNames[b], a, t],
          Quiet[Get[y]]; c = MemberQ6[Set[d, CNames[b]], a, t];
                            Map[ClearAll[#] &, d]; $ContextPath =
                          ReplaceAll[$ContextPath, b -> Nothing];
                            Unprotect[$Packages]; $Packages =
 Complement[$Packages, Contexts[StringTake[b, {1, -2}] <> "*"]];
                          SetAttributes[$Packages, Protected]; c]]
```

```
In[3333]:= ToolsInMxQ[{Vz, mm, Gn, nn}, "Agn.mx", t42]
Out[3333]= False
In[3334]:= t42
Out[3334]= {mm, nn}
```

The procedure call ***ToolsInMxQ[x, y, t]*** returns *True* if a tool ***x*** or their list belong to a file ***y*** of ***mx***-type with the user package, and *False* otherwise. At that, through the ***3rd*** optional argument ***t*** – *an undefined symbol* – the list of elements of ***x*** that are absent in the ***y*** file are returned. The procedure uses an useful enough ***MemberQ6*** procedure whose sourse code is represented below.

```
In[2]:= MemberQ6[x_ /; ListQ[x], y_ /; ListQ[y], t___] :=
            Module[{a = {}, b = {}}, Do[If[MemberQ[x, y[[j]]],
                AppendTo[a, True], AppendTo[a, False];
                    AppendTo[b, y[[j]]]], {j, Length[y]}];
                        a = AllTrue[a, # == True &];
                    If[{t} != {} && ! HowAct[t], t = b, 77]; a]
In[3]:= {MemberQ6[{a, b, c, d, g, h}, {a, d, h, u, t, s, w, g, p}, t], t}
Out[3]= {False, {u, t, s, w, p}}
```

The call ***MemberQ6[x, y, t]*** returns *True* if all elements of a list ***y*** belong to a list ***x***, and *False* otherwise. In addition, through the third optional argument ***t*** – *an undefined symbol* – the list of elements of the ***y*** list that are not in the ***x*** list are returned.

In a sense the procedures ***ContextMfile*** and ***ContextNBfile*** are inverse to the procedures ***FindFileContext, FindFileContext1*** and ***ContextInFile,*** their successful calls ***ContextMfile[w]*** and ***ContextNBfile[w]*** return the context associated with a package located in a file ***w*** of formats "***.m***" and {"***.nb***", "***.cdf***"} accordingly; the ***w*** file is set by means of name or full path to it [8,10-16].

Unlike of the procedure ***DeletePackage*** [16] the procedure ***RemovePackage*** is that the symbols determined by the package, removes *completely* so that their names are no longer recognized in the current session. The call ***DeletePackage[x]*** returns *Null,* i. e. nothing, providing removal from the current session of the package, determined by a context ***x,*** including all its exported symbols and accordingly updating the lists determined by the ***$Packages, $ContextPath*** and ***Contexts[]*** variables. Fragment below represents source code of the ***DeletePackage*** procedure along with accompanying examples.

```
In[3331]:= BeginPackage["Package7`"]
        W::usage = "Help on W."
        Begin["`W`"]
        W[x_Integer, y_Integer] := x^2 + y^2
        End[]
        EndPackage[];
In[3337]:= $Packages
Out[3337]= {"Package7`", "DocumentationSearch`", ..., "Global`"}
In[3338]:= $ContextPath
Out[3338]= {"Package7`", "DocumentationSearch`", ..., "Global`"}
In[3339]:= MemberQ[Contexts[], "Package7`"]
Out[3339]= True
In[3340]:= CNames["Package7`"]
Out[3340]= {"W"}
In[3341]:= ? W
Out[3341]= "Help on W."
In[3342]:= DeletePackage[x_] := Module[{a},
    If[! MemberQ[$Packages, x], $Failed, a = Names[x <> "*"];
                          Map[ClearAttributes[#, Protected] &,
  Flatten[{"$Packages", "Contexts", a}]]; Quiet[Map[Remove, a]];
                          $Packages = Select[$Packages, # != x &];
                    $ContextPath = Select[$ContextPath, # != x &];
      Contexts[] = Select[Contexts[], StringCount[#, x] == 0 &];
                          Quiet[Map[Remove, Names[x <> "*"]]];
               Map[SetAttributes[#, Protected] &, {"$Packages",
                                                   "Contexts"}];]]
In[3343]:= DeletePackage["Package7`"]
In[3344]:= $Packages
Out[3344]= {"DocumentationSearch`", ...,"System`", "Global`"}
In[3345]:= $ContextPath
Out[3345]= {"DocumentationSearch`", ..., "System`", "Global`"}
In[3346]:= CNames["Package7`"]
Out[3346]= {}
In[3347]:= ?W
Out[3347]= Missing["UnknownSymbol", "W"]
In[3348]:= MemberQ[Contexts[], "Package7`"]
Out[3348]= False
```

Context management is discussed in sufficient detail in [4, 6,8-15] along with a number of software means focused on the operating with contexts and associated with them objects. In particular, the procedure below is quite interesting whose call ***AllContexts***[] returns list of contexts that contain in the system packages of the current ***Mathematica*** version, whereas the call ***AllContexts***[*x*] returns *True*, if *x* is a context of the above type, and *False* otherwise. The fragment represents source code of the procedure along with typical examples of its application.

```
In[2247]:= AllContexts[y___] := Module[{a = Directory[], c, h,
                    b = SetDirectory[$InstallationDirectory]},
                    b = FileNames[{"*.m", "*.tr"}, {"*"}, Infinity];
  h[x_] := StringReplace[StringJoin[Map[FromCharacterCode,
  BinaryReadList[x]]], {"\n" -> "", "\r" -> "", "\t" -> "", " " -> "",
                                              "{" -> "", "}" -> ""}];
              c = Flatten[Select[Map[StringCases[h[#],
              {"BeginPackage[\"" ~~ Shortest[W__] ~~ "`\"]",
                     "Needs[\"" ~~ Shortest[W__] ~~ "`\"]",
                     "Begin[\"" ~~ Shortest[W__] ~~ "`\"]",
                     "Get[\"" ~~ Shortest[W__] ~~ "`\"]",
   "Package[\"" ~~ Shortest[W__] ~~ "`\"]"}] &, b], # != {} &]];
   c = DeleteDuplicates[Select[c, StringFreeQ[#, {"*", "="}] &]];
              SetDirectory[a]; c = Flatten[Append[Select[Map[
            StringReplace[StringTake[#, {1, -2}], {"Get[" -> "",
          "Begin[" -> "", "Needs[" -> "", "BeginPackage[" -> "",
            "Package[" -> ""}, 1] &, c], # != "\"`Private`\"" &],
                {"\"Global`\"", "\"CloudObjectLoader`\""}]];
  c = Map[ToExpression, Sort[Select[DeleteDuplicates[Flatten[
        Map[If[StringFreeQ[#, ","], #, StringSplit[#, ","]] &, c]]],
StringFreeQ[#, {"<>", "]", "["}] && StringTake[#, {1, 2}] != "\"`" &]]];
                                     f[{y} != {}, MemberQ[c, y], c]]

In[2248]:= AllContexts[]
Out[2248]= "AnatomyGraphics3D`", ..., "ZeroMQLink`"}
In[2249]:= Length[%]
Out[2249]= 1633
In[2250]:= AllContexts["PresenterTools`PresenterTools`"]
Out[2250]= True
```

As it was noted in [15], for each exported object of a certain package for it it is necessary to determine an ***usage.*** As a result of loading of such package into the current session all its *exports* will be available whereas the local objects, located in a section, in particular ***Private,*** will be inaccessible in the current session. For testing of a package loaded to the current session or loaded package which is located in a ***m–***file regarding existence in it of global and local objects the procedure ***DefInPackage*** can be used, whose the call ***DefInPackage[x],*** where ***x*** defines a *file* or *full path* to it, or *context* associated with the package returns the nested list, whose the first element defines the package context, the second element – the list of local variables whereas the third element – the list of global variables of the ***x*** package. If the ***x*** argument doesn't define a package or context, the procedure call ***DefInPackage[x]*** is returned unevaluated. In a case of an unusable ***x*** context the procedure call returns *$Failed.* Fragment represents source code of the ***DefInPackage*** procedure with the most typical examples of its application.

```
In[7]:= DefInPackage[x_/; MfilePackageQ[x] | | ContextQ[x]] :=
  Module[{a, b = {"Begin[\"`", "`\"]"}, c = "BeginPackage[\"", d,
                                                  p, g, t, k = 1, f, n = x},
  Label[Avz];
          If[ContextQ[n] && Contexts[n] != {}, f = "#"; Save[f, x];
                 g = FromCharacterCode[17]; t = n <> "Private`";
              a = ReadFullFile[f, g]; DeleteFile[f]; d = CNames[n];
                                            p = SubsString[a, {t, g}];
  p = DeleteDuplicates[Map[StringCases[#, t ~~ Shortest[___] ~~ "["
                          <> t ~~ Shortest[___] ~~ " := "] &, p]];
                    p = Map[StringTake[#, {StringLength[t] + 1,
            Flatten[StringPosition[#, "["]][[1]] - 1}] &, Flatten[p]];
  {n, DeleteDuplicates[p], d}, If[FileExistsQ[n], a = ReadFullFile[n];
            f = StringTake[SubsString[a, {c, "`\"]"}], {15, -3}][[1]];
                  If[MemberQ[$Packages, f], n = f; Goto[Avz]];
                                         b = StringSplit[a, "*)(*"];
  d = Select[b, ! StringFreeQ[StringReplace[#, " " -> ""], "::usage="] &];
 d = Map[StringTake[#, {1, Flatten[StringPosition[#, "::"]][[1]] - 1}] &, d];
             p = DeleteDuplicates[Select[b, StringDependAllQ[#,
```

```
                              {"Begin[\"`", "`\"]"}] &]];
   p = MinusList[Map[StringTake[#, {9, -4}] &, p], {"Private"}];
   t = Flatten[StringSplit[SubsString[a, {"Begin[\"`Private`\"]",
               "End[]"}], "*)(*"]]; If[t == {}, {f, MinusList[d, p], p},
               g = Map[StringReplace[#, " " -> ""] &, t[[2 ;; -1]]];
                            g = Select[g, ! StringFreeQ[#, ":="] &];
g = Map[StringTake[#, {1, Flatten[StringPosition[#, ":"]][[1]] - 1}] &, g];
g = Map[Quiet[Check[StringTake[#, {1, Flatten[StringPosition[#,
                  "["]][[1]] - 1}], #]] &, g]; {f, g, d}], $Failed]]]
In[8]:= DefInPackage["C:\\Mathematica\\MathToolBox.m"]
Out[8]:= {"AladjevProcedures`", {}, {"AcNb", "ActBFM", ...,
  "$UserContexts1", "$UserContexts2", "$Version1","$Version2"}}
In[9]:= Length[%[[3]]]
Out[9]= 1327
```

In a number of cases there is a need of full removal from the current session of a package loaded to it. Partially the given problem is solved by the standard functions ***Clear*** and ***Remove,*** however they don't clear the lists that are defined by variables ***$ContextPath, $Packages*** along with the call ***Contexts***[] off the package information. This problem is solved by means of the ***DeletePackage*** procedure whose the call ***DeletePackage***[*x*] will return *Null,* in addition, completely removing from the current session a package defined by *x* context, including all exports of the *x* package and respectively updating the above system lists. Fragment below represents source code of the ***DeletePackage*** procedure with the most typical example of its application.

```
In[2247]:= DeletePackage[x_] := Module[{a},
     If[! MemberQ[$Packages, x], $Failed, a = Names[x <> "*"];
                            Map[ClearAttributes[#, Protected] &,
                            Flatten[{"$Packages", "Contexts", a}]];
Quiet[Map[Remove, a]]; $Packages = Select[$Packages, # != x &];
                $ContextPath = Select[$ContextPath, # != x &];
     Contexts[] = Select[Contexts[], StringCount[#, x] == 0 &];
                          Quiet[Map[Remove, Names[x <> "*"]]];
Map[SetAttributes[#, Protected] &, {"$Packages", "Contexts"}];]]
In[2248]:= DeletePackage["AladjevProcedures`"]
In[2249]:= ?DeletePackage
Out[2249]= Missing["UnknownSymbol", "DeletePackage"]
```

Natural addition to the ***DeletePackage*** and ***RemovePackage*** procedures is the procedure ***DelOfPackage*** providing removal from the current session of the given tools of a loaded package. Its call ***DelOfPackage[x, y]*** returns the *y* list of tools names of a package given by its *x* context which have been removed from the current session. Whereas the call ***DelOfPackage[x, y, z]*** with the third optional *z* argument - a ***mx***-file - returns 2-element list whose the first element defines ***mx***-file *z*, while the second element defines the *y* list of tools of a package *x* that have been removed from the current session and have been saved in ***mx***-file *z*. At that, only tools of *y* which are contained in *x* package will be removed. The fragment below represents source code of the ***DelOfPackage*** procedure with typical examples of its use.

```
In[7]:= DelOfPackage[x_/; ContextQ[x], y_/; SymbolQ[y] ||
     (ListQ[y] && AllTrue[Map[SymbolQ, y], TrueQ]), z___] :=
        Module[{a, b, c}, If[! MemberQ[$Packages, x], $Failed,
                    If[Set[b, Intersection[Names[x <> "*"],
             a = Map[ToString, Flatten[{y}]]]] == {}, $Failed,
          If[{z} != {} && StringQ[z] && SuffPref[z, ".mx", 2],
        ToExpression["DumpSave[" <> ToString1[z] <> "," <>
                    ToString[b] <> "]"]; c = {z, b}, c = b];
        ClearAttributes[b, Protected]; Map[Remove, b]; c]]]
In[8]:= DelOfPackage["AladjevProcedures`", {Mapp, Map1}, "#.mx"]
Out[8]= {"#.mx", {"Map1", "Mapp"}}
```

The ***IsPackageQ*** procedure [8] is intended for testing of any ***mx***-file regarding existence of the user package in it along with upload of such package into the current session. The call of the ***IsPackageQ[x]*** procedure returns $*Failed* if the ***mx***-file doesn't contain a package, *True* if the package that is in the *x* ***mx***-file is uploaded to the current session, and *False* otherwise. Moreover, the procedure call ***IsPackageQ[x, y]*** through the *second* optional *y* argument - *an indefinite variable* - returns the context associated with the package uploaded to the current session. In addition, is supposed that the *x* file is recognized by the testing standard function ***FileExistsQ***, otherwise the procedure call is returned unevaluated. The use examples the reader can found in [8-15].

5.3. *Additional tools of operating with the user packages*

Tools of the ***Mathematica*** for operating with datafiles can be subdivided to two groups conditionally: *the tools supporting the work with files which are automatically recognized at addressing to them,* and *the tools supporting the work with files as a whole*. This theme is quite extensive and is in more detail considered in [8], here some additional tools of working with files containing the user packages will be considered. Since tools of access to files of formats, even automatically recognized by ***Mathematica,*** don't solve a number of important problems, the user is compelled to program own means on the basis of standard tools and perhaps with use of own means. Qua of a rather useful example we will represent the procedure whose call ***DefFromPackage[x]*** returns **3**–element list, whose first element is definition in string format of some symbol ***x*** whose context is different from {"***System`***", "***Global`***"}, the second element defines its usage while the third element defines attributes of the ***x*** symbol. In addition, on the symbols associated with **2** specified contexts, the procedure call returns only list of their attributes. The fragment represents the source code of the ***DefFromPackage*** procedure with examples of its typical application.

```
In[327]:= DefFromPackage[x_/; SymbolQ[x]] := Module[{b = "",
    a = Context[x], c = "", p, d = ToString[x], k = 1, h},
  If[MemberQ[{"Global`", "System`"}, a], Return[Attributes[x]],
   h = a <> d; ToExpression["Save[" <> ToString1[d] <> "," <>
    ToString1[h] <> "]"]];
  For[k, k < Infinity, k++, c = Read[d, String];
   If[c === " ", Break[], b = b <> c]];
  p = StringReplace[RedSymbStr[b, " ", " "], h <> "`" -> ""];
  {c, k, b} = {"", 1, ""};
  For[k, k < Infinity, k++, c = Read[d, String];
   If[c === " " || c === EndOfFile, Break[], b = b <>
    If[StringTake[c, {-1, -1}] == "\\", StringTake[c, {1, -2}], c]]];
  DeleteFile[Close[d]]; {p, StringReplace[b, " /: " <> d -> ""],
   Attributes[x]}]

In[328]:= DefFromPackage[StrStr]

Out[328]= {"StrStr[x_] := If[StringQ[x], StringJoin["\"", x, "\""],
```

```
ToString[x]]", "StrStr::usage = "The call StrStr[x] returns an
    expression x in string format if x is different from string;
        otherwise, the double string obtained from an
                expression x is returned.", {}}
```

The ***DefFromPackage*** procedure serves for obtaining of full information on ***x*** symbol whose definition is located in the user package uploaded into the current session. Unlike the standard functions ***FilePrint*** and ***Definition*** this procedure, first, doesn't print, but returns specified information completely available for subsequent processing, and, secondly, this information is returned in an optimum format. At that, in a number of cases the output of definition of a symbol that is located in an active package by the standard means is accompanied with a context associated with the package which complicates its viewing, and also its subsequent processing. Result of the ***DefFromPackage*** call also obviates this problem. The algorithm realized by the procedure is based on analysis of structure of a file received in result of saving of a *"y'x"* context, where ***x*** – a symbol at the call ***DefFromPackage***[***x***] and *"y'"* – a context, associated with the uploaded package containing the definition of ***x*** symbol. In more detail the algorithm realized by the ***DefFromPackage*** is visible from its source code.

As the *2nd* example extending the algorithm of the previous procedure in the light of application of functions of access it is possible to represent an useful ***FullCalls*** procedure whose the call ***FullCalls***[***x***] returns the list whose *1st* element is the context associated with a package loaded in the current session, while its other elements – the symbols of this package which are used by the user procedure or function ***x,*** or nested list of sublists of the above type at using by the ***x*** of symbols *(names of procedures or functions)* from several packages. Source code of the ***FullCalls*** procedure and an example of its application are represented in the following fragment.

```
In[7]:= FullCalls[x_/; ProcQ[x] || FunctionQ[x]] :=
            Module[{a = {}, b, d, c = "::usage = ", k = 1},
                Save[b = ToString[x], x];
```

```
For[k, k < Infinity, k++, d = Read[b, String];
If[d === EndOfFile, Break[], If[StringFreeQ[d, c], Continue[],
AppendTo[a, StringSplit[StringTake[d,
{1, Flatten[StringPosition[d, c]][[1]] - 1}], " /: "][[1]]]]]];
a = Select[a, SymbolQ[#] &]; DeleteFile[Close[b]];
a = Map[{#, Context[#]} &, DeleteDuplicates[a]];
a = If[Length[a] == 1, a, Map[DeleteDuplicates, Map[Flatten,
Gather[a, #1[[2]] === #2[[2]] &]]]]; {d, k} = {{}, 1};
While[k <= Length[a], b = Select[a[[k]], ContextQ[#] &];
c = Select[a[[k]], ! ContextQ[#] &];
AppendTo[d, Flatten[{b, Sort[c]}]]; k++];
d = MinusList[If[Length[d] == 1, Flatten[d], d], {ToString[x]}];
If[d == {Context[x]}, {}, d]]
In[8]:= FullCalls[DefFromPackage]
Out[8]= {"AladjevProcedures`", "GenRules", "ListListQ", "Map3",
"Map13", "Map9", "RedSymbStr", "StrDelEnds", "StringMultiple",
"SuffPref", "SymbolQ", "SymbolQ1", "ToString1"}
```

Thus, the procedure call ***FullCalls*[*x*]** provides possibility of testing of the user procedure or function, different from built-in means, regarding using by it of means whose definitions are in packages loaded into the current session. In development of the procedure the ***FullCalls1*** procedure can be offered with whose source code and typical examples of its use the interested reader can familiarize in [8,16]. In addition, both procedures ***FullCalls*** and ***FullCalls1*** are rather useful at programming a number of appendices with which can familiarize in [7-12,14,15].

In a number of cases there is a necessity for uploading into the current session of the system ***Mathematica*** not entirely of a package, but only separate tools contained in it, for example, of a procedure or function, or their list. In the following fragment a procedure is represented, whose call ***ExtrOfMfile*[*x, y*]** returns *Null*, i.e. nothing, loading in the current session the definitions only of those tools that are defined by an ***y*** argument and are located in a file ***x*** of ***m***–format. In addition, at existence in the ***m***–file of several tools of the same name, the last is uploaded in the current session. While the call ***ExtrOfMfile*[*x, y, z*]** with the third optional ***z*** argument – *an indefinite variable* – in addition, through *z* returns the list of definitions of *y* tools which will be located in the *m*–file *x*. In a case of absence in the *m*–file *x* of *y* tools the procedure call returns *$Failed*. The following fragment represents source code of the ***ExtrOfMfile*** procedure along with typical examples of its application.

```
In[6]:= ExtrOfMfile[f_/; FileExistsQ[f] && FileExtension[f] == "m",
   s_/; StringQ[s] | | ListQ[s], z___] := Module[{Vsv, p = {}, v, m},
                                            m = ReadFullFile[f];
   If[StringFreeQ[m, Map["(*Begin[\"`" <> # <> "`\"]*)" &,
                                   Map[ToString, s]]], $Failed,
   Vsv[x_, y_] := Module[{a = m, b = FromCharacterCode[17],
   c = FromCharacterCode[24], d = "(*Begin[\"`" <> y <> "`\"]*)",
         h = "(*End[]*)", g = {}, t}, a = StringReplace[a, h -> c];
                                   If[StringFreeQ[a, d], $Failed,
   While[! StringFreeQ[a, d], a = StringReplace[a, d -> b, 1];
   t = StringTake[SubStrSymbolParity1[a, b, c][[1]], {4, -4}];
                  t = StringReplace[t, {"(*" -> "", "*)" -> ""}];
   AppendTo[g, t]; a = StringReplace[a, b -> "", 1]; Continue[]];
                                 {g, ToExpression[g[[-1]]]}]];
   If[StringQ[s], v = Quiet[Check[Vsv[f, s][[1]], $Failed]],
   Map[{v = Quiet[Check[Vsv[f, #][[1]], $Failed]], AppendTo[p, v]} &,
                                             Map[ToString, s]]];
   If[{z} != {} && ! HowAct[z], z = If[StringQ[s], v, p]]; ]]
In[7]:= Clear[StrStr]
In[8]:= Definition[StrStr]
Out[8]= Null
In[9]:= ExtrOfMfile["c:/mathematica/MathToolBox.m", "StrStr"]
In[10]:= Definition[StrStr]
Out[10]= StrStr[x_] := If[StringQ[x], " <> x <> ", ToString[x]]
```

It should be noted that this procedure can be quite useful in a case of need of recovery in the current session of the damaged means without uploading of the user packages containing their definitions. In a certain measure, to the previous procedure the ***ExtrDefFromM*** procedure adjoins whose call ***ExtrDefFromM[x, y]*** in tabular form returns an usage and definition of a means *y* contained in a *m*–file *x* with the user package. This tool doesn't demand loading of the *m*–file *x* in the current session, allowing in it selectively to activate the means of the user package.

At last, the procedure ***ContextsInFiles*** provides evaluation of the context ascribed to a file of the format {***"m", "mx", "cdf", "nb"***}. The procedure call ***ContextsInFiles[w]*** returns the single context ascribed to a file ***w*** of the above formats. At absence of a context the call returns *$Failed*. In addition, it must be kept in mind that the context in files of the specified format is sought relative to the key word *"BeginPackage"* that is typically used at beginning of a package. A return of list of format {***"Context1", ..., "Contextp"***} is equivalent to existence in a ***m***–file of a certain construction of format ***BeginPackage["context1`", {"context2`", ..., "contextp`"}]*** where {***"context2`", ..., "contextp`"***} determines uploadings of the appropriate files if their contexts aren't in the ***$Packages*** variable. The next fragment represents source code of the procedure with the most typical examples of its use.

```
In[47]:= ContextsInFiles[x_/; FileExistsQ[x] &&
              MemberQ[{"m", "mx", "cdf", "nb"}, FileExtension[x]]] :=
                Module[{a = StringReplace[ReadFullFile[x], {" " -> "",
                                           "\n" -> "", "\t" -> ""}], b, b1,
                               d = Flatten[{Range[65, 90], Range[96, 122]}]},
                            If[FileExtension[x] == "m", b = StringCases[a,
                            Shortest["BeginPackage[\"" ~~ __ ~~ "`\"]"]];
  If[b === {}, b = $Failed, b = Map[StringTake[#, {15, -3}] &, b][[1]]];
  b1 = StringCases[a, Shortest["BeginPackage[\"" ~~ __ ~~ "`\"}]"]];
     If[b1 === {}, b1 = $Failed, If[! StringFreeQ[b1[[1]], {"{", "}"}],
       b1 = StringReplace[b1[[1]], {"{" -> "", "}" -> "", "\"" -> ""}];
    b1 = StringSplit[StringTake[b1, {14, -2}], ","], b1 = $Failed]]];
                              b = DeleteDuplicates[Flatten[{b, b1}]];
                                   SetAttributes[ContextQ, Listable];
         b = Select[b, AllTrue[Flatten[ContextQ[{#}]], TrueQ] &];
    If[ListQ[b] && Length[DeleteDuplicates[b]] == 1, b[[1]], b],
    If[FileExtension[x] == "mx", Quiet[Check[b = StringCases[a,
                      Shortest["CONT" ~~ __ ~~ "ENDCONT"]][[1]];
  b = Flatten[Map[ToCharacterCode, Characters[StringReplace[b,
                              {"CONT" -> "", "ENDCONT" -> ""}]]]];
                        StringJoin[Map[FromCharacterCode[#] &,
                           Select[b, MemberQ[d, #] &]]], $Failed]],
    Quiet[Check[a = StringCases[a, Shortest["BeginPackage\",
```

```
\"[\",\"\\\"\\<" ~~ __ ~~ "`\\>\\\"\",\"]\"}]"]][[1]];
                    a = StringReplace[a, "BeginPackage" -> ""];
        b = Flatten[Map[ToCharacterCode, Characters[a]]];
              StringJoin[Map[FromCharacterCode[#] &,
              Select[b, MemberQ[d, #] &]]], $Failed]]]]
```

```
In[48]:= ContextsInFiles["C:\\mathematica\\mathtoolbox.mx"]
Out[48]= "AladjevProcedures`"
In[49]:= ContextsInFiles[$InstallationDirectory <>\\SystemFiles\\
              components\\ccodegenerator\\CCodeGenerator.m"]
Out[49]= {"CCodeGenerator`", "CompiledFunctionTools`",
          "CompiledFunctionTools`Opcodes`", "SymbolicC`",
          "CCompilerDriver`"}
```

In addition to the previous ***ContextsInFiles*** procedure the ***ContextsFromFiles*** procedure allows to extract contexts from files of any format that are located in the set directories or are given by own full or short names. The call ***ContextsFromFiles*[]** without arguments returns the sorted list of contexts from all files located in the catalog ***$InstallationDirectory*** and in all its subdirectories whereas the call ***ContextsFromFiles*[*x*]** returns the sorted list of contexts from all files located in a directory ***x*** and in all its *subdirectories*, at last the call ***ContextsFromFiles*[*x*]** on an existing ***x*** file returns the sorted list of contexts from the ***x*** file. The unsuccessful means call returns *$Failed* or is returned unevaluated. The next fragment represents source code of the procedure with the most typical examples of its application.

```
In[2226]:= ContextsFromFiles[x___String] :=
    Module[{a = If[{x} == {}, FileNames["*", $InstallationDirectory,
          Infinity], If[DirQ[x], FileNames["*", x, Infinity],
    If[FileExistsQ[x], {x}, $Failed]]], b}, If[a === $Failed, $Failed,
 b = Select[Map[Quiet[StringReplace[#, {": " -> "", " " -> "", "\"" -> ""}]] &,
    Flatten[Map[StringCases[Quiet[Check[ReadFullFile[#], ""]],
  (Shortest[": " ~~ __ ~~ "` "] | Shortest["\"" ~~ __ ~~ "`\""]) ..] &, a]]],
          ContextQ[#] &]; Sort[DeleteDuplicates[b]]]]
```

```
In[2227]:= ContextsFromFiles[$InstallationDirectory <>
          "\\AddOns\\Applications\\AuthorTools\\Kernel"]
Out[2227]= {"AuthorTools`", "AuthorTools`MakeBilateralCells`"}
```

Note, the above procedure operates on platforms *Windows* ***XP*** *Professional* and *Windows* ***7*** *Professional.* The performance of the procedure is higher if it is applied to a ***mx***-file.

The binary ***mx***–files are *optimized* for fast loading. Wherein, they cannot be exchanged between different operating systems or versions of the ***Mathematica.*** Any ***mx***–file contains version of ***Mathematica,*** the type of operating system in which it has been created and the context if it will exist. The procedure call ***ContextMathOsMx*[*x*]** returns the three–element list whose the first element determines the context if it exists *(otherwise,* **$***Failed is returned),* the second element defines the list whose elements define version, releases of the ***Mathematica*** and the *3rd* element defines operating system in which a ***mx***–file ***x*** has been created.

In view of distinctions of the ***mx***–files created on different platforms there is a natural expediency of creation of the tools testing a ***mx***–file regarding the platform in which it was created in virtue of the ***DumpSave*** function. The ***TypeWinMx*** procedure is one of such tools. The procedure call ***TypeWinMx*[*x*]** in string format returns type of operating platform on which a ***mx***–file ***x*** was created; correct result is returned for a case of the *Windows* platform, whereas on other platforms **$***Failed* is returned. This is conditioned at absence of a possibility to carry out debugging on other platforms. The next fragment represents source code of the ***TypeWinMx*** procedure with examples of its application.

```
In[3339]:= TypeWinMx[x_ /; FileExistsQ[x] &&
                    FileExtension[x] == "mx"] := Module[{a, b, c, d},
        If[StringFreeQ[$OperatingSystem, "Windows"], $Failed,
                    a = StringJoin[Select[Characters[ReadString[x]],
  SymbolQ[#] | | Quiet[IntegerQ[ToExpression[#]]] | | # == "-" &]];
                    d = Map[FromCharacterCode, Range[2, 27]];
                    b = StringPosition[a, {"CONT", "ENDCONT"}];
                                      If[b[[1]][[2]] == b[[2]][[2]],
        c = StringCases1[a, {"Windows", "ENDCONT"}, "___"],
                    b = StringPosition[a, {"Windows", "CONT"}];
                    c = StringTake[a, {b[[1]][[1]], b[[2]][[2]]}]];
                    c = StringReplace[c, Flatten[{GenRules[d, ""],
        "ENDCONT" -> "", "CONT" -> ""}]]; If[ListQ[c], c[[1]], c]]]

In[3340]:= TypeWinMx["c:\\mathematica\\mathToolBox.mx"]
Out[3340]= "Windows-x86-64"
```

A quite certain interest is the question of occurrence in the definition of the user tools of the tools calls other than built-in tools. The ***FullContent*** procedure solves this problem. Calling ***FullContent*[*x*]** procedure returns the sorted list containing all names in string format of the user tools whose calls are in definition of a tool *x*. Whereas the call ***FullContent*[*x, y*]** with the *2nd* optional *y* argument – *an indefinite symbol* – additionally through it returns the nested list of the above tools with contexts ascribed to them; the list is gathered according to the contexts. In addition, a context is the first in the list of the tools names with this context. Indeed, the name *x* is included in the returned list too. The following fragment represents the source code of the ***FullContent*** procedure with examples of its application.

```
In[42]:= FullContent[x_, y___] := Module[{a, b, c, n, m},
  If[MemberQ[{FullContent, "FullContent"}, x],
    c = FullContent[ProcQ], a = Save["###", x];
  a = StringReplace[ReadString["###"], {"\n" -> "", "\r" -> ""}];
  b = StringCases[a, Shortest[" /: " ~~ __ ~~ "::usage ="]];
  DeleteFile["#"]; c = Map[{n = StringReplace[#, "::usage =" -> ""];
    m = Flatten[StringPosition[n, " /: "]];
    StringTake[n, {m[[-1]] + 1, -1}]} &, b];
  c = Sort[DeleteDuplicates[Map[StringTrim[#, "\\"] &, Flatten[c]]]]];
  If[{y} != {} && ! HowAct[y], y = Map[{#, Context[#]} &, c];
    y = Gather[y, #1[[2]] == #2[[2]] &];
  y = Sort[Map[Sort[DeleteDuplicates[Flatten[#]]] &, y],
    If[ContextQ[#1], #1, #2] &]; c, c]]
In[43]:= FullContent[ProcQ, gs]
Out[43]= {"Attributes1", "BlockFuncModQ", "ClearAllAttributes",
"Contexts1", "Definition2", "HeadPF", "HowAct", "ListStrToStr",
"Map3", "Mapp", "MinusList", "ProcQ", "ReduceLists", "ProtectedQ",
"PureDefinition", "StrDelEnds", "SuffPref", "SymbolQ", "SysFuncQ",
"SystemQ", "ToString1", "UnevaluatedQ"}
In[44]:= gs
Out[44]= {{"AladjevProcedures`", "Attributes1", ..., "Map3", ...,
"SymbolQ", "SysFuncQ", "SystemQ", "ToString1", "UnevaluatedQ"}}
In[45]:= {FullContent[LoadMxQ, vg], vg}
Out[45]= {{"LoadMxQ", "MxOnOpSys", "StrDelEnds", "StringCases2",
"SuffPref", "ToString1"}, {{"AladjevProcedures`", "LoadMxQ",
"MxOnOpSys", "StrDelEnds", "StringCases2", "SuffPref", "ToString1"}}
```

The *mx*-format is serialized package format. As a rule it is used for the distribution of both system and user packages. The binary file format is the optimized for fast loading. Meantime, as noted above, the *mx-format* files can`t be exchanged between operating platforms which differ from the predefined variable *$SystemWordLength* which gives the number of bits in machine words on the computer system where ***Mathematica*** is running. Furthermore, the *mx*-format files created by newer versions of ***Mathematica*** may not be usable by older versions. This raises the issue of testing the ability to load an arbitrary file of the *mx*-format into the current session. The following procedure solves this problem. The fragment below represents the source code of the ***LoadMxQ*** procedure with examples of its application.

```
In[7]:= LoadMxQ[x_/; FileExistsQ[x] && FileExtension[x] == "mx"] :=
                                        Module[{a, b, c, MxOnOpSys},
  MxOnOpSys[y_/; FileExistsQ[y] && FileExtension[y] == "mx"] :=
        Module[{a = ReadString[y], b = "Get.*)", c = "CONT", d},
                                   d = StringCases2[a, {b, c}][[1]];
  d = StringReplace[d, {b -> "", c -> "", "\n" -> "", "END" -> ""}];
                 d = StringJoin[Map[If[MemberQ[Range[32, 127],
       ToCharacterCode[#][[1]]], #, Nothing] &, Characters[d]]]];
                             g[t_] := t; DumpSave["###.mx", g];
                If[MxOnOpSys[x] == MxOnOpSys["###.mx"],
     DeleteFile["###.mx"]; True, DeleteFile["###.mx"]; False]]
In[8]:= LoadMxQ["C:\\Mathematica\\MathToolBox.mx"]
Out[8]= True
In[9]:= LoadMxQ["dump.mx"]
Out[9]= True
```

Calling procedure ***LoadMxQ[x]*** returns *True* if a *mx*-type file ***x*** was created on the current operating platform and can be loaded into the current ***Mathematica*** session by the ***Get[x]*** call, and *False* otherwise. In our works [8-16] a number of means for various processing of *mx*-files with interesting examples using in programming of various applications is presented. However, these tools have been debugged on *Windows* ***XP*** and *Windows* ***7*** platforms, in other cases requiring sometimes re-debugging.

References

1. ***Aladjev V.Z., Vaganov V.A.*** *Modular programming:* ***Mathematica*** *vs* ***Maple****, and vice versa.*- USA: Palo Alto, Fultus Corporation, 2011, ISBN 9781596822689, 418 p.

2. ***Aladjev V.Z. et al.*** Programming: System ***Maple*** or ***Mathematica?***- Ukraine: Kherson, Oldi-Plus Press, 2011, ISBN 9789662393460, 474 p.

3. ***Aladjev V.Z., Boiko V.K., Rovba E.A.*** Programming in systems ***Mathematica*** and ***Maple:*** A Comparative Aspect.- Grodno, Grodno State University, 2011, 517 p.

4. ***Aladjev V.Z., Grinn D.S., Vaganov V.A.*** The extended functional tools for system ***Mathematica.***- Kherson: Oldi-Plus Press, 2012, ISBN 9789662393590, 404 p.

5. ***Aladjev V.Z., Grinn D.S.*** Extension of functional environment of system ***Mathematica.***- Kherson: Oldi-Plus Press, 2012, ISBN 9789662393729, 552 p.

6. ***Aladjev V.Z., Grinn D.S., Vaganov V.A.*** The selected system problems in software environment of system ***Mathematica.***- Ukraine: Kherson: Oldi-Plus Press, 2013, 556 p.

7. ***Aladjev V.Z., Vaganov V.A.*** Extension of ***Mathematica*** system functionality.- USA: CreateSpace, An Amazon.com Company, 2015, ISBN 9781514237823, 590 p.

8. ***Aladjev V.Z., Vaganov V.*** Toolbox for the ***Mathematica*** programmers.- USA, CreateSpace, An Amazon.com Company, 2016, ISBN 1532748833, 630 p.

9. ***Aladjev V.Z., Boiko V.K., Shishakov M.L.*** The Art of programming in ***Mathematica*** System.- Estonia: Tallinn, TRG Press, 2016, ISBN 9789985950890, 735 p.

10. ***Aladjev V.Z., Boiko V.K., Shishakov M.L.*** The Art of programming in ***Mathematica*** system. *2nd edition.*- USA, Lulu Press, 2016, ISBN 9781365560736, 735 p.

11. ***Aladjev V.Z., Shishakov M.L.*** Software etudes in the ***Mathematica.***- CreateSpace, An Amazon.com Company, 2017, 614 p., ISBN 1979037272

12. ***Aladjev V.Z., Shishakov M.L.*** Software etudes in the

Mathematica.- Amazon Digital Services, ASIN: B0775YSH72, 2017, ***www.amazon.com/dp/B0775YSH72***

13. *Aladjev V.Z., Shishakov M.L., Vaganov V.A.* Practical programming in ***Mathematica.*** Fifth edition.- USA: Lulu Press, 2017, 613 p.

14. *Aladjev V.Z., Boiko V.K., Grinn D.S., Haritonov V.A., Hunt Ü., Rouba Y.A., Shishakov M.L., Vaganov V.A.* Books miscellany on Cellular Automata, General Statistics Theory, ***Maple*** and ***Mathematica.***- Estonia: Tallinn, TRG Press, *CD-edition*, 2016.

15. *Aladjev V.Z., Boiko V.K., Gostev A., Hunt Ü., Rouba E., Shishakov M.L., Grinn D.S., Vaganov V.A.* Selected Books and software published by members of Baltic branch of the Intern. Academy of Noosphere.- Tallinn: TRG press, 2019, *CD-edition*, ISBN 978-9949-9876-3-4

16. *Aladjev V.Z.* Package of Procedures and Functions for ***Mathematica.***- TRG: Tallinn, 2018; this package can be freely downloaded from sites ***https://yadi.sk/d/oC5lXLWa3PVEhi***, ***https://yadi.sk/d/2GyQU2pQ3ZETZT***.

17. *Aladjev V.Z.* Modular programming: ***Mathematica*** *or* ***Maple*** - A subjective standpoint / Int. school «*Mathematical and computer modeling of fundamental objects and phenomena in systems of computer mathematics*».- Kazan: Kazan Univ. Press, 2014.

18. *V.Z. Aladjev, V.K. Boiko.* Tools for computer research of cellular automata dynamics / Intern. school «*Mathematical modelling of fundamental objects and phenomena in the systems of computer mathematics*»; Int. scientific and practical conference «*Information Technologies in Science and Education*» *(ITON-2017)*, November 4 - 6, 2017, Kazan, pp. 7 - 16.

19. *https://bbian.webs.com/Our_publications_2019.pdf*

20. *Aladjev V.Z., Shishakov M.L.* Introduction into mathematical package ***Mathematica 2.2.***- Moscow: Filin Press, 1997, 363 p., ISBN 5895680046 *(in Russian with English summary)*

21. *Aladjev V.Z., Vaganov V.A., Hunt Ü.J., Shishakov M.L.* Introduction into environment of mathematical package ***Maple V.***- Minsk: International Academy of Noosphere, the Baltic Branch, 1998, 452 p., ISBN 1406425698 *(in Russian)*

22. ***Aladjev V.Z., Vaganov V.A., Hunt Ü., Shishakov M.L.*** Programming in environment of mathematical package ***Maple V.***- Minsk-Moscow: Russian Ecology Academy, 1999, 470 p., ISBN 4101212982 *(in Russian with English summary)*

23. ***Aladjev V.Z., Bogdevicius M.A.*** Solution of physical, technical and mathematical problems with ***Maple V.***- Tallinn-Vilnius, TRG, 1999, 686 p., ISBN 9986053986 *(in Russian)*

24. ***Aladjev V.Z., Vaganov V.A., Hunt Ü.J., Shishakov M.L.*** Workstation for Mathematicians.- Minsk-Moscow: Russian Academy of Natural Sciences, 1999, 608 p., ISBN 3420614023

25. ***Aladjev V.Z., Shishakov M.L.*** Workstation of Mathematician.- Moscow: Laboratory of Basic Knowledge, 2000, 752 p. + CD, ISBN 5932080523 *(in Russian)*

26. ***Aladjev V.Z., Bogdevicius M.A. Maple 6:*** Solution of Mathematical, Statistical, Engineering and Physical Problems.- Moscow: Laboratory of Basic Knowledge, 2001, 850 p. + *CD*, ISBN 593308085X *(in Russian with English summary)*

27. ***Aladjev V.Z., Bogdevicius M.A.*** Special questions of work in environment of the mathematical package ***Maple.***- Vilnius: International Academy of Noosphere, the Baltic Branch & Vilnius Gediminas Technical University, 2001, 208 p. + *CD with Library*, ISBN 9985927729 *(in Russian with English summary)*

28. ***Aladjev V.Z., Bogdevicius M.A.*** Interactive ***Maple:*** Solution of mathematical, statistical, engineering and physical problems.- Tallin: International Academy of Noosphere, the Baltic Branch, 2001-2002, *CD with Booklet*, ISBN 9985927710

29. ***Aladjev V.Z., Vaganov V.A., Grishin E.P.*** Additional software of mathematical package ***Maple*** of releases **6** and **7**.- Tallinn: Intern. Academy of Noosphere, the Baltic Branch, 2002, 314 p. + *CD with Library*, ISBN 9985927737 *(in Russian)*

30. ***Aladjev V.Z.*** Effective work in mathematical package ***Maple.***- Moscow: BINOM Press, 2002, 334 p. + *CD*, ISBN 593208118X *(in Russian with English summary)*

31. ***Aladjev V.Z., Liopo V.A., Nikitin A.V.*** Mathematical package ***Maple*** in physical modeling.- Grodno: Grodno State University, 2002, 416 p., ISBN 3093318313 *(in Russian)*

32. ***Aladjev V.Z., Vaganov V.A.*** Computer Algebra System ***Maple:*** A New Software Library.- Tallinn: Intern. Academy of Noosphere, the Baltic Branch, 2002, *CD*, ISBN 9985927753

33. ***Aladjev V.Z., Bogdevicius M.A., Prentkovskis O.V.*** A New Software for mathematical package ***Maple*** of releases **6, 7** and **8**.- Vilnius: Vilnius Technical University and International Academy of Noosphere, the Baltic Branch, 2002, 404 p.

34. ***Aladjev V.Z., Vaganov V.A.*** Systems of computer algebra: A New Software Toolbox for ***Maple***.- Tallinn: Intern. Academy of Noosphere, the Baltic Branch, 2003, 270 p. + *CD*, ISBN 9985927761

35. ***Aladjev V.Z., Bogdevicius M.A., Vaganov V.A.*** Systems of Computer Algebra: A New Software Toolbox for ***Maple. 2nd*** *edition*.- Tallinn: Intern. Academy of Noosphere, 2004, 462 p.

36. ***Aladjev V.Z.*** Computer algebra systems: *A new software toolbox for* ***Maple***.- USA: Palo Alto: Fultus Corporation, 2004, 575 p., ISBN 1596820004

37. ***Aladjev V.Z.*** Computer algebra systems: *A new software toolbox for* ***Maple***.- USA: Palo Alto: Fultus Corporation, 2004, Adobe Acrobat eBook, ISBN 1596820152

38. ***Aladjev V.Z., Bogdevicius M.A. Maple:*** Programming, physical and engineering problems.- USA: Palo Alto: Fultus Corporation, 2006, 404 p., ISBN 1596820802, Adobe Acrobat eBook *(pdf)*, ISBN 1596820810

39. ***Aladjev V.Z.*** Computer Algebra Systems. ***Maple:*** *Art of Programming*.- Moscow: BINOM Press, 2006, 792 p., ISBN 5932081899 *(in Russian with English summary)*

40. ***Aladjev V.Z.*** Foundations of programming in ***Maple:*** *Textbook*.- Tallinn: International Academy of Noosphere, 2006, 300 p., *(pdf)*, ISBN 998595081X, 9789985950814 *(in Russian)*

41. ***Aladjev V.Z., Boiko V.K., Rovba E.A.*** Programming and applications elaboration in ***Maple:*** *Monograph*.- Grodno: GRSU, Tallinn: International Academy of Noosphere, 2007, 456 p., ISBN 9789854178912, ISBN 9789985950821 *(in Russian)*

42. ***Aladjev V.Z.*** *A Library for* ***Maple*** *system: The Library can be freely downloaded from* ***https://yadi.sk/d/hw1rnmsbyfVKz***

About the authors

Aladjev V.Z.

Professor dr. ***Aladjev V.Z.*** was born on June 14, 1942 in the town *Grodno (West Belarus)*. He is the First vice-president of the *International Academy of Noosphere (IAN, 1998)* and academician-secretary of *Baltic branch of the IAN* whose scientific results have received international recognition, first, in the field of cellular automata (homogeneous structures) theory. Dr. ***Aladjev V.Z.*** is known for the works on cellular automata theory and computer mathematical systems. Dr. ***Aladjev V.Z.*** is full member of the *Russian Academy of Cosmonautics (1994)*, the *Russian Academy of Natural Sciences (1995)*, *International Academy of Noosphere (1998)*, and honorary member of the *Russian Ecological Academy (1998)*.

He is the author of more than ***500*** scientifical publications, including ***90*** books and monographs in fields such as: general statistics, mathematics, informatics, *Maple* and *Mathematica* that have been published in many countries. ***Aladjev*** *V.Z.* established Estonian School *of mathematical theory of homogeneous structures (cellular automata theory)*, whose fundamental results received international recognition and formed the basis of a new section of modern mathematical cybernetics.

Many applied works of dr. ***Aladiev V.Z.*** relate to computer science, among which are widely known books on computer mathematics systems. Along with these original editions, he has developed a rather large library *UserLib* of new software tools *(over **850** tools)*, awarded with the web-based *Smart Award*, and the unified package *MathToolBox (over **1320** tools)* for ***Maple*** and ***Mathematica***, respectively, to enhance the functionality of these computer mathematics systems.

Aladjev V.Z. repeatedly participates as a guest lecturer in the different international scientific forums in mathematics and cybernetics or a member of the organizing committee of them. In *2015* dr. ***Aladjev V.Z.*** was awarded by ***Gold*** medal *"European Quality"* of the European scientific and industrial consortium for works of scientifical and applied character.

Shishakov M.L.

Dr. ***Shishakov M.L.*** was born on October 21, 1957 in *Gomel* area *(Belarus)*. For his scientific activity Dr. ***Shishakov M.L.*** has more than **66** publications on information technology in various application fields, including more **26** books and monographs. Fields of his main interests are cybernetics, theory of statistics, problems of *CAD* and designing of mobile software, artificial intelligence, computer telecommunication, along with applied software for solution of different tasks of manufacturing and technical nature. In *1998* dr. ***M.L. Shishakov*** was elected as a full member of the *IAN* on section of the information sciences and information technologies.

At present, ***M.L. Shishakov*** is the director of the *Belarusian–Swiss* company *"TDF Ecotech"*. *TDF Ecotech* company builds and operates the appropriate facilities for production of renewable energy through its subsidiary branches *(with a focus on the Belarus region)*. Above all, the company works in the field of so-called "*green*" energy, combining the essential manufacturing activity with active scientifical researches.

Vaganov V.A.

Dr. ***Vaganov V.A.*** was born on February 2, 1946 in *Primorye Territory (Russia)*. Now dr. ***Vaganov V.A.*** is the proprietor of the firms *Fortex* and *Sinfex* engaging of problems of delivery of the industrial materials to different firms of the Estonian republic. Simultaneously, dr. ***V.A. Vaganov*** is executive director of the Baltic branch of the *IAN*. In addition, dr. ***Vaganov V.A.*** is well-known for the investigations on automation of economic and statistical works. ***V.A. Vaganov*** is the honorary member of the *IANSD* and the author of more than **62** applied and scientifical publications, at the same time including ***10*** books. The sphere of his scientific interests includes statistics, economics, problems the institution of the family, politology, cosmonautics, theory of sustainable development and other natural-scientific directions.

www.ingramcontent.com/pod-product-compliance
Lightning Source LLC
LaVergne TN
LVHW060210210926
848481LV00008B/2688